Our Moonlight Revels

STUDIES

IN

THEATRE

HISTORY

AND

CULTURE

EDITED BY

THOMAS

POSTLEWAIT

A MIDSUMMER NIGHT'S DREAM IN THE THEATRE

GARY JAY WILLIAMS

Our Moonlight Revels

UNIVERSITY OF IOWA PRESS Ψ IOWA CITY

University of Iowa Press,
Iowa City 52242
Copyright © 1997 by the
University of Iowa Press
All rights reserved
Printed in the United States of America

Design by Richard Hendel

http://www.uiowa.edu/~uipress

This book has been supported by a grant
from the National Endowment for the
Humanities, an independent federal agency.

Printed on acid-free paper

Library of Congress
Cataloging-in-Publication Data
Williams, Gary Jay.

Our moonlight revels: A midsummer
night's dream in the theatre /
by Gary Jay Williams.

p. cm.—(Studies in theatre history
and culture)

Includes bibliographical references and
index.

ISBN 0-87745-592-9

1. Shakespeare, William, 1564–1616.
Midsummer night's dream.
2. Shakespeare, William, 1564–1616—
Stage history. 3. Theatre—
History. I. Title. II. Series.
PR2827.W59 1997
822.3′3—dc21   97-21764
01 00 99 98 97 C 5 4 3 2 1

For Josephine Sayers Williams

CONTENTS

ACKNOWLEDGMENTS

This book has enjoyed many blessings along the way, but most especially the unselfish interest, humane criticism, and enduring patience of Josephine Sayers Williams, my wife. To her I dedicate it. My indebtedness to the many scholars whose works have lighted my way is recorded in the notes, but I want to express special gratitude to colleagues who generously shared their knowledge and time: Eugene Waith, Charles Shattuck, John Andrews, Stanley Wells, George Walton Williams, and Gary Taylor. For final rigorous critiques of the full manuscript, I am grateful to my editor, Thomas Postlewait, who has been unflinching in his faith, and to Edward Pechter. Among others who have been supportive are Oscar Brockett, Joseph Donahue, Don Wilmeth, Bruce McConachie, Dennis Kennedy, Margaret Ranald, D. Allen Carroll, Glynne Wickham, Douglas Schoenherr, Werner Habicht, Jeanne Newlin, Nancy Maguire, Simon Williams, Marvin Carlson, and Catherine Belsey.

Yale University fellowships made it possible to begin the project, and a Folger Shakespeare Library Fellowship made it possible to complete it. Grants from the National Endowment for the Humanities (NEH) and the Catholic University of America (CUA) helped sustain the research along the way, and NEH helped support the final publication. I am grateful to my understanding colleagues at CUA: William H. Graham, Donald Waters, Gitta Honegger, Eugene Kennedy, and Antanas Suziedelis. I want to acknowledge *Theatre Survey*, *Theater*, and *Theatre Studies*, in which portions of chapters 3, 4, 5, and 7 appeared.

I am indebted to many librarians but especially to Betsy Walsh of the Folger Shakespeare Library, Sylvia Morris and Mary White of the Shakespeare Centre Library, Richard Buck of the New York Public Library of Performing Arts at Lincoln Center, the late George Nash of the Victoria and Albert Museum, Christopher Robinson of the Bristol University Theatre Collection, Margaret Benton of the Theatre Museum, London, and Magarete Opel of the Goethe Collection of the Stiftung Weimarer Klassik. My Shakespeare seminar students at CUA over the years have always helped, especially Verleah Kosloske and Jack Hrkach, on whose research I have drawn.

Prologue

OUR MOONLIGHT REVELS

Titania: If you will patiently dance in our round
And see our moonlight revels, go with us
If not, shun me, and I will spare your haunts.

In the four hundred years from its probable premiere around 1596, William Shakespeare's *A Midsummer Night's Dream* has undergone more metamorphoses in our theatres than Ovid could have dreamed of. From Henry Purcell's *The Fairy Queen* of 1692 to Peter Brook's Royal Shakespeare Company production of 1970, the play has been extraordinarily responsive in the theatre to the cultural energies in every era, whether they flow from monarchies, from the social margins, or, as often happens, from both at once. This book is an account of the play's many lives in Western theatre over these four centuries and the ways in which theatre artists have brought to bear on the play the culture's negotiations of gender, class, sexuality, love, the supernatural, and even national identity.

My primary interest throughout this performance history has been to understand each major production in its cultural moment. Often my method has been to work from a selected production outward, mapping its cultural genetic markers as it were, and then stepping back to identify the parents and cultural lineage. I have preferred to retain a chronological framework, though at first glance this may seem unpromising for the work of cultural studies. Keeping the spectrum in view while focusing closely on selected productions and themes will, I hope, help foreground the story of our remarkably varied cultural transactions with this play. This particular play's performance history offers special opportunities to examine all the languages of theatrical production. An astonishing variety of scenery and music, from baroque to postmodern, has been created for its fairy and mortal worlds. These visual and musical vocabularies are always read here as cultural texts that mediate the play.

This account of *A Midsummer Night's Dream* in the theatre is not, then, a teleological history in search of a definitive production. It is the story of our uses of the play and of the intricate and radical cultural contingency that is intrinsic to the theatre. It is also a story of the dance between the ephemeral theatre and cultural mutability. The reader is invited to enter the account in the spirit that Titania invites Oberon to her moonlight revels: "If you will patiently dance in our round, / And see our moonlight revels, go with us" (2.1.140–141).

This account, of course, has its limits of coverage and cultural perspective. I have treated mainly performances in the English-speaking theatre over the four centuries. But productions in German-speaking countries often are important and closely related to that history, so I have described many of them, from the seventeenth-century German versions of *Pyramus and Thisbe* through Ludwig Tieck's nineteenth-century production, which gave us Felix Mendelssohn's score for the play, down to the some dozen stagings of the play by Max Reinhardt in the first third of the twentieth century. The story of the play in Germany under the Nazis, who attempted to erase Mendelssohn's music from history, also belongs in the cultural narrative here, as do the productions and influential criticism of the play in the once-Communist countries of Eastern Europe. The account seeks to situate culturally the major operas based on the play, from Henry Purcell's *The Fairy Queen* (1692) to Benjamin Britten's *A Midsummer Night's Dream* (1960), and the ballets that it has inspired. I offer some cultural perspective on the 1935 Warner Brothers film, directed by Max Reinhardt and William Dieterle, and analyze selected films and television productions. Some productions in the regional theatres and in the Shakespeare festivals that blossomed in the United States from the 1970s to the 1990s are covered here, although many were beyond the reach of this scholar's resources and a single lifetime. (In one three-year period in the 1980s, at least fifteen of the forty distinct Shakespeare festivals in the United States were producing the play.) I have selected productions that I think mark the intersections of imaginative theatre artists with significant cultural forces in the West.

All citations from this play and other of Shakespeare's plays are taken from *William Shakespeare, The Complete Works*, edited by Stanley Wells and Gary Taylor (Oxford: Clarendon Press, 1986). Most of my promptbook analyses of the way managers and directors handled the text were completed prior to the publication of the Oxford edition, and for these I used Horace Howard Furness's Variorum edition of the play. In illustration captions, the act and scene indications are based on the Oxford edition, not on the particular production's act/scene division.

Our Moonlight Revels

Chapter one

THE WEDDING-PLAY MYTH AND
THE *DREAM* IN FULL PLAY

Bottom: A calendar, a calendar — look in the almanac,
   find out moonshine, find out moonshine.

A Midsummer Night's Dream engages us today in ways we could not have imagined only fifty years ago. The play now seems remarkably open to such late-twentieth-century perceptions as "it is the world of words that creates the world of things,"[1] that between desire and mortality, we are ever busy about the construction of meaning and the representation of ourselves. The cultural changes by which we have come to such perceptions within the last half century offer a lesson in the hazards of speculating about how Shakespeare's audiences might have experienced this play four hundred years ago. But the changes also offer opportunities for fresh perspectives on certain traditions of staging and criticism that this play has enjoyed but which for a long time stood, as I hope to show in this chapter, between us and the play in Shakespeare's theatre.

The first part of this chapter examines one theory that has entwined itself around the critical literature on, and theatrical productions of, this play for a century and a half: the long-standing theory that the play was conceived as an entertainment for an Elizabethan court wedding at which Elizabeth was present. In most versions, England's greatest queen is surrounded by her court and the young newlyweds, virgin mother to all, watching the play by England's greatest poet in an oak-beamed Tudor great hall where the fairies dance by firelight. This vision is, of course, a mirror image of the play's last act, in which a beneficent Greek ruler, Theseus, and his court watch the play *Pyramus and Thisbe* on an ancient nuptial night in Athens. The vision has been a beguiling one, to use Samuel Schoenbaum's word.[2] One measure of the fascination with it is the fact that no fewer than eleven court weddings have been put forward as candidates for the premiere. (The appendix lists the weddings proposed and the scholarship surrounding them.) The evidence is adduced largely from the play itself; none of the other evidence offered for any one of these cases is more than circumstantial. But the theory has persisted, recurring with the power of myth. Myths, as Roland Barthes has suggested, effectively naturalize historical intentions and cultural constructions, turning history into nature, the contingent into the inevitable.[3]

I shall show that the theory has never been convincingly supported, and I shall argue on the grounds of Elizabethan theatre practice that it is very unlikely that the play was topically designed. I shall also show why the wedding-play myth has persisted despite its evidentiary weaknesses and explain (in this chapter and thereafter) the cultural work the myth has been doing — both in the academy and in the theatre. Several important matters are at stake in disentangling the play from the theory. The wedding-play myth affects the way we think in general about who Shakespeare was and about the audience for whom he wrote. The theory silently creates a picture of Shakespeare and his company as court dependent and tends to discount his public playhouse audience. The myth also affects our experience of the play itself. Scholars who find congenial the idea that the play was designed for a court wedding tend to see the play as a passage from sensual to neo-Platonic love, from irrational love to rational marriage and a stable society under a strong ruler. Indeed, this would make it concur with Tudor doctrine on the patriarchal family. But relatively suppressed in such readings, as they have been in much of the play's theatrical history, are the play's repeated explorations of complex gender relations, which, if Louis Montrose is right, echo the complexly gendered power relations of Queen Elizabeth as a woman ruler in a patriarchal culture. The play also is rich in explorations of its characters' tenuous hold on meaning and identity, which it has in common with other of Shakespeare's plays. (Not to pay close attention to this is also to miss in this play the way that Shakespeare exploits his nonillusionistic, open stage.) Such suggestions about human instability are not wholly congenial to the wedding-play myth's vision of domestic and court tranquility, which affirm a traditional patriarchy. They are also not congenial to the idealizing humanistic vision of a homogeneous Elizabethan England to which the wedding-play myth has long been the companion. (Because it serves that vision, the myth has repeatedly resurfaced in connection with assertions of national identity.)

More comprehensive cultural explanations of the forces at work in the play are to be found in Louis Montrose's ideological analysis (1983), now widely recognized, and in the recent works by Montrose and by Penry James.[4] These help us understand, in part, what caught the intuitions of the wedding-play advocates in the first place. The play is permeated by what Montrose describes as the "cultural presence" of Queen Elizabeth. It reproduces and enlarges upon the dimensions of the cultural field of the Elizabethan gendered political system and Elizabeth's powerful place within it. Her relation to her subjects is at the heart of *A Midsummer Night's Dream*'s fascination with unstable hierarchies and gender categories. Montrose sees the play as the poet's complex re-presentation of a realm in which males found themselves in an uncertain and sometimes eroticized relationship with their female monarch; the play participates in the discourse of what was a patriarchal culture in every way, except that a woman was on top. "The woman to whom *all* Elizabethan men were vulnerable was Queen Elizabeth herself," writes Montrose. Resonating throughout the play are the problematic gender relations of the queen who represented herself as both virgin and mother, both desirable and unattainable, both in service to a patriarchal order and in control of it. From the play's sources in the legends of Theseus, Medea, and Hippolyta the Amazon to its fantasy of a fairy queen brought under control by a fairy king and glimpsed in an erotic relationship with an artisan/actor, the play transmits and reproduces this complex cultural formation and, at times, critiques it. Montrose's overarching ideological argument, to which I will return, helps explain much. But the theatre historian still has both a theatrical and cultural interest in the particular work of critiquing the wedding-play myth because of its effects on our understanding of Elizabethan theatre practice and Shakespeare's audience and because of the cultural work the myth has often done in connection with major theatrical productions since.

The first proposal of the wedding theory came from Ludwig Tieck, in the late bloom of German romanticism. There is no inkling of a wedding premiere for the play in Nicholas Rowe, who did report the legend of Elizabeth wanting more of Falstaff. Edmund Malone did not suggest it, nor did any other commentators on Shakespeare in the eighteenth century. Not even amid that century's boomlet of Shakespearean editing or David Garrick's revivals of the plays or his Shakespeare jubilee do we find a suggestion of it. Scholars from Rowe (1709) to the present have seen compliments to the virgin queen in Oberon's references to the "fair vestal thronèd by the west" (2.1.158) and "the imperial vot'ress" (2.1.163) who was untouched by Cupid's arrow.[5] But no one before Tieck tried to associate these or the design of the play with a specific wedding.

In his notes to Schlegel's translation of *A Midsummer Night's Dream* in 1830, Tieck proposed that the "germ or first sketch" of Shakespeare's play was a "felicitation [*Glückwunsch*] . . . in the shape of a mask" for the wedding of Shakespeare's patron, Henry Wriothesley, Earl of Southampton, to Elizabeth Vernon in 1598, the year of Francis Meres's mention of the play.[6] No evidence is offered, other than the correspondence of the dates and general circumstances. The theory would have appealed to Tieck's imagination. In his novel *Dichterleben* (1825–1829), Shakespeare, Southampton, Marlowe, and the Dark Lady all appear in a sentimental and inaccurate picture of a romanticized Elizabethan England.[7] Of course, the theory would have been congenial to the general German appropriation of Shakespeare. It abetted the construction of a spiritual national identity bound up with art-loving rulers. As I show in chapter 3, Tieck's theory is almost certainly bound up with his production of the play in 1843, sponsored by Friedrich Wilhelm IV and premiered in the court theatre. For it Felix Mendelssohn was commissioned to write the incidental score that included his famous "Wedding March." On the whole, this production conferred upon its patron the status of a modern Theseus/Elizabeth.

After Tieck, the wedding theory was passed along, with occasional variations, by various Victorian scholars.[8] It received its fullest scholarly attention yet in the years bracketing World War I, probably because it offered a fond, comforting image of a golden age of the British Empire. John Masefield wrote in his 1911 *William Shakespeare* (published for the Home University Library of Modern Knowledge) that in *A Midsummer Night's Dream*, "Shakespeare set himself free to tell his love for the earth of England that had ministered to his mind with beauty through the years of youth."[9] E. K. Chambers advanced his case for the 1595 wedding of William Stanley and Elizabeth Vere, daughter of the Earl of Oxford, in a 1916 Shakespeare tercentenary tribute anthology, *A Book of Homage to Shakespeare*. The lavish, white, leather-bound volume also carried verses by Kipling and others in which Shakespeare was celebrated as the national poet and enlisted in the war against Germany.[10] Chambers suggested as an alternative the 1596 wedding of Elizabeth Carey, granddaughter of Henry Lord Hunsdon, patron of Shakespeare's company, and Thomas, son of Lord Berkeley.

The court-wedding hypothesis next received major attention in the prestigious 1924 Cambridge edition of the play, edited by Sir Arthur Quiller-Couch and John Dover Wilson. The frontispiece of their edition was a portrait of Elizabeth Vernon, bride to Shakespeare's patron, the Earl of Southampton. Like Tieck, they connected the play to her 1598 wedding but suggested Shakespeare had written it earlier and undertook a revision for this occasion. Dover Wilson stopped short of placing the queen at the performance. He believed the play might have been written as early as 1592 and twice revised, in 1594 and 1598, the last stage of which Dover Wilson believed showed a more mature hand. His ingenious analysis of mislineations in Theseus's speech about imagination in 5.1, now widely accepted, demonstrated a holograph revision in the source from which the Quarto of 1600 was printed; the revision included Shakespeare's additions about the poet's imagination. Dover Wilson tied these revisions and the closing of the play ("Through the house give glimmering light" [5.2.21]) to the ostensible rehandling of the play for the 1598 wedding.

In the introduction to the edition, Quiller-Couch provided a fanciful account of Shakespeare working out his idea for the play for a wedding in some great private house.[11] Quiller-Couch won his knighthood in 1910 for his services to English literature, among which was his *Historical Tales from Shakespeare*, which told young readers during the years of the Boer War that "patriotism" was the "great lesson" in the history plays.[12]

It will be helpful at this point to provide an overview of the arguments of the modern wedding-play advocates in general, after which I will critique them. As Tieck apparently had, all take their first cues from selected features of the play itself and couple these with the circumstances of the court patronage of Shakespeare's company. They stress that the play is concerned with love and marriage throughout; contains compliments and allusions to Queen Elizabeth that Shakespeare devised, knowing she would be present at the wedding to hear them; includes the festive celebration of a triple court wedding, which includes a play at court; and closes with a fairy blessing of "this palace" and its noble owner. In addition to the references to the virgin queen already cited, scholars have pointed to the compliment to her in Theseus's praise of chastity in his Act 1 charge to Hermia: "Thrice blessèd they that master so their blood" (1.1.74). Oberon speaks of once hearing a mermaid singing on a dolphin's back (2.1.150), which is almost certainly an echo of the spectacular court entertainments for Queen Elizabeth during her progresses. Her visit to Leicester's Kenilworth in 1575 has had special appeal. Some scholars have maintained that certain characters in the play are based on actual court figures (Titania as Queen Elizabeth or Egeus as George Carey, the Lord Chamberlain, for example). Others have suggested that the play's internal time scheme and references to the moon point to a particular date when astrological conditions were favorable for a particular court wedding, conditions to which, it has been argued, Elizabethans paid close attention. Chambers proposed that the play's need for more boys than usual demonstrates the necessity of support from a noble household, which could have provided the music-trained boys to play Titania's four singing fairies.[13]

Dover Wilson has argued that the final fairy blessing of the palace was designed for a performance in the noble household; Puck's epilogue, allegedly redundant, has been said to be an alternative ending for public playhouse performances.[14] Shakespeare must have provided this alternative ending, Chambers then further reasoned, because the extra children were not available to him on the public stage.[15]

Of the eleven weddings nominated for the play's premiere, six fall within a time frame now widely accepted for the composition of the play (1594–1596). Of all the weddings nominated, the two for which the best arguments have been advanced are those of Elizabeth Vere and William Stanley, Earl of Derby, probably on 26 January 1595, and of Elizabeth Carey and Thomas Berkeley on 19 February 1596. These being the best cases, and most of the arguments for them being typical of those offered for the other weddings proposed, I will focus primarily on these two.

Elizabeth Vere, daughter of Edward de Vere, was the granddaughter of Lord Burghley (on her mother's side) and the goddaughter of, and a maid of honor to, the queen. We can establish that the queen was present at the Vere-Stanley wedding, whether at Greenwich or Burghley house, and that four days later she visited Burghley house in the Strand.[16] Chambers more than once promulgated the Vere-Stanley wedding as the likely occasion for the play's premiere.[17] The Vere connection has been attractive to some who claim that the Earl of Oxford wrote the plays ascribed to Shakespeare. In 1931, Eva Turner Clark advanced arguments that Oxford wrote *A Midsummer Night's Dream* between 1581 and 1583, presenting it before the queen no later than 1584. Clark claimed that it contains many allusions to the unrealized match between Elizabeth and François, Duke of Alençon. Clark contended that Oxford might have written it as an entertainment for the French ambassadors who were in London in 1581 to negotiate this match and suggested that the play was played again later, perhaps in altered form, at the wedding of Oxford's daughter in 1595. Theseus and Hippolyta are said to represent Alençon and Queen Elizabeth, and the truth about their courtship is supposedly represented in the love affair between Bottom and Titania. When Bottom calls Titania's fairies "Monsieur Cobweb" and "Monsieur Mustardseed," this, for Clark, clinches the argument that Bottom is the Frenchman.[18] More recently, Marion A. Taylor described a similarly intricate network of allusions in the play to the aborted match of the queen and Alençon and sought to relate the play generally to topical, allegorical literature, from court masques to *Richard II*. Elizabeth is Titania, Bottom is the French duke, and some of the other mechanicals are his envoys. Peter Quince, for example, is named for one Monsieur De Quincé.[19]

The other favored wedding, that of Elizabeth Carey and Thomas Berkeley, was first suggested by Chambers as a possible alternative to the Stanley-Vere wedding.[20] Harold Brooks makes this case anew in his Arden edition of the play (1979), and David Wiles makes an astrological case for it in his *Shakespeare's Almanac* (1993). The Carey-Berkeley advocates argue that Shakespeare would have been obliged to provide a play for this occasion, given the fact that the bride was the granddaughter of his company's patron (and her father succeeded him). Elizabeth also was one of the queen's goddaughters. The case benefits from the probability that *The Merry Wives of Windsor* served as an occasional piece marking her father's election to the Order of the Garter in 1597, according to Leslie Hotson's generally accepted theory.[21] The marriage took place at Blackfriars, presumably at the Carey home there, on 19 February 1596, and court records show payments to both the Lord Chamberlain's and Lord Admiral's companies for court performances near that date, on 22 February.[22]

A major component of David Wiles's book-length advocacy of the Carey-Berkeley wedding is his attempt to correlate all the play's references to the moon and Venus to the astrological readings for 19 February.[23] William B. Hunter before him had noted that there was a new moon the day before the Carey-Berkeley wedding. Pointing to Theseus's reference to a new moon in four days (1.1.1–4), he placed the play's performance at court for the newlyweds on St. Valentine's Day.[24] Wiles builds on the fact that Elizabethans took great interest in astrology and that poets repeatedly paid attention to it in their epithalamiums (Spenser being the prime example). Wiles suggests that members of these particular families would have carefully considered planetary motions in the planning of this wedding. Thomas Berkeley reportedly gave great credence to astrological readings, and his mother and wife both consulted astrologers at important junctures in their lives. Wiles sees 19 February as "an ideal day" for the wedding, because, just before five P.M., the new moon was conjunct with Venus in Pisces, a happy position in general for weddings according to Elizabethan almanacs, such as Leonard Digges's. Theseus's comment in the first scene that four days will bring a new moon for their marriage is not precise, but, Wiles contends, Hippolyta's corrective response is, for she is careful to note four nights also: "Four days will quickly steep themselves in night, / Four nights will quickly dream away the time; / And then the moon, like to a silver bow, / New bent in heaven, shall behold the night / Of our solemnities" (1.1.7–11). As Wiles calculates it, this places the wedding and the play's premiere on 19 February 1596, when a new moon and Venus would have been visible in the western sky. Wiles observes that the date is also five days after St. Valentine's Day, which Theseus notes in Act 4 "is past" (4.1.138), when he wakes the lovers in the wood.

(Wiles suggests, too, that traditional rites of St. Valentine's Day are reflected in the plot structure.) Wiles assures us that when Bottom calls for an almanac to determine whether the moon would shine on performance night, he "did precisely what those who planned the wedding must have done." [25]

One argument for a wedding premiere could be adduced from my account in the next chapter of Henry Purcell's opera of 1692, *The Fairy Queen*. I believe that opera to have been devised in large part as a tribute to the marriage of William and Mary. This, it might be said, would suggest the persistence of a tradition in the late seventeenth century in which the play was associated with a court wedding. But the wedding-play theory had not yet been born, and the play's general evocation of the cult of Elizabeth would have been sufficient reason for bringing out the play as a tribute to royalty, which has been the case many times since. In the nineteenth century, the play was produced for the first anniversary of Queen Victoria's marriage and in the twentieth century on the occasions of Queen Elizabeth II's coronation and her silver jubilee.

To assess the wedding-play arguments, we may begin with the title page of the 1600 Fisher Quarto, which tells us only that the play was "sundry times publikely acted, by the Right honorable, the Lord Chamberlaine his servants." It does not say that the play was performed at any time before Her Majesty, let alone the first time, as do certain Quartos for *Love's Labour's Lost* (1598) and *The Merry Wives of Windsor* (1602). Such advertising practices were not consistent, however, so this is not conclusive. Records of payment to Shakespeare's company for performances at court offer enticing, but still circumstantial, evidence. The company was paid for six performances in late December 1594 and early January 1595 and for five between 26 December 1595 and 22 February 1596. Chambers, continuing his advocacy for the Vere-Stanley wedding in his 1923 *The Elizabethan Stage*, entered a performance of the play by the Lord Chamberlain's company into his Court Calendar for 26 January 1595 (accompanied with a speculative question mark), a date not given in the payment records. Also, the records only occasionally list play titles, but it must be noted that *A Midsummer Night's Dream* is not mentioned. [26]

We do have evidence, however, that a masque was planned for the Vere-Stanley occasion (whether it was performed is not certain). Chambers documents that Arthur Throgmorton planned a masque of nine muses for the wedding, in which Throgmorton hoped to regain the queen's favor for himself or perhaps for Sir Walter Raleigh (who had seduced and married Throgmorton's sister). [27] True, both this masque and *A Midsummer Night's Dream* might have been performed on the wedding day at Greenwich; John Stow says the "marriage feast was there most royally kept." [28] Or both might have been performed at Burghley house a few days later, when the queen visited there.[29] But we have a record of a masque, or at least of its planning, and not a play, and a masque would be more consistent with Elizabethan court wedding customs.

The entertainments at court weddings in these years were more often masques than plays, as Stanley Wells first pointed out.[30] An early example is the masque at the wedding of Sir Henry Unton in 1580, portrayed in the well-known painting of scenes from Unton's life.[31] Masques, not plays, were the entertainments at five weddings attended by Queen Elizabeth during her reign, including that of Anne Lady Russell and Henry Lord Herbert in June 1600, another of the weddings proposed for the premiere of *A Midsummer Night's Dream*.[32] On this occasion, Elizabeth saw a masque of eight muses, she, apparently, becoming the missing ninth.[33] At this elaborate and best documented of the court weddings attended by Elizabeth, there was no play.[34]

This is not surprising. The masque, with its flattering allegory and abstraction, was a genre much more appropriate for a court occasion, more malleable for compliments than the drama, with its relative realism and independent fictive life. Andrew Gurr has pointed out that poets themselves (including Ben Jonson) were well aware of that difference.[35] Some scholars have strained to metaphorize *A Midsummer Night's Dream* into a masque (for example, by citing the mechanicals as an antimasque element), but while it echoes court celebrations of royal power and has cultural affinities with court entertainments, the play is not a masque.[36] From the fact that *Pyramus and Thisbe* is among the offerings for the court-wedding entertainment in the last act, one could argue that Shakespeare was following a court practice of having plays on such occasions. But *Pyramus and Thisbe* is the exception among the offerings, and its performance by the artisans is intrinsically related to the whole play.

The fact that the queen was godmother to a particular bride or groom is often used by wedding advocates, including Chambers, as evidence of Elizabeth's likely presence at a given wedding.[37] It is true that Elizabeth Vere, Thomas Berkeley, and Elizabeth Carey were the queen's godchildren. But, as Marion Colthorpe has pointed out, so were over a hundred other court progeny. Colthorpe also notes that the queen is known for certain to have attended the weddings of only two of those godchildren, one of which was Lady Vere's.[38] Similarly, the queen had numerous maids of honor, and the fact that one or another of them was a bride is no assurance of the queen's presence at any of their weddings.

For the Carey-Berkeley wedding there is a brief contemporary account, but it says nothing of a play, as Colthorpe has pointed out. The account is that of

Berkeley family historian John Smyth, a contemporary of the groom, who spent much of his life in service of the family and was a meticulous record-keeper in royal matters. Whether or not he witnessed the actual wedding, he was well informed about the match between Thomas Berkeley, to whom he was a some-time personal servant, and Elizabeth Carey. Smyth tells us the match developed rapidly. Thomas came with his father to London in Michaelmas term, 1595, and saw Elizabeth at her family home in Blackfriars.

> Such affection (upon motion formerly made) grew between him (then lodg-ing with his father at Thomas Johnson's house in Fleet street) and Elizabeth Carey, only child of Sir George Carey, then knight marshall and governor of the Isle of Wight, then living at his house in the Blackfriars, that on Thursday the 19th of February following, Anno 1595 [1595/96], in the said 38th of Elizabeth, they were married together. The articles of agreement concerning which marriage were drawn and sealed the same morning.[39]

This description, as Colthorpe observes, "suggests that lawyers rather than players were at hand and gives no hint of any great festivities on the wedding day."[40] Nor is there any hint of entertainments in the days after. Smyth does not say where the vows were exchanged; Colthorpe found no mention of the marriage in nearby church registers.

Smyth's only mention of the queen is by way of his decorous dating of the marriage as taking place in the thirty-eighth year of Elizabeth's reign. As Colthorpe notes, "If the Queen had honoured this wedding with her pres-ence, Smyth would surely have mentioned it."[41] Indeed, the pedigree-conscious Smyth was careful to note in his biography of Thomas, within which his account of the wedding occurs, that the queen was Thomas's godmother, that Thomas had been born on 11 July 1575 at Callowdon, six miles from Kenilworth Castle, just at the time that Queen Elizabeth was being feted there by Robert Dudley.[42] David Wiles argues that Smyth did not think it worthwhile to mention in his family history something so minor as the appearance of a company of players at Thomas's wedding.[43] But Wiles wants us to believe everywhere else that the play was politically important and astrologically correct, with eager court audi-ences gleaning its every allusion to the moon, stars, court affairs, and particular family members.

The astrological arguments lean heavily on literal readings of the relevant lines of Theseus and Hippolyta. Most wedding advocates have stopped short of attributing precise astrological programming to the playwright. That there was a wide interest in astrology in England in Tudor times is not disputed. John Dee, astrologer to Queen Elizabeth, selected her coronation day, and many almanacs were published in her reign.[44] Ornamental zodiac motifs were painted on the ceilings of some great houses, and in some theatres the ceiling of the stage may have been painted with a zodiac or in some other way decorated as the "starry gallery" that Flamineo refers to in *The White Devil* (5.4). But historians of English astrology carefully discriminate among the variations in contemporary beliefs and practices. Astrologers did not always agree with each other in their interpretations of the effects of planetary positions, as even Wiles himself acknowledges at one point.[45] There also was skepticism about particularized prophesying by the stars (few were as lucky, or as shrewdly ambiguous, as Nostradamus). Earnest astrologers, like Johannes Kepler, warned against charlatans, who were nicely satirized in the theatre in figures such as Ben Jonson's Subtle in *The Alchemist* and Thomas Middleton's Weatherwise in *No Wit, No Help Like a Woman*.[46] Weatherwise regulates his whole life by the almanac. Bottom and friends do indeed look to an almanac to find out if the moon will shine through the chamber window on the night of their court performance; clearly Shakespeare intends the amateurs' preoccupation with versimilitude to be amusing. There were even parodic almanacs.[47] What was widely accepted was the general influence of the heavens and fortune, and Elizabethan poets and playwrights were quick to turn such influences into conceits.[48] Shakespeare does so with his star-crossed lovers. The allusions to the planets by characters in his plays from *Twelfth Night* to *Timon of Athens* do not make them all occasional plays. When Shakespeare writes in sonnet fourteen, "Not from the stars do I my judgment pluck, / And yet methinks I have astronomy," he is speaking of being able to derive dependable knowledge from the constant stars in his friend's eyes.[49]

On the issue of Shakespeare's ostensible allusions to the progress entertainments at Kenilworth or Elvetham, something like a whole branch of Shakespearean scholarship developed in the nineteenth century. Horace Howard Furness surveyed it in his 1895 Variorum edition in a sixteen-page footnote to Oberon's speech (2.1.153–175). But no amount of line sifting for explicit allusions to one particular progress entertainment over another ever produced a consensus.[50] Such allusions to the queen's progress entertainments are better read within a larger cultural frame such as Montrose offers. For Wiles, however, Shakespeare was surely alluding to Kenilworth, providing a politic reminder of the bonds in the past between the crown and the Berkeleys, bonds that had long since eroded:

Shakespeare ingeniously suggests that the marriage of 1596 is predicated upon Leicester's failed bid in 1575. The Elizabeth of 1575 is transformed into the young Elizabeth who marries in 1596. Thus is the tension between Venus and Diana magically resolved, under the happy influence of the planets.[51]

One also wonders how politic it would have been for Shakespeare to remind the queen in public of the failed alliance at Kenilworth. All this complex astrological and political programming was done ostensibly by the playwright who, to our knowledge, never wrote a masque or a civic entertainment.

To believe with Eva Turner Clark that the Earl of Oxford wrote the play and that it alluded to the match between Elizabeth and Alençon requires a much earlier dating of the play's composition. Clark's scheme of allusions involves the kind of strained decoding operations that often figure in, and damage, the arguments of the champions of Oxford-as-Shakespeare. Neither of Oxford's two other major champions, J. Thomas Looney (1920) and Charlton Ogburn (1984), pressed the issue of the Stanley-Vere wedding as the occasion for which Oxford might have created the play, though Ogburn seems to have accepted it.[52]

Both Steven W. May and Wiles have argued that the play abounds in allusions to the Careys. To mention a few, May sees Philostrate as Lord Hunsdon, the Lord Chamberlain; Lysander's reference to a "dowager aunt" is an allusion to either Elizabeth's aunt, the Dowager Countess of Derby, or great aunt, the Dowager Lady Russell.[53] Wiles sees the Folio's Egeus as George Carey. He also finds an allusion to Thomas Berkeley's physical disability (affecting his head and neck) in the promise made in the concluding fairy blessing that the newlyweds' children would not be marked: "And the blots of nature's hand / Shall not in their issue stand" (5.2.39–40).[54]

Even supposing that Shakespeare programmed all this and astrology, too, into his play, one wonders what he would have to gain by pushing a comparison between the cranky Egeus and his company's patron. And if Wiles is right, the audience might well have gathered that Elizabeth had disobeyed her father in the choice of her husband, as the unruly Hermia does. The play treats what were probably topical issues: the extent to which sons and daughters were the property of the father to manage to the best advantage and the extent to which love should be considered in arranged marriages. Most aristocratic fathers probably expected, as Egeus does, to have their will with their daughters.[55] But this play clearly seeks to elicit sympathy for young lovers, not fathers; this is one of the ways the play critiques the system of patriarchy even as it stages the anxieties of that system. The play echoes the love tragedy of *Romeo and Juliet* in many ways, even in *Pyramus and Thisbe*. Hermia and Lysander catalog the obstacles to true love, lamenting on how forced matches, war, death, or sickness "lay seige to it," how quickly "the jaws of darkness do devour it up / So quick bright things come to confusion" (1.1.142, 148–149).

Wiles's answer is that court censors were indeed concerned with the identification of Carey with Egeus, and this explains Egeus's absence from the last scene of the 1600 Quarto. Wiles thinks that Shakespeare returned to his original intention in the Folio version, in which Egeus takes over the role of Philostrate. The censorship scenario is not persuasive if only for the fact that the ostensible wedding audience would have already seen the irascible Egeus of the Quarto's 1.1 and 4.1.

Both May and Wiles attempt to connect the Carey-Berkeley wedding and James Burbage's planned theatre at Blackfriars, on premises that abutted the Carey residence. Wiles grows so bold near the end of his book as to ask us to believe that the professional company acquired this particular space so that they would have "a base in which to prepare their material [*A Midsummer Night's Dream*] under supervision."[56] The doubtful economics of this aside, it is widely accepted that Burbage's interest in acquiring this property arose not because of the impending wedding and production plans but because of the failing negotiations with Giles Allen over the nearly expired lease on the land on which Burbage's public theatre stood.[57] Further, Burbage's purchase in Blackfriars was not Farrant's original theatre space, as Wiles says, but an area not yet adapted. Nine months later, in November, Burbage's neighbors filed a petition with the Privy Council against his use of the space for a theatre. Among the successful petitioners was the bridegroom, George Carey, now the new patron of Shakespeare's company.[58]

For the argument that *The Merry Wives of Windsor* served a particular occasion, the evidence is much better, whether we date the play's composition with Leslie Hotson in 1597, the year of the Garter ceremony involving George Carey, or with Stanley Wells and Gary Taylor a year later.[59] The references in the Folio text's last scene to Windsor Castle and its worthy owner and to the Order of the Garter are, indisputably, topical allusions. Rowe reported that Elizabeth so enjoyed the Falstaff of the two parts of *Henry IV* that she asked for more.[60] This may only repeat a legend built up from the allusions in the Folio text of *Merry Wives* itself.[61] But Hotson's linking of the play's premiere with the particular Garter feast of 1597 involving Carey has been generally accepted.

We should not jump to the conclusion, however, that *A Midsummer Night's Dream* presents the same kind of evidence of having been an occasional play. The blessing by the fairies of "this palace" and "the owner of it" (5.2.45–50), for example, is internally applicable to Theseus and his household, not an obvious topical allusion. As to the lines alluding to Elizabeth, Dover Wilson once noted that several lines in the play might not have been pleasing to the ears of the virgin queen, such as Theseus's threat to punish Hermia by sentencing her to a life as a vestal virgin (1.1.83–90).[62] But all this is better seen in the larger frame of Elizabeth's cultural presence and her power as the virgin queen. If *Merry Wives* was *designed* for the Carey occasion and thereafter transferred to the public stage, I strongly suspect that this was an exception. This would have reversed the normal, more practical sequence, which was for a company to perform at court a play already in its repertoire.[63] *A Midsummer Night's Dream* could have been taken from the company's repertoire for a court-wedding occasion rather than being originally created as a court-wedding entertainment. But most wedding advocates have wanted nothing less than a premiere and (saving Dover Wilson) have wanted Queen Elizabeth present.

Stanley Wells refuted the argument for Elizabeth's presence at the play's premiere in the preface to his 1967 edition of the play, which offered the only serious challenges to the wedding theory to that time: "Admittedly the Queen did not attend the public theatres; but an allusion to her does not imply that she was expected to be present at the play's first, or any other, performance."[64] Harold Brooks countered Wells: "It is not impossible to imagine the compliments as paid [Elizabeth] *in absentia*; they would then reach her by hearsay or at a revival at court; but it is more natural to imagine that Shakespeare knew she would hear them at the original performance."[65]

By this point, a basic critical issue has come into focus. Because we are dealing with a professional theatre company, whose daily livelihood was in the professional, public playhouse, we must ask: Would Shakespeare's original purpose have been to provide a play "designed to grace a wedding in a noble household," in Brooks's terms, with Elizabeth present? A liveried company had its obligations to do command performances, and no doubt the resulting prestige had good effect on the company's public playhouse box office. The ten pounds that seems to have been the customary payment for a performance of a play at court under Elizabeth certainly would have been welcome income.[66] But between 1595 and 1602, the Lord Chamberlain's men played at court on an average of only three times a year.[67] Professional companies existed by the grace of the court, as Glynne Wickham has stressed, having traced their growing professionalism, but at this rate, Shakespeare's company was not making a living designing plays for court occasions in the late Elizabethan years.[68] It was at the public playhouse that Shakespeare's company made its living in the mid-1590s. Nor was the company prepared to give up their public Southbank venue even when it was performing more frequently at court under James I, as the King's Men, nor again after the company expanded its winter operations to the Blackfriars in 1610. When the Globe burned in 1613, the King's Men rebuilt it more elaborately.

Shakespeare's first priority throughout his career seems likely to have been to provide plays for the public playhouse, rather than plays-to-order for court occasions. We know that *The Tempest* was performed at Whitehall before the king in 1611, probably the year in which it was written.[69] But as Stephen Orgel has observed, "A record of a performance at court implies neither a play written specifically for the court nor a first performance there."[70] *The Tempest* was also performed at court a year and a half later for the wedding of James's daughter, Elizabeth, to the Elector Palatine, along with thirteen other plays. It seems likely that in the interim it would have been performed at the Blackfriars and the Globe. From all that we know of the company's operations, I suspect that plays tightly programmed to the circumstances of specific court occasions would have ill suited a professional company that had to move between the public playhouse and court, and probably quickly at that. Brooks grants that "Shakespeare would not mean [*A Midsummer Night's Dream*] to be laid aside after its one wedding performance."[71] But this hedge is in a footnote to his long argument that the play was "designed" for a court-wedding premiere.

That the wedding-play theory has never been tested against the practical imperatives of playhouse practices, as I have done here, points to some antitheatrical bias in the academic discourse to which the theory has been congenial. In the modern academy, Shakespeare's literary credentials have had to be impeccable.[72] As late as 1971, Gerald Eades Bentley, in his study of the profession of the playwright in Shakespeare's time, thought it necessary to call attention to the "anti-professional attitude" he believed long common among Shakespeare scholars.[73] This bias can affect our understanding of who Shakespeare was and the audience for whom he wrote. Consider Chambers's particular suggestion (which Brooks found congenial) that the extra boy actors required for Titania's singing fairies would have had to have been furnished by a noble household. The argument implies that Shakespeare created a play that his own company did not have the resources to produce in its own public theatre. It paints a picture of a company attached to, and dependent upon, the court.[74] Consider Dover Wilson's argument, which Chambers sought to reinforce (and Brooks seconded), that the play comes to us with a double ending, with Robin's epilogue having been used for the public theatre and the fairy blessing finale ("Through the house give glimmering light . . .") having been created later for a court-wedding performance. Not only have editors since Dover Wilson seen the play as the product of one period of composition, not two.[75] This double-ending theory assumes that a diminished form of the play was good enough for the public theatre. It implies, too, as Wells pointed out, that the final fairy blessing is dramatically extraneous, requiring something external — the royal-wedding occasion — to be understood,[76] when the benediction is intrinsically appropriate for Theseus's "palace" and the three-nuptial night.[77] One hardly recognizes here the company that by 1595 – 1596 was operating what was becoming London's most successful public theatre. Chambers's strong inclination to associate the play with a court wedding, whether it be the Vere-Stanley or the Carey-Berkeley wedding, may be seen as consistent with the whole fabric of his four-volume *The Elizabethan Stage*, which begins with a lengthy study of the organization of the royal household for its entertainments. Never far from the wedding-play myth and its court orientation is the celebration of Shakespeare as England's national poet. Chambers's first essay proposing the Vere-Stanley wedding in the nationalistic *Book of Homage* of 1916 was timely and in appropriate company.

The sharp distinction between court and public playhouse audiences, which is embedded in the wedding-play theory, was reiterated very strongly in the essays of two American scholars in the 1950s who suggested that a court-wedding audience would have been the ideal audience for the play. One proposed that the Elizabethan court-wedding guests "could not miss the flattering similarity between the Elizabethan bridal couple and the gracious, exalted pair of legendary antiquity." The court audience would have seen, in the wedding of Theseus and Hippolyta, a historical analogy with the present wedding, "a feature of which was this very play, which was to stir them, the choicest of English aristocratic youth, to merriment." Theseus's "gracious condescension" to Quince's company would have consciously flattered the "lordly graciousness" of these aristocratic spectators.[78] The other scholar maintained that the play was suited to a court-wedding audience because it embodied, in various ways, neo-Platonic tradition, Christian marriage doctrine, classical literature, Spenser's *The Faerie Queene*, and Philip Sidney's *Arcadia*, all familiar to the educated courtiers. The court audience would have understood that the first movement of the play is toward "an orderly subordination of the female [Hippolyta, the Amazon] and her passions to the more reasonable male [Theseus, the rational Greek]," of whom Chaucer's Theseus is the model. The play is said to be related to John Lyly's court comedies and to Jonson's masques to come, requiring "the sophistication of minds swift in catching emblematic meanings." Shakespeare's symbols are said to come not "from the Celtic twilight but from more conscious and intellectual literary traditions." These symbols were derived from the classics, Lyly, and Spenser, which were "the property of the court."[79]

Such literary influences are, of course, part of the whole cultural field of the play; the subordination of Hippolyta, the irrational Amazon, to the rational Theseus is especially congenial to Montrose's analysis. Employing these influences in the service of the court-wedding argument to suggest that the play was designed to court tastes obscures the fact that the play had a life in the public playhouse, probably a long one. The notion that the playwright might have drawn on popular traditions ("the Celtic twilight") is rejected with something like aristocratic distaste. It is perhaps worth noting that these essays were written in the context of American Anglophilia following World War II and the crowning of Elizabeth II in 1953. But the arguments had a long lineage in the discourse of the academy and were doing the approvable work of celebrating England's national poet and distancing him from the hurly-burly of the public theatre, from what another American scholar as late as 1964 was calling "the odium of the stews."[80]

At the other extreme on the issue of Shakespeare's audience is Alfred Harbage's argument, offered during the post-Depression years, that Shakespeare was something of a Roosevelt Democrat who wrote for a middle-class audience at the Globe and whose plays were the better for it than those of his effete successors who wrote for the private theatres.[81] Ann Jennalie Cook's 1974 economically based study of audiences presented a different picture. Only a well-to-do 15 percent of the London population could have afforded a ticket and an afternoon off at the public playhouse, Cook concluded. While Cook seems to have had no bias against the public theatres, her conclusion leads us to envision a singularly elite audience.[82]

My line of argument here finds support in Andrew Gurr's suggestion that Harbage's and Cook's pictures of Shakespeare's audiences oversimplify, stressing differences too much. Surveying what is known about individual spectators in the public theatre, Gurr shows the audience to have been quite varied, and different playhouses may have appealed to different constituencies.[83] Gurr points out, as I have here, that Shakespeare's company did not forget its public theatre audience even as it expanded its operation under James I: "Nothing in the available evidence suggests that the King's Men's pre-eminence and their possession of the playhouse most frequented by the privileged [the Blackfriars] altered in any way their assumption that they catered for the whole range of society."[84] In its narrowness, the wedding-play myth can only impair our understanding of Shakespeare's audience.

To summarize, the hypothesis that Shakespeare designed *A Midsummer Night's Dream* to celebrate a court wedding, attended by Queen Elizabeth, has never been convincingly supported, even in the two best cases of the proponents. There is no record of the play having been performed for a court wedding. The allusions to Elizabeth do not assure her presence at such a wedding, nor is it assured by the fact that Elizabeth's many godchildren or maids of honor may have been involved. Masques, not plays, were the customary court-wedding entertainment during her reign. Arguments that the play was internally timed to the astrological conditions prevailing on the wedding night lean heavily on literal readings and an audience occupied with careful decoding, as do the arguments that the play contains allusions to particular persons and circumstances of the court. Both lines of argument attribute a complex programmatic agenda to the playwright. We would do better to seek the context of the play in larger cultural formations, such as Louis Montrose has suggested. As to comparisons to the composition of the Folio *Merry Wives of Windsor*, we should be cautious about concluding from what may have been a special case that *A Midsummer Night's Dream* was similarly designed for a court occasion. Testing the wedding-play theory against playhouse practices, I have suggested that plays programmed closely to court occasions would have ill suited a professional company that was primarily dependent for its livelihood on its public playhouse and that moved, probably quickly, between its public and court venues. The wedding-play myth, being congenial to the idea of a sharp distinction between the audiences in these two venues, impairs our understanding of Shakespeare's audience. The myth has been congenial to romantic, national, and academic discourses over the last two centuries. It has been compatible with those idealizing visions of a homogeneous Tudor England under Elizabeth that have served the construction of German and British national identities and served the notion of Shakespeare as the loyal, national poet. More of its cultural work in the theatre will be seen in the chapters to come.

More complex dimensions of this play were available to Shakespeare's audiences than the wedding-play discourse would suggest, both in the play's figuring of the cultural field of gender relations under Elizabeth and in its comic representations of the precarious grasp we have on reality.

Most of the principal characters in *A Midsummer Night's Dream* try, most of them endearingly, to negotiate a world subject to misapprehension and misfiguring. One cannot trust one's own eyes; R. W. Dent noted that eyes are mentioned far more frequently in this than in any other of Shakespeare's plays.[85] Egeus is sure that Lysander has deceived his daughter with verses by moonlight and any number of other false signifiers of affection.[86] Hermia wishes her father "look'd but with my eyes" (1.1.56). Theseus replies that she must choose by her father's eye; she is "but as a form in wax / By him imprinted, and within his power / To leave the figure or disfigure it" (1.1.49–51). Helena cannot understand why Demetrius does now not find her as fair as Hermia. (For Helena's soliloquy in 1.1, many actresses have used a mirror to reassess their image.) Under the spell of Puck's charm, both Lysander and Demetrius pursue Helena, and she has no way of determining which is sincere or who is who. (The frequent critical cavil that we cannot tell the young lovers apart misses a point. Neither can they.) And, of course, Oberon and Titania are estranged because of "the *forgeries* of jealousy" (2.1.81, emphasis mine). The catalog need not be extended much further, but I want to call attention to one of several instances, not usually noted, when Shakespeare made his audience aware that they also were not in firm command of their negotiations of reality. In the last act, during the play at court, cross references to the fairy forest world surface, as if all somehow had been dreaming a common dream. When Theseus says, "I wonder if the lion be to speak," Demetrius replies, "No wonder, my lord — one lion may when many asses do" (5.1.151–153). The rational Theseus comments after watching Bottom act the death of Pyramus: "With the help of a surgeon he might yet recover and prove an ass" (5.1.305–306). Demetrius and Theseus never have seen Bottom in the ass's head. But how do these characters come so near such knowledge, Shakespeare's audience might well have asked, not wholly confident of their own perceptions. The forest dream seems to have invaded the palace even as the courtiers (and the playhouse audience) laugh so confidently at the mechanicals' empirical attempts at verisimilitude.

Shakespeare exploited his open platform stage for this dimension of the play, including his conscious destabilizing of his audience's assumptions about their knowledge of reality. This nonillusionistic stage (as we must characterize it today after three hundred years of proscenium theatres and elaborate scenery) was essentially a space awaiting the transformation of language, becoming in the audience's imaginations what the poetry said it was. It accommodated both realistic and relatively stylized representations, changing with language styles that ranged from the prosaic language of the tavern to elevated soliloquies.[87] On this stage, matters involving representation, identity, and perception could become key issues.

A brief comparison of the nonillusionistic stage and Shakespeare's uses of it with the contemporary Italian court stage, where the proscenium tradition began, will help show how congenial the open stage was to such issues. At the courts of the Medici and Farnese in Shakespeare's lifetime, Italian designers were developing mechanized stages of changeable scenery to serve the *intermezzi*. These court entertainments were lavish allegorical pageants that moved

scenic ideographs of heaven and earth to position the ruler-patron in the hier-
archy of gods or, at least, as their earthly delegate. The *intermezzi* were based in
the classical mythology in which the court elite had been educated (ostensibly),
and the most advanced scenic technology money could buy was deployed to
create spectacular representations of the doctrine of absolutist rule. It was for
these "power plays" that the proscenium arch and the towering stage house
behind it, with its engines for the manipulation of illusion, came into being.[88]
The Italianate stage was imported to the English court in 1605 for the masques
for James I. The proscenium stage prevailed everywhere in Western theatre from
the mid-seventeenth century to the mid-twentieth, its engines supporting the
architectural fantasies that framed baroque opera and later (with alterations) the
romantic pictorialism that illustrated melodrama and Shakespeare in the nineteenth century. When Shakespeare's plays came to be staged with these illusion-
making machines, a theatrical dimension intrinsic to the plays was lost, arguably
affecting meaning as much as did the alterations of Shakespeare's texts about
which text-centered Shakespearean scholars complained for so long.

Shakespeare could use the English open stage to explore the problems of
representation and the very process of knowing. Bottom could be "translated,"
and Prince Hamlet and Macbeth could sort between the truth and its appearances. Pairs of twins from Ephesus and Syracuse could throw into comic confusion the very notion of individual identity. Richard II, a king of words and
ceremonial representations, could call for a mirror after being deposed, to see
whether his appearance had changed. The very nature of kingship could be the
subject. It is something of a truism that, on the daylight stage, the poetry created
the moonlit wood where Oberon and Titania are ill met. But it bears emphasizing that in this process, Shakespeare not only relied on his audience to construct
such fictions, he at times made sure the audience was aware of the instability of
such constructions. As Barbara Freedman has shown, in his comedies, including
this one, he often lured spectators into a stable position of mastery and then
undermined it.[89] When the mechanicals arrive at their forest spot to rehearse
later in the play, Quince remarks: ". . . here's a marvelous convenient place for
our rehearsal. This green plot shall be our stage, this hawthorn brake our tiring-
house"(3.1.2–4). Up to this point, the audience had been asked to imagine just
the reverse. This comic undercutting of the audience's supposedly stable perception is integral to the play's interest in the audience's unfirm grasp of reality and identity. This issue, so accessible to Elizabethans, was lost on the illusionistic Victorian stage, which labored to provide edifying visions of ancient
Greece and an almost scientifically literal fairy world.

Again, in the mechanicals' preparations for, and performance of, *Pyramus and Thisbe*, Shakespeare was making clear not only the limits of literal representation of reality in the theatre but the larger issue of misrepresentation. The artisans fret over how to bring in a wall and how to create a lion that will not frighten the court ladies, and they consult the almanac to see if the moon will shine through the chamber window on the night of their performance. On that night, Starveling tries in some bewilderment to explain his arcane symbolic props to the laughing court audience: "All that I have to say is to tell you that the lantern is the moon, I the man i'th' moon, this thorn bush my thorn bush, and this dog my dog" (5.1.252–254). It may be said that by demonstrating how not to stage a play, Shakespeare reminded his audience that imagination was required of them to make his own play work. But there is more in all this than a poetics of theatre; the mechanicals' playing of *Pyramus and Thisbe* is one of many instances in which the play offers a reminder of our inadequate figurings of reality.

The other dimension of the play suppressed by the wedding-play discourse is its fascination with unstable hierarchies and male anxiety about gender categories. Unruly women who have challenged male perogatives are prominent in the play. Montrose argues that Elizabeth's relation to her subjects is at the heart of it. He goes so far as to suggest that the festive conclusion of the play depends upon the success of the process by which "misanthropic warriors, possessive mothers, unruly wives, and willful daughters are brought under the control of lords and husbands." [90] The play opens with Theseus's reference to subduing Hippolyta with his sword, and Titania, too, must be brought under the control of her lord. Montrose writes: "Theseus' defeat of the Amazonian matriarchate sanctions Oberon's attempt to take the [Indian] boy from an infantilizing mother and to make a man of him." [91] Titania's speech on raising the Indian boy for his deceased mother paints a picture of female fecundity and the bonds between women, a counterpoint to the paternalistic ownership and shaping of Hermia played out by Theseus and Egeus in the first scene — which Montrose suggests is one representation of a whole compensatory process in which an anxious patriarchy asserted itself as the progenitor, seed provider, and proper master. Theseus advises Hermia, "To you your father should be as a god, / One that composed your beauties, yea, and one / To whom you are but as a form in wax, / By him imprinted, and within his power / To leave the figure or disfigure it" (1.1.47–51). [92] Hermia and Helena have only fathers in this play; their mothers never appear. Montrose argues that the play resonates with echoes of problematic gender relations, from Shakespeare's borrowings of Seneca's *Medea* and Euripides' *Hippolytus* to the entertainments offered to Theseus in the final act, which include the battle of the phallic centaurs, accompanied by an Athenian eunuch on the harp, and the riot of the "tipsy bacchanals / Tearing the Thracian singer in their rage" (5.1.48–49).

Behind all this, according to Montrose, is Elizabeth's complex and sometimes threatening relation to the men of her court. Montrose richly mines Elizabethan sources of this consciousness, ranging from Simon Forman's erotic dream of Elizabeth through the mythology of Amazons to Sir Walter Raleigh's stragegy for persuading his queen to support a colonial conquest. Montrose sees the liaison between Titania and "the assified artisan as an outrageous theatrical realization of a personal fantasy that obviously was not Forman's alone." [93] One may add that it plays out an archetypal male dream of the ethereal beauty and the hairy beast. To take a more conventional example from Montrose, Elizabeth's interest in controlling court marriages was well known, and in this "the Queen reserved to herself the traditional power to give or withhold daughters." [94] On the other hand, she had an interest in not seeming to threaten male hegemony and at times took pains to represent herself as the exceptional woman whose first interest was not traditional marriage and maternity but to nurture her nation.

To recognize these issues and cultural forces operating in the play is to view it quite differently from the tradition of criticism that has seen it as a site of the Renaissance debate between reason and imagination and has viewed its ending as a resolve into comfortable closure and domestic and state stability. (To this line of criticism, the wedding-play theory has been understandably congenial.) Some have argued that the play challenges the orthodox Renaissance view of the superiority of reason, and others have seen in it an affirmation of the value of reason over the precarious world of imagination. [95] R. A. Foakes found in it "a splendid balance between the two." [96] While many productions in the last three decades have emphasized the play's unsettling dimensions, influential critical analyses of the play have stressed the movement of the play toward social harmony and argued that the play's form offers a corresponding aesthetic perfection. [97] (Jan Kott's 1964 *Shakespeare Our Contemporary* is the very important exception.) [98] Harold Brooks saw the major theme as "love aspiring to, and being consummated in marriage," with all the couples moving toward stability. [99] David Young, in his influential full-length study of the play, argued that Hippolyta defends art as well as the consistency of the lovers' stories of the night, and he suggested that the "something of great constancy" (5.1.26) which Hippolyta finds in the lovers' stories refers to both the coherence of nature and the poet's art, art and nature working hand in hand. [100] Brooks and Foakes, influenced by Young, found in the final fairy blessing of Theseus's house a comfortable aesthetic closure that confirms the social order of the rational court: "So these triumphs of the poet's imagination at the close confirm the stability of the ordered society for which Theseus and his 'cool reason' stand, reminding us that the continuance of society depends upon marriage," wrote Foakes.[101]

But constructing this play as a contest in which one of the two forces "wins" erases our actual theatrical experience of its dialectics. Seeking comfortable closure and domestic and state stability at the end of the play leads us away from recognition of the play's constant figuring of complex gender relations and its comic but sometimes unsettling representations of our precarious constructions of reality. The fairy king and queen who lead the blessing of the nuptial beds have a long history of quarrels, and Theseus and Hippolyta are likely to continue theirs. The fairies' final invasion of the palace — and the palace cannot hold them or the mechanicals out — does not set the seal on state power and terminal domesticity. The moment is a midsummer night's amnesty, the momentary concord of all discord that the artifice of art can render. (Shakespeare will call attention to art as artifice more forcefully in *The Winter's Tale* and *The Tempest*.) It is no more than that. Puck's epilogue is not perfunctory; in it Shakespeare foregrounds the fictional character of the play: this miraculous dispensation beneath the hurrying moon has been a vision, "No more yielding but a dream" (Epilogue 6). In the Elizabethan daylight theatre, where production was not under the postromantic imperatives of organic unity and a play was not subject to the manipulations of nineteenth- or twentieth-century theatrical technology, the play's dialectics were probably more accessible. Elizabethan audiences apparently were expected to negotiate them.

The play would have made no exceptional demands upon the Elizabethan stage or staging methods. It was written to be played on a completely bare stage platform, as were over 80 percent of the plays Shakespeare wrote for the Globe, if Bernard Beckerman's estimate is correct.[102] The first scene is self-evidently a "court" scene in Theseus's "palace" (later so designated by Bottom [4.2.33] and Oberon [5.2.48]). Preset throne chairs, perhaps on a dais, for Theseus and Hippolyta might have been used to help establish Theseus's authority and the formality appropriate to his juridical handling of Egeus's complaint. The two tiring house doors up right and left would have accommodated all the necessary exits and entrances in this and other scenes. The meeting of Quince and company in 1.2, which nineteenth-century editors and producers will locate in Quince's house or carpentry shop, requires no setting other than simple stools or a bench that the actors could have carried on and off stage.

There are, to be sure, emblematic trees on Philip Henslowe's properties list, but there would have been no more need for them to create the moonlit wood than there was for an orchard and orchard wall for the balcony scene in *Romeo and Juliet*.[103] The entrances of the fairy monarchs are simply noted: "Enter Oberon the King of Fairies at one door, with his train, and Titania the Queen at another, with hers" (following 2.1.57). Nineteenth-century productions have Puck enter by riding a mushroom up through a trap, and a trap was available to Shakespeare. But a tiring-house door seems to have sufficed: "Enter a Fairy at one door and Robin Goodfellow, a puck, at another" (following 1.1.104). The pillars supporting the "shadow," or roof over the stage, might have served for Puck's hiding places.

Did Titania's train include the Indian boy? Neither the stage directions nor the texts of the Folio or Quarto indicate his presence, but it seems very likely. Puck describes him as her "attendant" (2.1.21), and he is the focal point of the central argument between the fairy king and queen. Shakespeare seems to take some pains to account for his absence late in the play, when Oberon tells Puck that Titania, under the charm, yielded the boy, "and her fairy sent / To bear him to my bower in fairyland" (4.1.59–60). It seems unlikely that an Elizabethan theatre company would have missed the opportunity to use an attractive child, at least in an early scene.[104] We can establish firmly the presence of the Indian boy on stage in Purcell's 1692 opera (see chapter 2).

Shakespeare's use of an Indian boy might derive in particular from Spenser's *The Fairie Queene*, Book II, where the founder of Oberon's royal line "Was Elfin: him all India obayd."[105] But his choice no doubt echoes the larger matter of English interest in India in the 1590s; the British East India Company was established in 1600. The India where Titania and the Indian boy's mother gossiped at night "in the spicèd Indian air" (2.1.124) was an exotic other-world to Elizabethans, and Shakespeare appropriated this erotic geography for the air of the fantastic that it would lend to Oberon and Titania, who in their adventures seem to commute regularly between there and fairyland.

Some current readers may see traces of colonialist attitudes in the use of the Indian boy, whom Oberon/England wishes so jealously to possess and who could be described as the subject of a quarrel between sovereigns. But the play counters such weighty distrust. Titania's interest in him is humanized in her description of the relationship she had with his mother (2.1.122–137), who "being mortal, of that boy did die" and for whose sake Titania has taken him into her care. In nineteenth-century productions, however, the presence of the Indian boy will become more problematic, not only because this passage is cut but because of the context of the unmistakable scenic images of empire the pictorial stage will provide.[106]

Shakespeare's forest is elusive in its geography and perhaps intentionally so, as Homer Swander has suggested.[107] There is clearly a difference between the fairyland of which Titania and Oberon speak (2.1.65, 122 and 4.1.60, respectively) and the forest itself, and even between Titania's canopied bank where the wild thyme grows and her bower. She has her fairies lead Bottom *from* her canopied bank and *to* her bower (3.1.189). The lines of the lovers in their forest chase give the impression that they are going deeper into the forest, to different locales, distinct from Titania's bank. In fact, of course, they would have simply re-entered each time onto the unchanged stage. On the pictorial stage of the nineteenth century, however, distinct scenic locales will be created for each point of the forest chase. But the play itself is not constructed with such logic of locale. Plotted literally, the forest spot where the young lovers fall asleep at the end of their chase cannot be the same place as Titania's canopied bank where Bottom awakes after the lovers and Titania have left. Localizing these scenes, nineteenth-century producers had to change settings two or three times and rearrange Shakespeare's sequence of scenes in order to account for the sleeping lovers, Titania's bank, the entrance of Theseus's hunting party, the waking of Bottom, and his return to Quince's house.[108] On the Elizabethan stage, Titania's canopied bank, where the fairies sing her to sleep in 2.1, may have been located in one of the tiring-house doors. She could have then wakened to Bottom's singing some seventy lines later, after the scenes of the lovers and mechanicals (who would not see her, especially if a curtain had been drawn across the opening), and exited with Bottom to her bower. Returning to her flowery bed to hold the sleeping Bottom in her arms in 4.1., Titania could then have been released from the charm by Oberon, with whom she would have exited, leaving Bottom asleep, out of plain sight when Theseus and his party next entered and awakened the lovers (4.1.102–140).

In connection with the lovers' chase, the First Folio supplies a problematic stage direction between 3.3 and 4.1: "They sleep all the Act." The direction may well indicate that the lovers were to remain asleep on stage during an interval between acts. The direction is not in the Quarto, and its insertion in the First Folio may reflect the relatively new practice (beginning around 1607) by the adult companies of having act intervals, during which music was often supplied. (Intervals had been a regular practice in the children's companies long before.) Such intervals would have represented a change in practice for the King's Men, perhaps in conjunction with their move into the Blackfriars around 1609–

1610.[109] We should not imagine that these new intervals were long, however, given the self-evident predilection for swift, continuous action on the unlocalized stages.[110]

Several significant, well-integrated dances are called for in the play. Far from being mere adornments, the play stands to lose an unrecoverable dimension without them. Near the end of the forest sequence, just before night, Oberon calls for a dance to make and mark the reconciliation between Titania and him: "Sound music. Come my queen, take hands with me, / And rock the ground whereon these sleepers be" (4.1.84–85). We do not know the type of dance done originally or to what music, but clearly it would have consisted of vigorous, vital motions, reestablishing their dynamic, complementary relationship, broadcasting this synergy to the elements that their quarrels had once so disturbed. At the end of this dance, Oberon had to be able to say convincingly, "Now thou and I are new in amity" (4.1.86).

The bergamask that two of Quince's company perform after *Pyramus and Thisbe* was a country dance, a cousin to the morris. Probably involving a dance with a hobbyhorse between the legs, it was comically, sexually suggestive and likely to have had fertility associations. Andrew Sabol has indicated that it would have been an appropriate, rustic invocation of blessings on the newly wedded couples.[111] As Skiles Howard suggested, in her essay on reading the dances in the play as cultural discourse, the mechanicals' dance probably would not have been done ineptly and not performed as a condescending joke at the expense of the uneducated artisans, which was the practice common in most productions until the 1960s.[112] In the larger picture, the mechanicals' dance, derivative of entertainments on medieval feasts of misrule, can be seen as an insertion of their folk world into the court of Theseus. It seems an irresistable, natural force, as does the final ritual dance of the fairies who invade the palace.

The fairies' blessing of the newlyweds at the end of the play probably would have involved a more courtly folk dance: "Hand in hand with fairy grace / Will we sing and bless this place," says Titania (5.2.29–30), preceded by Oberon's

> Through the house give glimmering light.
>   By the dead and drowsy fire,
> Every elf and fairy sprite
>   Hop as light as bird from brier,
> And this ditty after me
> Sing, and dance it trippingly. (5.2.21–26)

In itself the blessing dance can be seen, as Brooks and others have, as a lyric coda on domestic harmony.[113] But it is framed by Puck's intimations of mortality in his speech before it ("In remembrance of a shroud" [5.2.8]) and in his reminder after it of the limitations of art:

> If we shadows have offended,
> Think but this, and all is mended:
> That you have but slumbered here,
> While these visions did appear;
> And this weak and idle theme,
> No more yielding but a dream,
> Gentles, do not reprehend. (Epilogue, 1–7)

Perhaps, as Quiller-Couch and Dover Wilson suggested, the fairies wore crowns of candles, similar to those called for in *The Merry Wives of Windsor*, where Mistress Page says she will dress the fairies "with rounds of waxen tapers on their heads" (4.4.50).[114] Lantern-carrying fairies are common in Elizabethan fairy lore. Robert Burton, in the *Anatomie of Melancholie* (1621), reports the lore of night-walking spirits called "pucks" who led people astray, and Puck seems to be such a "Jack-o'-lantern" as he misleads Demetrius and Lysander (3.2.397–414). The fairies might have used the gallery above the main stage to fulfill their charge to "each several chamber bless." The play supplies no clues that a second level was available to the company, but *Romeo and Juliet*, written within a year of it, required it.[115] Such costuming and movement as the text indicates (5.2.21–26) suggest a dance that blended popular folk traditions and court dances.

The original production may have included more music here than the texts record. In the Quarto, the lines beginning "Now until the break of day" (5.2.31–53) are assigned to Oberon; in the Folio they are not, and they are italicized, centered, and preceded with the italicized heading *The Song*. Most editors, from Samuel Johnson through Brooks, Foakes, and Taylor, believe a song is missing here, rather than that these lines were the actual song lyrics. Presumably, the Folio printer mistook a prompter's added note and set the lines following the heading as if a lyric.[116] Oberon's "Now" probably indicates a resumption of speech after "The Song."

The text gives us only a few precious clues to the costuming of the original production. The Elizabethans saw their tales of the ancient Greeks through the lens of the chivalric romances, a tradition exploited in Sidney's *Arcadia* and Spenser's *Faerie Queene*, and the costumes of the Greeks were probably a fanciful blend of Greco-Roman and knightly elements. Titania refers to Hippolyta as Oberon's former "buskined mistress and your warrior love" (2.1.71). Oberon, giving Puck orders to anoint the eyes of the lovers, says, "Thou shalt know the man, / By the Athenian garments he hath on" (2.1.263–264), which allows

Puck to confuse Demetrius and Lysander. The young men may have worn simple, short, sleeveless, girdled chitons and sandals; or, as they were probably armed with swords (3.2.403), perhaps they (and Theseus) wore some elements of Greco-Roman armor, such as the cuirass, skirt, and plumed helmet (as may be seen in the frontispiece of John Stow's 1615 *Annales*). Helena and Hermia might have worn longer, long-sleeved chitons and sandals, and for the Amazon Hippolyta, some elements of armor would be likely.

The text gives us no costume clues for the fairies, but for Shakespeare's audience, the fairy tribe would have been at home among the Greeks. The mingling of fairyland and classical figures was common in fairy traditions of the age, and we may suspect that the dressing of Titania and her train echoed that of the classical sylphs. As we have seen, in *Metamorphoses* Ovid gives Diana the name Titania, and King James VI, in his 1599 *Daemonologie*, represents a common belief when he writes of "that fourth kinde of spirites, which by the Gentiles was called Diane and her wandering court and amongst us was called the Pharies." [117] Titania says the Indian boy's mother "was a *vot'ress* of my order" (2.1.123, emphasis mine). Reginald Scot, in his 1584 *The Discoveries of Witchcraft*, provides some costume clues in recording a charm to achieve invisibility, naming three sisters of fairies, Milia, Achilia, Sibylia: "I charge you that you doo appeare before me visible, in forme and shape of faire women, in white vestures, and to bring with you to me the ring of invisibilitie." [118] In 1598, Philip Henslowe bought the Lord Admiral's company "a robe for to goo invisibell." [119] Oberon might have relied upon such a costume at his line "I am invisible" (2.1.186), although given Shakespeare's playfulness in matters of illusion, Oberon's simple declaration might have been intended to suffice, together with other actors pretending not to see him; the strategy would have made the audience an accomplice in the illusion making. The moment is commonly played that way today. For a masque of about 1610, Inigo Jones's costume design for a cloud-borne woman shows her in a flowing ankle-length skirt, sandals, and an embroidered, quasi-Elizabethan bodice, with four pairs of insectlike wings attached to her back (fig. 1). [120] For the fairy teasing of Falstaff in *The Merry Wives of Windsor*, Mistress Page tells her husband that she will dress their daughter as queen of all the fairies in a silk white robe (4.4.70–72), but, to match her up with the doctor, she really plans for Ann to be in green, "loose enrobed, / With ribbons pendant flaring 'bout her head" (4.6.40–41). All these fairies are to be "masked and visorèd" (4.6.39). From these clues, we might envision Titania and her followers in flowing green or white robes, perhaps winged and masked. Puck says the king of the fairies wants Titania's Indian boy to be a "Knight of his train"

FIGURE 1. Inigo Jones's costume design for an unidentified winged masque character, ca. 1610. Devonshire Collection. Trustees of the Chatsworth Settlement.

FIGURE 2. Inigo Jones's final design for the costume of Oberon in Ben Jonson's *The Masque of Oberon*, 1610. Devonshire Collection. Trustees of the Chatsworth Settlement.

(2.1.25), and it seems likely that Oberon's costume would have been a fantastic blend of knightly armor and Greco-Roman elements, perhaps winged. Jones's designs for Oberon in his 1611 masque of that name shows such a heroic mix (sans wings) (fig. 2).

Puck, or Robin Goodfellow, was familiar as a creature in ballads and plays belonging to the mischievous hobgoblin category of fairies, distantly related to what King James's *Daemonologie* called "the Brownie."[121] The title page engraving of *The Life of Robin Goodfellow* (1628) shows Robin as a bearded satyr figure, with a goat's hooves and legs, a hairy skirt, full frontal phallus, a horn on his belt, a broom in one hand and a torch in the other, dancing in a ring of small figures (fairies?).[122] But this randy fellow is a distant relative of Shakespeare's Puck, who is a gentler spirit of no lascivious mischief and whom Shakespeare has rendered more poetically and with a touch of Cupid. In the play *Grim, the Collier of Croydon* (1600), a servant to the devil enters disguised as Robin Goodfellow in "a suit of leather close to his body, his face and hands coloured russet-colour, with a flail."[123] But this, too, seems closer to folk traditions of medieval demons than to the spirit of Puck.[124]

The mechanicals are clearly Elizabethan artisans, perhaps dressed in appropriate, contemporary work clothes. Puck's "hempen homespuns" is the chief clothing clue (3.1.71), and the mechanicals were probably equipped with tools of their trades. Shakespeare links the name and trade of each, with Quince's name probably referring to quoins or wedges a carpenter used for leveling or tightening a joint and Snug the Joiner's name similarly apt for a carpenter. Bottom the Weaver's name derives from the "bottom," or core, on which a weaver's yarn is wound; Flute the bellows-mender may be a comic reference to a mender of organ pipes; and Snout the Tinker is surely a mender of kettle spouts. The name of Starveling the Tailor conforms to a proverbial Elizabethan image of tailors as slender and effeminate, as is Francis Feeble, the woman's tailor in *2 Henry IV* (3.2.146–168).[125] In *Pyramus and Thisbe*, Bottom would have worn some elements of Greco-Roman armor, including his sword (5.1.291), and Thisbe needs her classical mantle (5.1.277) for Lion to snatch. Half of Snug's face is to be seen at the neck of his lion costume (3.1.33–34). It is not clear precisely how Snout represents a wall with roughcast and stone (5.1.130); later productions give us a wide array of possibilities, from a suit of painted brick to handfuls of brick and mortar. To represent the moon, Starveling carries a lantern and bush of thorn, and he is accompanied by his dog (5.1.134–135), emblems of a legend of the man in the moon, perhaps arcane by this time, which Theseus and the court recognize and find hilariously employed here.[126] Latter-day Starvelings have often used toy dogs, perhaps to protect themselves from being upstaged, but I suspect Starveling's original dog was real. In *Two Gentlemen of Verona*, a play then in the company's repertoire for at least a year, Launce had to have had a live dog for his memorable "dogologues" with Crab (2.3.1– 32 and 4.4.1–38). If Launce and dog and Starveling and dog were played by the same twosome, Starveling's protest that "this dog [is] my dog" (5.1.254) would have been all the more amusing for the regulars in Shakespeare's audiences.

We can only speculate on the original cast. Starveling may have been played by John Sincklo, who did thin men's roles.[127] Oberon and Puck likely would have been played by adult actors. Oberon is arguably a role for Burbage, who could carry the poetry and the romantic appeal.[128] The Puck in *Grim, the Collier of Croydon*, who is there a servant of the devil, was played by an adult actor.[129] And the First Fairy does refer to Puck as "thou lob of spirits" (2.1.16). Younger or smaller actors probably played other fairy roles, including Peaseblossom, Cobweb, Moth, and Mustardseed. In *The Merry Wives of Windsor*, Mistress Page thinks it apt to employ little children to play the "urchins, oafs, and fairies" (4.4.49) who will affright Falstaff in the woods.[130] The fairies in Oberon's so-called train are never enumerated, except for Puck, and we can only surmise that he had some, who would have joined the final fairy blessing song. Hippolyta, Hermia, Helena, and Titania would have been the "boy actor" roles. Of the actors playing Hermia and Helena, we know only the long and short of what their lines in the forest quarrel reveal about Hermia's diminutive, "puppet" stature and Helena's "maypole" height (3.2.289–306). Will Kemp, the company's foremost clown, is likely to have created Bottom, especially since he also played Dogberry in *Much Ado About Nothing*.[131]

The possibility that some of the company doubled in this play, performing two roles, is very likely, and one arrangement offers an alternative to the hypothesis that extra boys were required. There are twenty speaking roles (twenty-one if the Quarto's Philostrate is included), plus the possible supernumeraries for the fairy trains. Doubling was a common practice in the early Elizabethan companies, as is evident from the many interludes that were published with a dramatis personae indicating the specific doubling arrangements. In the best known of these, Thomas Preston's *Cambises King of Persia* (1569), for example, the "Division of the Partes" shows that five men in the company did six or seven roles each.[132] David Bevington demonstrates that, on the basis of extant "plots" for four plays between 1590 and 1602, the practice of doubling was alive in the 1590s.[133] Companies had grown in size, and while their leading players were more likely to be assigned to single roles, actors in supporting roles probably were still doubling heavily.[134] The large casts of Shakespeare's *Henry VI* (1589–1591) would suggest that doubling was common when he began his career. Scott McMillin's study of *Sir Thomas More* (1594–1595) shows that all but one of the speaking roles in the revision could have been played by thirteen men and five boys and that several revisions — some of which make doubling possible — probably were done in order to reduce the company size.[135] Gary Taylor has shown that some of the variations in the memorially reconstructed 1600 "bad" Quarto of *Henry V* are probably the result of doubling arrangements.[136]

William Ringler Jr. has proposed that, with doubling, *A Midsummer Night's Dream* and other of Shakespeare's plays written between 1594 and 1599 could have been performed by a company of eleven or twelve adults and four boys.[137] He doubts that there was doubling in the roles of Theseus/Oberon and Hippolyta/Titania but suggests that the adult actors who played four of the mechanicals — Flute, Starveling, Snout, and Snug — may have doubled as the four fairies who serve Titania — Peaseblossom, Cobweb, Moth, and Mustardseed, respectively.[138] This would obviate the need for the extra boy actors from a court household. Ringler also suggests the doubling of Theseus and the fairy who speaks to Puck in 2.1, but, as T. J. King shows, the role of Theseus is the largest male role in the play (218 lines), and actors in principal roles in Shakespeare's company were less likely to double.[139] In addition, patently different qualities are wanted of the actors in these two roles. Not every doubling arrangement that is geometrically possible in Shakespeare's plays would have been theatrically desirable. King's casting does not double Theseus/Oberon or Hippolyta/Titania nor the fairies and mechanicals, but he does offer the credible idea that one of the boy actors doubled as Hippolyta and the fairy who speaks to Puck in 2.1.[140]

Doubling in the roles of Theseus/Oberon, Hippolyta/Titania, the fairies/mechanicals, and Puck/"a Lord" is, in fact, indicated in the dramatis personae of the interregnum droll, *The Humours of Bottom the Weaver*. As published in Francis Kirkman's collection of drolls, *The Wits, or, Sport upon Sport*, in 1673, the list of characters notes explicitly that the actors playing Oberon and Titania may also play "the Duke" and "the Dutchess" — Theseus and Hippolyta — and that three of the mechanicals, Bottom, Flute, and Snout, "likewise may present three Fairies." The list also indicates that the actor playing Pugg also plays "a Lord."[141] Two unnamed lords appear in the final scene, one of whom is clearly Egeus.[142] The Folio lines for Egeus, Lysander, and Demetrius are split between these two lords. There is no determining from the text which lord was played by the actor playing Puck, but, assuming that one of the lords was, like Lysander or Demetrius, younger than Egeus, the doubling of Puck and Egeus seems the most likely arrangement. The role of Egeus would have afforded the actor who has played Puck the opportunity to then disguise himself with some aging.

If Shakespeare's company doubled the four mechanicals and four fairies, Puck and Egeus, and Hippolyta and the fairy in 2.1, the play could have been acted by twelve men and four boys (not counting any extras for the fairy "trains"), well within the norm for Elizabethan companies. The key component in this is the doubling of the fairies/mechanicals. The boys cannot play both the women's roles and the four fairies, so unless four boys were added to the company, the four fairies had to have been acted by the adults/mechanicals. No other doubling arrangement works to reduce the size of the company sufficiently. If, in addition, the roles of Theseus/Oberon and Hippolyta/Titania were doubled, the play could have been played by eleven men and three boys.[143] But if the normal company size was twelve men and four boys, the doubling of Theseus/Oberon and Hippolyta/Titania would not have been necessary.

In recent years, thematic arguments have been advanced for doubling in the roles of Theseus/Oberon and Hippolyta/Titania. Modern directors began to experiment with the doubling of Theseus/Oberon and Hippolyta/Titania in the 1960s, and the practice has been commonplace since Peter Brook's 1970 production.[144] Stephen Booth maintained that this double vision, as it were, is apt for the play's irrational forest dream world, with its other "changes and confusions of persona," and reflects Shakespeare's experimentation with double consciousness of the performance and the performed.[145] James L. Calderwood offered an elaborate view of the doubling as intrinsic to Shakespeare's creation of our anamorphic view of the action, in which the forest experience is necessary to resolve the problems in Athens.[146] Graham Bradshaw has contended that this doubling allows an integration of reason and the mystery necessary to the play, while John Russell Brown and Ralph Berry have objected stoutly on the grounds that doubling minimizes the considerable differences between these pairs.[147] Such doubling seems doubtful on another ground. Theseus and Hippolyta must enter at 4.1.102, immediately on the heels of Oberon's and Titania's exit. While costume changes can and have been done in an instant, the moment becomes theatrically self-conscious in a blatant way that one finds nowhere else in the play. Any doubling that occurred proceeded, I believe, from pragmatic interests. Keeping this in mind, I want to turn to the differences between the 1600 Quarto and First Folio involving the roles of Egeus and Philostrate. With this issue, I close on considerations of the Elizabethan production of the play.

Barbara Hodgdon has proposed that there is thematic significance in the changes in the Folio, in which Egeus has replaced Philostrate in Act 5, and she sees Shakespeare's revising hand in them.[148] In the Quarto, Egeus is absent from the last act; his name is not included in the opening entrance directions, and he is given no lines. In the Folio, he enters at the top of the last act and is given the lines that the Quarto assigns to Philostrate (save one, which editors since Furness generally agree is a speech heading error). Also, in the Folio, the reading of the amusing catalog of entertainments offered to Theseus (5.1.42–57) is shared between Egeus and Lysander. Hodgdon suggests that Egeus is thereby participating as a joyful father in the wedding celebration and that there has been an appropriate resolution to the family conflict that set the play in motion. At the opposite pole is the stage business of the 1970 Peter Brook production, in which Egeus stalked off stage after Theseus's decision in 4.1 to overrule him in favor of the lovers' wishes.

Hodgdon is certainly right that the changes in question are deliberate rather than evidence of compositor carelessness in the Folio. She argues that economy could not have been the motive because the change would not have reduced the company by one actor; Philostrate's presence is still required in the Folio Act 1, and Egeus enters only four lines after Philostrate's exit, so these roles cannot be doubled. But there is a doubling option here not considered by Hodgdon. Philostrate has no lines in Act 1; he is present with the court at the opening of the play and simply exits to carry out Theseus's command (1.1.15). The actor playing Puck easily could have doubled as Philostrate here, in this walk-on role, were Egeus to have taken over Philostrate's lines in Act 5. This arrangement eliminates one actor and would have been economically attractive. That may well have been the casting arrangement in the interregnum droll, as we have seen, and the roles of Philostrate and Puck have been played by the same actor in numerous modern productions, including the Royal Shakespeare Company's (RSC) productions of 1970, 1981, and 1995, and the Stratford, Ontario, production of 1977. As to the Folio's division of the lines between Lysander and Egeus describing the entertainments, I suggest that this change from the Quarto followed logically. Egeus was now present in the last act, and this had to be acknowledged. The sharing of the entertainment descriptions between Egeus and Lysander provided some opportunity, as Hodgdon notes, for showing their relationship. Perhaps Egeus tutored his new son-in-law as a future Master of Revels, handing him the list of entertainments to read. Or perhaps Lysander asserted his own voice, even interrupting Egeus.[149] But a choice would have had to have been made. I suspect the antagonism continued, comically handled. In sum, I am suggesting that the Folio changes were the result of the company's collaborative process in which a casting economy was turned to good dramatic account. We cannot know when the change was made or whether Shakespeare participated in or acceded to it. In any case, the Folio's use of Egeus in Act 5 offers modern actors and directors more options.

We have only a few clues about the stage life of *A Midsummer Night's Dream* from 1596 to the closing of the theatres in 1642. It probably was in the company's repertoire for many years. Francis Meres mentioned it in 1598, some three years after the probable date of its writing, and the 1600 Quarto title page claimed to give the reader the text "as it hath been sundry times publikely acted."[150] There is the possibility, but no assurance, that *A Midsummer Night's Dream* was the "play of Robin goode-fellow" that was performed for King James — probably at Hampton Court — in January 1604.[151] It does sound like a memory of well-known stage business when a character in Edward Sharpham's play of 1607, *The Fleire*, says "like Thisbe in the play, 'a has almost kil'ed himself with the scabberd."[152] We may infer some continuing popularity of the play from the fact that it was one of the ten plays by Shakespeare (or attributed to him) reprinted in quarto in 1619 by William Jaggard, before Jaggard became involved in plans for the First Folio. The added stage directions in the 1623 Folio may be evidence of recent stage life, including the entrance stage direction, "Tawyer with a Trumpet before them" (5.1.125). This probably refers to William Tawyer, "Mr. Heminges man," who was named among musicians and attendants of the King's Men in 1624.[153] John Taylor, the Water-poet, may have been remembering the play in the theatre when he wrote in the foreword to his *Sir Gregory Nonsense* in 1622: "I say, as it is applausefully written, and commended to posterity, in the Midsummer-Night's Dream, If we offend, it is with our good will, we came with no intent but to offend, and show our simple skill."[154]

The most solid evidence that the play remained in the King's Men's repertoire for over three decades is that "Midsomers Night's Dreame" occurs in a list of four plays done by the company for King Charles at Hampton Court on 17 October 1630.[155] For this occasion, if we wish, we can imagine the performance in a candle-lit and perfumed great hall, which is how Peter Cunningham described the theatrical performances he saw in Hampton Court hall in about 1572.[156] In either 1629 or 1631, the play or a portion of it probably was performed on a Sunday for the Bishop of Lincoln, John Williams, and his guests at Buckden Palace, near Huntingdon. The host was fined for this Sunday entertainment, and the court also decreed that a principal player of the unnamed play be put in the stocks, wearing an ass's head, with a bundle of hay at his feet, as punishment for his "brutish" impersonation.[157]

In the prologue to his 1646 masque, *The Triumph of Beauty*, James Shirley is clearly borrowing crudely on *Pyramus and Thisbe* when he has a character named Bottle lead his shepherd friends in farcical preparations for a performance of the tragedy of the Golden Fleece to entertain the prince.[158] In 1624, John Gee, in *New Shreds of Old Snares*, is unmistakably referring to Quince's comedy of *Pyramus and Thisbe*.[159] Had the mechanicals' play been separated from the rest of the play by this time? We cannot be sure, but it soon would be. In the interregnum, the rehearsal and performance of *Pyramus and Thisbe* were apparently prominent among the drolls, those short entertainments brought out furtively to lighten that dark period of Puritan zeal that leveled most theatres.

Chapter two

SHAKESPEARE ABSOLUTE

FAIRIES, GODS, AND ORANGES IN

PURCELL'S *FAIRY QUEEN*

Theseus: How shall we find the concord of this discord?

For almost two hundred years, from 1642 to 1840, *A Midsummer Night's Dream* was never seen in its entirety in the English or continental theatre. In the mid-seventeenth century, strolling players in England and Germany played *Pyramus and Thisbe*, lifted from the play, and in eighteenth-century England the mechanicals' play was borrowed to satirize the opera. In England, Shakespeare's blend of mythological Athenians, courtly lovers, supernatural fairies, and earthy artisans was incompatible with the rationalistic neoclassical rules for straight drama. His plays with supernatural elements were more properly to be treated in operatic adaptations, where music could carry the fantastic. The English semi-opera of 1692, *The Fairy Queen*, with its sublime music by Henry Purcell, was the play's first significant production under the new order, and it is the primary subject of this chapter. To appreciate this semi-opera (a problematic label) in its cultural moment, we will need to read all three of its texts: the music, the libretto, and the visual vocabulary of its original staging. This reveals what has not been seen clearly before: *The Fairy Queen* reshaped Shakespeare's play to feature royal tributes to William and Mary, most especially in its lavish climax, which paid tribute to their marriage.

Before turning to Purcell's ethereal court music, I want to consider briefly the mid-seventeenth-century's popular uses of the play — the appropriations of *Pyramus and Thisbe*. During the interregnum, after Cromwell's crews had dismantled most public playhouses, the playlet turned up among the drolls, which were given clandestinely under the pretense of "rope-dancing" or the like. Audiences filled the Red Bull playhouse for these,[1] apparently sometimes at risk. On at least one occasion, they had to pay off Cromwell's soldiers both on the way in and on the way out the theatre doors.[2] The drolls' appeal is explained by Francis Kirkman in the introduction to his 1673 anthology of them, *The Wits, or, Sport upon Sport*:

> When the publique Theatres were shut up, and the Actors forbidden to present us with any of their Tragedies, because we had enough of that in earnest; and Comedies, because the Vices of the Age were too lively and smartly represented; then all that we could divert our selves with were these humours and pieces of plays.

Pyramus and Thisbe was apparently one of the more popular drolls, for it was published twice, the second time in Kirkman's 1673 anthology.[3] It begins with the artisans' first meeting to cast *Pyramus and Thisbe* and ends with their performance of the play and the bergamask for Theseus and Hippolyta. The young lovers' scenes are all omitted; the cutting alternates the mechanicals' scenes with those involving Oberon, Titania, and "Pugg." The mechanicals head the edition's dramatis personae.

Slight things that they were, Kirkman remembers such drolls gratefully and praises especially one of their actors, "the incomparable Robert Cox, who was not only the principal Actor, but also the contriver and Author of most of these Farces." Kirkman's collection is a kind of early Samuel French acting edition, marketed to aspiring thespians: "Players who intend to wander and go a stroleing, this very Book, and a few ordinary properties is enough to set them up, and get money in any town in England."[4]

Resourceful English players already had long since carried versions of the mechanicals' play to towns in Germany. It is well established that English actors traveled to numerous German cities from the mid-1590s to about 1620.[5] Ovid's tale of the tragic lovers may have been familiar to some in the German audiences, and the burlesquing of such tales was the familiar stuff of the Pickelherring clowns. The mechanicals were not far from the peasant comedy tradition of Hans Sachs. A traveling English-speaking company could carry off *Pyramus and Thisbe* in broad action and business that would overcome the language barrier. Evidence of performances in Germany in the mid-seventeenth century that were unmistakably derived from the playlet includes one published text.[6] Andreas Gryphius's *Absurda comica; oder, Herr Peter Squentz, Schimpff-Spiel* came into print no later than 1657. Squentz is Shakespeare's Quince transformed into a small-town German schoolmaster at Rumpelkirchen. He is a broadly parodied, pretentious pedant who introduces himself *"cum titulius plenissimis"* and as "a *Universalem*, that is, experienced in all branches of learning."[7] Gryphius's first act corresponds to 1.2, the first meeting of the artisans to cast *Pyramus and Thisbe*, the second to 5.1, the performance of their play at court. Pickelherring plays Pyramus. Bottom is a bellows-maker named Master Bulla-Butain and plays Wall. Master Clod-George, a spoolmaker, plays Thisbe. Master Lollinger, weaver and "*Meistersanger*," plays the fountain by which Ovid's original lovers meet, which here becomes a singing and spraying fountain, a spoof on classical town fountains. The farcical business described in the plentiful stage directions is reminiscent of the commedia dell'arte and is clearly aimed at carnival and street-fair audiences. Pickelherring/Pyramus and Bulla-Butain/Wall thrash each other in a violent quarrel. Thisbe, mourning over the dead Pyramus, says, "See how my hair I tear and rend," after which the stage direction reads, "She scratches under her armpits (ridet)."[8] This version of *Pyramus and Thisbe*, and variations on it, is all that Germans saw of *A Midsummer Night's Dream* in performance for almost two centuries.

The play had no significant life on the English stage from the Restoration of Charles II in 1660 until Purcell's opera in 1692.[9] The only record of the play in the theatre in those years comes in Samuel Pepys's diary entry for 29 September 1662:

> To the King's Theatre where we saw "Midsummer Night's Dream," which I had never seen before, nor shall ever again, for it is the most insipid ridiculous play that ever I saw in my life. I saw, I confess, some good dancing & some handsome women, which was all my pleasure.[10]

Pepys was twenty-nine; he was removed two generations and a civil war from the age of Elizabeth, and his tastes were those of the court whose king he served, ultimately as Secretary to the Admiralty. His utter distaste for *A Midsummer Night's Dream* seems directed at the play itself, probably in an adaptation, more than at the performance at Thomas Killigrew's simple theatre on Vere Street.[11] The handsome women who came under Pepys's male gaze could have been the actresses in the roles of Hermia and Helena; women had been on the London stage for at least two years. From his mention of dancing, one can speculate that he saw a musical adaptation. But all we really can conclude is that the 1662 production that Pepys saw was not altered far enough for his taste.[12] London managers did not venture the play again soon; after 1662, there is no sure evidence that *A Midsummer Night's Dream* was performed, in any version, for thirty years.[13]

The first significant production of the play in the new order was an idealizing celebration of royal power — the appropriation seems irresistible. The resonance of the play's allusions to Elizabeth would have been sufficient reason; the wedding theory had not yet been born. *The Fairy Queen, an Opera* was first produced on 2 May 1692 at the Queen's Theatre (formerly Dorset Garden Theatre).[14] In this semi-opera, the play text proper, in its adapted form, is largely spoken; it features at the end of Acts 2 through 5 four lavish, masquelike spectacles of song, ballet, and elaborate scenic displays. It was for these that Purcell created his score, widely regarded today as containing some of his most sublime music. Produced in all likelihood under the guidance of Thomas Betterton, with the United Company, the opera was one of the most expensive productions in an era of expensive English operas. Purcell's full score was lost soon thereafter, being recovered only around 1900.[15] Since then, *The Fairy Queen* has had life chiefly as a concert piece and in recordings, quite separated from the adaptation and the spectacles for which Purcell created his music. Only rarely since has the opera been staged fully.[16]

We also have lost some keys necessary for unlocking the full meaning of the opera as staged in its time. Opera historians, troubled by Purcell's non-Italian form, have not recovered these meanings, nor have music scholars concerned with formal appreciations of Purcell's aesthetic achievement, nor have Shakespearean scholars, who have been inclined to deprecate any operatic adaptation of Shakespeare's text (except perhaps Verdi's).

Shakespeareans and theatre historians of modern times have mocked this opera's text, its spectacles, and Restoration audience taste. Horace Howard Furness, in his 1895 Variorum edition of the play, summarily dismissed what he called a "witless opera."[17] Theatre historian George C. D. Odell, in his 1920 *Shakespeare from Betterton to Irving*, despaired of Restoration adaptations of Shakespeare in general as "atrocities," perpetrated by Judas-like adapters who "kissed him ere they killed him." Odell confessed to being unable to make any "historical readjustment" to Restoration operas such as *The Fairy Queen*. A dutiful stage historian, he cited the lengthy stage directions from the extant libretto. Neither Furness nor Odell would have heard Purcell's lost score; neither seems to have even inquired after it. For Odell, *The Fairy Queen* violated Shakespeare's sacred text, offering mere operatic spectacle for a Restoration audience "mad for such entertainment and largely fed on it by Betterton."[18] Hazelton

Spencer, in his ironically titled *Shakespeare Improved* (1927), fully cataloged the textual alterations and stage directions as evidence of the play's having been "tortured into an opera" (a phrase borrowed from Odell). The scenic embellishments, he wrote, "do not call for serious criticism," and the music he did not consider at all.[19] Constant Lambert, who thought the music deserved attention and produced a shortened adaptation of the opera at Covent Garden in 1946, referred to the original text as "a seventeenth century hotch-potch."[20] In 1959, W. Moelwyn Merchant offered some background on the baroque scenic context of the opera but lamented that Shakespeare's play had been made into "a mere scaffolding to carry a wholly unrelated series of spectacles."[21]

Modern music historians have been much concerned with formalistic appreciations of the music of *The Fairy Queen* and with discussions of the generically troubling English semi-opera — a genre whose proper identity was the subject of even more dispute among Restoration critics, composers, and librettists themselves. *The Fairy Queen* combined the spoken play text with Purcell's act-ending musical spectacles; the former was delivered by a cast of actors and actresses quite distinct from the singers and dancers who performed in the latter. It did not follow the model of the all-sung Italian opera developed at the end of the sixteenth-century and so is regarded by some modern commentators as a generic mistake along the road to the modern ideal of opera, a rather troublesome work in which to find so much immortal theatre music. Robert Moore, Roger Savage, and Curtis Alexander Price have concentrated, for the most part, on formalistic appreciations of the opera's music.[22] Moore expands upon the opera's context, even giving some attention to Restoration scenecraft. But this effort is finally subsumed in his endeavor to demonstrate the formalistic coherence of Purcell's score. His agenda is never clearer than when he tries (several times) to add aesthetic stature to the opera by devaluing the original play: Shakespeare's dialogue is "feeble," and his young lovers "wrangle," while Purcell "creates music which lifts the whole work from the realm of mediocre farce to that of ethereal enchantment."[23]

Such concerns have not taken us far enough toward understanding the design of *The Fairy Queen* as royal entertainment. Like other English Restoration operas, *The Fairy Queen* is a late entry in the European allegorical court entertainments that extend from the Italian intermezzi through the Jacobean and Caroline court masques. Compared to some of the English semi-operas not long before it, such as *King Arthur*, it was, in fact, as Price and Eric Walter White have observed, something of a retrenchment in its separation of the act-ending musical spectacles and the spoken dramatic text.[24] The mission of the court entertainments traditionally was to show how the earthly rulers who were their patrons were, in effect, divinely empowered joint partners with the classical deities in the governance of an orderly universe. In these "mighty shows," as Ben Jonson called the English masques, the connection between divine and royal power was made palpable by awe-inspiring multimedia theatrical effects of the new scenic technology, underwritten by the vast wealth of the absolutist state. Such shows gave expression to a vision of a neo-Platonic marriage of ideal and real; they were the religious rituals of the new secular state. If the earth was no longer the center of the universe, Copernicus's heliocentrism offered the useful idea of a divine ordering power at the center of all things, scientific sanction for centralized political power. The allegorical demonstration of this relation between heaven and earth was something the new theatre of magnificent scenic transformations and music could do. Stephen Orgel has shown the principle at work in his analysis of several court entertainments, including *News from the New World*. Orgel demonstrates that in such shows,

> the court and the aristocratic hierarchy expand and become the world, and the King is in turn abstracted to Pan the Universal god, to the life-giving sun, to Hesperus the evening star, or even, in an extraordinary example, to a physical principle, pure potential, through whom the ultimate scientific mysteries of perpetual motion and infinite power are finally solved.[25]

The creators of *The Fairy Queen* have debts to the operas of Jean-Baptiste Lully, created for the French court of Louis XIV, most especially to the *tragédie-ballet Psyché* (1671), as Robert Moore has shown.[26] These works featured singing, ballets, and scenic spectacles in which stage machinists brought heaven to earth in massive shows of absolute power — three hundred deities strong in *Psyché*. *Psyché*'s stage machinery had been used previously in *Hercules in Love*, an operatic compliment to Louis, created for his marriage celebrations in 1662 and featuring, for the finale, the descent from the clouds of *le Roi Soleil* and his whole family. The immense *Salle des Machines* that Cardinal Mazarin had Carlo Vigarani build for these works was not designed purely to advance the aesthetic development of opera (nor, as it turned out, acoustics). The English creators of *The Fairy Queen* also had behind them a strong native tradition of the pre-Commonwealth English masques and, in the Restoration, previous tributary operas, all in the service of Stuart rulers who had held strongly to the principle of the divine right of kings.

The "glorious revolution" that brought William and Mary to the throne in 1689 was, to be sure, the beginning of a less centralized monarchy and more parliamentarian participation in governance, as well as religious tolerance. But in 1692, a traditional climate of absolutism still obtained in some respects, including expectations that the arts would serve the monarchy. William once had been a keen admirer and imitator of Louis XIV, destined though he was to oppose his expansionism. In 1668, when William was eighteen, he gave a *Ballet de Paix*, in which he played Mercury, who intervened to unite a quarreling England and France.[27] William maintained a French troupe of actors and then an opera company at the Hague in the 1670s and 1680s.

When William came to the English throne, Purcell became composer to His Majesty. The immediate operatic predecessors of Purcell's *Fairy Queen* celebrated Britannia. John Dryden's *Albion and Albanius* (1685) was planned as a symbolic history of the reign of Charles II, its prologue framed in praise of Charles and James. Purcell's *Dido and Aeneas* (1689) contained allusions to the ascendance of William and Mary in the form of Phoebus and Venus; *The Prophetess, or, The History of Dioclesian* (1690) alluded to William's mission to subdue the Irish in the Battle of the Boyne.[28] In *King Arthur* (1691), Dryden and Purcell aimed at a British national opera (or as Dryden decided to subtitle it, a "dramatic opera"). The agenda for the masques in *The Fairy Queen* is not as obvious as are the intentions in these works or in the earlier Caroline masques, *Coelum Brittanicum* (1634) and *Brittania Triumphans* (1637). But the musical spectacles in *The Fairy Queen* are compliments to William and Mary in the tradition of these. Purcell's music is more personally expressive; Queen Mary herself may have been a particular source of inspiration to him. (Perhaps she was shown the work in advance, as was the case with *King Arthur*.) Purcell and the other creators of *The Fairy Queen* remodeled Shakespeare's fairy play as a tribute to Mary and as an allegory on marital harmony, the model of which, the opera demonstrates, was to be found in William and Mary's marriage.

Shakespeare's text is cut and rearranged to serve this intent and to be theatrically efficient. The play proper is trimmed to the bare essentials of dramatic action, with much of the original poetry sacrificed. The opening scene is streamlined from 265 to 157 lines. In Act 2, much of Titania's poetry on discord of the elements proceeding from the estrangement between Oberon and her is gone (2.1.81–117), as are her description of the Indian boy's mother ("His mother was a vot'ress of my order" [2.1.123–137]) and Helena's description of her childhood bond with Hermia (3.2.193–220). A new, climactic spectacle at the end of the opera results in the major alteration of Shakespeare's Act 5. The mechanicals' play is moved to the forest rehearsal, where it is performed in its entirety. Robin scatters the actors after Thisbe's death, after which he brings on Bottom in the ass's head. Bottom and his companions are reunited later, as in Shakespeare, with Bottom announcing that "our play shall be preferr'd." Something more grand and politic is in order for the Act 5 finale, however, so the adapters used the mechanicals' play in the forest rehearsal rather than losing it altogether. The fairy song and dance ("Through the house give glimmering light" [5.2.21]) and Puck's epilogue are cut entirely for the new ending.

Two careful pieces of surgery are the elimination from the play of any mention of Athens and the total elimination of the character of Hippolyta. Gone are the references to "the ancient privilege of Athens," "Diana's altar," and "the sharp Athenian law" (1.1.41, 89, 162). Lysander's aunt's house is not seven leagues from Athens (1.1.160) but a mile outside "the town." Oberon tells Puck he will know Demetrius "by the embroidered garments he has on," not by his Athenian garments (2.1.264). And the name of Theseus is replaced by the title "the Duke" in all his speech prefixes and in all references. Theseus was, in fact, as much English duke as Greek Argonaut even in Shakespeare's play, where, in several Act 5 speech headings (Quarto and Folio), we find him identified as "Du." or "Duk." and Hippolyta as "Dut."

There were probably two reasons behind this consistent "Englishing" of the play. It tidied up Shakespeare's romantic mix of ancient Greeks, gothic fairy mythology, and Elizabethan artisans, anachronisms that Samuel Johnson criticized in his later *Preface to Shakespeare*.[29] More important, it served the opera's allegorical focus on William and Mary, as did the omission of Hippolyta and all references to her marriage to Theseus. The opera climaxes with a scenic spectacle that educates the Duke in the possibilities of love in this kingdom: the royal couple to be focused on at this point is William and Mary, not Theseus and Hippolyta.

Throughout the adaptation, Shakespeare's verse has also been "modernized." It is pruned of what, in the Restoration, seemed archaic diction and syntax, and the verse is regularized in meter and rhyme. About half of the original text is cut, probably to make time for the musical spectacles. Shakespeare's text consists of 2,134 lines; the 1692 edition of the spoken text consists of about 1,200 lines, modified Shakespearean and non-Shakespearean.[30]

An often overlooked point must be made about the adaptation. While the cutting and rearranging of the text and the modernizing of the language have scandalized purists, the play as spoken drama was still there; 1,200 lines of it were not set to music. The aim, clearly, was to give the spoken play its due, together with the music and spectacle. There was considerable debate among the English throughout the Restoration and beyond over what the best English form of "opera" should be (even the Italian term is problematic for the English), a debate that manifests considerable anxiety about the national identity. But in general it may be said that the English did not wish to see the spoken word completely sublimated to those less than rational seductions of music that the "soft" Italians favored.[31] Matthew Locke, in his preface to his score of the English version of *Psyche* (1675), defended a mixture of spoken dialogue and musical elements as "more proper to our [English] genius."[32] Peter Motteaux, writing in the *Gentleman's Journal* in 1692 about Purcell's operatic works, said:

> Other Nations bestow the name of Opera only on such plays whereof every word is sung. But experience hath taught us that our English genius will not relish that perpetual Singing. . . . It is true that their *Trio's*, chorus's, lively Songs and *Recits* with *Acompaniments* of Instruments, Symphony's, Machines, and excellent Dances make the rest be borne with, and the one sets off the other: But our English Gentlemen, when their Ear is satisfy'd, are desirous to have their mind pleas'd, and Music and Dancing industriously intermix'ed with Comedy or Tragedy.[33]

In the years between these two statements, there was much nuanced debate, and operatic works themselves varied in form. But defenses of a semi-opera form that served the English taste for the spoken word resurfaced time and again. In *The Fairy Queen*, the spoken text not only provided the structural framework, it got a high proportion of the performance time — probably roughly 40 percent. The emphasis, then, by Shakespearean scholars on how much of Shakespeare's play was or was not cut obscures the fact that this adaptation represents an English preference for "operas" in which the spoken word was an equal with the music, dance, and scenic spectacle. The sentiment is still alive, to judge from BBC commentator Nicholas Kenyon, who, on the occasion of the tercentary of Purcell's death in 1995, characterized Purcell's semi-operas as "extended plays with musical interludes, theatre-plus rather than opera-minus."[34]

To come to Purcell's music, audiences first heard two short pieces played before the curtain by an orchestra of at least twelve and perhaps as many as thirty instruments. In Purcell's "First Music," there are light, gracefully flowing melody lines and semiquavers on strings and harpsichord. A hornpipe follows, its folklike melody and rhythm formally orchestrated. The "Second Music" evolves to passages that anticipate the opera; it includes a memorable, tender rondeau. It closes with a short overture consisting of a trumpet fanfare, suitable perhaps for the entry of royalty to the royal box; this is then elaborated by trumpets and strings. The music evokes a strong sense of ceremony, of the formal ambience of an intimate Restoration theatre with the court in attendance. We are far from the public theatre of Shakespeare's time.

The curtain then opens and the action proceeds — in dialogue: Egeus brings Hermia before the Duke, and the dramatic action proceeds through Helena's exit, as it does in Shakespeare. Act 1 of the 1692 text includes no songs (the 1693 revision included songs and will be examined later), nor does it end with a musical spectacle as do Acts 2 through 5.

The first act's scenic requirements are less elaborate than those to come; the
"palace" called for in the opening stage direction (p. 1) probably was a stock flat-and-shutter setting behind the proscenium. That *The Fairy Queen* depends on a stage that can provide such pictures distinguishes it, of course, from the interests of Shakespeare's play in issues of perception. But the English Restoration pictures were generically emblematic rather than illusionistic. In the Restoration theatres, actors played on the relatively large apron platform downstage of the proscenium; the scenic pictures came and went upstage within the proscenium frame. The effect was an English compromise between a theatre of words and one of sensual spectacle, quite comparable in spirit to the English semi-opera compromise between the spoken word and singing.

The mechanicals' first meeting is incorporated in the opera's first act, with no indication of a change of setting. The printed text indicates an act break after the mechanicals exit, but neither the length of the first act (less than ten minutes is required to play its 157 lines) nor the preparations for the coming scene change would have made an intermission necessary. For Act 2, the palace set was replaced by "a Wood, by Moonlight."

The sequence of action in Act 2 is much as it is in Shakespeare, from the entrance of Robin and the fairy through the quarrel between Oberon and Titania and her reentrance to sleep in her canopied bed. The quarrel over the Indian boy is highlighted with some novel scenic trickery. A 1692 variant issue of the libretto reveals business probably used in the premiere: Titania enters first, "leading the Indian boy, fairies attending." When a sentinel enters to warn that Oberon is coming, she commands the earth to open and receive the Indian boy. Judging from the next stage direction, "He sinks," it did.[35] Oberon then enters in perplexed pursuit of the boy.

When Titania reenters later (probably through one of the proscenium doors), she commands that the setting (behind the proscenium) be transformed into fairyland: "All delights this place surround, / Every sweet Harmonious Sound, / That e'er Charmed a skilful Ear, / Meet and Entertain us here" (p. 15). This introduces the first musical spectacle of the opera. The stage directions describe a well-ordered fairyland: a symmetrical palace garden, with grottoes and arbors, rendered in single point perspective — a neat, neoclassical version of the bank where the wild thyme grows, "nature methodized," to use Pope's phrase:

The scene changes to a Prospect of Grotto's, Arbors, and delightful Walks: The Arbors are Adorn'd with all variety of flowers, the Grotto's supported by

Terms, these two lead to two Arbors on either side of the Scene, of a great length, whose prospect runs toward the two Angles of the House [stage house]. Between these two Arbors is the great Grotto, which is continued by several Arches, to the farther end of the House [stage]. (p. 14)

We are nearer to William and Mary's new symmetrical gardens for Hampton Court than to a wood near ancient Athens.[36]

Purcell's music provides a brief prelude of flutes in birdlike runs, after which comes the opera's first song, sung by a fairy (tenor), "Come all ye Songsters of the Sky" (p. 15). Answering this summons, birds enter to dance a ballet in three-quarter time, led by flutes and oboes. Titania's fairy chorus requests that Echo join them, and the flutes and oboes cleverly echo the birds' refrains during the Echo Dance. This delicate music then breaks into a light, tripping song by a soprano and full chorus, "Sing, sing while we trip it, / trip it upon the green" (p. 16).

From this light-footed fairy world, Purcell moves to the mysterious and sublime, making the Fairy Queen the center of focus. Allegorical figures of Night, Mystery, Secrecy, and Sleep enter, each one singing a verse around the sleeping queen. Night's song is one of tenderest solicitude, the soprano accompanied with muted violins and violas. The song of Sleep (bass solo and chorus) includes dramatic pauses of two full seconds of hushed silence between phrases: "Hush [silence], no more [silence], Hush [silence] no more . . . Sweet repose [silence] has closed her eyes, / soft as feathered snow does fall! / Softly, softly steal from hence, / no noise disturb her sleeping sense" (pp. 17–18). The chorus of sopranos and altos repeats the bass's lines, almost like a benediction, as Robert Moore notes. A ballet for Night and her followers closes the movement, choreographed by Josiah Priest, as were all the dances. The movement is Purcell's elegant, elaborate replacement of the lullaby called for in Shakespeare, beginning, "You spotted snakes with double tongue" (2.2.9–30). Purcell's Fairy Queen sleeps serenely in a hushed world of ethereal beauty, divine tranquility. His score requires highly trained opera voices and exacting attention to choral balance and phrasing; the orchestration of Night's ballet is technically sophisticated, with first violins in canon with basses at the same time that second violins are in canon with violas. In all, it is sublime, sophisticated music that could be a fitting tribute to the living queen. Moore suggests that it elevates Titania to the Spenserian, Elizabethan associations of her title,[37] but the masque seems much more likely to have been a tribute to Queen Mary. She was frequently compared to Elizabeth I, as Thomas Shadwell did in his text for Purcell's birthday ode for

Queen Mary in 1689.[38] This tribute would be sufficient to account for the choice of the opera's title. It is not surprising that the opera's most sublime music celebrates Mary, who inspired more loyalty and affection in general than did her somewhat dour husband.

After the masque, the action proceeds as in Shakespeare, but much compressed. Oberon enters to squeeze the juice of the magic flower on Titania's eyes, and the weary Lysander and Hermia enter and sleep. The second act ends with the entrance of Robin to charm Lysander. Act 3 begins with the lovers' chase, their dialogue cut to the bare necessities of exposition. Quince and company run through all of *Pyramus and Thisbe*, near the end of which Puck scatters them and translates Bottom. Titania wakes to Bottom's ousel cock song (if Purcell provided a new tune, it has been lost) and exits with him. Oberon and Puck observe the confusion of the quartet of lovers (whose lines are much reduced) and exit to make amends. Omission of a large section of the lovers' quarrel (3.2.122–413 and 3.3.1–48), which will be used in Act 4, brings the action to the reentrance of Titania with Bottom (4.1) and the climaxing of Act 3 with a masque. Titania asks her fairies to prepare "a Fairy Mask / To entertain my Love," and she commands that they "change this place / to my Enchanted Lake." With this, the scenery changes (in full view) to

> a great Wood; a long row of large Trees on each side: A River in the middle; Two rows of lesser Trees of a different kind just on the side of the River, which meet in the middle, and make so many arches: Two great Dragons make a Bridge over the River; their Bodies form two Arches, through which two Swans are seen in the River at a great distance. (p. 7)

This perspective setting would have been carried out on flats and a backcloth, with profile (or cutout) pieces of the trees and bridge, set at different planes in front of the backdrop landscape featuring the river. Dancers as swans then enter under the arched trees and "turn themselves into Fairies and Dance." At the same time, arched trees return to upright positions, and the painted dragon bridge upstage vanishes — flown out or pulled off on sliding flats that met at center stage. For his swan ballet music, Purcell opens with stately string basses and provides what Anthony Lewis describes as "a miniature French overture based on smoothly gliding figures."[39] Then, downstage, "a troupe of Fawns, Dryades and Naiades" enters to entertain Titania and Bottom. A soprano and chorus sing Purcell's now famous, "If Love's a Sweet Passion, why does it torment?" The amorous lyrics of this two-stanza love song are coyly set to a piquant melody in three-quarter time: "Yet so pleasing the Pain is, so soft is the

Dart / That at once it both wounds me and tickles my heart."[40] Titania and Bottom are the ostensible occasion for this song, a patent set piece that proved a favorite with audiences.[41]

A short, dainty dance for the fairies follows, which is then interrupted by the entrance and vigorous dance of "the Green Men" — a kind of comic anti-masque, whose music is folkish and sprightly, with flutes, oboes, and basses pizzicato. It marks a transition to a pastoral interlude featuring two comic rustics, Coridon and Mopsa, who enter with a troupe of haymakers. The original Folio stage directions call here only for "rural music" (4.1.34), not this extensive an evocation of arcadia. The dance is a rustic interlude, done in Purcell's own stylish fashion and tongue-in-cheek. In a song about kissing, a moaning Coridon implores the shepherdess Mopsa for her kisses, and she resists: "I'll not trust you so far, I know you too well; / Should I give you an inch you'd soon take an ell. / Then lordlike you rule, and laugh at the fool" (p. 31). Mopsa was played by "Mr. Pate (in woman's habit)," the intent of this cross-dressing apparently being to raise laughter by mocking male-female courtship.[42] Present-day recordings follow this tradition, having the role of Mopsa sung by a countertenor, which Pate probably was. A "nymph" (soprano) then sings of finally yielding to her lover, vowing that if he is inconstant, she will be, too. The haymakers do a vigorous dance, and Coridon, Mopsa, and chorus close this scene and the act with a happy song on rural life: "A thousand, thousand ways we'll find / To entertain the hours, / No two shall e'er be known so kind, / No life so blest as ours" (p. 32). Titania and Bottom exit to "a bank strew'd o'er with violets."

The beginning of Act 4 picks up the young lovers' trail (using the omitted portions of 3.2 and 3.3), with Puck ultimately leading them back on stage, one by one, to fall asleep. Oberon releases Titania from her spell, and they are reconciled. In response to Oberon's call for music ("Sound music. Come my queen, take hands with me / And rock the ground whereon these sleepers be" [4.1.84–85]), Purcell provides a masque of the four seasons, symbolizing a return to natural order with the reconciliation of the Fairy Queen and King. Roger Savage is surely right in his suggestion that Purcell took his theme from Titania's speech,[43] cut from the opera, on the disorder of the elements proceeding from the quarrel between her and Oberon: "The spring, the summer, / The childing autumn, angry winter change / Their wonted liveries, and the mazèd world / By their increase now knows not which is which; / And this same progeny of evils comes / From our debate, from our dissension. / We are their parents and original" (2.1.111–117). Figures of the four seasons are a common motif in baroque art. They surround William and Mary in Sir James Thornhill's huge painting in the great hall of Greenwich Hospital, *Allegory of the Protestant Succession*.[44] A scene change accompanied Purcell's masque:

> The Scene changes to a Garden of Fountains. A Sonata plays while the Sun rises, it appears red through the Mist, as it ascends it dissipates the Vapours, and is seen in its full Lustre; then the Scene is perfectly discovered, the Fountains enriched with gilding, and adorn'd with Statues: The view is terminated by a Walk of Cypress Trees which lead to a delightful Bower. Before the Trees stand rows of Marble Columns, which support many Walks which rise by Stairs to the top of the House; the stairs are adorn'd with Figures on Pedestals, and Rails; and Balasters on each side of 'em. Near the top, vast Quantities of Water break out of the Hills, and fall in mighty cascades to the bottom of the Scene, to feed the Fountains which are on each side. In the middle of the Stage is a very large Fountain, where the Water rises about twelve Foot. (p. 40)

This Versailles-like garden of fountains would have been painted in perspective on the flats and on an opaque backdrop, behind which a sun would have been hoisted, its "lustre" provided by candlepower. The "vapours" would have been provided by transparent gauzes (scrims), flown out as the sun ascended. The large fountain at center stage may well have been a practical, working one.[45]

With the coming of dawn, Titania and chorus call for a salute to the sun, who has chased the night away, as Purcell develops his allegory. A countertenor duet calls for "fifes, clairions, and shrill trumpets" to sound, "and the arch of high heaven the clangour resound." In response, there is a thundering trumpet and tympany fanfare, twenty-four measures in length, greeting Phoebus: "A Machine appears, the clouds break from before it, and Phoebus appears in a chariot drawn by four horses" (p. 40).

The sun god sings of his power to give all things birth, life, warmth, and vigor: "Even love, who rules all things in earth, air and sea, / would languish and fade and to nothing would fall, / the world to its chaos would return but for me." After these lines, dear to the heart of any absolute monarch, the chorus sings "Hail! Hail! great parent, hail!" to Phoebus, and the four seasons, on stage to greet him, begin their tribute songs.

All this constitutes a celebration of absolute power and cosmic order familiar to a Restoration audience. Phoebus was a quickly recognizable icon, associated not only with Louis XIV in particular but with centralized monarchy in general: power, life, and order flowed from the king. In Purcell's *Dido and Aeneas* three years earlier, audiences would have associated William with Phoebus and Mary with Venus, "regent of the night," in a masque in that opera, which was an allegory on their joint sovereignty in the first year of their rule.[46]

The next song in the opera requires this association of William with the sun. Titania concludes the sunrise sequence with a birthday song to her partner: "Tis that happy, happy day, / the birthday of King Oberon" (p. 40). The lines are repeated numerous times in numerous variations by the soprano and chorus. This birthday song, which commentators on the opera have passed over, has nothing to do with either Shakespeare or Oberon, of course; it can only be for the English Sun King, William III.[47] The likelihood of this reference increases given the fact that a copy of *The Fairy Queen* was registered with the Stationers' Company on 2 November 1691, two days before the king's forty-first birthday.[48] There are other instances of birthday tributes to the king being incorporated in English operas. Franklin B. Zimmerman, in his discussion of topical allusions in Purcell's *Dido and Aeneas*, notes there an otherwise inexplicable reference to "this genial day."[49] In Charles Gildon's *Measure for Measure, or, Beauty the Best Advocate* (1700), Eschalus presents a four-part masque to Angelo on his birthday, which seems similarly suspect.[50]

Act 5 opens on the same garden setting, with the Duke entering with Egeus (sans Hippolyta), bragging of his hounds. They discover the sleeping lovers, who are then awakened by hunting horns. The Duke forgives them, and so does Egeus, whom Shakespeare left silent. After the Duke and his party exit, Bottom awakens and remembers his dream. Quince and company enter, happily discover Bottom, and all exit. The Duke and Egeus now reenter (with no scene change), followed by the lovers. The Duke expresses to Egeus his skepticism about the lovers' stories of the night. Hippolyta, as previously noted, is missing, as are her lines about there being "something of great constancy; / But howsoever, strange and admirable" (5.1.26–27) in the lovers' stories of the night. But the Duke is about to be cured of any skepticism about constancy in the opera's spectacular finale, so different from Shakespeare's.

After the Duke's "How easy is a bush suppos'd a bear?" Oberon, Titania, Robin, and all the fairies enter "while a short symphony plays." The Duke at first only hears the music but sees nothing, and then Oberon comes forward to explain:

Tis Fairy Musick, sent by me
To cure your Incredulity.
All was true the lovers told,
You shall stranger things behold.

Mark the wonders shall appear,
While I feast your eye and ear. (p. 47)

The skeptical Duke is about to experience a revelation, a conversion by spectacle and music — a dramatic effect that is at the heart of baroque aesthetics.[51]

Titania tells the Duke to cast his eyes upward, and from the stage heavens Juno descends "in a machine drawn by peacocks" (associated with her in mythology). While a "symphony" plays, "the Machine moves forward and the Peacocks spread their tails, and fill the middle of the Theatre [stage]" (p. 47). Apparently, her chariot touches down upstage and moves to center, where the birds open their fan tails, colorfully framing their passenger. Oberon explains that this goddess, "who does still preside / Over the Sacred Nuptial Bed," has come to bless the days and nights of the young lovers "with all true joys and chaste delights" (p. 47). In her epithalamium, Juno frees them from jealousy and the errors of the past night and "all that anxious Care and Strife / That attend a married Life" (p. 48). She then ascends.

Oberon has one final demonstration to perform. He calls for Puck to overcast the day with "thick darkness" and usher in "a glorious light." He says, "Let a new transparent world be seen." His commands bring the opera's most remarkable scene change:

> While the scene is darken'd, a single Entry is danced; Then a Symphony is play'd; after that the Scene is suddainly Illuminated, and discovers a transparent Prospect of a Chinese Garden, the Architecture, the Trees, the Plants, the fruit, the Birds, the Beasts, quite different from what we have in this part of the World. It is terminated by an Arch, through which is seen other Arches with Close Arbors, and a row of Trees to the end of the View. Over it is a hanging garden, which rises by several ascents to the top of the House [stage]; it is bounded on either side with pleasant Bowers, various Trees, and numbers of strange Birds flying in the Air, on the Top of a Platform is a Fountain, throwing up Water, which falls into a large Basin. (p. 49)

This, as Robert Moore has observed, is a version of an Edenic paradise for the lovers. For Restoration audiences, it would have been all the more exotic for its suggestions of China, with whom western Europe had recently developed trade. In art and the popular imagination, China was a remote, exotic land of palm trees, monkeys, pagodas, and tropical birds. Decor in the Chinese style became fashionable in England in the late seventeenth century and throughout the eighteenth.[52] The scene painter for this exotic garden may have been Robert Rob-

inson, a well-known decorator who specialized in the painting of *chinoiserie*.[53]
China was imaged as an untamed paradise of splendid bounty, ripe for the pick-
ing, not unlike the exotic new world of America. The Orient had been exploited

in Restoration heroic tragedies such as John Dryden and Robert Howard's *The
Indian Queen*. In a mezzotint by W. Vincent, entitled *The Indian Queen*, actress
Anne Bracegirdle is seen in the role of the Indian Queen in *The Widow Ranter*
by Aphra Behn. Some portion of Behn's colorful life was spent in Suriname, and
she had once given the King's Company feathers from Suriname, used in Dryden and Howard's *The Indian Queen*.[54] The actress-queen is displayed as an exotic delectation, wearing a costume that blends a Western dress with a feather
headdress, feather fan, and sandals, walking beneath an oriental-looking fringed
sun umbrella carried by one of two small African attendants in feathered headdresses. In a remarkable parallel with Titania and her Indian boy, Queen Mary
at one time had a Javanese dwarf attending on her. When he died in 1681, his
elegy, written by a Dutch poet, contained the lines, "Of the East Indian man-
nequin I tell / Who by his lowness pleased his Highness well."[55]

Into Eden come a Chinese man and woman. He sings of the creation we have
just witnessed:

> Thus, thus the gloomy world
> At first began to shine,
> And from the power divine
> A glory round about it hurled
> And made it bright and gave it birth in light. (p. 51)

In this exotic paradise, free of pride, ambition, and fame, the archetypal Adam
and Eve (tenor and soprano) together sing of their love and bliss. There is, of
course, nothing oriental in Purcell's music. In a further suggestion of the Edenic
wilderness, six monkeys (costumed dancers) come from among the trees to
dance. Two women appeal in song for Hymen to appear, which the Greek god
of marriage then does, singing:

> My torch has long been out. I hate
> On loose dissembled vows to wait,
> Where hardly love outlives the wedding night. (p. 51)

At this point, a stage direction tells us that "six pedestals of China-work rise
from under the Stage; they support six large Vases of Porcelain, in which are six
China-Orange trees" (p. 51). The women instruct Hymen to "turn then thine
eyes upon those glories here," promising that his torch will then surely catch

flame. Hymen responds, singing, "My Torch, indeed, will from such Brightness shine: / Love ne'er had yet such Altars, so divine" (p. 51). Has Hymen changed his mind upon seeing the six young lovers now onstage — Demetrius, Lysander, Helena, Hermia, and the Chinese couple? What has all this to do with the six orange trees, now on the move again? "The Pedestals move forward [*sic*] the front of the Stage, and the Grand Dance begins of twenty-four Persons." Hymen and the two women then sing together:

> They shall be as happy as they're fair;
> Love shall fill all the Places of Care:
> And every time the Sun shall display
> His Rising Light,
> It shall be to them a new Wedding Day;
> And when he sets, a new Nuptial Night. (p. 51)

While the Chinese man and woman dance, the chorus joins the refrain for the finale.

This spectacle has baffled historians, but Queen's Theatre audiences of 1692 would have understood its text. First, the orange trees in the oriental Eden would have made some literal sense to English audiences: the common sweet orange was then popularly known as the China-orange.[56] It may have originated in India, but for English audiences of the time, the Orient was all one. More important, audiences also would have recognized the orange tree as a familiar icon representing William of Orange and his queen.[57]

Jacob de Hennin's portrait of Mary (ca. 1677) shows her standing beside, and pointing to, an orange tree in a large vase.[58] Mary had orange trees brought from Holland for her gardens at Hampton Court and Kensington Palace.[59] Orange trees decorated one of the triumphal arches erected in London for William in 1690, for an entry celebrating his landing at Tor Bay and his victory in Ireland.[60] Orange trees were emblems in the pageants for William's entry into the Hague in 1691, his first return to his homeland as England's king. In one, Queen Mary was shown sitting on her throne beneath an orange tree, providing protection for persecuted French Protestants (see fig. 3.).[61] In the theatre, orange trees in vases had previously emerged from under the stage in a last-act scenic spectacle visualizing the triumph of love in Purcell's *Dioclesian* in 1690.[62] The theatre in Whitehall Palace was even equipped with an orange-colored curtain after William and Mary came to the throne.[63]

The orange trees make their entrance in the finale with precise, significant timing. The moment that they emerge, Hymen is to turn to see "those glories

FIGURE 3. A rather fierce Queen Mary sits beneath an emblematic orange tree, Jupiter's thunderbolts in hand, offering protection and sanctuary to persecuted Protestants. The engraving by R. De Hooge derived from a painting on a triumphal arch erected for the entry of William and Mary into the Hague in 1691. Folger Shakespeare Library.

there." It is usually assumed that Hymen's change of heart comes as a result of seeing the young lovers, but the well-timed appearance behind them of the unmistakable orange trees of William and Mary surely symbolizes the model royal marital union central to the stability of the kingdom.[64] It is this that assures Hymen that love endures; in the sunlike radiance of William and Mary's marriage, the love of the young couples will flourish in the garden of England-Eden. Once the orange trees have moved to their prominent downstage position, the grand concluding dance can begin, with Hymen and the two women singing the lines, "And every time the Sun shall display / His Rising Light, / It shall be to them a new Wedding Day."

The skeptical Duke thereby receives a lesson on the harmony of the spheres and the endurance of love. As spectator to the baroque spectacle, he functions like a classical chorus or like Bernini's nobles in their box watching the ecstacy of St. Teresa.

Franklin B. Zimmerman, in his biography of Purcell, was near the mark when he speculated that the opera was "conceived as a tribute" to Queen Mary. He noted that she was referred to by poets of her time as Gloriana, a name once given Elizabeth I, that the opera was first announced in March, when she had taken up the reins of government, and that the opera's premiere fell on 2 May, only two days after Mary's birthday.[65] While Lutrell, whose diary of state affairs is our source for that date, makes no mention of such an association, Zimmerman was on the right path.[66] If we look not only at the premiere date but also at the opera's Phoebus sequence, its birthday song for Oberon, and its compliment in the finale to the marriage of the reigning couple, its tributary elements clearly allude to William and Mary. In this connection, 4 November 1691 was the date of both their fifteenth wedding anniversary and William's birthday. As I noted, it was just two days before this date that the opera libretto was entered in the Stationers' record. The shared date could explain the opera's tribute to their marriage and the song for Oberon's birthday. We know that there was no performance then, however. Lutrell records that on 5 November 1691 there were celebrations in London commemorating William's birthday, William and Mary's anniversary, and William's safe return a few days before from the battlefields on the Continent, but he mentions only a ball at court and no opera.[67] While the opera was not produced upon that busy occasion, its homage to William and Mary would have been scarcely less appropriate on its eventual premiere date the next May, near Mary's birthday.[68]

The preface to the 1692 libretto included a plea for the kind of support for opera in England that it enjoyed in France and Italy, which was to say court support:

That a few private Persons shold venture on so expensive a Work as an Opera, which none but Princes, or States Exhibit 'em abroad, I hope is no Dishonour to our Nation: And I daire affirm, if we had half the Encouragment in England, that they have in other countries, you might in a short time have as good Dancers in England as they have in France, though I despair of ever having as good Voices among us, as they have in Italy. . . . If this [opera] happens to please, we cannot reasonably propose to ourselves any great advantage, considering the mighty Charge in setting it out, and the extraordinary expense that attends it every day 'tis represented. If it deserves their Favour? [*sic*] if they are satisfied we venture boldly, doing all we can to please 'em? [*sic*] We hope the English are too generous not to encourage so great an undertaking. (p. A4v)

It seems likely that the unidentified author of the preface was Thomas Betterton, who, as producer, would have had the most reason for concern with its daily expense.

The Fairy Queen was, as Betterton said, extraordinarily expensive to mount, even by comparison with other costly works. Lutrell reported that the opera "exceeds former playes: the clothes, scenes, and musick cost 3000 £."[69] John Downes also reported that, in comparison to *Dioclesian* (1690) and *King Arthur* (1691), *The Fairy Queen*

in ornaments was superior to the other two; especially in cloaths for all the Singers and Dancers, Scenes and Machines, and Decorations; all most profusely set off; and excellently perform'd, chiefly in the instrumental and vocal part. . . . The court and Town were wonderfully satisfy'd with it; but the expences on setting it out being so great, the company got very little by it.[70]

Apparently, the production did little better than break even. Nor did the opera win the patronage Betterton hoped for. What Richelieu and Mazarin had done in enlisting the arts as the dress guard of centralized monarchy probably was becoming less appropriate for the rule of William and Mary. Stuart absolutism was passing, and William and Mary and the English parliament were evolving toward rule by compromise and conscience. Jeremy Collier's attack on the immorality of the stage in 1698 was a part of this process of democratization, as he appealed to the need for a more rigorous morality in the national interest. Collier found no conscience or religion for the nation in the machines of Purcell and Dryden's *King Arthur* (1691) or in Dryden's "fairy way of writing."[71] While the writing of English semi-opera or wholly sung opera in the Italian style did not cease immediately after the death of Purcell in 1695, the opera, with its expensive theatre machines, separated from theatre repertoires, had to become financially self-supporting.[72] By the turn of the century, English music and theatre were on the cusp of a new marketplace entrepreneurialism.

The Fairy Queen was briefly revived in 1693, with major alterations in the first act, as is evident in a variant issue of the text in 1693.[73] The first scene is dropped, as are the introduction to the young lovers and any explanation of their flight to the forest; we meet them for the first time in the forest chase. Instead, we have a song inviting us to a kind of fête champêtre, after which Titania enters and instructs her fairies to torment any mortal who comes near the bower. They reenter leading three drunken poets, one of whom is blind, whom they torment with a pinching song. Its lyrics echo the fairy pinching songs in John Lyly's *Endimion* (1591) and Jonson's *Entertainment at Althorpe* (1603). But here the poet is pinched for the crime of his doggerel rhymes. If there was a topical, literary joke here, the queen may have been in on it. She and her maids of honor attended this rendition on 16 February 1693.[74] Purcell added a few songs to this 1693 rewrite, and present-day recordings use this version, notwithstanding the fact that, given the alteration of the first act, the necessary preliminary exposition of the plot is missing. After 1693, Purcell's semi-opera completely disappeared from view, with the exception of concert performances of portions of it.

The issue of the libretto authorship remains, and I will treat it briefly. The title page of the 1692 libretto gives no author. F. C. Brown's attribution to Elkanah Settle should now be regarded as weakly supported and doubtful.[75] David Dyregrov has argued that the actor Jo. Haines was responsible.[76] But Roger Savage's suggestion, based on his experience in staging the opera in 1973, that *The Fairy Queen* was originally a "committee" effort puts the issue in its proper context.[77] As noted, it is likely that Betterton was involved in the conception of the very important scenic text. As Judith Milhous and Robert D. Hume have shown, Betterton was paid a handsome fifty pounds for staging the operatic *Indian Queen*, which suggests his importance to the staging of operas at Dorset Garden.[78] Also, bibliographical evidence points to the kind of committee collaboration in which he likely was involved. In two different autograph scores, a song in Act 5 begins with the lines "Yes, Daphne, in your looks I find / the charms by which my heart's betrayed." By the time of the final score, Daphne had become Xansi.[79] Nothing in the lyrics otherwise and nothing in Purcell's music, of course, suggest anything Chinese. Daphne almost certainly became Xansi as a result of the choice of the scenic world of an exotic, quasi-Chinese Eden for the last act; it seems likely that this choice was made during the production process by Betterton, together with his scene designer and perhaps in consultation with the rest of the production team. In the theatre, authorship is not always a simple issue.

In the fairies, gods, and Chinese oranges of *The Fairy Queen*, there was nothing that would not have made sense to the Queen's Theatre audiences of 1692. But the culture fostered by absolute monarchies out of which it came was changing, and Purcell's semi-opera all but disappears from the stage for over two centuries.

Chapter three

"SIGNOR SHAKESPEARELLI"

Semibreve: Never wonder at that, for we that have studied the Italian opera may do anything in this kind. — *The Comick Masque of Pyramus and Thisbe,* 1716

On the few occasions that *A Midsummer Night's Dream* reached the English-speaking stage at all in the eighteenth century, it was still in the form of operatic adaptations. Two of these borrowed *Pyramus and Thisbe* to create musical parodies of the new Italian opera, the new London vogue. Three more elaborate musicalized adaptations were produced at David Garrick's Drury Lane, each of which used only selected elements of the play — the fairies, the lovers, or the mechanicals — in various matchups. The adaptation closest to Shakespeare's text was the least successful. For Augustans, the play's mix of heroic Greeks, woodland fairies, and hard-handed mechanicals violated neoclassical rules. Under neoclassicism's grave rationalism, the supernatural fairies put the play beyond the reach of drama and into the special sphere of the lyrical. Then, too, there was little useful in this play for promulgating the philosophy of natural law and the general moral reform of the theatre that Sir Richard Steele, Joseph Addison, and George Lillo were advocating in the first third of the century. Shakespeare was being brought to the new American colonies at midcentury by the company of the entrepreneurial Lewis Hallam, but not yet this play; nor would it be staged in America until well into the nineteenth century.

This chapter examines the three opera versions produced under Garrick. As a purveyor of the plays in the decades of England's consolidation as a mercantile empire under the Hanoverians, Garrick simultaneously championed a universal, immortal Shakespeare while naturalizing him for mid-eighteenth-century London audiences. It was an intriguing performance in his own era, and it still is.

In the first half of the eighteenth century, when Italian opera had become the London rage, two English composers borrowed *Pyramus and Thisbe* from Quince and company to spoof the fashion. Richard Leveridge's *The Comick Masque of Pyramus and Thisbe*, composed "in the high stile of Italy," was produced as an afterpiece by John Rich at Lincoln's Inn Fields in 1716.[1]

The piece is one in spirit with essays mocking Italian opera that had appeared in the *Tatler* and the *Spectator* a few years before, when Steele and Addison were chiding audiences for their adoration of the foreign opera with all its extravagances.[2] In Leveridge's little piece, Semibreve, a composer, rehearses the rustics in the tedious brief play (using lines from Shakespeare's 1.2, 3.1, and 5.1) for the benefit of two other characters — also musicologically named — Crotchet and Gamut.[3] Leveridge "made bold to dress out the original in Recitative and Airs after the present Italian mode," so there are nine songs, and even Wall sings. When asked whether Lion would sing, too, Semibreve replies, "Never wonder at that, for we that have studied the Italian opera may do anything in this kind." Pyramus dies singing "like a hero in an Italian opera to very good time and tune" and rises again for a closing duet with Thisbe.[4] Leveridge (1670–1758), who had composed theatre music and sung bass roles in Purcell operas, sang Bottom doing the role of Pyramus; a comedian performed as Bottom up to that point. Audiences apparently enjoyed the spoof; Rich got ten performances out of Leveridge's piece.[5] It made no dent in the popularity of Italian opera, however. Two hundred and fifty years later, this musical joke was repeated in kind. Benjamin Britten, in his 1960 opera version of the play, had Bottom and friends perform their tragedy for Theseus's court after the manner of nineteenth-century Italian opera.

Leveridge's spoof was expanded in 1745 by John Frederick Lampe (ca. 1703–1751), a composer of sixteen works for the stage, including several other burlesque operas. Produced by Rich at Covent Garden, *Pyramus and Thisbe: A Mock-Opera* offered an overture and fourteen songs. Lampe featured more of Shakespeare's dialogue for the mechanicals; Rich secured well-known tenor John Beard for Pyramus and Mrs. Lampe for Thisbe.[6] Bottom sings out his bombast over the dead Thisbe, "Approach you Furies fell! / O Fates! Come, Come, / Cut Thread and Thrum, / Quail, crush, conclude, and quell." After this, Lampe's composer, Semibrief, exclaims happily: "If this won't fetch a subscription, I'll never pretend to compose Opera or Masque again while I live."

Thisbe has the longest air, singing eighteen lines of her lament over the dead Pyramus, beginning, "These lilly lips, / This cherry nose." Lampe's musical cartoon had no less than thirty-seven performances of record between 1745 and 1754.[7] In 1723, *Pyramus and Thisbe* was also grafted onto a Shakespeare branch, Charles Johnson's *Love in a Forest*, derived from *Love's Labour's Lost* and produced at Drury Lane.[8]

But generally by this time, Shakespeare's texts were being taken more seriously, at least in print. The reading public had grown considerably since the Restoration, and, with the increasing democratization of England and the emergence of a merchant middle class, the creation and dissemination of a national literary canon became almost as important as the development of the new civil code. Great literature could be a civilizing instrument and knowledge of it a mark of good citizenship. It was in the national interest that Shakespeare's texts be made accessible, and this the growing book trade did. The eighteenth century saw a boom in the editing and competitive marketing of Shakespeare's complete works, with a grand succession of editors from Nicholas Rowe (1709) through Alexander Pope, Lewis Theobald, Thomas Hanmer, William Warburton, Samuel Johnson, Edmond Malone, and George Steevens.[9] In the *Tatler* and the *Spectator*, the new print-media guardians of moral rectitude and good literary manners, quotations from Shakespeare's tragedies were offered as beacon lights to guide the new "man of reason" and a right heart. Steele and Addison argued that the theatre in particular had the power to move all those Lockean benevolent feelings that resided in the bosom of humankind. Jeremy Collier's widely supported fundamentalist condemnation of the stage (1698) was thereby answered with the claim that the theatre could, in Pope's words, "make mankind in conscious virtue bold, / Live o'er each scene, and be what they behold." These lines occur in Pope's prologue to Addison's *Cato* (1713), which Pope concludes with an exhortation to audiences that may stand as a concise explanation of the purposes of a new drama of moral sentiment: "Britons, attend: be worth like this approved, / And show you have the virtue to be moved."[10]

A Midsummer Night's Dream was not seen as offering much of substance for these neoclassic and moral agendas. Samuel Johnson thought the play "wild and fantastical," although he did praise its stylistic variety.[11] Elizabeth Griffith, minding the national interest in *The Morality of Shakespeare's Drama Illustrated*, looked upon *A Midsummer Night's Dream* with some embarrassment in 1775. She believed that this play and *The Tempest* were among Shakespeare's very earliest works, written when his "youthful imagination must naturally be thought to have been more sportive and exuberant than his riper judgment might have permitted the indulgence of." Griffith said of *A Midsummer Night's Dream*, "I can see no general moral that can be deduced from the Argument; nor . . . is there much sentiment to be collected even from the Dialogue."[12] She dedicated her volume to David Garrick (who had produced her plays as well as his adaptation of Shakespeare's) with the commendation: "Your action has been a better comment on his text than all his editors have able to supply. You mark his beauties; they but clear his blots."

During Garrick's thirty-year reign at Drury Lane (1747–1776), three different versions of *A Midsummer Night's Dream* were tried, the most successful of which bore the least resemblance to Shakespeare's play. In these decades, in which England was consolidating itself as a commercial empire under the Hanoverians, Garrick was promoting Shakespeare as the national poet. He was, in fact, constructing the several Shakespeares that England needed in its national poet — a universal Shakespeare, a morally correct Shakespeare for a growing middle class, and where necessary an operatic Shakespeare. The story of the adaptations of *A Midsummer Night's Dream* produced under Garrick's management provide a cameo of Garrick and of the cultural forces he embodied.

Some twentieth-century theatre historians have tended to construct Garrick as a model Enlightenment figure of impeccable literary taste, emphasizing his avowed reverence for Shakespeare, his frequent revivals of the plays, and the immortal greatness of his acting. In this way, Garrick could be a legitimate subject for the developing discipline of theatre history as it sought respectability as the natural companion of canonical literary studies. In this view, when Garrick produced adaptations of Shakespeare's plays, he was doing, with good-natured sufferance and shrewd management, only what the tastes of his age required.[13] But Garrick was of an age in which England was constructing a new national identity. As Michael Dobson has demonstrated, the transformation of Shakespeare's status from the comparative neglect of the Restoration to his celebration as the national poet "constitutes one of the central cultural expressions of England's own transition from the aristocratic regime of the Stuarts to the commercial empire presided over by the Hanoverians."[14] Garrick was the major player in this at midcentury, providing the Shakespeare England now needed.

Garrick's successes in this derived not only from his acting genius but also from his genius in the role of the new natural man of sense and sensibility. Physically attractive, graceful, and intelligent, Garrick offered a model image of a well-educated, self-possessed man of reason and right instincts, blending the literary taste and social sophistications of an elite gentry with the virtue and easy resourcefulness of a Lockean natural man. He was, in effect, an English gentleman by nature rather than by title. In his acting style, he eschewed the declamatory, heroic, aristocratic pomp that had gone before him and offered instead a new, individualized persona. Giving an easy, congenial, contemporary voice to the classics, Garrick appealed to a nation still negotiating its way from Stuart absolutism toward a relatively democratized monarchy. Britain's future depended upon such negotiations and on alliances between the older, titled aristocracy and the new merchant class.

Marriage couplings across these class lines are prominent in the era's sentimental comedies. One of Garrick's most memorable roles was in one of them — that of Archer in George Farquhar's *The Beaux' Stratagem*. The charming young Archer aims opportunistically at marriage with the wealthy daughter of Lady Bountiful. Ultimately, he resigns his crass designs, having been affected by the natural goodness in her heart. Having thus discovered and responded from the natural goodness in his own heart, he is rewarded with her hand, and more. In the next moment, Archer learns that he has inherited, unexpectedly, a gentleman's rank and wealth. Heaven thus smiles its timely approval, providing him with the outward seals of rank and wealth on his inner nobility. The role was a signature one for Garrick.

Actor, natural gentleman, and Shakespeare's promoter, Garrick became the darling of London, perhaps the first modern commodified celebrity. His image was everywhere in the works of contemporary painters and printmakers. Among the major artists who did portraits of Garrick were Thomas Gainsborough, Francis Hayman, Joshua Reynolds, John Zoffany, Nathaniel Dance-Holland, Angelica Kauffmann, Robert Edge Pine, and William Hogarth. Some were of the actor himself and some in stage character, many of which were Shakespearean. According to Kalman A. Burnim, Garrick was the subject of more portraits than any figure in British history save Queen Victoria.[15] It is not surprising to find him a patriot, too. During the Seven Years War, during which so many symbols of British culture were born, he wrote a ballad that began, "Heart of oak are our ships / Heart of oak are our men," which historian Keith Thomas remembered learning two hundred years later in a south Wales grammar school.[16]

Garrick espoused publicly and often his dedication to both Shakespeare and the national moral agenda. He framed them as one and the same and cast himself as Shakespeare's earthly representative. At the opening of the 1750–1751 season at Drury Lane, he declared from the stage: "Sacred to Shakespeare was this spot design'd, / to pierce the heart and humanize the mind."[17] Over his career, he staged twenty-six of Shakespeare's plays, playing seventeen roles in fourteen of them. He referred to his theatre as "the house of William Shakespeare," consulted with Edward Capell on early editions, and had himself painted by Gainsborough enfolding a bust of Shakespeare, a painting which he gave to the town of Stratford-upon-Avon, leaving at Shakespeare's birthplace an image of himself and Shakespeare as immortal collaborators.[18] Garrick may well have posed for the statue of Shakespeare he commissioned from Louis-François Roubilliac.[19] With his 1769 Shakespeare "Jubilee," he made Stratford a shrine for literary pilgrimages, capping the general promotion of Shakespeare as the national poet. The jubilee was a media event so well managed that its impact could not be undone either by the disastrous rains that blanketed Stratford during the days of the celebration or the absence from the ceremonies of a single line from the works of its honoree.[20] At Garrick's death, his longtime friend, the conservative Edmund Burke, wrote an epitaph praising him as the actor who "raised the character of his profession to the rank of a liberal art."[21]

But even as he was championing a universal Shakespeare, Garrick was simultaneously naturalizing and nationalizing him. He readily adapted the plays to the neoclassical, moral, and musical tastes of his mid-eighteenth-century London audiences. He left the comic gravediggers out of *Hamlet* as readily as he wrote the bawdry out of Wycherley.[22] He domesticated and sentimentalized *The Taming of the Shrew* and *The Winter's Tale*.[23] He helped make English semi-operas of *The Tempest* and *A Midsummer Night's Dream*, and he readily used the adaptation of *King Lear* by Nahum Tate which gave audiences an ending that assured succession to the throne and the future of the kingdom rather more than Shakespeare had. In his construction of the national poet, Garrick may be compared generally to John Boydell, whose proud national project was the Shakespeare Gallery on Pall Mall (1789), in which hung paintings of scenes from all the plays that he commissioned from "Artists of Great Britain."[24] Garrick's revivals of and many successes with Shakespeare, as well as his great personal popularity, meant that only a few could criticize him for altering the plays, and fewer did so publicly.

Garrick's naturalizing and nationalizing of Shakespeare can be seen in many details of the three adaptations of *A Midsummer Night's Dream* done at Drury Lane. The first, *The Fairies*, was produced on 3 February 1755 as an afterpiece. The title page describes it as "An opera. Taken from *A Midsummer Night's Dream*, Written by Shakespear."[25] An opera it was, in the modern Italian sense that it was wholly sung, with alternating recitative and songs. John Christopher Smith, pupil to George Frideric Handel (and later his amanuensis), provided the music for the twenty-eight songs, dances, and recitative for the three-act adaptation.[26] Neither the published text nor the score identifies an adaptor, almost certainly a deliberate omission. Garrick wrote a prologue for it and even delivered it himself, perhaps evidence that he thought his presence would be helpful for easing the adaptation into acceptance. From the apron, he asked his audiences to excuse an Englishman's attempt at opera, saying that Smith had been empowered with "sparks he caught from his great Master's blaze." On the issue of who had actually rewritten Shakespeare's text for the libretto, Garrick had to be coy, given his position as promoter of Shakespeare: "I dare not say *who* wrote it — I could tell ye, / to soften matters, Signor Shakespearelli."[27] It seems likely that Garrick and Smith "patched it up together," as Roger Fiske put it, and Garrick scholars are agreed that Garrick's hand is in it.[28]

Garrick did not misjudge his audience in offering a musical adaptation of the play. While a sarcastic Horace Walpole complained that this new Italianate opera was "crowded by all true lovers of their country," Walpole allowed that Shakespeare's play itself was "forty times more nonsensical than the worst translation of any Italian opera."[29] The work is a slight pastoral pastiche of a few elements of the plots of Shakespeare's moon-crossed lovers and the quarrel of Oberon and Titania. Only 560 of the original 2,134 lines remain, delivered recitative in combination with Smith's twenty-eight songs. Bottom, his friends, and his ass's head are all omitted. Puck comes to Oberon with a report that Titania has awakened to love "a clown," which might have puzzled audiences. But Bottom and the mechanicals were hardly fit subjects for a fairy kingdom fashioned according to Handel. Also, an advertisement in the text explained that one reason for so many omitted lines from Shakespeare was that the dialogue was delivered in recitative (unlike many English operas, such as *The Fairy Queen*): "It was feared that even the best poetry would appear tedious when only supported by Recitative." One notable passage of poetry not set was Oberon's "I know a bank where the while thyme blows" (2.1.249–267), which would become a set-piece song of the nineteenth century. Most of Act 5 was cut, including *Pyramus and Thisbe*. The opera ends with the discovery of the sleeping lovers, the exit of Theseus and the court to the nuptials, and a rousing choral finale with monarchical overtones. Taken from George Granville's semi-opera, *The British Enchanters* (1705), it is at many removes in spirit from Shakespeare's hushed midnight invasion of fairies and midsummer amnesty:

Hail to love and welcome joy!
Hail to the delicious boy!
See the sun from love returning,
Love's the flame in which he's burning.
Hail to love, the softest pleasure;
Love and beauty reign for ever.[30]

The advertisement in the text noted, "Where Shakespeare has not supplied the Composer with Songs, he has taken them from Milton, Waller, Dryden,

Lansdown, Hammond, &c and it is hoped they will not seem to be unnaturally introduced."[31]

For seven of his twenty-eight songs, Smith used lines from the play itself. Music was provided for the fairy lullaby, of course. Oberon sang all of the lines of his charm over Demetrius, "Flower of this purple dye" (3.2.102 ff), and Puck sang his "Up and down, up and down, / I will lead them up and down" (3.2.397–400). Among the young lovers' airs, Helena sang six lines of her speech to Hermia, "O happy fair! / Your eyes are lodestars" (1.1.182 ff), and the six lines beginning "Love looks not with the eyes, but with the mind" (1.1.234–251) from her speech closing Shakespeare's 1.1. Hermia sang four lines, beginning with "Before the time I did Lysander see / Seemed Athens as a paradise to me" (1.1.204 ff). In Garrick's Act 2, Oberon sang part of Shakespeare's Act 5's closing lines, "Now until the break of day" (5.2.31 ff). Four other lyrics came from four of Shakespeare's other plays. Puck also was given Ariel's "Where the bee sucks, there lurk [*sic*] I," (differently treated than it is in Thomas A. Arne's still well known setting).[32] Titania borrowed lines from a song in *Henry VIII*, "Orpheus with his lute made trees" (3.1.3–14). Before sending Puck to unconfuse the lovers, Oberon sang, "Sigh no more, ladies, sigh no more," a song from *Much Ado About Nothing* (2.3.61–76). Lysander sang to Helena six lines of Dumaine's sonnet in *Love's Labour's Lost* (4.3.98–118), and Lysander and Hermia sang eleven lines of Milton's "L'Allegro," beginning "When that gay season did us lead / To the tann'd haycock in the mead" (11.89 ff).[33] Lysander sang two more songs by Waller and Hammond, and the title page credit to Lansdowne (William Petty) is for the final choral stanza. The cumulative effect is of a moderately diverting, innocuous love pastoral with an expansive ending in which mildly erotic love moves toward matrimony in an assurance of continuing state harmony. Shakespeare's unruly women are domesticated, wholly subservient to male love interests. Such domestication served Britain's interest in the stability of its new middle class. Smith's score is in general undistinguished. Roger Fiske's assessment is that "one can say little more for the music than that it is in rather tepid good taste."[34]

There are few contemporary complaints on record about the adaptation itself. Theophilus Cibber, who attacked Garrick's *Catherine and Petruchio* and *Florizel and Perdita* (his version of *The Winter's Tale*), also wrote that *A Midsummer Night's Dream* had been "minc'd and fricaseed into an indigested and unconnected thing called *The Fairies*." But Cibber knew his criticism of Garrick's "bottling" of Shakespeare would be of little avail. "This lucky Son of Fortune," Cibber wrote with some intuition about Garrick's role as national icon, "was so in fashion that it became a kind of Treason, among some People, even to hint a Possibility of his being in error."[35] One of Garrick's contemporary biographers, Arthur Murphy, defended the musical rendering of the play: "The aerial beings, of which Shakespere was the father, could not, it must be acknowledged, be rendered more fit for representation by any other contrivance."[36] At one point, Garrick was brought to denying privately that he himself had done the tampering with Shakespeare's text. In a letter to James Murphy French in 1756, he wrote:

> I received your letter, which indeed is more facetious than just — for if you mean that I was the person who altered the Midsummer Night's Dream, and the Tempest, into operas, you are much mistaken. — However, as old [Colley] Cibber said in his last epilogue, "But right or wrong, or true or false — 'tis pleasant."[37]

Garrick biographer George Winchester Stone sought to vindicate Garrick from the charges of stage historian John Genest and the later Shakespeare purists who ridiculed Garrick's self-proclaimed zeal for Shakespeare.[38] Stone credited Garrick's denial and placed the burden for the adaptation on Smith.[39] The matter seems to have troubled Garrick less than it did Stone. If Garrick's "Shakespearelli" prologue is any indication, he produced the version with no serious remorse and afterward was happy that the piece had been a modest success with audiences, as is clear from the last sentence of Garrick's letter, a sentence that Stone omitted.[40]

The opera played nine times in the 1754–1755 season and twice the next, with receipts above the norm.[41] *The Fairies* "was well performed and with good success," according to Tate Wilkinson. The Italian opera singers who were enlisted for the roles of Lysander (Signore Guadagni) and Hermia (Signora Passerini) gave particularly valuable service.[42] In addition, there were strengths in John Beard's Theseus and the Bottom of comedian Richard Yates. Helena was played by the teenage Jenny Poitier, who soon after married her Demetrius, Joseph Vernon.[43] Judging from the cast list and Horace Walpole's account, "chapel boys" sang and acted some of the fairy roles.[44] By March, audiences could buy the book of Smith's songs, which came to be among his best-known work.[45] These songs formed the core of the next two adaptations at Drury Lane; producers of the play continued to borrow on Smith's songs well into the nineteenth century.

The Fairies even had one curious consequence lasting into the twentieth century. When Charles and Mary Lamb wrote their famous *Tales From Shakespeare* in 1807, they were apparently looking not at Shakespeare but Garrick when they came to write their prose summary of *A Midsummer Night's Dream*. In their

sugar plum version, all that remains of the rude mechanicals is Garrick's reduction of them to the report of Oberon that Titania has awakened to love a
"clown." And the Lambs' *Tales* are still in wide publication.[46]

Garrick later came back to the play. His preparation copy of the text, together
with other related manuscripts in his hand, show him working in the spring of
1763 on a new adaptation that preserved more of the original.[47] When the play
finally came to the Drury Lane stage again in the fall of 1763, however, Garrick
was absent, refreshing himself on the Continent in the wake of the half-price
riots that had shaken his management. (Garrick had tried to do away with ticket
discounts to latecomers.) He delegated the adaptation to playwright George
Colman, the elder, from whose hand the final production and the published text
came. In a letter to Colman about this and other plays-in-the-planning for the
season, Garrick wrote from Paris on 8 October 1763:

> Many thanks to you for the trouble you take about the *Invasion*, cut as you
> please — I leave it to you — as for Midsummer Nights &C. I think my pres-
> ence will be necessary to get it up as it ought — however, if you want to, do
> for the best — & I'll ensure its success.[48]

The 1763 version offered more of the original text than did the 1755 opera,
some of which was now spoken. It included more of Shakespeare's blend of Grecian heroes, courtly lovers, woodland fairies, and earthy artisans than had been
seen in a century. It was even offered under the original title.[49] But Garrick could
not put Shakespeare's romance together again for a mid-eighteenth-century
London audience. Even with its thirty-three songs, the work failed so utterly on
opening night, 23 November 1763, that it played only that one night.[50]

Both the play and the performers displeased. A critic in the *St. James Chronicle* called it "an odd romantic Performance, more like a masque than a Play, and
presenting a lively picture of the ungoverned imagination of that great Poet."
While this critic found the fairy portion of the play "most transcendentally
beautiful," the love plots, including the marriage of Theseus,

> were flat and uninteresting; even the very fine speeches of Theseus, towards
> the conclusion of the Piece, are fitter for the closet than the Stage, where
> they receive no great Addition by coming from the deep mouth of our old
> friend, Mr. Bransby.

This critic also found much of the dialogue badly spoken:

> I never at one time saw at the Playhouse so much good and so much bad
> acting. The Children [fairies] were admirable, most of the *Grown Gentlemen*

and *Ladies* execrable. Three or four of the Performers showed themselves incapable of delivering Blank Verse, except in Recitative. It is a thousand pities that such sweet Children should be thus overlaid.

The critic then offered a four-stanza ode of sympathy for the suffering children, written by his theatre companion of the evening.[51]

Prompter William Hopkins left this assessment in his diary:

Upon the whole, never was anything so murder'd in the speaking. Mr. W. Palmer [Demetrius] and Mrs. Vincent [Helena] were beyond Description bad; & had it not been for the Children's excellent performance [as fairies] and particularly Miss Wright [first fairy] who sung delightfully, the Audience would not have Suffer'd 'em to have gone half thro' it. The Sleeping Scene particularly displeas'd. Next day it was reported[:] The Performers first Sang the audience to Sleep, and then went to Sleep themselves. Fairies pleas'd — Serious parts displeas'd — Comic between both.[52]

Twelve of the songs and the overture were brought over from Smith's earlier score. According to the rare Table of Songs (fig. 4) in the Folger Shakespeare Library copy, fourteen new ones were composed by Charles Burney, organist of St. Paul's and eminent music historian. He also may have compiled the score.[53] Its other seven songs came from Michael Arne (three), Jonathan Battishill (two), George Frideric Handel (one), and Theodore Aylward (one). Eleven songs set Shakespearean verse to music (five by Burney), but only nine of those used lines from the original play. Lysander and Hermia sang the air by Smith that used lines from Milton's "L'Allegro." Some of Burney's new melodies may have set lyrics by Garrick himself, but it is difficult to sort out Garrick's contributions given the fact that it was Colman who actually staged the opera and made many adjustments in the process. Edward Capell may have offered a song for a fairy, but his name does not appear in the Table of Songs.[54] Helena sang a new Burney song, "Our softer sex can't fight for love," and she and Hermia later sang a new Burney duet, "With various griefs my mind is torn." The result of these and of the cutting was to emphasize further the women's passivity, while the men remained the brave agents of action, conventional eighteenth-century renderings of gender, again in the service of English domestic stability.[55]

The published text of the 1763 adaptation does not bear the names of Garrick or Colman; Shakespeare was, after all, the house playwright. George Winchester Stone may be right in concluding from Garrick's preparation copy that, had Garrick been present, this version would have had fewer songs (twenty-seven rather than thirty-three) and more of Shakespeare's poetry (561 lines more).[56]

A TABLE of the SONGS, with the
Names of the several Composers.

ACT I.

An OVERTURE *by Mr.* SMITH.

		Page.	Composers.
1.	*With mean disguise let others nature hide*	9	*Mr.* Smith.
2.	*When that gay season did us lead*	10	*Mr.* Smith.
3.	*O Hermia fair, O happy, happy fair*	11	*Mr.* Smith.
4.	*Before the time I did Lysander see*	11	*Mr.* Smith.
5.	*Against myself, why all this art*	12	*Mr.* Burney.
6	*Most noble Duke to us be kind*	15	*Mr.* Burney.

ACT II.

7.	*Kingcup, daffodil, and rose*	17	*Mr.* Mich. Arne.
8.	*Yes, yes, I know you, you are he*	18	*Mr.* Mich. Arne.
9.	*Away, away, I will not stay*	20	*Mr.* Burney.
10.	*Forbid the stormy sea to roll*	21	*Mr.* Batershall.
11.	*Our softer sex can't fight for love*	22	*Mr.* Burney.
12.	*Come follow, follow me*	23	*Mr.* Handel.

ACT III.

13.	*You spotted snakes with double tongue*	24	*Mr.* Smith.
14.	*Not the silver doves*	25	*Mr.* Smith.
15.	*If, oh, if no flame return*	27	*Mr.* Burney.
16.	*Sweet soothing hope, whose magic art*	28	*Mr.* Smith.
17.	*The ousel-cock so black of hue*	31	*Mr.* Burney.

ACT IV.

18.	*These looks, these tears, these tender sighs.*	34	*Mr.* Burney.
19.	*I'll range all around till I find out my love*		*Mr.* Burney.
20.	*Flower of this purple dye*	35	*Mr.* Smith.
21.	*How can these sighs and tears seem scorn to you*		*Mr.* Burney.
22.	*How calm my soul in this blest hour*	36	*Mr.* Batershall.
23.	*Let him come, let him come, &c.*	37	*Mr.* Burney.
24.	*With various griefs my mind is torn*	38	*Mr.* Burney.
25.	*Up and down, up and down*		*Mr.* Burney.
26.	*Sigh no more, ladies, sigh no more*	40	*Mr.* Smith.

ACT V.

27.	*Sweetest creature, pride of nature*	41	*Mr.* Burney.
28.	*Welcome, welcome to this place*	42	*Mr.* Mich. Arne.
29.	*Be as thou wast wont to be*	43	*Mr.* Burney.
30.	*Orpheus, with his lute*		*Mr.* Smith.
31.	*Hark, hark, how the hounds and horn*	45	*Mr.* Smith.
32.	*The dream is o'er, as day appears*	46	*Mr.* Aylewood.
33.	*Pierce the air with sounds of joy*	47	*Mr.* Smith.

FIGURE 4. List of the songs from the 1763 opera adaptation of the play by David Garrick and George Colman, the elder, staged at Theatre Royal, Drury Lane. The adaptation ran only one night, even with thirty-three songs. Folger Shakespeare Library.

But Garrick's preparation copy still shows approximately 450 lines cut, including most of Titania's "These are the forgeries of jealousy" speech (2.1.81–117) and all of Oberon's "Since once I sat upon a promontory" (2.1.149–174), some of the play's most valued lines for their imagery and sound. Garrick also suggested the final fairy revel be cut, which Colman objected to, hoping for a pleasant spectacle, but ultimately Colman, too, abandoned it. The play ends, as Garrick suggested it should, with the discovery of the lovers and a few concluding lines from Theseus's speech on the lunatic, the lover, and the poet. Garrick would have retained *Pyramus and Thisbe*, but Colman wanted as little of it as possible and suggested that songs be interspersed to "enliven it."[57] So it was that Colman has Quince produce a pitch pipe at the end of the artisans' first scene (1.2) and lead the mechanicals in a song in which they self-consciously demean themselves in a manner that Shakespeare's originals, in their innocent confidence, never do.

> Most noble Duke, to us be kind;
> Be you and all your courtiers blind,
> That you may not our errors find,
>   But smile upon our sport.
> For we are simple actors all,
> Some fat, some lean, some short, some tall.
> Our pride is great, our merit small;
>   Will that, pray, do at court?[58]

The adaptation was in trouble throughout rehearsal, with Colman struggling all the while, according to the prompter, William Hopkins:

> The piece of Shakespear's was greatly Cut & Alter'd: the 5th Act Entirely left out & many Airs introduced all through — got up with a vast deal of trouble to everybody concern'd in it but particularly to Mr. Coleman, who attended every Rehearsal & had alterations innumerable to make.[59]

With the one-night flop and gross earnings of only £98 7s., Colman decided to try to salvage "so much Pains and Expense as was bestowed on the Midsummer Night's Dream."[60] He extracted from the failure a short musical afterpiece, which he called *A Fairy Tale*. This hasty adaptation, which he opened three days later, was an unusual pairing of the mechanicals and the fairies, with the mortals dropped.[61] In some four hundred lines, the mechanics rehearse, Puck disperses them in fright, not with Bottom in the ass's head but with a thunderstorm, and Titania and Oberon are reconciled. In the thirteen songs brought over from the

FIGURE 5. Jane Barsanti as Helena, engraving, *Bell's British Theatre*, 1776. Pictured here in the formal contemporary fashion worn by actresses in classical plays, Barsanti herself probably never actually played Helena. Folger Shakespeare Library.

fuller version, Titania is serenaded by the First Fairy with "Sigh no more, my lady," from *Much Ado*, and the sleeping Bottom is carried offstage while "Orpheus with his lute made trees" is sung.[62] Such afterpieces gave audiences some variety in an evening's bill, and this one, said Hopkins, turned out to be "as pleasing a farce as most that are done." It played twenty-one times that season and twenty-three times over the next three seasons.[63] Colman brought it out again for six performances in 1777 under his summer patent at the Haymarket. The text then was even shorter, though there were added songs composed by Arne, Smith, James Hook, and Samuel Arnold.[64]

The scenery for all three operas consisted of little more than still-life backgrounds to the words and music on the forestage: generic, stock palaces and painted forests on flats and drops. Even the fairies entered at the doors downstage of the proscenium frame.[65] For the 1763 adaptation, Garrick's preparation copy called for "lamps down" for the Lysander-Demetrius chase in the woods, led by Puck, a slight foreshadowing of romanticism's illusionistic forests.[66] As to costuming, Garrick's practice was to dress Greek and Roman plays in "Roman shapes," as he called them.[67] In this Shakespearean comedy, the cast probably wore a mixture common for classical plays: "Roman shapes" for the men and contemporary eighteenth-century formal dresses for the women. Two editions of the play in the late 1770s carry engravings of Jane Barsanti as Helena in typical, elegant, formal contemporary dress (fig. 5).[68]

In all, in the Garrick-era variations on *A Midsummer Night's Dream* one glimpses the cultural negotiations of mid-eighteenth-century Britain in the performance of its favorite theatrical son, as he championed a universal Shakespeare and simultaneously naturalized and nationalized him, providing England with the Shakespeare it needed. Garrick was not the first to do so, of course, nor would he be the last. The first major version of the play in the next century, as we shall see, is a nationalistic opera of 1816 celebrating the British Empire after Waterloo.[69]

Chapter four

THE SCENIC LANGUAGE
OF EMPIRE

A GRAND PAGEANT, commemorative of *The Triumphs of Theseus* . . .
— Covent Garden playbill, 1816

For the critics and poets of the romantic movement, Shakespeare was the bright particular star. He is a key reference point for August Wilhelm von Schlegel in his "Lectures on Dramatic Art and Literature" (1809–1811), for example, as Schlegel critiques the received ideas of classical tragedy and describes romantic poetry as "the expression of the secret attraction to a chaos which lies concealed in the very bosom of the ordered universe, and is perpetually striving after new and marvelous births." Shakespeare's plays are clearly in Schlegel's mind as he rejects neoclassicism's rationalistic concept of verisimilitude and observes that "the theatrical as well as every other poetical illusion, is a waking dream, to which we voluntarily surrender ourselves."[1] Romanticism's quest for access to an infinite realm of the spiritual led it to explorations of the marvelous and the mysterious and to ideas about the essences of national culture.

A Midsummer Night's Dream had many attractions for the romantics. Here Shakespeare gave the supernatural a local habitation and a name, locating the numinous in nature, and did so with delicate lyricism. In contrast with the classical insistence on homogeneity and generic purity, he mingled folklore and classical myth and fairies, courtiers, and artisans in the kind of organic mixture of things antithetical that was proof to the romantic mind of the superhuman unifying powers of the poet's imagination. Goethe incorporated Oberon, Titania, Puck, and Ariel into *Faust*, Part I, where they appear in the supernatural melange of his intermezzo, "Walpurgis Night's Dream." Goethe may even have considered staging Shakespeare's play at Weimar. In England in the 1790s, artist Henry Fuseli envisioned Titania, Bottom, and the fairies in a lush, forest dreamworld that is one of the earliest of what became a minor English genre of fairy painting.[2] (To the modern eye, Fuseli's forest is alive with sexual symbolism, but not until the twentieth century would the theatre explore the play's suggestions of the erotic.)

The theatre, however, lagged behind, with the first identifiably romantic staging of *A Midsummer Night's Dream* coming in 1816 in the form of a Covent Garden production of an operatic adaptation by Frederick Reynolds and Sir Henry Rowley Bishop. Although it is romantic in its attempts at greater illusionism in pictorial scenery — in this respect the production is seminal for the century — it is the production's nationalistic tropes that mark it especially. Both scenically and in the adaptation of the text, the opera is ripe with the language of British colonial expansionism following the Napoleonic wars. For this opera to be understood — and theatre historians from George C. D. Odell to the present have not understood it — it must be read in the light of empire. Unlikely as it may seem for Shakespeare's fairy play, it became a medium for the representation of British national identity throughout the nineteenth century.[3] This chapter explains the vocabulary of the production of this seminal 1816 opera and two subsequent minor incarnations of it, one of them in America — the first time the play in any form had ever been seen there.

The Reynolds opera opened at the Theatre Royal, Covent Garden, on 17 January 1816.[4] Some of the text and music came from the Garrick-Colman operatic version of 1763, but the new scenes and the new scenic text were significant.[5] By 1816, an adaptation of a Shakespeare play that eliminated any of his poetry and then loaded it with spectacular scenery could draw heavy fire from English romantic critics.[6] On this occasion, a famous, flaming critical arrow came from the bow of William Hazlitt. In his review for the *Examiner*, Hazlitt, homilist of the high Anglican, romantic church of Shakespeare, mourned the loss of sacred text that had been cut, and he also rejected the theatre's new visual vocabulary for the play:

> We have found to our cost, once and for all, that the regions of fancy and the boards of Covent Garden are not the same thing. All that is fine in the play is lost in the representation. The spirit was evaporated, the genius was fled; but

the spectacle was fine: it was that which saved the play. Oh, ye scene-shifters, ye scene painters, ye machinists and dress-makers, ye manufacturers of moon and stars that give no light, ye musical composers, ye men in the orchestra, fiddlers and trumpeters and players on the double drum and loud bassoon, rejoice! This is your triumph; it is not ours: and ye full-grown, well-fed, substantial, real fairies . . . we shall believe no more in the existence of your fantastic tribe.[7]

John Genest, who witnessed the production, also described it with sarcasm, saying "the real friends of Shakespeare" could never approve, though he did allow its "fine scenery."[8]

But not all critics objected in 1816. The *Theatrical Inquisitor and Monthly Mirror* applauded the "sublime scenery, splendid processions, and everything that constitutes the pomp and magnificence of the stage."[9] Henry Crabb Robinson, barrister, sometime *Times* correspondent, diarist, and friend of many English and German writers of his day, enjoyed the opera.[10] Hazlitt's complaints had a negligible effect. The production was fairly popular; it had eighteen performances and was revived in the next season.[11] And Reynolds was emboldened to adapt five more of Shakespeare's comedies, with music by Bishop.[12]

George C. D. Odell was outraged when he came to write about this 1816 adaptation and was as baffled as he had been by Purcell's 1692 *The Fairy Queen*. He cited Reynolds's textual trespasses and ridiculed the interpolated scenic pageants as foolish excrescences of pantomime and spectacle for the thoughtless, irrelevant to the play.[13] But Reynolds's interpolated pageants would not have seemed irrelevant to London audiences of 1816; the pageants' vocabulary becomes quite clear when read within the discourse of the British Empire in the year following Napoleon's fall.

A brief characterization of Reynolds's three-act adaptation and of Bishop's music will bring us to its two spectacles of cultural and theatrical interest. Reynolds acknowledged his debt to the Garrick-Colman opera on his playbill for the first few performances, probably to dress himself in Garrick's armor the first time out. He dropped the credit from the bills once success was assured, and in his preface to the 1816 edition of his libretto, he even affected to deplore the Garrick-Colman version.[14] For himself, he tells us he was "compelled to alter" Shakespeare's "divine drama." In his autobiography, he boasted that his own version, with its twenty performances, had had more success than Garrick's.[15]

There were at least twenty-four vocal pieces in his opera, including several from the Garrick-Colman version. Ten new song settings came from Bishop, a prolific composer of theatre music who later would give Victorians the melody for "Home, Sweet Home." Bishop collaborated with Thomas Simpson Cooke on two more.[16] Among the Shakespearean words newly set were those in the opera's first song: in Act 1, Hermia sang her vow to elope with Lysander, beginning with "By the simplicity of Venus's doves." Demetrius sang Helena's lines of praise for Hermia, beginning "Oh happy fair! / Your eyes are loadstars," perhaps set by Bishop. Oberon sang his "Flower of this purple dye," perhaps using Smith's music of 1763. The fairies sang two quartets derived from the original text, one by Richard Stevens for the lullaby to Titania and one using the last two lines of Shakespeare's last song, "Trip away, make no stay; / Meet me all by break of day." Reynolds used Shakespeare's Act 5 fairy blessing but moved it to the end of the forest sequence. Among the non-Shakespearean lyrics, Hermia sang Handel's "Hush ye pretty warbling choir," addressed to "sylvan songsters," which Bishop's orchestra rendered on a cue marked "bird symphony."[17] Hermia was played by Kitty Stephens, who, with tenor John Sinclair, carried the music for the young lovers. Neither Helena nor Lysander was assigned a solo, the assignment of songs probably being determined by the musical talent available — or not.

Reynolds cut the text crudely. In Act 1, Helena was never brought on to be told of Hermia's elopement plans, and this omitted the basic exposition of how she and Demetrius have come to be in pursuit of Lysander and Hermia in the forest. Reynolds eliminated much of the lovers' quarrels in the wood, a cut to which Genest had no objection, nor did most Victorian critics.[18] Hazlitt was so indignant over the omission of Helena's recollection of her childhood friendship with the now "injurious Hermia" (3.2.196–220) that he reprinted it in his review to restore it.[19] Reynolds did retain Titania's description of the mother of her Indian boy but with a prudish adjustment in one passage: "When we have laughed to see the sails conceive / And grow big-bellied with the wanton wind" (2.1.128–129) was altered to "and grow all pregnant with the wanton wind."[20] Shakespeare's line was not to be heard thereafter on the nineteenth-century stage, even in modified form.

Reynolds also structurally altered the play in order to end his opera not with the mechanicals' *Pyramus and Thisbe* and the fairy blessing of Theseus's palace but with a pageant of *The Triumphs of Theseus*. At the beginning of Reynolds's last act, Theseus enters, saying that the "palpable gross play" has already "beguiled our time." After Hermia pays obeisance to her father, Egeus, a trumpet sounds, and Theseus exclaims, "Hark! They approach! / My hardy veterans! / My brave companions in the toils of war!" At his request, Hermia sings them "a harmonious greeting," beginning, "Warriors! March on! March on! and hear the praise / A grateful nation to your valor pays."[21] Theseus then tells the court that his new bride, Hippolyta, has requested a pageant in honor of all his conquests, which follows. The playbill advertised it as

A GRAND PAGEANT, commemorative of *The Triumphs of Theseus, Over the Cretans — the Thebans — the Amazons — the Centaurs — the Minotaur. Ariadne in the Labyrinth — the Mysterious Peplum, or Veil of Minerva — the Ship Argo — and the Golden Fleece.*[22]

(See figure 6 for an 1817 playbill containing a slight variant on the same advertisement.) The opera closed with a chorus to "Great Theseus's Name."

Theseus's conquests were of relatively limited interest to Shakespeare. Why end the opera with this visual classical catechism? Did it better set the universe in order than the fairies yet could in 1816? The traditional response of theatre historians would be to look to theatrical style: this is an era of increasing scenic spectacle, with the development of melodrama and romantic pictorialism. In the huge, five-galleried Covent Garden, such pageants were common, and Theseus's pageant would have offered an impressive visual climax more effective than the delicate word music of Shakespeare's fairy blessing. But such explanations do not take us very far into the labyrinth with Theseus, much less out of it.

The purposes of the Theseus pageant become clear when the scenic vocabulary is read within British colonialist discourse. The figure of Theseus loomed large in romantic art and literature's constructions of the ancient world. Within that general enthusiasm for the Hellenic world that marks romanticism in England, Germany, and France, we find the Greek argonaut refigured in poetry and statuary as a paradigmatic protector of civilization against barbarism. The legendary ancient, who was victorious over the Minotaur and who was Phaedra's suffering husband, is figured as the handsome embodiment of the muscular force of reason in the struggle against the irrational. All aspects of this construction involve quite selective uses of Greek legend qua history. It begins as early as the fifth century, when Athenians themselves were eager to construct Theseus as their founder and patriarch.[23] As mythic founder of Athens and paradigm of power and reason, Theseus enjoyed wide popularity in Europe from the last decades of the eighteenth century through at least the end of the nineteenth. Simon Tidworth, tracing the Theseus myth from the Renaissance through romanticism, has observed that Theseus, the conqueror, was reborn, "appropriately enough, in the age of Napoleon and the beginnings of nationalism."[24] G. W. F. Hegel, who treated myth and religion almost as art, called for "a new Theseus" to unite Germany.[25] Sculptor Antonio Canova created his *Theseus Triumphant* in 1781–1782, a classically styled piece, now in the Victoria and Albert Museum, in which a young, noble, muscular male figure sits atop the Minotaur

THEATRE ROYAL, COVENT-GARDEN

This present SATURDAY, Feb. 15, 1817, (in 3 acts) Shakspeare's Play of

A MIDSUMMER NIGHT's DREAM

The Overture composed by Mr. BISHOP.—The original Musick by Arne, Battishill, and Smith—with Additions by Handel, Dr. Cooke, Steven, Liston, &c.
The SCENERY painted by Meff. Phillips, Whitmore, Grieve, Pugh, Hollogan, Hodgins, and their affiftants.
The Machinery by Mr. SAUL. The Decorations by Mr. BRADWELL.
The Dreffes by Mr. Flower and Miss Egan The Dances by Mr. NOBLE.

ATHENIANS

Theseus, Duke of Athens, Mr EGERTON, Egeus, Mr. CHAPMAN,
Lysander, Mr. ABBOTT, Demetrius, Mr. SINCLAIR, Philoftrate, Mr JEFFERIES,
Quince, the Carpenter, Mr EMERY, Snug, the Joiner, Mr. TOKELY,
Bottom, the Weaver, Mr. LISTON, Flute, the Bellows Me der, Mr SIMMONS,
Snout, the Tinker, Mr. BELLAMY, Starveling, the Tailor, Mr. MENAGE,
Hippolita, Miss LOGAN, Hermia. Miss STEPHENS, Helena, Miss FOOTE.

FAIRIES

Oberon, Mr. DURUSET, Titania, Mrs FAUCIT, Puck, or Robin Goodfellow, Miss S. BOOTH
First Fairy, Mrs. LISTON, 2d Fairy, Miss MATTHEWS, 3d Fairy, Mrs. BISHOP,
4th Fairy, Mrs STERLING, 5th Fairy, Miss CAREW, 6th Fairy, Mrs MAC ALPINE
CHORAL FAIRIES, Meffe Coates, Chipp, Corri, Finelay, Grimaldi, Herbert, Hibbert, Iliff, Norman, Weft, Whitmore.
Meff. Treby, King, Tinney, Norris, Crumpton, Everard, Higman, Lee, Linton, Power, Terrr, Tett, Watson,

The Songs, Choruses, &c. will be sung in the following succession:

Grand Chorus.
Song, Hermia—'By the simplicity of Venus' doves.'
Air, 2d Fairy—'Kim up, daffodil and rose.'
Song Demetrius—'Forbid the so my sea to roll.'
Air, 1st Fairy—'Come, follow, follow me.'

ACT II.——Quartetto—'Ye spotted snakes.'
Air, Bottom—'The ousel cock.'
Chorus—'Hail, mortal, hail'
Duet, Demetrius & Hermia—'These looks.'
Song, Oberon—'Flowers of the purple dye.'
Recit Fairy—'Oberon, no more despair.'

Attendant Spirits, Meff. VEDY, BERTHET, BEGRAND,—Meff. PLOURDEAU, BRADWELL, MORI,
Chorus—'Pierce the air with founds of joy.'

ACT III.——Quartetto—'Welcome to this place.'
Air, Oberon—'Be as thou wast wont to be.'
Chorus of Hunters—'Hark, each spartan hound.'
Song, Demetrius—'Sweet cheering hope.'

Solo, Obe on—'To the best bride bed will we.'
Chorus—'In Thefeus' house give glimmering light'
Recit. & Song, Hermia—'Warriors, march.'
Chorus—'His fame proclaim.'

The Play to conclude with

A GRAND PAGEANT,

COMMEMORATIVE OF

THE TRIUMPHS OF THESEUS,

In which is introduced the Cretans, the Thebans, the Amazons, the Centaurs, Ariadne in the
Labyrinth—Mysterious Peplum, or Veil of Minerva—the Ship Argo—& the Golden Fleece.
After which, 7th time, a New Ballet Divertisement (composed by Mr. NOBLE) called

AURORA;

Or, THE FLIGHT OF ZEPHYR.

Zephyr by Mr. NOBLE,
Cupids, Misses Parsloe, F. Boaden, C. Boaden, R. Boaden,
Shepherds—Meff. Vedy, Berthet, Begrand
Attendants on Zephyr—Meff. Goodwin, Grant, Platt, Sarjant, Sutton White
Flora by Miss LUPPINO, Nymphs by The Miss DENNETTS,
Pastoral Nymphs—Misses Worgman, Shotter, L. Boaden,
Shepherdesses—Mesdames Plourdeau, Bradwell. Mori
To which will be added the Melo-Drama of The

MILLER AND HIS MEN.

The characters as before

☞ ALL ORDERS must be REFUSED at the DOORS.

Printed by E. Macleish, r Bow-street, London

MR. BOOTH,

In his second Performance of

KING RICHARD,

was again most loudly and universally called for to repeat the Character—
but from the great fatigue attending his exertions, he cannot have the honour
of appearing again till Monday.

The new Ballet of AURORA; or the Flight of Zephyr,
having been received throughout with every expression of applause and satisfaction,
will be repeated every night—Monday excepted.

The New HIGHLY POPULAR PANTOMIME

will be repeated on Monday.

On Monday, Shakspeare's Tragedy of KING RICHARD the THIRD.

King Richard by Mr. BOOTH,

On Tuesday (27th time) the New Musical Drama of The SLAVE.
With (9th time) the Melo-Drama of The RAVENS: or, The Force of Conscience.

A NEW OPERATICK PIECE

in two acts, is in rehearsal, and will be produced immediately.

FIGURE 6. Playbill for a performance in 1817 of the 1816 opera adaptation by Frederick Reynolds and Sir Henry Rowley Bishop, Theatre Royal, Covent Garden. The scene painters get almost top billing, and the bill features the Act 5 spectacle, "A Grand Pageant, Commemorative of the Triumphs of Theseus." Folger Shakespeare Library.

FIGURE 7. *Theseus Triumphant*, by Antonio Canova, 1781–1782. Theseus was frequently figured as the patriarchal protector of civilization in art and poetry in Europe in the first half of the nineteenth century. Trustees of the Victoria and Albert Museum.

FIGURE 8.
Theseus, by Antoine-Louis Barye.
Musée des Beaux-Arts, Bordeaux.

83
*The
Scenic
Language
of Empire*

he has just slain, victory in repose (fig. 7). Later Canova sculpture groups show
Theseus fighting a centaur. In 1846, Antoine-Louis Barye created two romantic
bronzes, *Theseus* (fig. 8), in which Theseus is about to slay the Minotaur, and
Theseus Slays the Centaur, Bianor.[26] Both Barye groups show an idealized, muscular Greek male figure efficiently subduing the bestial, writhing creature. Two
minor English poets, Barry Cornwall (Edmund Kean's biographer) and Felicia
Hemans, celebrated Theseus. In her *The Shade of Theseus*, Hemans drew upon
legend to place his inspiring ghost at Marathon, helping to drive out the invad-
ing Persians: "And the foaming waves grew red, / And the sails were crowded
fast, / When the sons of Asia fled, / As the Shade of Theseus passed!"[27] Theseus
is also present in many nineteenth-century treatments of Ariadne, Phaedra, and
Hippolytus, including those of Leigh Hunt, Algernon Swinburne, Christina
Rosetti, and Robert Browning.[28] So familiar was Theseus by midcentury that, in
1848, James Robinson Planché could even spin off, as one of his "classical extravaganzas," a spoof on the Theseus and Ariadne story.[29]

Of course, Britain's appropriations of the classical past in general were as old
as the Renaissance and as familiar on the London landscape as Wren's St. Paul's

or the new Covent Garden Theatre itself, designed by Robert Smirke after Athenian acropolis temples. Art historian Hugh Honour has noted the long appropriation of classical architecture by the West in the design of foreign embassies. Honour reminds us that, just as Doric temples had marked the Greek presence among the barbarians and classical orders had followed the Roman occupations from North Africa to northern Europe, so too have classical columns, entablatures, and pediments signified modern European empires in Africa, India, and Southeast Asia.[30]

In 1816, the year following Napoleon's defeat at Waterloo, when England was on the brink of a long era of expansionism, the British were taking their Greek heritage very seriously. John Keats's first look into Chapman's Homer was the least of it that year. The issue of the so-called Elgin marbles was high in public consciousness. The Elgin marbles were, of course, the sculpture groups from the pediments of the Athenian Parthenon and portions of a frieze from its metopes that Lord Elgin (Thomas Bruce) had taken down and shipped back to England. The Parthenon had been seriously damaged by Turkish bombardments, and Elgin regarded the preservation of the marbles as the British Empire's duty to civilization, if not something of a cultural windfall. (English country homes of the aristocracy were currently being decorated with antique marbles, and Elgin was planning his own mansion in Scotland.) Elgin's removal of the marbles, which entailed massive engineering and shipping operations between 1803 and 1812, was possible because of shifts in the balance of power in the Mediterranean during the wars with Napoleon. The Turkish government, which still controlled Greece, had come to favor the British. Elgin was the British ambassador to Constantinople and capitalized on his position to secure the necessary permissions. Today, many regard Elgin's removal of the Parthenon marbles to London as one of the most notorious cultural thefts in modern history, giving rise to the term "Elginism."[31]

Even at the time, not all admired Elgin's feat, and it was in response to criticism that Elgin put the marbles on public display, first at his London home and then at Burlington house. Probably the most damning censure came from George Gordon, Lord Bryon, including his poem, "The Curse of Minerva." Minerva confronts the English poet as he meditates on the Parthenon: "I saw successive tyrannies expire. / 'Scaped from the ravage of Turk and Goth, / Thy country sends a spoiler worse than both," who "basely stole what less Barbarians won."[32] Early in 1816, Elgin, having decided to sell the figures, asked the House of Commons for an inquiry into their value, and the matter was hotly debated. Byron, who would die at Missolonghi supporting Greek liberation, continued

FIGURE 9. Marble figures from the eastern pediment of the Athenian Parthenon removed to England by Lord Elgin between 1803 and 1812 and first shown publicly at the British Museum in 1816. The reclining male figure at center was thought to be Theseus. British Museum.

his attack on the Scotsman Elgin, crying, "What the goths spared, the Scots destroyed."[33] On the other side, Elgin was praised and defended by Canova and in James Stuart and Nicholas Revett's *The Antiquities of Athens, Measured and Delineated*.[34] Parliament conducted a formal inquiry in 1816 and finally soothed its uneasy conscience by taking the marbles into the public trust, reimbursing Elgin somewhat, and turning them over to the British Museum. Their first public showings at the museum occurred just after Christmas of 1816.[35] One major figure among the marbles, situated in a sculpture group on the eastern pediment of the Parthenon, was thought at the time to be that of Theseus (fig. 9).[36] Today the figure is referred to as Dionysus or, occasionally, Heracles. Barry Cornwall wrote of this putative Theseus as a "proud and mighty figure" in his poem "On the Statue of Theseus."[37] Keats, in his poem "On Seeing the Elgin Marbles for the First Time," languished in reflections on his own mortality and that "most dizzy pain, / That mingles Grecian grandeur with the rude / Wasting of old Time."[38] Today, the Elgin marbles, designated as such, are exhibited still in the British Museum, in the Duveen Gallery, notwithstanding the pleas in the 1980s of Greece's Minister of Culture, Melina Mercouri, for their return to Athens.

Frederick Reynolds's creation of a theatrical litany of Theseus's conquests with which to climax his 1816 *A Midsummer Night's Dream* was more than topical and opportunistic. It was a natural move, flowing from the discourse of empire. Further, it not only reiterated Britain's most recent appropriation of the classical past but connected it with Shakespeare, the nation's own greatest cultural capital, furthering the parallels between England and Greece. Samuel Johnson had long since said in his famous *Preface* to his edition of the plays (1765) that Shakespeare had begun "to assume the dignity of an ancient," and in Reynolds's move, England and Athens were effectively conflated in a popular and accessible theatrical spectacle.[39] *A Midsummer Night's Dream*, with its blend of Greeks and English fairy lore, court lovers and Elizabethan artisans, was, of course, wholly congenial to this marriage.

Having seen the pageant of Theseus within the discourse of empire, we now can understand better the choice — and the language — of the other major scenic spectacle in Reynolds's opera. In Shakespeare, the quarrel between Oberon and Titania over possession of the Indian boy is quietly resolved in Act 4, when we are told that Titania has finally surrendered her Indian boy to Oberon. The surrender is not shown; Oberon reports it to Puck, concluding with the lines, "I then did ask of her her changeling child, / Which straight she gave me, and her fairy sent / To bear him to my bower in fairyland" (4.1.58–60). Reynolds decided to depict the Indian boy's return, staging it elaborately at the end of his Act 2. No pictorial evidence of the scene survives, but we can unpack the interesting text of this spectacle by closely considering the dialogue, lyrics, and stage directions for the scene.[40]

> Music
> *(Clouds descend and open. A fairy is discovered, who chaunts the following lines.)*
> Finale
> Fairy.   Oberon!
> Oberon.   Appear!
> Fairy.   Oberon! No more despair!
>   Titania wafts him to your care!
>   Borne by each propitious gale,
>   From India's shores her gallies sail.
>   Nor storms, nor quicksands can they meet,
>   For Zephyrs fan the fairy fleet!
>   And silv'ry seas the treasure bear, —
>   The Boy! — the Indian Boy is near!
>   *(Clouds begin to ascend again.)*
> Oberon.   Her vessels waft him to my care,
>   The joy I own, to all be known;
>   And join with me, in dance and revelry!

Then — Titania's charmed eye release
From Monster's view — and all things shall
be peace.

Music.

(Clouds having ascended, the Sea is discovered. A Fairy Palace in the Distance.
Titania's galley and other gallies in full sail. Dance — During which, Indian Boy
is brought forward.)

CHORUS

Pierce the air with sounds of joy!
Hail Titania's treasur'd Boy![41]

This pictorial and musical narration of galleys sailing from India with their
treasure for Oberon and England ended on a Handelian coda, and it is an unmistakable reiteration of Britain's interest in exotic India. Britain had been long
absorbed in "the Indian question," from the 1709 reorganization of the original
East India Company into the United Company of Merchants of England trad-
ing to the East Indies, through Robert Clive's establishment of the British Empire in India in 1765 and the subsequent controversies over India in the 1780s.
At Eton, Cambridge, and Oxford, young Englishmen competed for prizes with
essays or Latin verses on such subjects as "The Probable Design of the Divine
Providence in subjugating so large a portion of Asia to the British dominion."[42]
Parliamentary disputes had raged over the alleged exploitation of Indians, first
under Clive and then Warren Hastings, and both men were impeached in the
1780s. Clive committed suicide, and Hastings had a trial lasting seven years, at
the end of which he was honorably acquitted. British historians agree that the
British public sentiment was that Hastings, for all his faults, had saved India for
England.[43] In 1813, Parliament debated whether to renew the United Company's charter (which it did), and the elderly Hastings, his reputation somewhat recuperated, had returned to testify.[44] Reynolds's 1816 pictorial and musical elaboration on the return of the Indian boy, with Titania's galleys sailing to
England from India's shores, reproduced the very familiar discourse of colonial
conquest. The spectacle narrates the mastering of the disobedient Titania and
oriental India, combining colonialism and sexual domination in a familiar manner.[45] This scene speaks the same language as the production's pageant of the
conquests of Theseus. The Indian boy is delivered to the King of English fairies
as readily as Theseus was brought to London from the eastern pediment of the
Athenian Parthenon. The device is somewhat reminiscent of Betterton's appropriation of the exotic East in the Chinese Eden that he created for the last act of
Purcell's The Fairy Queen.

Other features of the Reynolds opera now come into focus. Hermia's song, greeting Theseus's "brave companions in the toil of war" ("Warriors! March on! March on! and hear the praise / A grateful nation to your valor pays"), is an echo of the many public tributes "a grateful nation" was paying to Wellington and his forces in 1815 and 1816.[46] And there is a notable piece of stage business. The mechanicals' *Pyramus and Thisbe* was not dropped completely but incorporated into their forest rehearsal scene. Theseus watched it there, secretly, from behind a tree. When Theseus was disclosed, Bottom, played by comedian John Liston, fainted, crying, "Mercy! the King! dead! dead in earnest!" At this point, according to the stage directions, Liston "Falls on the stage, at the King's feet."[47] Theseus, of course, is not a king. Even in Shakespeare's own anachronistic speech headings and line references, he is at best a duke. But in Reynolds's mind in 1816, England and ancient Greece were one, and after Waterloo, much was at the English king's feet. One likes to think that for some in the Covent Garden audience, Liston's business might have been comic relief from all the flattering royal pomp of this production.

The role of the old patriarch, Egeus, is enlarged in Reynolds's opera, not surprisingly. For his last act, Reynolds created a scene that is not in Shakespeare: a reconciliation between Egeus and his daughter, Hermia (see chapter 1). Hermia kneels at her father's feet, seeking pardon and permission to marry Lysander, which Egeus grants.[48] Reynolds thereby not only assures that the father is not displaced but takes care that the new order has the patriarch's blessing. Such family reconciliations were moral keystones in the sentimental drama of the eighteenth century and the melodrama of the first half of the nineteenth.

Given the importance of the scenic text in this production, it is not surprising to find that Reynolds's playbill not only advertised the spectacles but listed the names of scene painters near the top (see fig. 6), just below those of the adaptor and composer.[49] He was profoundly right to do so, more than he could have known. By their visual text, the painters were as much the mediators of Shakespeare as the textual adaptors and composers so complained of by theatre chroniclers, such as Genest and Odell. And in Hazlitt's complaint that the new scenery was too literal for the fairy play, he either failed to read or chose to ignore the chauvinism in the production. It is a critique that privileges idealist romantic aesthetics and renders Hazlitt as silent as Keats about such imperial appropriations.

We can understand better now, too, the grandiloquent language of Reynolds's stage directions for the setting for 1.1: "A Grand Doric Colonnade appertaining to Duke Theseus' Palace." The setting for the finale was "Theseus' Grand Hall of Audience — Throne."[50] When *Julius Caesar* was produced on this stage under John Philip Kemble in 1812, Kemble had insisted upon the stylistic architectural features of the empire over those of the republican style, against the advice of his consultant in antiquarian matters, Francis Douce.[51] Kemble's health was failing by 1816, but it is likely that Theseus's palace, too, was rendered in a style closer to the Roman Empire than to Pericles' Athens. One promptbook in Kemble's hand, probably prepared for the revival of the production in 1817, during Kemble's last season, calls for Theseus to enter in Act 1 accompanied by twelve guards and six officers.[52]

For the forest scenes in the play, the necessary scenic corollary to the mythopticon for Theseus was an illusionistic, romantic forest landscape. The fairies, too, were royally outfitted. In the first forest scene, Titania and Oberon entered to processional music, each "in a Car," Oberon from one wing and Titania from the other. Oberon's costume was rendered in classical style. The only surviving engraving of this production shows John Duruset as Oberon in a belted Grecian tunic, mantle, and sandals, with a spear in hand (fig. 10). Forty-six fairies danced attendance upon the fairy royalty, probably wearing the short gauze dresses of the developing romantic ballet, romantic descendants of Diana's sylphs.[53] An attempt was made to create an illusionistic, continuous picture-sequence of distinct locales in the wood, an effect we would describe today as cinematic. After the meeting of Oberon and Titania ("A Wood — Moonlight"), the set changed to Titania's bower in "Another part of the Wood," which featured "the Duke's Oak" (2.2.105). The Lysander and Hermia chase scene was set in yet another forest locale. At one point, there was a cinema-like "dissolve" from one forest locale to another. After Puck taunted Lysander and Demetrius (with "stage lamps down"), the picture changed, and Oberon entered to wonder about the outcome of Puck's mission. The scenic picture then altered again before the audience's eyes: Puck's voice was heard as he began his incantation over the sleeping Lysander, and, with music beneath, another part of the wood opened, and the two were gradually revealed behind translucent gauzes. The stage directions read:

Music
(*A part of the Wood opens — a Mist is seen — the Mist gradually disperses, and Lysander is discovered asleep on a flowery Bank, Puck standing by him, with the Herb in his hand.*)[54]

Here, in 1816, stage technology has begun to provide material representations of a fairy forest world, quite different in spirit from the word-conjured world of Shakespeare's open stage. The romantic theatre can create a virtual, alternative reality.

Painted by J. Boaden.   Engraved by Chas Picart.

Mr Duruset as Oberon.

"Ill met by moon-light, Proud Titania."
Midsummer night's Dream.

FIGURE 10. John Duruset as Oberon in Reynolds's opera, *A Midsummer Night's Dream,*
Theatre Royal, Covent Garden, 1816. His Greco-Roman costume reflects the emerging antiquarian interest in "historically correct" scenery and costumes. Yale-Rockefeller Collection
of Theatrical Prints, Yale School of Drama Library.

For the remainder of the century, such palaces and forests become obligatory for productions of *A Midsummer Night's Dream*, and they grow ever more ostentatious. From Reynolds's opera, the Grieve family dynasty of scene painters carry the scenic vocabulary to the productions of Elizabeth Vestris (1840), Charles Kean (1856), and Charles Calvert (1865).[55] The watercolors of Kean's production capture this tradition at midcentury (see plates 1–5). We see this vocabulary again, inflated, in the photographs of the productions of Augustin Daly (see figs. 16, 19–21) and Sir Herbert Beerbohm Tree at the end of the century (see figs. 22, 24, 26).

Reynolds's opera had two more incarnations. When the play was performed for the first time in the United States in 1826, it was almost certainly a pared down version of this opera.[56] The *New York American* advertised the play as being presented at the Park Theatre for the first time in America and "as performed in London with unbounded applause," and it was offered "with Music, Dances, and various Scenic Displays."[57] One finds no good Jacksonian denunciations of its British chauvinism. Instead, an American critic echoed Hazlitt's complaint that the fairy world was "too light, changing and ethereal for actors of flesh and blood and the clumsy contrivances of the stage."[58] The perfection of illusion will be as much America's business as it is England's. Interested in illusion, this critic recorded some business that was probably common throughout the century but seldom mentioned. Bottom (Thomas Hilson) manipulated the ears on the ass's head with a string behind his back, business this critic objected to only because the trick was all too visible. It is not so far from here to Disney animations. The production was a benefit for the well-liked Ellen Hilson, who played Puck, and it does not seem to have had much, if any, repetition.

In London, manager Alfred Bunn modified the Reynolds version for an ignominious and short-lived revival in 1833, a year in which the quarrelsome producer was trying to make ends meet by managing both Covent Garden and Drury Lane.[59] Bunn's promptbook shows a reshuffling of the 1816 text and the deletion of twelve pages. Bunn used fourteen of its twenty-four songs, and he billed it as Shakespeare's play with music, "Compressed into Two acts."[60] Not only was Helena still missing from Act 1, but so was most of the lovers' chase in 3.2 and 3.3. This compression resulted in Oberon entering to release Titania from her spell immediately after she had exited with Bottom and the fairies. Oberon waved his wand in the general direction of the offstage Titania, singing "Be as thou wast wont to be" into the wings. Titania's galley did not sail, nor was Theseus celebrated with a final pageant. According to the promptbook, Bunn was amused to take Quince literally at 3.1.2–4: "here's a marvellous convenient place for our rehearsal. This green plot shall be our stage, this hawthorn brake our tiring-house." Bunn arranged a tiring-house out of bushes for the mechanicals' forest rehearsal, which, of course, entirely undid Shakespeare's little joke on how we construct our realities. An admired comedian of the company, William Dowton, played Bottom. One feature of the Bunn production is a notable historical first. The playbill for the opening night promised audiences that prior to the play, "the Band will perform Mindelssohn's [*sic*] Celebrated Overture." Bunn's is the earliest record of the use of any of the Mendelssohn music with a production; in this instance, he would have borrowed on the overture that Mendelssohn had composed in 1826.[61]

Chapter five

"THESE ANTIQUE FABLES . . .
THESE FAIRY TOYS"

Theseus: More strange than true. I never may believe
These antique fables, nor these fairy toys.

The productions of *A Midsummer Night's Dream* of Lucia Elizabeth Vestris in London in 1840 and Ludwig Tieck in Potsdam in 1843 were not only successful but created visual and musical vocabularies for the play that became nearly inseparable from it for the rest of the century.[1] Vestris offered more of the text than had been performed in two hundred years and sophisticated advancements in the romantic scenic vocabulary (fig. 11). It was for Tieck's production that Felix Mendelssohn created his famous incidental score.

Vestris also set another precedent. She took the role of Oberon (fig. 12), adroitly capitalizing on both her musical talent and, dressed in a revealing costume, her sexual appeal. Succeeding managers followed Vestris's model in more than text and staging; after Vestris, the role of Oberon was played by a woman in every major English and American production of the play until 1914, with one exception.[2] Attractive brunette contraltos played Oberon to blond sopranos as Titania (see figs. 17 and 23).

A woman fairy king would have addressed the patriarchal Victorian culture in complex, fascinating ways. Once again a woman was on the English throne, and in this production of a play resonant with the anxieties of Elizabethan men

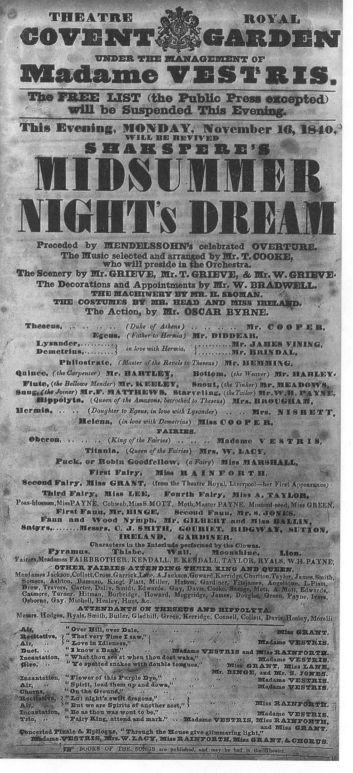

FIGURE 11.
Playbill for the opening performance of Elizabeth Vestris's production, Theatre Royal, Covent Garden, 16 November 1840. Vestris staged the relatively complete text of the play for the first time in more than two centuries. Folger Shakespeare Library.

MADAME VESTRIS

AS OBERON.

In the Midsummer Night's Dream!

FIGURE 12. Elizabeth Vestris as Oberon in her 1840 production, Theatre Royal, Covent Garden. Lithograph by W. Clerk. Harvard Theatre Collection.

not in control of their women, as Louis Montrose has suggested, an eroticized woman theatre manager stepped into the role of a male ruler.[3] Victorian males perceived women in terms of their sexuality, their reproductive role, and their emotions, and women were regarded as closer to nature and the irrational; they were, at one and the same time, eroticized as sexual companions, feared as predators, and idealized as creatures of the spirit.[4] The idealization is exemplified in a male critic's assessment of Julia Neilson's Oberon in Sir Herbert Beerbohm Tree's production of 1900: "Her Oberon is truly regal, while the mere fact of her being woman just differentiates it from humanity."[5] A female fairy king was just that much more ethereal. On the other hand, a woman in this role was unquestionably sexually appealing; she was the adorable, diminutive enchantress in a child's fairy world, Lolita as well as angel.

Vestris was well aware of her sexual capital. She had won fame in her youth as a light opera darling of London, especially appealing in cross-dressed roles such as the title role in *Giovanni in London*, Moncrieff's burlesque of Mozart's opera. By all contemporary accounts — and all of them are male accounts — her face and figure, her French charm, and her sweet contralto voice won her a large male following.[6] In one Victorian male's memoir, she is remembered admiringly as being "just the height and build of the Medicean Venus," and another recalled that enterprising vendors sold plaster casts of "le jambe de Vestris" outside theatres where she appeared.[7] Vestris and the women who succeeded her played the role of Oberon in costumes that were exceptionally revealing for the era (see figs. 12 and 17).

The fairy trains attending Oberon and Titania at mid century consisted of adult women (see plate 5), all of whom were costumed in the short, white gauze dresses and white silk stockings of the romantic ballet, in the manner of dancer Marie Taglioni's costume for *La Sylphide* (1832). In the context of respectable Shakespeare, the actresses were relatively free from reproach, and the male gaze was free to play. Victorian male critics, of course, rarely acknowledged that there was such sexual appeal in the church of Shakespeare. But one male critic in a New York sporting newspaper, which was clearly aimed at a roughcast male readership, exclaimed of the female Oberon in Laura Keene's 1859 production, "Ye gods! such a figure." He also recommended the rest of the fairy troupe to his readers: "hosts of handsome girls, all having well-formed limbs and wearing the same kind of tights."[8] American critic William Winter inadvertently revealed the erotic appeal when he objected to a disturbing transformation scene featuring flying women fairies; it relied chiefly for its success, he wrote, upon "representing female loveliness in suspense."[9]

In Vestris's case, her seeming sexual accessibility came in tandem with her position as a theatrical manager, the eminent domain of males. As Kathy Fletcher has noted, the fact that Vestris could both run theatres (the Olympic, Covent Garden, and the Lyceum) and play the coquette on stage "must have enhanced her fascination."[10] As the Woman on Top, she would have been simultaneously as appealing and disturbing to men as a dominatrix. In one point in her cross-dressed performance, she waved her fairy wand and the forest scenery changed behind her, her triple powers in play in a single moment; the one surviving engraving of her in the role shows her at this moment (fig. 12). As Oberon, Vestris was both inside the conventional parameters for Woman and outside them, both compliant and in charge, Woman and monarch. She obviously had to negotiate her performance carefully, as did the young queen who came to see her perform.

At the same time that Vestris was aware of her physical appeal, she could hope that a Shakespearean success would provide respectability and legitimacy for her management of Theatre Royal, Covent Garden. Her restored-text version of *Love's Labours Lost* in the previous season had been only a *succès d'estime*. Also, with *A Midsummer Night's Dream*, Vestris and her collaborator in this production, James Robinson Planché, could draw on their previous successes with innumerable fairy extravaganzas at the Olympic Theatre on Wych Street, a theatre limited to noncanonical entertainments but which they made popular enough to draw the young Princess Victoria. Among their fairy works had been Planché's elegant *The Sleeping Beauty*. The fertile Planché also had created the libretto for Carl Maria von Weber's distantly related *Oberon*, which had premiered at Covent Garden in 1826. These, like Vestris's production of *A Midsummer Night's Dream*, came in the midst of a wave of fairy literature, operas, ballets, and paintings that included Grimm's fairy tales (which appeared in English with illustrations by George Cruikshank in the 1820s); the ballet *La Sylphide*; Richard Wagner's 1834 opera, *Die Feen*; and some of the works of Hans Christian Andersen.[11] Also, with *A Midsummer Night's Dream*, Planché could continue his earnest campaign for historically correct dress for Shakespeare, first realized in his costumes for Charles Kemble's 1823 *King John*, a campaign that Vestris, seeking legitimacy, gladly supported. Vestris also had at her disposal scenic artist John Henderson Grieve, who had painted for the Reynolds opera, together with his two sons, Thomas and William.

But perhaps the key circumstance behind the choice of *A Midsummer Night's Dream* was the marriage of the eighteen-year-old Queen Victoria to Prince Albert in February 1840. On the occasion, Vestris and Planché designed a Covent

Garden pageant, *The Fortunate Isles*, as a compliment to them and gave a command performance of it.[12] Now, in the succeeding season, Vestris offered *A Midsummer Night's Dream*. Victoria and Albert attended the production in February 1841, within a few days of their first anniversary.[13]

Vestris's relatively restored text of the play was prepared by Planché, according to the contemporary Shakespearean scholar J. O. Halliwell, who was a vigorous defender of Vestris and Planché against those who complained of the new pictorial scenic system. "The alterations . . . are few," he wrote, "and made with that good judgment which characterizes everything that Mr. Planché undertakes."[14] However, had a male actor-manager been in Vestris's place, one doubts that Planché would have been given all the credit. In all, 390 lines were omitted, unexceptional in the century. The production's thirteen songs set only Shakespearean text, and no scenes were omitted.[15] Vestris's text — not forgetting her songs — falls within the century's average reduction of the play's text by 17 to 19 percent, slightly above Samuel Phelps's and well below the cuttings of Charles Kean, Augustin Daly, and Sir Herbert Beerbohm Tree.[16]

The Planché-Vestris text is also cut with more sensitivity than subsequent Victorian texts. It leaves relatively complete Titania's "forgeries of jealousy" speech in Act 1 (which Garrick cut), Helena's lines on her childhood with Hermia in Act 1, and Theseus's Act 5 lines on the lunatic, the lover, and the poet. Oberon's final speech, beginning "Now until the break of day" (5.2.31–52), was intact, as was Puck's epilogue. None of these may be taken for granted subsequently. Phelps, for example, cut thirty of the thirty-seven lines of Titania's speech, as did William Burton and Daly; Kean left only three lines of it. Oberon's final speech was cut entirely by Phelps, Burton, Kean, and Daly.[17]

The Planché-Vestris cutting became the Victorian pattern: shorten and soften the lovers' wrangles in the forest, remove arcane references, shorten lyrical elaborations that do not move the plot, omit any shade of the suggestive and any shadow of the unpleasant. To illustrate briefly the latter two, the text omits Titania's three lines on the pregnant mother of her Indian boy, and Puck loses all his references to screech owls, shrouds, gaping graves, and Hecate's team (5.2.6–10, 14). Hermia was, however, allowed to refer to her "virgin patent" (1.1.80), but in the Daly and Tree productions later, she referred instead to her "maiden heart." In 1840, Theseus could still say "Lovers, to bed" (5.1.357), but in Kean's 1856 production, this became "Lovers, away."

For all of the relative care with the text, there remained what the young Victoria described in her diary entry on this production as those "stupid duets and songs."[18] Vestris and Planché tried to turn the songs to intrinsic dramatic purpose, giving all of them to the fairies to help distinguish them from the mortals.

Also, in the huge theatre, they probably believed singing would count for more than the speaking of Shakespeare's delicate verse. Several song-settings came from the Reynolds-Bishop opera; Vestris's music director was Thomas Simpson Cooke, who had collaborated with Bishop. Among the songs were those for "Over hill, over dale," the fairy lullaby to Titania, and the music for the final fairy blessing. One new melody was used for Oberon's speech, "I know a bank where the wild thyme blows" (2.1.249 ff), sung by Vestris and the First Fairy (Miss Rainforth) and written by Charles Edward Horn, who had been music director for Vestris's first seasons at the Olympic. It probably was to this song in particular that Victoria objected, as did the *John Bull* critic:

> Now if these [words] are not set to music by the poet himself, then there is no music in poetry. Yet, instead of Vestris delivering them with the accompaniment of her own rich speaking voice, you hear irreverent fiddlers preludizing to the butchery, and she and Miss Rainforth quaver on "the nodding, nodding, vio-o-lets" till you are tempted to forswear Christendom and become Turk.[19]

But the duet was given encores that evening and praised by other critics, and Horn's song appeared repeatedly thereafter in productions throughout Christendom, prevailing over all protests.[20]

The elaborate scenic pictures "illustrating" Shakespeare impressed London critics, who compared them favorably to those in William Macready's *The Tempest*. The first picture to appear on the huge Covent Garden stage, after the playing of Mendelssohn's overture, was a "hall in the Palace of Theseus — with distant view of Athens."[21] The *Spectator* described the view as "looking up a long perspective of fanes to the Acropolis towering in the distance, the polychrome decorations of the Greek architecture being visible in the foreground."[22] For such views, scenic artists went to the "best authorities," among which would have been the recent editions of James Stuart and Nicholas Revett's oversize volumes of engravings, *Antiquities of Athens*. A view of Athens that sounds like the descriptions of Vestris's scene appears in the watercolor rendering of the backdrop for this first scene in Charles Kean's 1856 production, which Kean's acting edition describes as "a Terrace adjoining the palace of Theseus, Overlooking the City of Athens" (see plate 1).[23] The scene in Vestris's production, said the reviewer for the *Theatrical Journal*, was

> calculated to raise one to a contemplation of the finer portion of the mind. . . . I was on classic ground . . . what a remembrance to a well-stored mind to see the glories of this city . . . to be for awhile Greek in heart and hand.[24]

Planché's costumes for the Athenian court called for tunics with Grecian borders, mantles, laurel wreaths, and sandals.[25] Just prior to this production, Planché had contributed notes on ancient Grecian costume to accompany this play in Charles Knight's illustrated edition of Shakespeare: "We must look to the frieze of the Parthenon," he begins there, and, of course, that frieze rested safely nearby in the British Museum.[26]

100
*"These
Antique
Fables . . .
These Fairy
Toys"*

The second scene, in which the mechanicals meet to cast their play, would have been played far downstage in front of a painted drop of Quince's workshop, a typical "carpenter's scene" that allowed stage carpenters to erect the upcoming full-stage setting behind the drop.[27] In the forest scenes of Shakespeare's Acts 2 through 4, there were full-stage woodland settings by the Grieves that underwent a sequence of gliding transformations. Essential to these was the use of a panorama, a continuous roll of painted canvas unspooled from one vertical roller to another across the back of the stage.[28] After the moonlight meeting of Oberon and Titania, the manager herself, in limelight, waved her wand, and the forest glided behind her to change to Titania's bower, formed by the overhanging branches of moon-illumined trees. She then ascended, flown off as Titania's fairies danced on.[29] The *Times* critic remembered Vestris's Oberon

> as she stood with her glittering armour and fantastic helmet on an eminence, with a blue tinted wood gliding by her in the background, presenting different aspects of the same sylvan scenery . . . the marked out but remoted figure on a dark ground . . . shone on by some artificial light . . . a supernatural appearance.[30]

She wore a translucent, star-flecked dress of yellow and gold, descending only to the knee, tightly belted at the waist, and pinned at the shoulders, exposing arms and neck; on her head was a plumed Grecian helmet with translucent wings appended, and she carried a gold spear topped with a butterfly (fig. 12).

The remaining sequence of forest scenes brought more complex changes, as Vestris attempted to differentiate pictorially each forest locale. The lovers met in another part of the forest, with a stream and a raised bank in the background, under a mist-veiled moon that slowly sank, its reflection disappearing in the stream.[31] Near the end of this gradually darkening scene, Puck led the confused male lovers, vaunting their threats, in and out of the mists, achieved by means of transparent gauzes. The mists cleared to reveal another part of the forest, conveying the spectator, almost cinematically, to a new locale. The *Spectator* said of the forest sequences, "all is sylvan and visionary; the wood scenes change like the phases of a dream," and even the *John Bull* critic agreed.[32] Here the production advanced the techniques of illusionism, moving from representation toward reproduction, offering a material fairy forest almost as a reality. Vestris's songs would have been among the few remaining vestiges of theatrical playfulness.

Vestris's localization of the forest scenes entailed a reordering of Shakespeare's text. On his nonillusionistic stage, all four of the exhausted lovers could reenter and fall asleep at the end of their forest chase, near each other and the sleeping Titania and Bottom. Oberon then entered to awaken Titania and exited with her, after which Theseus and his hunting party entered and discovered the sleeping lovers. Once the hunting party had exited, the previously unseen Bottom could awaken. But with Vestris's literal localization, Titania's bower and the sleeping lovers were now in two different parts of the forest. Vestris, therefore, had to have Bottom wake after the exit of Oberon and Titania, instead of after the exit of the hunting party, and have him then rejoin his joyful friends at Quince's house. Putting the "carpenter's scene" here allowed Vestris to change the upstage setting and return us to the full stage forest scene where the sleeping lovers had last been seen and where Theseus's hunting party could discover them. In consequence, Bottom's gleeful announcement to his friends that "our play is preferred" at the multiple weddings at court (4.2.34) came prematurely, before Theseus had discovered the sleeping lovers and called for the nuptials. Nonetheless, Charles Kean used this same sequence in 1856, and every Victorian manager hereafter, except Phelps, somehow altered Shakespeare's scene sequence at this point, encumbered by pictorial scenery.[33]

Vestris's other special staging features included Puck rising from a trap at center stage on a toadstool and Titania and Bottom exiting together in a floral car. Most of the fairy troupe of fifty-two were dressed in silver-spangled white gauze dresses to just below the knee, white silk stockings, chaplets of flowers, and not-very-aerodynamic insectlike wings. Titania's fairies were identifiable by their yellow scarves, Oberon's by blue ones. But the fairy tribe also included fauns in goatskins and satyrs in fur, and Puck was an elfish creature in a light brown plush shirt, with long ears and with his arms and legs in coverings the same color as his flesh.[34] Oscar Byrne choreographed a ballet around the sleeping lovers, and Vestris arranged a forest sunrise over them, prior to Theseus's entrance. "The morning descends in pearls among the waving foliage of the forest," wrote one critic.[35] John Moore, later a stage manager for Burton and Daly, recorded the effect in his promptbook:

The back scene was a drop painted entirely on linen — a large opaque tree C. which was supposed to hide the sun itself — but made a magnificent contrast to the rest of the scene which was pervaded by a powerful white Sunlight. Sunlight mediums — yellow silk.[36]

102

*"These
Antique
Fables . . .
These Fairy
Toys"*

In Vestris's final act, the curtain rose on more Periclean splendor: Theseus's "Hall of Statues, with raised stage in the centre, hung at the back with curtains." The *Spectator* spoke with reverence of "the severe forms of the marble Caryatides relieved by the chaste richness of antique draperies and classic costumes conveying a lively idea of the 'pomp of elder days.'"[37] The quartet of young lovers entered with wreaths of white roses in their hair to a court peopled with "lords and ladies" in Athenian attire. Theseus and Hippolyta reclined classically on couches to watch *Pyramus and Thisbe*, performed on the raised stage at center.

After the court had exited following the entertainment, the setting was transformed for the fairy blessing. Planché devised the staging, as he proudly tells us in his autobiography, inspired by Oberon's command, "Through the house give glimmering light" (5.2.21). The *Times* critic described it:

> The vanishing of the theatre in which the clowns act their tragedy, and discovery of the interior of the palace, with fairies crowded in every part, gliding along galleries, ascending and descending steps, soaring in the air with blue and yellow torches, which produce a curious light, is one of the most beautiful and highly wrought fairy scenes ever introduced on the stage.[38]

This description and the Pattie edition stage directions suggest pictures very similar to those of the Kean production, preserved in watercolors (see plates 4 and 5).

Understandably, with the fuller text, the thirteen songs, and the inevitable pauses for even the most efficient of scene changes, the production ran three and a half hours, and some complained about the length.[39] Moreover, for some critics the spectacle and music were not enough. The *Athenaeum* said, "The material attractions of a pageant, however gorgeous, are no substitute for spiritual essence," though the writer did not say what that might be. The *Times* charitably commended "the struggle":

> As far as theatrical representation of this ethereal drama is possible, it was achieved last night, and a gorgeous spectacle was produced. . . . Cobweb, Moth, and Mustardseed, with their shrill trumpet voices, were but inadequate likenesses of their shadowy originals; but in the conception of the whole, a fine poetical feeling was apparent, a consciousness of the difficulties with which the struggle was to be made, and a resolution to conquer them if possible. If the minute elves could not be obtained, it was still left to give a shadowy unreal character to the scenery; if the individuals could not be realized, it was still possible to give a fairy grace to the troupes and impart to the whole tableau what could not be bestowed on its parts.[40]

Vestris had not yet proved that Hazlitt was wrong; that would be left to the perfection of illusionism to come in Samuel Phelps's production of the play.

In addition, in the vast Covent Garden spaces, the poetry itself was lost; several critics described actors struggling unsuccessfully to project simple meaning, "labouring to fill an area too large to allow a complete governance of the voice."[41] John Cooper's Theseus, counting his imaginary hounds with his forefinger, was in the best John Kemble classical manner, "a too didactic and formal declaimer for the fluent phrase of poetry," said the *Spectator*.[42] It found only Vestris distinct and musical.

But the pictures were impressive, and the production was praised repeatedly for its good taste.[43] It enjoyed a relatively long run, with fifty-nine performances that season and eleven the next.[44]

Neither the long run nor the prestige, however, repaid the immense costs. The play was mounted in the second season of Vestris's three-season management with her new husband and lessee, comedian Charles James Mathews. In his autobiography, Mathews wrote of the hopelessness of meeting the accumulating debts and loans of their three seasons, indebtedness that ultimately led him to debtors' prison. Specific and poignant evidence of this debt can be seen in a page from Mathews's ledgers for the 1840–1841 season, which was reproduced in his autobiography, posthumously edited by his friend Charles Dickens. In the last week of December, during which *A Midsummer Night's Dream*, *The Merry Wives of Windsor*, and a pantomime were running, Mathews was struggling to meet the salaries of 684 persons, including 199 in the scenic department and 116 in wardrobe. The fifty-two supernumeraries that are an item on the ledger page would have been the fairies from *A Midsummer Night's Dream*.[45] Vestris and Mathews were operating that season at a loss of at least ten pounds a night for 221 nights. And that season, with *A Midsummer Night's Dream* and the debut of Dion Boucicault's *London Assurance*, proved to be the most financially successful of their three at Covent Garden.[46]

Future managers would have to carry the material burdens of the new scenic vocabulary; Shakespeare deserved no less. They would continue to add to the illusion until it collapsed of its own weight.

The Tieck-Mendelssohn production of 1843 marks the beginning of the production of the play in its entirety on the German stage and of its long life as a favorite in Germany and Austria. Commissioned by the king of Prussia, Friedrich Wilhelm IV, it premiered on 14 October in Potsdam's court theatre, together with Mendelssohn's incidental score, opus 61. Mendelssohn had written the overture to the play in 1826 and premiered it in Stettin in 1827. In 1829, the twenty-year-old composer had conducted the overture's first London performance, at the beginning of his enormous popularity in England, and in 1835 dedicated the published score of it to the then Prince Friedrich.[47]

104
*"These
Antique
Fables . . .
These Fairy
Toys"*

Theatre historians have been much occupied with the physical stage of the Tieck-Mendelssohn production as an early German attempt at a *Shakspear-Bühne*. German scholarship has framed Tieck's effort within a narrative of the recovery of the Elizabethan open stage.[48] In the wider cultural perspective in which I wish to view it, the Tieck-Mendelssohn production has interest as one of the most prominent occasions of the German appropriation of Shakespeare as cultural capital. With August Wilhelm von Schlegel's translation, Mendelssohn's music, and Tieck's direction, a popular, major Shakespeare play was fully converted into German currency. King Friedrich also commissioned at this time court productions of other canonical works — Sophocles' *Oedipus at Colonus* and Racine's *Athalie*. His state theatre projects, like those of preceding German-speaking rulers, from Moritz of Hesse through Goethe's patron at Weimar, Duke Karl August, to Austria's Emperor Josef II, were at once artistically idealistic and bound up with establishing German cultural identity and status. Mendelssohn's score has been customarily treated by Shakespeare scholars and music historians in aesthetic terms as the ultimate musical realization of Shakespeare's intentions in *A Midsummer Night's Dream*. It, too, needs to be understood in light of the occasion of this production.

Shakespeare in Germany was already *unser Shakespeare*. Christoph Martin Wieland's translations of the plays in the 1760s, which had included *Ein Sommernachstraum* in verse, had been widely read. Schlegel's translations of seventeen of the plays (1797–1810) and the relatively complete works in the Schlegel-Tieck collection (1839–1840), had effectively given Germany adoption rights.[49] By the time the seventy-year-old Tieck came to stage *A Midsummer Night's Dream* in 1843, he had been a lifelong Shakespeare devotee.[50] In addition to his work as translator, he had been dramaturg to the court theatre in Dresden for a series of Shakespearean revivals and had long dreamed of offering Shakespeare on a stage such as that for which Shakespeare had originally written, a stage without pictorial scenery, which Tieck believed would better engage the audiences' imaginations.[51] In Tieck's novel of 1828, *Der junge Tischlermeister*, he portrayed a young carpenter helping to realize the dream of his mentor: the building of an Elizabethan-style stage in a great hall for a production of *Twelfth Night*. In 1836, Tieck developed, with architect Gottfried Semper, a reconstruction of the Fortune Theatre.

But Tieck's staging of *A Midsummer Night's Dream* was ultimately a compromise between his Elizabethan project and the nineteenth-century pictorial stage. The production had to be staged within the proscenium arch stage of the Potsdam court theatre, and later it was moved to a proscenium theatre in Berlin. Designer J. C. Gerst provided Tieck a single architectural unit of three levels that remained in position throughout his three acts, a structure with elements of the Tieck–Semper Fortune stage reconstruction.[52] Two staircases, right and left, ran up to the second- and third-level galleries. Titania slept beneath them. Curtains could be drawn over sections of the galleries.[53] The setting was framed at far right and left, not by flats but by tapestries, hanging at right angles to the proscenium. Tieck did not fully abandon pictorial elements. Classical columns were lowered in to frame the second gallery for the palace scenes, and, for the forest scenes, the second gallery was backed with a painted landscape of trees and hills, with shrubbery placed all around the unit (fig. 13). A painted drop was lowered in downstage of this unit for the artisans' workshop. This compromise between the Elizabethan and pictorial stage resembles two set sketches found among Goethe's papers, probably dating from 1828, when Tieck was considering staging the play in Dresden. Tieck probably discussed it with Goethe when he visited him that year.[54] The sketches show a changeable unit setting of staircases and levels, one of which could be converted from a balustraded gallery to a backdrop of trees. Vertical hangings seem to frame the settings right and left (fig. 14). (Down center is the prompter's box on Goethe's small Weimar stage.) The costumes were a mix of Greek, old German, and sixteenth-century Spanish elements. A full orchestra, required by Mendelssohn's un-Elizabethan score, occupied the pit in front of the stage. Overall, the theatrical vocabulary of the production was a mélange, given Tieck's Elizabethan stage elements, the pictorial scenic elements, the assorted costumes, and Mendelssohn's light romantic score.

Mendelssohn's 1827 overture was already popular and, like Schlegel's translations, regarded as a perfect marriage of German and English genius, a fact certainly not lost on Tieck and Wilhelm IV. Not a measure of Mendelssohn's new incidental music went unused, though by mistake he had provided a few extra measures. Because Mendelssohn and Tieck worked independently on their preparations of the score and the production text, discrepancies resulted. Eduard Devrient, Tieck's Lysander, remembered that Tieck divided his production into three acts, with Acts 1 and 3, respectively, being the opening and closing scenes in Theseus's palace and Act 2 comprising the forest scenes (Shakespeare's Acts 2 through 4). Mendelssohn, however, based his score on Schlegel's four-act division, resulting in extra *entr'acte* pieces. Rather than omit them, Tieck incorporated both. The A-minor intermezzo (*allegro apassionato*) was used to accompany an interpolated pantomime of Hermia in search of her

106

*"These
Antique
Fables . . .
These Fairy
Toys"*

dem Globetheater in London, mit gerauer Nachweisung der Quellen, aus denen der Verfasser geschöpft, beschrieben war. Die öffentliche Aufführung, welche der ersten, die nur vor dem königlichen Hofe in Potsdam stattgefunden, bald nachfolgte, zeigte indessen, daß L. Tieck zwar die Einfachheit der Bühnenmittel auf jenes, damals bekannte Minimum zurückgewünscht, aber andererseits doch auch die Kunst der scenischen Ausschmückung nichts weniger als verschmäht hatte.

Zunächst war die Bühne so wenig tief, als die Darstellung und die Anhäufung der Personen auf derselben es ir-

den ganzen Seitenraum. Dies war der ganze scenische Apparat, in welchen nach Tieck's Angaben der geschickte Regisseur der königl. Bühne, Staminsky, den theatralischen Vorgang hinein baute.

Im ersten Acte war der Palast des Theseus darzustellen. Alles, was auf der Zeichnung Baum und Busch ist, war hier Säule und Mauer. Die Treppen führten zu einem Säulengange, durch welchen das Auf- und Abtreten der Darsteller geschehen konnte, und der von den Treppen eingeschlossene Mittelraum stellte eine Art von Portikus dar, durch

werden könnte, wodurch allein schon die vorgefaßte Me wie dieser Bühnenapparat auf historischen Grundlagen berichtigt wurde. Hat nun Tieck durch die Scenirung Sommernachtstraums wirklich beweisen wollen, daß es haupt geht, die scenischen Mittel auf ein Minimum zwar ein feststehendes zurückzuführen, so hat die führung eben bewiesen, daß es nicht geht, weil bei nur drei Decorationen ein Ab- weichen von dem festste Apparat und ein Zurückkehren zu der gewöhnlichen T vorrichtung nöthig wurde.

Sommernachtstraum: Act II.

gend erlaubt, wodurch Tieck einen in seinen Schriften oft ausgesprochenen Wunsch verwirklichte. Man sah den Boden der Bühne mit einem grünen Teppich bedeckt, der sich auch über zwei ungefähr 20 Stufen zählende Doppeltreppen fortzog, welche von rechts und links auf eine 7 Fuß hohe Estrade oder Balcon führten. Die Treppen wendeten sich nach 10 oder 12 Stufen rechts und links gegen die Mitte zu, und schlossen so den Raum ein, den wir auf der Zeichnung von der Bogenlaube ausgefüllt sehen, in welcher Titania mit Squenz schlummert. Neben den Treppen und statt der sonst gewöhnlichen Coulissen bedeckten zwei große Teppichgardinen

welcher man in das Innere des Palastes gelangte. Theseus und Hyppolita traten durch diesen Mittelraum auf; Egeus und die Liebespaare durch die Teppichgardine rechts vom Zuschauer. Das Ganze erschien, bis auf die bunten Teppiche, statt der Coulissen, wie eine für diesen Zweck nach dem neuesten Stande der Decorationsmalerei aufgestellte Decoration. — So leicht sich diese Form nun auch den Waldscenen anschloß, so bewies doch gleich darauf, am Ende des ersten Actes, das Herablassen einer gewöhnlichen Decorationsgardine, die das Innere einer Handwerkerstube darstellte, daß mit diesen feststehenden Mitteln nicht allen Erfordernissen genügt

Im zweiten Acte, welcher bei der Berliner Aufführ aus einer Zusammenziehung des zweiten, dritten und v des Originals bestand, war das Gerüst des Palastes mit einer Walddecoration bekleidet. Da, wo früher Balcon Säulen ein Mauergesims trugen, verbreitet Baumstämme und Laubkronen den Palast. Der Po unten in der Mitte war, wie wir auf der Abbildung, in eine tiefe Laube verwandelt, die grün belegten Te aber und die Teppichgardinen statt der Coulissen bie geblieben. In dieser Decoration entwickelten sich die ff lichen Scenen zwischen den Liebespaaren, den Elfen u

FIGURE 13. Setting by J. C. Gerst for Ludwig Tieck's production, Potsdam, 1843. Engraving, Leipzig *Illustrirte Zeitung*, 21 December 1844.

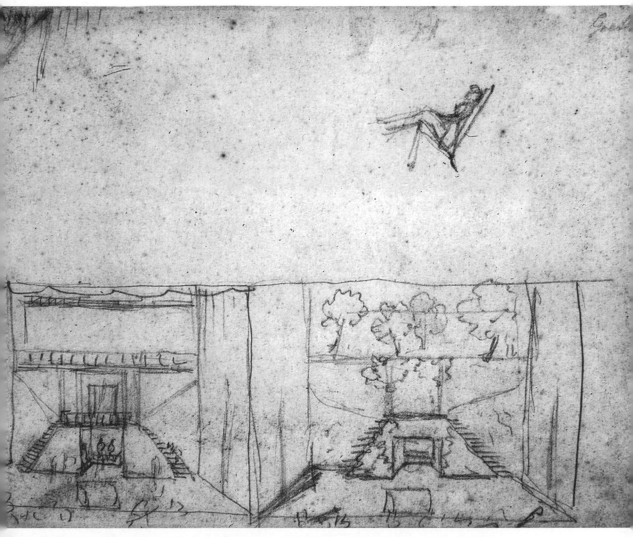

FIGURE 14. Sketches for settings for *A Midsummer Night's Dream*, perhaps drawn about 1828, when Ludwig Tieck discussed the play with Goethe during a visit to Weimar. Goethe Collection, Stiftung Weimarer Klassik, Weimar.

lost Lysander, which caused no difficulties. But the other piece, the E-major nocturne, was played as the four young lovers slept, and this entailed an awkward concealing of the sleeping lovers with shrubbery, apparently so that they would not be too long in view while Mendelssohn's nocturne was played.[55]

The incidental music is as programmatic as nineteenth-century pictorial scenery was in general illustrative. Thirteen numbers comprise the score (after the overture), six of which are melodramas — music coordinated with specific passages in the play. The score begins with the fairies' entrances in Act 2. No music is provided for the first act — none of the plaintive songs for Lysander or Helena of which audiences in the eighteenth century had been so fond. Among the score's most familiar specific segments are the fairy march for the entrances of Titania and Oberon and their trains, the bassoon-led theme for the artisans, the dirge for their tragedy, the lullaby for Titania, and the "Wedding March" for the last act. This march is used also for the court's exit, and it then fades and segues to the scurrying string scherzo passages that bring on the fairies for the finale.

108
"These
Antique
Fables . . .
These Fairy
Toys"

In Mendelssohn's 1827 overture, there was no hint of the "Wedding March" that is so prominent a feature of the incidental score. The march is clearly the result of a production conception of an elaborate entrance procession at the beginning of the last act of the three newly married couples, Theseus and Hippolyta, Lysander and Hermia, and Demetrius and Helena.

The C-major march, with its royal trumpet fanfares and full complement of strings, is fully five minutes in length, music for a processional entrance of proportions fit for real royalty.[56] Emphasizing as it does the pomp and circumstance of court and power, the march is essentially a celebration of Theseus as a beneficent Elizabethan Greek hero, with Prussian overtones. The tributary march reflects that special regard the nineteenth century had for Theseus as founder and protector of Athens and his appropriation as a role model for empire, which in the case of *A Midsummer Night's Dream* began, as we have seen, in the 1816 opera, with its conclusion of a pageant honoring Theseus's triumphs. Moreover, Mendelssohn's celebration of royal power was in perfect harmony with the discourse of Tieck's theory that Shakespeare's play was originally created for a court wedding at which Elizabeth I was present (see chapter 1). The benevolent, artistically enlightened Theseus is a kind of stand-in for the queen. Further, on the court occasion of the royally commissioned Tieck-Mendelssohn production, Shakespeare's play, the music, and the pageantry would have conferred, masquelike, upon Tieck and Mendelssohn's patron, King Friedrich, who was known as "the Royal Romantic King," the status of a modern Theseus/Elizabeth. That this was, indeed, the sense of this occasion is confirmed in the account of Feodor Wehl, who was among the invited audience of court and glitterati on opening night. He wrote of it in exalted prose: "Verily, we seemed transported to the age of Versailles in the days of the Louises. It was a gala-day for the realm . . . the highest pinnacle of the reign of Friedrich Wilhelm the Fourth. Who could have dreamt that behind this glittering play of poetic fancy there stood dark and bloody revolution, and fateful death?"[57] There is more in his comparison than mere snob appeal.[58] German romantic criticism had conferred the highest spiritual status upon art, and Shakespeare was its touchstone.

The commissioned Tieck-Mendelssohn project was a contribution to the validization of German culture, a project that could be compared to the practice in the twentieth century in which emerging countries have built museums stocked with Western holdings to signal to major powers their legitimate national status.[59]

The Tieck-Mendelssohn production was moved to Berlin and was performed a total of 169 times before being abandoned in 1885.[60] Tieck's methods did not result in a reform in the staging of Shakespeare. But in Germany, England, and America, Mendelssohn's score became as inseparable from productions of *A Midsummer Night's Dream* as the vistas of Periclean Athens, both entwining the play in emblems of royal power. The score still was being used in major stage productions of the play through the mid-1950s. (The custom of playing the "Wedding March" for bridal processions dates from its use at the wedding of the princess royal in 1858.) As late as 1961, popular historians Will and Ariel Durant were characterizing the play itself as "powerful nonsense, only redeemed by Mendelssohn."[61] Just as theatrical productions of the play were beginning to break from nineteenth-century traditions in the early 1960s, George Balanchine, inspired by Mendelssohn's score, created a ballet, *A Midsummer Night's Dream*, in 1962. The Balanchine ballet, popular down to the closing decade of the twentieth century, restated and prolonged the life of the musical and scenic vocabulary for the play that romantic ideology and the aspirations of empire had constructed.

Chapter six

THE NATIONAL AND
NATURAL DREAM

Quince: Gentles, you wonder at this show,
But wonder on, till truth make all things plain.

By the 1850s, *A Midsummer Night's Dream* had become a major Shakespearean vehicle for inspiring spectacle, as the Victorian pictorial stage elaborated on the visions of stalwart Greeks and benevolent fairies. Heroic vistas of ancient Athens assured Victorians of their links with both an ennobling classical past and Shakespeare. Silent armies of stagehands coordinated carefully painted canvases, diaphanous gauzes, and gaslight to unfold picture-perfect moonlit fairy forests in lavenders and greens before audiences in darkened auditoriums, offering elaborate illusions of a benevolently designed world of nature.

The full play was seen on the American stage for the first time in the 1850s. American productions of the play, such as those of William Burton and Augustin Daly, emulated British models throughout the century, usually boasting only technological novelties, though occasionally freshened by American talent. By 1900, productions on both sides of the Atlantic were heavily invested in colossal pictures of Athens and lakeside forests aglow with electric fireflies, and the play had become an obligatory rite of reassurance.

This chapter begins with the production of Samuel Phelps in 1853, in which skillful stagecraft turned the simulcra of romantic forests and ancient Athens into the soothing virtual realities of a bourgeois romanticism. It closes on Sir Herbert Beerbohm Tree's lavish, imperial recapitulation at the end of the century.

Samuel Phelps's production of *A Midsummer Night's Dream* in 1853 wove a seamless web of illusion around the play. At Sadler's Wells Theatre, then well beyond the circle of the West End's fashionable audiences and the coverage of London's daily newspapers, Phelps sought and won the following of a relatively proletarian audience, offering modest scenery, carefully instructed young casts, and his own acting. Between 1844 and 1862, he produced a remarkable series of thirty-one Shakespeare plays. For *A Midsummer Night's Dream*, Phelps followed Vestris's pattern in general, but without her added songs, and he and his scenic assistant, Frederick Fenton, perfected the trend toward illusionism.

Phelps's scenes of Athens, painted by Fenton, were instructively Periclean. The backdrop was still in use at annual performances of classical plays at Westminster School in the 1890s.[1] In the forest scenes, Phelps and Fenton achieved a new, almost cinematic level of illusion. A curtain of green gauze was hung across the proscenium, through which spectators watched a dreamlike sequence of noiselessly gliding sylvan scenery. Scene changes were aided by a diorama. A canvas painted with night clouds and backed by a limelight moon was slowly unrolled from one vertical spool to another upstage, while downstage a canvas of cutout trees was unrolled in the opposite direction. "The moon was seen to rise, to shine between the boles of the trees, to be partially obscured by passing clouds, and then to swim, as it were, over and through the trees," according to Fenton's own account.[2] Semitranslucent gauzes were used to veil Titania's bower after Oberon had charmed her and to create the fog in which Puck led the rival lovers up and down.[3] Douglas Jerrold, who lovingly reviewed the production, wrote of the costumes:

> The living figures are so dressed as to harmonize with the scenery, looking as if they were inseparable parts of the same picture; thus, the fairies, as they glide in and out of the trees and foliage, give you a notion that they have actually stepped out of them, as though the trunks and flowers were their natural abiding places, and by long residence, they had been embued with the colour of them. They were none of your winged, white muslin fairies with spangles and butterfly wands, but were real, intangible, shadowy beings.[4]

Light sufficient to illuminate all the action behind the proscenium-wide green gauze was made possible by gas lighting, which Fenton installed at Sadler's Well

Theatre and used for the first time in this production.[5] The gauze ascended after Oberon and Titania made their final exit, before the dawn over the sleeping lovers.

Phelps's own much-praised performance as Bottom was described by the *Spectator* as "dreamy, dogged, and dogmatical." Critic Henry Morley described him as the dream-figure dreaming, and the *Athenaeum* characterized him as the perfect dream victim.[6] He was deliberate and elaborate, speaking slowly and with equal stress on all words. To Titania's "Thou art as wise as thou art beautiful" (3.1.140), he bowed profoundly, the donkey's ears working. After waking and giving his speech containing the lines "Methought I was . . . Methought I had . . ." (4.1.198–215), he left the stage "thoughtfully and slowly, feeling in the air for his long ears and nose, which he cannot comprehend quite how he can have lost," wrote Douglas Jerrold.[7] After he had rejoined his friends and made plans with them for their play, he parted, saying, "No more words, away, go away," delivered "in the tone of a man who had lived with spirits and was not perfectly returned to the flesh."[8]

In the final act, after the court had retired, servants put out the candelabras lighting the pillared hall, and back curtains opened to disclose a terrace and a view of Athens. Moonlight streamed into the hall, along with forty-two fairies with lanterns. The Grecian pillars, covered with waxed linen and illuminated by gas jets from within, began to glow as if illuminated by moonlight.[9] Phelps eschewed the songs that Vestris had featured and most likely used Mendelssohn's score to contribute to the spell.[10] No wonder Jerrold was dream-struck. He dismissed Hazlitt's famous complaint that the material stage could never embody this play:

> It is a play, in truth, to dream over. The best way to enjoy it is to half-close your eyes and resign yourself completely to the influence of the scene. It is our firm belief, from the hushed stillness that reigns at times through the house, that one-half the spectators are dreaming it without knowing it. . . . This belief is strengthened by the fact of the unusual sparingness of the applause. . . . Occasionally a loud laugh bursts out, but it is quickly succeeded by a deep stillness . . . something more than the mere reverence of attention. You would suppose from the silence that closes you in like a dark room, that you were all alone, with your senses far away, wandering you knew not where, but watching intently some strange illusion of a man with an ass's head being kissed by a Fairy Queen. . . . You feel quite disconcerted when you rub your eyes, and discover that there is a chandelier instead of the stars shining above you, and far from "blessing" Theseus's house with Oberon and Titania, that

you are in Sadler's Wells Theatre with loud cries of "Phelps! Phelps!" being hammered on all sides in your startled ears. The illusion is pulled, like a common cotton night-cap, from off your brow; and the ideal trance, in which you have been plunged for the last three hours, is followed by an awakening conviction that you have been fooled during that time not less completely than Bottom himself.[11]

Phelps's illusion-making was of a subtle order new even to Jerrold, who, at age fifty, was an experienced playwright, producer, and culture-watcher with the satirical *Punch*. His description suggests that he sat in a darkened auditorium for at least the forest scenes and the last fairy scene, immersed in solitary illusion. (Continuous darkening of the auditorium was not customary until those two later temples of illusion, Wagner's Bayreuth and Irving's Lyceum.) Sadler's Wells, a somewhat smaller theatre than Covent Garden, lent itself to relative intimacy. Henry Morley described the "subdued hush" of an "earnest" and "reverent" audience. He, too, gave way to the enchantment as "scenes melt[ed] dream-like one into another." Morley even found the lovers' quarrels so loud and real as to intrude upon the idyllic dream.[12] For Morley, Phelps's staging was closer to the "Shakespearean spirit" than Vestris's had been, and, like Jerrold, Morley thought Phelps had shown that the play belonged to the stage.[13] Under Phelps's spell, neither Morley nor any other critic commented on the 372 missing lines.[14]

More important, there was little awareness that the skillful illusionism had suppressed the complex transactions between audience and play that had been possible in Shakespeare's daylight playhouse. On the open stage, Shakespeare could playfully leave indeterminate the distinctions between illusion and reality. But Phelps sought a perfect material embodiment of a creditable fairy forest, making the proscenium a window onto another world. Resemblances passed fully into representation; the simulacra of romantic forests and a Periclean Athens were offered as realities, artifice as nature.[15] Roland Barthes has suggested that such confusion of the sign with the signified is "a duplicity peculiar to bourgeois art."[16] Careful that nothing should disturb the illusion for his audience, Phelps allowed scant place for self-conscious theatrical artifice. Oberon did not wave her wand to change the forest scenery or come downstage to sing her songs. The scenes unfolded in a continuum of illusion that discouraged any reflection on the means of representation, much less on problems of perception. Almost dream victims, the Sadler's Wells audiences were passive spectators who barely needed to engage in anything as strenuous as Coleridge's "*willing* suspension of disbelief."[17] The ironic project of Phelps and Fenton was an illusion so technologically proficient that it would seem to affirm the actual existence of an alternative world in which the supernatural and natural were comfortably reconciled. Their literal orchestrations sentimentalized the play, of course, rendering a tranquilized vision of a permanent world of stable Greeks and benevolent nature. Even while Phelps was offering Shakespeare's text relatively whole, he was subordinating it to a visual language that both carried its own meanings and reduced the possibilities of Shakespeare's. By the end of the century, this illusionism would feature real rabbits and fairies aglow with electric lights, the Disney-like animations of a culture straining for dominion over a material world. Phelps was not as heavy-handed in his staging as his sucessors would be, but he sealed the theatre's incarnation of the play in the terms of bourgeois romanticism.

Phelps's audiences and critics were enamored of the illusion. His production had fifty-five performances in the 1853–1854 season and revivals in 1855, 1856, and 1861. Jerrold recommended Phelps's Bottom to the queen ("hitherto our Elizabeth has not visited our Burbage") and so, apparently, did Charles Dickens, but to no avail.[18] Phelps repeated his performance of his moonstruck Bottom at the Gaiety Theatre in London in 1875, by which time his acting style seemed to critic Dutton Cook to be of an older school, though critic Clement Scott and historian Barton Baker thought it among the finest performances they had seen.[19] Memories of Phelps's staging remained into the 1890s. Fenton's explanation of how the magic had been done was published in J. Moyr Smith's edition of the play in 1892. Sir Herbert Beerbohm Tree borrowed Fenton's illuminated columns for the final fairy scene of his 1900 production, electrifying them.

As recently as 1969, Phelps's staging was praised by a theatre historian as the ideal production, and Phelps was seen as a precursor of the best of the twentieth-century modernist directors who (ostensibly) faithfully served the author's intentions and his transcendant text with harmonious coordinations of all theatrical elements.[20] Of course, Phelps's staging was a version of the play, successfully addressing his era, no less culturally mediated than productions of any other.

In America, a summer revival of the play in New York's Park Theatre in 1841 was a hasty attempt to capitalize on Vestris's recent success. Manager Edmund Simpson's text was likely that of Reynolds's opera, which Simpson had produced in 1826.[21] A young Charlotte Cushman, trained in opera, played Oberon and sang the obligatory songs. But the American cast was poorly prepared, the small orchestra out of tune, and, on opening night, the mechanicals' *Pyramus and Thisbe* dissolved in a fight between Moonshine's real dog and Lion.[22]

In February 1854, two New York managers brought out the play simultaneously, opening and closing within a few days of each other.[23] One took the cultural high road and the other a middle path, and each was scenically spectacular in its way. Both managers no doubt took their cue from Phelps's recent success.

William Evans Burton took the high road, offering the production in his sixth season at his Chambers Street theatre. Under his management, this had become one of New York's most popular and critically acclaimed playhouses.[24] The genial, talented, English-born comedian had managed several American theatres, edited *Gentleman's Magazine*, and was an amateur bibliophile with a remarkable library of Shakespeareana, including copies of each of the four Shakespeare folios, several quartos, and a set of the plays extra-illustrated with pictorial material that he had collected. In the three seasons prior to 1854, Burton had given New York four other Shakespeare comedies and Milton's seldom-produced *Comus* as well. Burton was elected president of the new American Shakespeare Society on Shakespeare's birthday in 1852.[25] Not surprisingly, Burton's text of *A Midsummer Night's Dream* was more complete than New York had ever seen mounted.[26] Burton, who enjoyed successes in his career in the roles of John Falstaff, Toby Belch, Autolycus, and Micawber, played the role of Bottom.

The competing production was mounted at the Broadway Theatre under Thomas Barry and the lessee of the well-equipped and capacious theatre (capacity, four thousand), E. A. Marshall. Barry, an English-born actor who had played with William Macready, had staged the play in Boston in 1839 and stage-managed Edmund Simpson's hasty Park Theatre production of 1841.[27] The Barry version was more commercial and less canonical than Burton's, its text rather crudely cut, and its fairy scenes more in the pantomime vein.[28]

Taken together, the two productions are relatively unsophisticated American reiterations of the British cosmogony of idealized Greeks and pantomime fairies. They also provide a compendium of nineteenth-century spectacle and special effects for this play. In both, the argonaut Theseus arrived in Act 1 in a galley ship, and, on the Broadway's big stage, he and his landing party were met by thirty-two Athenian soldiers and twelve Amazons in facing ranks, with spears, shields, and banners.[29] Burton circulated a playbill shortly after Barry's production opened, boasting that his own production featured "entirely new scenery painted by Mr. Heilge expressly for this comedy, not dug up from the remains of a defunct Fairy Opera."[30] Burton then issued a twenty-four-page pamphlet that set out with numbing scholarly industry his effort to illustrate the play with historical accuracy. Theseus's warrior attendants were taken from "Willemin in his *Costumes des Peuples de l'antiquité*." Hippolyta and her Amazons were dressed according to representations on Etruscan vases and in Piranesi's prints, and the Athenian women wore "the long sleeveless tunic, the caladiris or stola, with the rich and varied peplum over the bust, and the crepida sandal." [31] Burton's Act 1 setting of "a Courtyard in the Palace of Theseus" was backed with a view of "the principal buildings of the Acropolis or Upper City, and the Hill of Mars," with "statues of the household gods . . . observable in the various avenues." [32] Aquaducts were painted in, too, more Roman, of course, than Athenian, but no less apt in the litany of classical icons. Burton even crowded his small stage with a working fountain. [33] Quince's house, his pamphlet assured readers, was "earliest Doric . . . , opening to the suburbs of Catapolis, or Lower City." In all of this, Burton put on the appearance of an American Charles Kean. Kean had brought thoroughly historical Shakespeare to New York for the first time in the 1845–1846 season with his *King John* and *Richard III*, and Burton's years on Chambers Street nearly parallel Kean's at the Princess's Theatre in London. [34] On both sides of the Atlantic, the striving for antiquarian authenticity conferred respectability, and the establishment press was quick to validate such efforts. High-class Shakespeare was especially welcome, said the *New York Sunday Dispatch*, after all of the "Uncle Tom Foolery" and "the rage for nigger literature," an ugly, bigoted reference to the recent success of *Uncle Tom's Cabin*. [35]

The forest scenes of both productions featured looking glass lakes and "working" moons that rose and fell in night skies. Puck made his entrance on a mushroom or flower rising from a trap. Burton's Oberon (Miss Raymond) entered descending in a dragonfly car, Titania (Mrs. Burton) in a butterfly car. Barry's Puck arrived in a peacock car, and his Oberon — "a French danseuse" named Mademoiselle Poinisi — and Titania entered in swan- and dolphin-drawn cars, respectively, from opposite sides of the stage. [36] They were greeted by twelve dancing fairies in silver-sprayed white muslin and wearing wings. [37] Both Titanias were accompanied by Indian boys. Some of Burton's fairy troupe (many of whom were children) were small satyrs, "costumed from Rubens' celebrated picture of the Bacchanals," said Burton in his pamphlet. He cast a boy as Puck and costumed him as a beetle-browed, bat-winged lob of spirits, rather than "a pretty piece of femininity in ringlets and muslin skirts." Burton's theatre could not match the Broadway's technology, which allowed for a moving panorama that took the swan-drawn Oberon on a flight through fairyland, ending with a water landing amid floating fairies. This, in itself, critics agreed, was "well worth a visit to the Broadway." [38] After charming Titania, Burton's Oberon exited by entering the trunk of a tree which then ascended, and Barry's Puck ascended on "Look how I go." Some of Burton's fairies wore bee or butterfly heads, and butterflies on springs were attached to the fairy garlands around Bottom's neck. When Burton's Bottom laid his ass's head on Titania's breast, he waggled his ears and winked a moveable eye at the audience; when Barry's Bottom, William Davidge, exited with Titania, he turned back to wink an ass's eye at the audience. In both productions, suns rose slowly over the sleeping lovers ("red mediums" and "gold tissue to revolve"), and in both, Theseus and his hunting party entered the forest with real hounds (quickly taken off by attendants).[39]

In Burton's last act, the curtain went up on a drop of "A Port in Ancient Greece," which John Moore noted in his promptbook was "a copy of Darley's arrival of Cleopatra." The *Daily Times* called it "the abomination of painted ship upon a painted sea." This rose to reveal "a lofty and magnificent hall" in Theseus's palace. Burton's court entered to recline on couches to watch *Pyramus and Thisbe*, and on Barry's stage, the mechanicals performed on a miniature nineteenth-century proscenium stage, complete with green floor cloth and curtain. Burton's hall underwent a transformation for the entrance of the fairies, who ran up and down staircases with illuminated flowers, effects replicating Vestris's.[40] Barry climaxed his staging with a transformation to fairyland. Oberon waved his wand and, with the sound of a gong, a sun-drawn cloud appeared and carried the fairy royalty downstage into a final fairy dance and tableau ("red fire in sun").[41]

Burton advertised on his playbill that, in his staging, the play was "graced for the first time on any stage by Mendelssohn's music . . . every note of it." Burton was wrong, of course, but he was the first American to use the score Mendelssohn had written for Tieck's production.[42] Burton used no extraneous songs, while Barry offered three, including one melody for Oberon's "I know a bank."

Burton's Bottom was certainly the best America had seen (fig. 15). The promptbook notes on his business and the critics' descriptions of his restraint and "mother-wit" suggest that he deserves comparison to Phelps rather than the lower Bottoms, such as that of his immediate rival, William Davidge.[43] Davidge annoyed critics with such business as ambling about the stage "like a four-footed beast, making feeble efforts at assinine brays," and for not learning his lines. Davidge fell into a public skirmish with the press over the criticism and was still trying to even the score in his autobiography a decade later.[44]

The *Tribune* critic complained of Shakespeare's treatment of the mechanicals. Could Shakespeare not "produce one ray of genius or polish, except in courtly Hamlets and gallant Petruchios? Why were his honest laborers always greasy, dirty, stupid, and slavish?"[45] But the fault lay less with Shakespeare than with nineteenth-century theatre practice, in which Bottom and his friends were commonly rendered as simpletons rather than simple men. Phelps and Burton were

FIGURE 15. William Burton as Bottom in Burton's production, Chambers Street Theatre, New York, 1853. Folger Shakespeare Library.

exceptional for their thoughtful Bottoms. More common was the kind of Bottom John Harley rendered in Vestris's production (and later in Charles Kean's), described as "a lively buffoon making fun of the character." Tree played him with a "bibulous visage" and "a voice thickened with indulgence in liquor," wearing "flesh-colored" hose with a hairy growth.[46] Not often among the mechanicals was there the kind of artistry seen in Vestris's Flute, Robert Keeley, of whom a *Spectator* critic wrote: "He shared in the general joy and sorrow like one whose obtuse intellect apprehended it the last, but whose good-natured heart felt it the most."[47]

Much stage business had already accumulated around the mechanicals by midcentury, some of it ingenious and some of it buffoonery. In the playing of *Pyramus and Thisbe*, both lovers usually died elaborately. Phelps stabbed himself on both sides and in the breast, fell, then raised his head and decorously placed his sword away from him, business that may have been traditional and that often was repeated thereafter. Phelps's Thisbe crawled over him to get his sword for her suicide, stabbed herself, and fell across his feet; after a pause, Phelps raised his head and, seeing her there, tried to kick her off.[48] Theseus lent his sword to one Thisbe when she could not find Pyramus's.[49] Such humor often deteriorated to the level of that in Tree's production, when Pyramus and Thisbe kicked each other in the backside during their curtain calls.[50] In Burton's performance, Pyramus's helmet repeatedly dropped over his eyes. Pyramus and Thisbe repeatedly changed the height of Wall's hand to speak through the chink, and, at Pyramus's death, Burton fell off the mechanicals' small stage, then got back on and arranged his legs to hang over the stage edge. His Thisbe died only after carefully covering her knees with her petticoats.[51] The Thisbe of the Olympic Theatre production of 1867 burlesqued the style of the popular French tragedienne, Rachel.[52] In Vestris's production, Thisbe was gowned and veiled, Moonshine wore a silvered gown and a mask, his dog was a real dog, and he carried his lantern on a pitchfork. Wall's long gown was painted to depict a stone wall, and he was masked.[53] Barry's lion had a tail that curled and wagged when he bowed, and Moonshine managed to tread on it.[54] The ass's head with maneuverable jaws, ears, and eyes was in service at least as early as 1826, and an example of it can be seen in a photograph of Augustin Daly's production of 1888 (see fig. 18).

Nothing in the competing American productions of 1854 departed from the British theatrical vocabulary for the play. America remained dependent on England for its Shakespearean models long after the riot at the Astor Place Opera House, which broke out in 1849 when William Macready, England's "eminent tragedian," competed for favor with Edwin Forrest, America's "national tragedian." In the minor, sometimes quirky variations of the New York productions of *A Midsummer Night's Dream*, one sees an American urge for a democratized and accessible Shakespeare. But its need for cultural approval also makes the United States a reverend respecter of English traditions.

Charles Kean's 1856 production was a restatement of Vestris's, yearning for respectability. At the end of the season in which he produced *A Midsummer Night's Dream*, the son of the romantic actor and tempestuous alcoholic Edmund Kean proudly accepted the honor of being made a Fellow of the Society of Antiquaries. His eleven Shakespearean productions at the Princess's Theatre between 1850 and 1859 were very nearly vehicles for pictorial travelogues: for *A Winter's Tale*, a well-documented Syracuse, ca. 330 B.C.; for *Richard II*, an interpolated procession of Bolingbroke and Richard through an authentic Tudor London; and for *The Tempest*, furies from Etruscan vases to chase Caliban.[55] Kean reverently documented his historical authorities in his playbills and editions of the plays. *Punch* magazine once offered a parody of a Kean playbill that included a note that all the police on duty at the Princess's Theatre were members of the Church of England.[56] Kean left posterity meticulous pictorial records of his productions in watercolors of major scenes, painted by the scenic artists who had executed the settings. In a curtain speech on the night of his retirement, he defended himself against the few critics of the "upholstered" drama at the Princess's Theatre with what amounted to a nineteenth-century twist on Horace's *ut pictura poesis*:[57]

> I have always entertained the conviction that in illustrating the great plays of the greatest poet who ever wrote for the advantage of men, historical accuracy might be so blended with pictorial effect, that instruction and amusement would go hand in hand; and that the more completely such a system was carried out, so much the more valuable and impressive would be the lesson conveyed.[58]

He was proud to claim that "in no single instance have I ever permitted historical truth to be sacrificed to theatrical effect."[59] Faced with the difficulty of factually illustrating Theseus's eighth-century Athens, he took pains to explain his alternative: "I have felt myself unfettered with regard to chronology," and he offered instead Athens "at a time when it had attained its greatest splendour in literature and art — when it stood in its pride and glory, ennobled by a race of illustrious men."[60] Not only were there the usual views (plate 1) of Periclean Athens ("On the hill of the Acropolis stands the far-famed Parthenon, the Erectheum, and the statue of the tutelary goddess Minerva or Athena"),[61] but Quince had an authentic carpenter's workshop, complete with "tools copied from discoveries at Herculaneum."[62] In his acting edition, Kean rendered Theseus an "Athenian prince" rather than an anachronistic English duke. His red act curtain was decorated with Grecian border motifs and two large emblems framed in laurel wreaths: on the left, a golden lyre, under which was written, "For Apollo," and on the right, a pedestal urn, under which was written, "For Dionysus."[63] Both were written in Greek, which the Eton-educated Kean would have known, but which relatively few in his audiences would have been able to read.

Behind the wood scene for the meeting of Oberon and Titania was a backdrop painted by W. Gordon that meticulously reproduced J. M. W. Turner's recent painting, *The Golden Bough*, helping to suggest an Edenic paradise (plate 2).[64] The formations of flying fairies hovering above the fairy trains of Oberon and Titania in the watercolor were not an illustrator's fancy, nor were they painted on gauzes; their airborne presence is verified by the promptbook's flight directions.[65] Kean used a panorama of forest scenes for transitions to other parts of the wood, as Vestris had. Painted by Thomas Grieve, the unrolling canvas displayed tree-covered hills, lush flowering foliage, and a small waterfall and pool, nestled among trees and rocky ledges.[66] Critic Henry Morley complained that Kean's Oberon stood beside the moving scene, waving his wand (as Vestris had), "as if he was the exhibitor or a fairy conjurer."[67] Before Titania slept, she danced with her fairies in a forest clearing by moonlight so bright that they could dance with their own shadows (plate 3). For the end of Act 3, after Puck had led the lovers up and down and finally put them to sleep, forty fairies danced a Maypole ballet around a palm tree that sprang from beneath the stage and rained down garlands of flowers. Morley objected, but audiences encored the ballet.[68] The choreographer for this and the other fairy dances, most of them to Mendelssohn, was Oscar Byrne, who had fashioned Vestris's dances.[69]

One notable and unusual fairy was Kean's Puck, the gawky preteen Ellen Terry, who made her first entry rising up through a trap sitting cross-legged on a mushroom. (She is seen near the feet of the armored Oberon in plate 2.) She was flown off on "Look how I go!" and flown away again with Bottom's ass's head. Queen Victoria liked her and also the "darling little children" who played Peaseblossom, Cobweb, Moth, and Mustardseed.[70] "We know them at once, these fairies!" one critic wrote.[71] But the visiting German writer Theodor Fontane found Terry to be "an altogether intolerable, precocious, spoiled, unchildlike child, raised in an English manner to be old before her years." But Fontane also said it would be impossible for him to imagine a full-bosomed adult woman in the role thereafter.[72]

Kean's finale featured a transformation from the court setting for *Pyramus and*

Thisbe to the setting for the fairy revel (plates 4 and 5) that was almost certainly borrowed from Planché. Ninety fairies carrying colored lanterns thronged the steps, stage, and platform, and some were painted on the backdrop.[73] The watercolors are idealized representations, of course, suggesting a stage more spacious than the Princess's, whose proscenium opening was twenty-seven feet wide. The ethereal troupe consisted entirely of women, and one account makes it clear that not all the appeals of Kean's production were antiquarian. Herman Charles Merivale, a long-time friend of the Keans's, remembered spending his holidays as a young man at the Princess's Theatre. Recalling watching the rehearsals for *A Midsummer Night's Dream*, he wrote:

> Kean had a wonderful eye for pretty girls, and this was a real bevy, headed by one who still remains in mind . . . as the loveliest woman in her youth I have ever seen . . . Carlotta LeClerq [Titania]. . . . As she had no special talent [she] rose from the ranks by sheer right of beauty . . . height, hair, limbs, figure and proportions, all in the fairest symmetry of womanhood. She couldn't act; but one can't have everything, and that didn't matter. As she could play nothing in particular, she played everything in general, and all well enough. Miranda, Titania, Perdita, Marguerita, or Lydia Languish.[74]

But London critics wrote mainly of Kean's momentous cultural efforts. A few complained that the play was at times overburdened with scenery.[75] The *Literary Gazette* critic thought the finale, with the trains of fairies moving in continuous lines up and down the stairs, "resembles much more the track of a colony of industrious ants than the midnight whiz and whirl of the sprites." Fontane was charmed and described it lovingly: "The whole effect is magical, spellbinding for even the most prosaic spirit."[76] The pictures did displace a good deal of the text of the "greatest poet who ever wrote for the advantage of men," however. Kean cut 838 lines, almost 40 percent of the play.[77]

Over the next two decades, Kean's staging was closely imitated by at least four successful English and American productions. Charles Calvert modeled his lavish version in Manchester in 1865 on it, using Kean's text and scenery painted by Thomas and Walford Grieve.[78] Edward Saker followed Kean in his 1880 production, seen in Liverpool and London.[79] Calvert and Saker each used sixty children as bewinged fairies, mirroring the increasingly popular Victorian iconography in which children were portrayed as radiant with angelic purity, sentimental evidence of a spirit world.

In the United States, Laura Keene emulated Kean's staging in her 1859 revival at her New York theatre and blended in more pantomime elements.[80] The English-born actress had trained at the Olympic Theatre under Vestris, who was apparently a role model for her.[81] She acted under manager James Wallack at New York's Lyceum Theatre and then managed her own playhouse from 1856 to 1863. Her lavish *A Midsummer Night's Dream*, her first Shakespearean venture, was underwritten by her recent profitable long run of *Our American Cousin*.[82] In her acting edition of the play (1863), Keene offered the by now obligatory scholarly window-dressing, acknowledging her indebtedness to "Mr. H—— of Harvard College" for assistance on Athenian antiquities and to "Mr. W——" for assistance with the text. Scholarly eminences needed to be careful about having their names associated with the frivolous theatre. "Mr. H—— of Harvard" may have assisted with matters such as Hippolyta's Amazon costume of red-and-gold armor with a leopard skin over it, which was based on a figure depicted on a Greek vase. The textual consultant would have been Richard Grant White, America's first Shakespeare scholar of consequence, who had recently edited the complete works and was a devout Anglophile.[83] Keene had good reason for a show of reverence. Editions of Shakespeare's works were proliferating — 162 were published between 1851 and 1860.[84] Keene's playing text, however, was actually based on Charles Kean's and Thomas Barry's, and she cut even more than Kean had. This gives her the distinction of omitting more Shakespeare than anyone in the century since Vestris restored the play.[85] During the production's opening week, the enterprising manager ran innovative, column-long advertisements describing the plot and scenery in the accessible terms of a modern melodrama. The first scene promised a sunrise over the terrace of Theseus's palace terrace and more:

> The approaching nuptials and their appropriate festivities. A discordant element. Paternal complaints. Love at cross purposes. Cupid bewitched. Ancient punishment of refractory daughters. The convent or the tomb. An unloved fair one. Contemplated flight from Athens. Misplaced confidence.

In the forest scenes she promised the usual panorama and a few other things:

> THE FAIRY KING and the NYMPH of the FOUNTAIN, introducing the wonderful effect of NATURE IN ANIMATION; Trees, shrubs, Beautiful Flowers, &c., SPRING INTO LIFE IN VIEW OF THE AUDIENCE. Fairy revelries. The incantation. Application of the love philter. Titania bewitched. Lovers caught napping.[86]

The spectacle was the star, and the individual members of Keene's company, experienced and popular as many were, won little attention for their performances, not even Keene, who played Puck, nor E. A. Sothern, who was playing Lysander just after his recent great success as Lord Dundreary in *Our American*

Cousin.[87] Actor William Blake, a conventionally rotund Bottom, was "exceedingly bad," said one critic.[88] But Keene's spectacle won audiences for forty performances in a season when New Yorkers could see productions of twelve of Shakespeare's plays, including Wallack's lavishly mounted *The Merchant of Venice* and *Antony and Cleopatra*, neither of which ran as long as Keene's *A Midsummer Night's Dream*.[89]

But we should not imagine that the scene painting for these American productions of the 1850s and 1860s yet matched the quality of the English stage. One reviewer of Keene's production wrote that the view of the Parthenon on the Acropolis "looks as if it were on the point of running violently downhill."[90] London *Times* theatre critic, John Oxenbury, visiting New York in the fall of 1867, commented on American audiences' appetite for scenic decoration and noted that, "whereas in London even the humblest theatres can boast of a well-executed drop curtain, such a luxury is rare in New York."[91]

Better scene painting and scenic novelties were clearly the priorities for the production of the play at the Olympic Theatre (formerly Keene's) in the fall of 1867, also modeled in part on Charles Kean's.[92] Joseph Jefferson, who oversaw the staging, thought New Yorkers craved spectacle and brought from London a commissioned panorama by William Telbin, Senior, an admired scenic artist who had painted for Macready and Kean.[93] The panorama was employed after Theseus's discovery of the sleeping lovers in the forest to illustrate the passage of the hunting party and the lovers out of the forest and back to Athens. Young William Winter, in the bud of his long critical career, described its views of "hill and valley, woodland and meadow, rock and stream, rural road and classical temple," and echoed the humanistic pieties of his earlier British counterparts:

> We march in the train of Theseus, as we gaze, we follow the flight of Oberon, and we breathe the pure air of Greece, and feel around us the golden spell of her ancient civilization. Technical blemishes might be found in the work here and there, but, as a whole, it is the admirable reflection of a true artistic spirit.[94]

Other scenes, painted by Americans James E. Hayes and Minard Lewis (who painted for Edwin Booth), were also praised, including a triple transformation for the fairy finale, the scenes of which the playbill listed as "The Golden Vineyard of Aurora Fairy Land; the Valley of Ferns; the Temples of Arcadia, with groups of winged Fairies upon Rising Pedestals."[95] Act 2 ended with a tableau reproducing Sir Edwin Landseer's painting of the translated Bottom in Titania's bower.[96] Jefferson's judgment about spectacle proved correct. The Olympic production ran for a hundred consecutive performances (far exceeding Keene's), the longest consecutive run of this play in America yet and one of the few very profitable Shakespearean productions of the era.[97] George L. Fox's broadly comic Bottom was the second reason for the success. Capitalizing on it, Olympic publicist Clifton Tayleure had the new granite curbstones being laid along Broadway stenciled with the query, "Have you seen Fox's Bottom?"[98]

The monumental scenic pictures of Augustin Daly and Sir Herbert Beerbohm Tree close the century.[99] Shakespeare had become ever more obligatory for a theatre manager aspiring to cultural status. Sir Henry Irving staged twelve of the plays, Daly sixteen, and Tree sixteen, all with lavish scenic illustration. One did not stage Shakespeare without the full rites of high culture. In his 1900 *A Midsummer Night's Dream*, Tree mocked William Poel, who had recently taken up the cause of staging Shakespeare without scenery on an Elizabethan-style stage. Tree's mechanicals appeared for *Pyramus and Thisbe* with quasi-Elizabethan placards hung around their necks reading, "This is a Lion," "This is a Wall," "This is a Maiden," and "This is a Youth" (see fig. 26). To Tree, the archaic Elizabethan staging, offered by "epicures in mediocrity," seemed bereft of all that a modern theatre, fully equipped for illusionism (such as Tree's new theatre was), should be doing for Shakespeare.[100] George Bernard Shaw, of course, disagreed. In a review of Poel's Elizabethan Stage Society's production of *The Tempest*, he wrote, "You can best do without scenery in *The Tempest* and *A Midsummer Night's Dream* because the best scenery you can get will only destroy the illusion created by the poetry."[101] But most Victorians wanted a picturable world for Shakespeare. Both Daly's and Tree's productions of *A Midsummer Night's Dream* were recapitulations of the play's sentimental, pictorial traditions, monumentalized and embellished with novelties, and both were popular. Tree's production in particular was offered as a kind of victory lap for Victorian Shakespearean staging.

The surviving photographs of Daly's production of 1888 show an ostentatiously lavish classical palace for Act 1, rendered in meticulous photographic realism (fig. 16). American audiences of the Gilded Age were taken into the interior of Theseus's palace, as if on a private tour of the Newport mansions of the rich and famous. Odell, who published two full pages of the photographs, admired it:

> Well do I remember the architectural beauty of the opening picture of the Palace of Theseus, the lofty Corinthian columns with their Grecian paintings of dull red hue for about one-third of their height, the rich sombre curtains pulled back to show an inner room of equal beauty, cut in two by another pair

FIGURE 16. Interior of Theseus's palace, 1.1, in Augustin Daly's production, Daly's Theatre, New York, 1888. Setting by Henry E. Hoyt. Billy Rose Theatre Collection, New York Public Library for the Performing Arts.

of graceful pillars, and the door in the extreme rear, opened, and giving by its vista an effect of almost unlimited spaciousness. [102]

Odell, who thought Daly's production "the best within my experience of half a century," also praised "the chief woodland scene," possibly for 2.1 (which can be seen behind the actors in figures 17 and 18):

Tall trees formed the middle distance, approached by slopes of rich growth and with an occasional tall flower of luxuriant bloom, and all the background was a sylvan stream of exquisite beauty, its rocky banks shaded by great trees, in whose dimly outlined forms the imagination loved to lose itself.[103]

Daly embellished the received traditions with elaborate, superficial novelties. The Indian boy was carried on in a curtained palanquin in 1.1, and when Oberon

FIGURE 17. Alice Hood as Oberon and Effie Shannon as Titania, 2.1, in Augustin Daly's production, New York, 1888. Billy Rose Theatre Collection, New York Public Library for the Performing Arts.

threatened to seize him, the curtains closed at Titania's gesture and reopened to show that he had vanished.[104] (He had disappeared through a trap in Purcell's opera.) Daly equipped his fairies with the new electric lights, which flickered in their hair and at the tips of their wands, powered by batteries on their backs. Dancing among Daly's fairies at one point was Isadora Duncan. "I tried to tell Mr. Daly that I could express wings without putting on *papier mâché* ones," she remembered, "but he was obdurate."[105] Electric fireflies glimmered through the mists around the sleeping lovers, and crickets chirped. Odell admired all the new effects, as did critic George Montgomery, who recorded the production in detail for the *Cosmopolitan*.[106]

The chief novelty was Daly's ending for the forest sequence. As the sun rose over the forest, the argonaut Theseus and his hunting party entered, disembarking from a ship. Daly was not the first to set Theseus afloat; Burton's and Barry's Theseus had disembarked from a ship in Act 1 in 1854. But after Daly's Theseus

FIGURE 18. Effie Shannon as Titania and James Lewis as Bottom in Augustin Daly's production, New York, 1888. Lewis manipulated the ass's features with strings, using one hand beneath his apron. Billy Rose Theatre Collection, New York Public Library for the Performing Arts.

awakened the lovers, he boarded everyone and made for the "port" of Athens. A complex diorama provided moving scenery behind the ship and a moving shoreline in the foreground (figs. 19–21); as the party arrives in port, even the caryatids seem to wave handkerchiefs in greeting (fig. 21). "The effect was much talked of," Odell wrote, though he objected to the voyage because the illusion was unconvincing.[107] For his finale, Daly departed from the traditional picture of lantern-bearing fairies scampering through galleries, offering instead an odd, midair apotheosis scene in which Oberon and Titania appeared surrounded by fairies and painted cupids, all framed by the huge caryatids. This

FIGURES 19, 20, 21. In Daly's 1888 staging, Theseus, the argonaut, set sail with his hunting party and returned the lovers from the forest back to Athens in this barge in a panorama sequence in 4.2. The moving scenery was painted by Henry E. Hoyt. Billy Rose Theatre Collection, New York Public Library for the Performing Arts.

was accompanied not by Mendelssohn's score but by Bishop's song from the 1816 opera for the lines "Through the house give glimmering light."[108]

The four young lovers were probably the best in half a century, with Daly's chief star, Ada Rehan, as Helena to John Drew's Demetrius and Otis Skinner as Lysander to Virginia Dreher's Hermia.[109] The sources allow us the best glimpse yet of Shakespeare's lovers as Victorians. According to Daly's promptbook, when Rehan's Helena entered in 1.1 and saw Lysander and Hermia, she "starts with a pang." At another point, she "throws herself on a seat and buries her head in her hands." After the court exited, Rehan, "regal and lovely in a Grecian robe of delicate salmon pink," reclined on the ornate couch in Theseus's palace (where we see Hippolyta in fig. 16) for her speech that ends the scene, "How happy some o'er other some can be! / Through Athens I am thought as fair as she" (1.1.226 ff).[110] William Winter saw her as the wronged, suffering maiden, alone and comfortless amid the splendor, notwithstanding the fact that Rehan appeared in a series of beautiful gowns.[111] Young men of the day saw in her portrayals, said Winter, "the fulfillment of that ideal of sensuous sentiment, piquant freedom, and impetuous ardor, combined with rich beauty of person and negligent elegance of manner, which they account the perfection of womanhood." Winter thought the "leap-year attitude of Helena impedes its ready access to sympathy," but Rehan made her "entirely noble and charming" by "sweet sincerity" and "fervent passion."[112] When Daly brought *A Midsummer Night's Dream* to London, George Bernard Shaw ridiculed it, from the scenery to the speaking of the verse, but he was smitten with Rehan. Only when Rehan was on stage, said Shaw, did "the play assert its full charm. . . . She gives us beauty of tone, grace of measure, delicacy of articulation . . . along with the rich feeling and fine intelligence without which those technical qualities would soon become monotonous. When she is at her best, the music melts in the caress of the emotion it expresses."[113] Lysander and Demetrius were ideal young Victorian males, Skinner and Drew winning the praise of Odell, Winter, and other male critics as "men of gallant bearing" and "pictures of manly grace."[114] Rehan brought humor to her quarrel with Hermia in the wood, but between the plaintive women and the manly men, there seems to have been much less room for laughter at the lovers than Shakespeare allows. Two textual alterations made by Daly and other Victorian managers are evidence of this. Shakespeare provides a stichomythic exchange of lines beween Lysander and Hermia on the course of true love (1.1.134 ff); its excessive rhetoric allows us to smile at their self-dramatization while not doubting their sincerity. Like managers before him, Daly turned the sequence into a monologue for Lysander, delivered with Victorian male solemnity.[115] Also, in the forest scenes, the quartet's quarrels were reduced, so that, as Winter wrote in the preface to Daly's edition of the play, "the spectator may not see too much of the perplexed and wrangling lovers."[116] Shakespeare in the theatre was responsible for providing Victorians with models of behavior.

Daly's lavish pictures succeeded in awing New York critics and audiences. Reviewers praised the "glory and wealth of scenic art such as Shakespeare never dreamed" and "the wealth of scenic attire and luxurious dressings in such profusion and with such taste."[117] The production had seventy-nine performances, was revived in 1890, and, after the London production in 1895, toured major American cities in 1895–1896. Later in 1888, Daly's chief scene painter, Henry Hoyt, painted for a successful Chicago production staged by John Albaugh.[118] In London, Daly was drubbed by the reformers Shaw and William Archer for the sins of heavy accessories and textual omissions (558 lines) and transpositions.[119] These earned him the title "Grandfather Daly" from Shaw, but Daly's sins differed little from those of his British contemporaries.[120]

Sir Herbert Beerbohm Tree's *A Midsummer Night's Dream* in 1900 was Tree's sixth Shakespearean production, his third in his new technologically advanced theatre, Her Majesty's. Tree was dauntless and rarely subtle in his efforts to stage Shakespeare impressively. Charles Kean was his role model. Tree's tastes ran to the obvious and literal: rumbles of thunder when Desdemona was smothered, real deer for *The Merry Wives of Windsor*, and the famous real rabbits for *A Midsummer Night's Dream* (added for the production's revival in 1911).[121] The Shakespeare playgoer Gordon Crosse observed that the actor-manager never let Shakespeare speak for himself.[122] Shakespeare never had, of course; no text goes unmediated, least of all in performance, and Tree's spectacle alone spoke volumes. Tree's promptbook shows 410 lines omitted, and this did leave 50 percent more of Shakespeare's text than Kean had used.[123]

Tree had the virtue of bluff certainty about his mission: Shakespeare deserved, and the public wanted, impressive staging. When *Blackwood's Magazine* stung Tree with criticism of his lavish production of *The Tempest* in 1904, Tree responded with a program note midway in the run, defending the whole pictorial scenic system for Shakespeare, saying, "Illusion is the whole business of the theatre." Illusion was indeed good business for Tree. Of the three Shakespearean plays he produced at Her Majesty's between 1897 and 1900, 240,000 people saw his *Julius Caesar*, 170,000 saw his *King John*, and 220,000 saw his *A Midsummer Night's Dream*.[124] He encouraged others to stage Shakespeare "as beautifully as they can afford," pointing out that "no single one of my Shakesperian [*sic*] productions has been unattended by a substantial pecuniary reward."[125] Tree once even defended his lavish staging in a paradoxical reference to *Pyramus and*

Thisbe as an example of "how Shakespeare himself, in this humorous lament of Adequacy, stood forth as the staunch advocate of a wider art." [126] Lavish Shakespeare was not merely good business, it was in the national interest, which Tree saw his theatre as representing. When he opened Her Majesty's Theatre, he dressed his staff in liveries of the royal household (which the royal household quickly halted). To his *King John* he added a scene of the king signing the Magna Carta. [127] From 1905 through 1913, he organized Shakespeare festivals at his theatre every spring for several weeks, bringing in companies such as Sir Frank Benson's and reviving his own productions. The most ambitious of these festivals was in 1911, the year of George V's coronation. [128]

Tree's famous production of *A Midsummer Night's Dream* in January 1900 was almost a patriotic occasion. Tree consciously intended that it should be a reaffirmation of traditions as the century clock turned twelve and amid the growing sense that an era was ending. In the previous twelve years, territories equal to twenty-four times the area of Great Britain had been added to the empire. But in December 1899, Britain experienced Black Week — a series of disastrous defeats in the Transvaal in its imperial war with the Boers for the Rand gold mines. Mrs. Tree (Helen Maud Holt) was doing readings of Rudyard Kipling, but, in Barbara Tuchman's words, "With Black Week went the last time Britons felt themselves unquestionably masters of the earth." [129] Tree's production offered the comforting old images of England as Theseus's Athens, source of civilization, the weighty pictures piling simulacra upon simulacra in a scenic rhetoric that was being emptied of its imperial mythology. Tree's tableau act curtains closed at every scene change to conceal the shifts from one romantic illusion to another. [130]

One can hardly miss the classical weight of Tree's first act setting (fig. 22). He even labeled it "Athens," in Greek, on the shield suspended above it, lest audiences miss it. *Punch*'s critic described the setting as "the Pantheon . . . on the Necropolis." [131] But for Shakespeare's *A Midsummer Night's Dream* at Her Majesty's in time of war, there were reasons for reviving once more the scenic text that conflated England and ancient Greece. Victorian children were reading such works as *Stories from Shakespeare* by Dr. Thomas Carter, a theologian and author of books for improving boys. Tree's setting is the visual corollary of the description with which Carter began his summary of *A Midsummer Night's Dream*: "On the great plain of Attica, watered by the Kaphisos and the brook Ilissus, and circled by its hills, Parnassus, Hymettus, Pantelicon, and Lycabettus, there stands the famous city of Athens." [132] Tree's Oberon, Julia Neilson, wore a spikey crown that rendered her very like the image of Britannia on British currency (fig. 23).

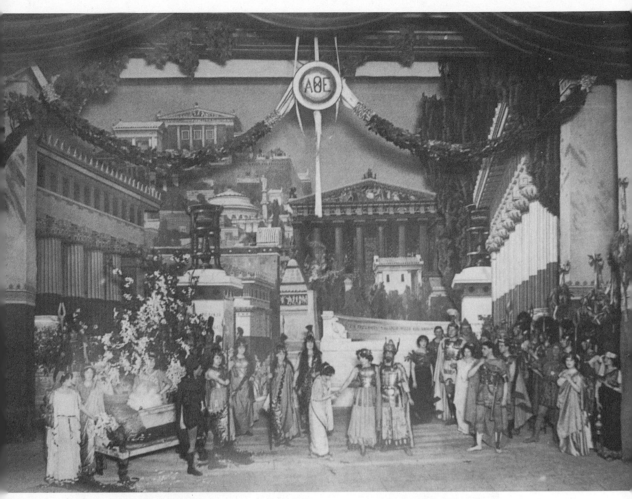

FIGURE 22. Exterior of Theseus's palace, 2.1, in Sir Herbert Beerbohm Tree's production, Her Majesty's Theatre, London, 1900. Setting by Joseph Harker. Theatre Museum, Victoria and Albert Museum.

In the forest scenes, mechanical birds sounded in English beeches, and the moon sent silver light through traceries of branches to light a fairy troupe of children, who danced in a fairy ring to Mendelssohn. The *Times* admired a Hawes Craven forest scene, with its "carpet of thyme and wildflower, brakes and thickets full of blossom, and a background seen through tall trees of the pearly dawn or the deep hues of the night sky. . . . The mind in recalling it seems to dwell upon some actual beauty of nature."[133] Craven's scene included a simulated stream in which Bottom checked his reflection for the ass's ears after awakening from his dream. Titania was sung to sleep in a honeysuckle bower by forty-seven fairies, one of whom hovered in the air above her, amid hanging

FIGURE 23. Mrs. Beerbohm Tree (Helen Maud Holt) as Titania and Julia Neilson as Oberon, Sir Herbert Beerbohm Tree's production, 1900. Costumes by Percy Anderson. Theatre Museum, Victoria and Albert Museum.

FIGURE 24. Titania's bank, Sir Herbert Beerbohm Tree's production, 1900. Setting by Hawes Craven. Theatre Museum, Victoria and Albert Museum.

boughs, while moonlight played on a background sea (fig. 24). Many of the fairies were children, consistent with the frequent images in late Victorian art of children as angelic and semidivine. Tree's costume chart listed ten "special flying fairies, 4 fireflies, 9 imps, 4 sea urchins, 8 wood elves, [and] 2 wood fairies." [134] Some fairies could switch on battery-operated glow lamps which they wore at such moments as Puck's incantation over the sleeping lovers. [135] Neilson as Oberon wore an electrically lighted breastplate and crown. She sang "I know a bank" and other songs with "a rich thrill [trill?] in her tones that

FIGURE 25. Sir Herbert and Lady Tree as Bottom and Titania in Sir Herbert Beerbohm Tree's production, 1900. Theatre Museum, Victoria and Albert Museum.

suggests some gorgeous Eastern bird," said the *Pall Mall Gazette*. It was on the occasion of Neilson's performance that this critic pinpointed one of the appeals of a woman fairy king for Victorians: "Her Oberon is truly regal, while the mere fact of her being woman just differentiates it from humanity."[136]

Theseus's palace in Tree's final scene (fig. 26) included a mosaic-painted floor and intricate Grecian border motifs running the width of each ceiling border. Accustomed as we now are to color-saturated video and cinema screens, it may be difficult for us, as we look at the early black-and-white photographs of Tree's settings taken under harsh electric light, to appreciate how impressive these carefully painted, stagewide pictures were to the eyes of Victorians. Percy Anderson's surviving designs for the costumes of Theseus (William Mollison) and Puck (Miss Louie Freear) help recover some of the production's color (plates 6 and 7). For the fairy invasion, Oberon touched each of the nine huge pillars with his wand, and they glowed from within. At the close, "slowly the light dies down as the fairies steal quietly away; and when all is darkness, the big curtain falls," wrote the enthralled critic of *Vanity Fair*.[137] Critic J. T. Grein lavishly praised Tree's pictures, saying their beauty brightened "these troubled times when there is much sorrow in the land."[138]

Tree played Bottom, demonstrating him broadly (fig. 25). His performance "distended till it spread over the whole play," wrote critic Percy Fitzgerald.[139] The *Times* praised Tree even while noting that he played the role with "the bibulous visage of a confirmed toper and voice thickened with indulgence in liquor," and *Punch* described him as wearing "flesh-colored hose" with a hairy growth.[140] He gave himself a late, prodigious entrance in the first mechanicals scene, going around to each of his friends to allow them to shake his hand in an idolizing way. Interpolated after many of his lines were the approval-seeking ejaculations, "Eh? Eh?" Sitting himself on a bench with the others, he knocked off an end man and then ate an apple while the parts in the play were being distributed. In the rehearsal, he threw down his script when corrected by Quince on "odours." At one point, Tree leaned on a pedestal in a tragic pose that was intended to parody the acting of actor-manager Sir John Hare.[141] London critics were unanimous in praising the other artisans — Franklin McLeay's Quince, Louis Calvert's Flute, E. M. Robson's Snug, and Fisher White's Starveling. But *Pyramus and Thisbe*, already heavy with accretions of traditional business (see chapter 4), was even further laden. Starveling was elderly and deaf as he had been in Benson's production, but in Tree's this occasioned the repetition of lines, shouted in Starveling's ear. When Quince tells Starveling he is to play Thisbe's mother, Starveling replied, "Thisbe's brother?" to which the troupe replied in unison, "Mother!"[142] Snug hiccuped after saying, "We are to utter

FIGURE 26. Interior of Theseus's palace and the performance of *Pyramus and Thisbe*, Sir Herbert Beerbohm Tree's production, 1900. Setting by Joseph Harker. Theatre Museum, Victoria and Albert Museum.

sweet breath"; Quince stuttered his prologue; Lion roared himself into coughing; and Bottom sneezed when Thisbe knelt over him and asked, "Dead, dead, my dove?" Moon dropped his too-hot lantern and picked it up again with Thisbe's mantle, leaving Pyramus without a mantle to apostrophize. At the end of the play, Pyramus and Thisbe could not settle into positions for their deaths, so Quince finally threw a blanket over them and sat on them.[143] The decline of the mechanicals to this low level of farce reminds us that they had not been integral to the play in any organic way since perhaps Phelps. They have been effectively displaced by the two worlds the nineteenth-century production vocabulary had constructed and privileged — a royal, imperialized Athens of Theseus and a naturalized fairy forest. The artisans have become only foolish, the butt of a class joke; perhaps it is not so surprising that the actors in these roles asserted the identity left to them. At times one feels that their aggressively low farce is a form of resistance to the pomposity and sentimentality around them.

The major critics outdid themselves with praise for the spectacle at Her Majesty's. Critics of the *Times*, the *Athenaeum*, and other mainstream periodicals wrote admiringly of the palaces and forests painted by Walter Hann, Joseph Harker, and Hawes Craven. The *Times* was awed by the expense and labor, and the *Athenaeum* believed that "no spectacle equally artistic has been seen on the English stage." Tree had achieved "what may, until science brings about new possibilities, be regarded as the limits of the conceivable." Critic Max Beerbohm of the *Saturday Review* had anticipated having to let his half-brother down gently, but he found the production charming and the illusion of true fairies fully achieved by the troupe of children.[144] The public kept Tree's production on the stage from January through the end of May, and eleven years later he revived it.

From the 1890s until well into the twentieth century, the play became a ubiquitous perennial. It was staged to celebrate Shakespeare's birthday at Stratford-upon-Avon, performed by young men in private schools, acted in public parks on summer evenings, and done as a Christmas confection for children at the Old Vic. A performance of this play, whether in an outdoor summer theatre or as a Christmas fairy fantasy, became a common experience of Shakespeare in the national cultural life of middle- and upper-class England, often a childhood experience. In the years just before and after World War I, the play became the more valued for its ability to stir visions of a golden age of Britain, when England's greatest poet celebrated the country's greatest queen. In 1924, John Dover Wilson and Sir Arthur Quiller-Couch revisited the theory that the play had been created for a court wedding in their prestigious Cambridge edition of the play.[145] Among Shakespeare's plays, perhaps only *Henry V* has had a comparable place in English life as a national play.

For many audiences outside London or New York, the experience of the play was supplied by the companies of Sir Frank Benson and Sir Ben Greet. They offered upcoming talent, scenery in the traditional mode but simplified, Mendelssohn, and even some of the old songs, such as "I know a bank." Benson, well-bred, handsome, athletic, and earnest, organized his Shakespearean company in the 1880s. He had behind him the solemn theatrical initiation of his Oxford University Drama Society production of *Agamemnon* (in Greek) and, to sustain him, the blessings of his idol, Sir Henry Irving. By 1886, Benson was charged by the new Memorial Council of Stratford-upon-Avon with control of all its theatrical productions. The Bensonians played there every summer save two until 1911 and toured the provinces during the year, ultimately performing most of the canon. George V knighted Benson for his Shakespearean services in 1916.

A Midsummer Night's Dream was frequently in the Bensonian repertoire.[146] William Helmsley provided an act drop with a picture of the Globe Theatre that evoked the requisite Shakespearean devotion. Theseus's palace, guarded by marble lions, came, in part, from Agamemnon's. Constance Benson, Benson's wife, remembered that the fairy costumes were based on "Walter Crane's beautiful designs in his book of flowers."[147] Forty or fifty children from local dancing schools would furnish Benson's fairy ranks; most were not more than four or five years old (before laws forbade children under fourteen to perform). Touring dictated scenic simplicity, but Benson could be more lavish in Stratford and London: thirty-nine supernumeraries as slaves, priests, Amazons, Athenian soldiers, and citizens; electric fireflies on the leaves and an electric crown for Puck; and a novel fight between a spider and a wasp.[148]

In a last-act rite that became a remembered Bensonian tradition, he had his young lovers enter to Mendelssohn's "Wedding March" on a path of rose petals, and they solemnly mimed marital vows before an altar on which a flame burned.[149] In Benson's company in 1889 was Otho Stuart as a manly Oberon — the first male to play the role since Vestris's production, though no one noticed, not even Shaw. In later casts, Henry Ainley played Oberon. Notable among Benson's mechanicals over the years were H. O. Nicholson as Starveling, poet Stephen Phillips as Flute, and George Weir's long-lived, low-comedy Bottom, memorialized in stained glass in the Benson window in the Royal Shakespeare Theatre art gallery in Stratford-upon-Avon. Weir's somewhat literal Bottom wakened from his dream to find hay in his pouch.[150] Helena was played by Kate Rorke, who Shaw thought rose above the mediocrity of the rest of the company — "not the illiterate, indifferent, professional mediocrity, but the literate, amateur, enthusiastic mediocrity."[151] Rorke eventually became Shaw's Candida. Benson himself played Lysander and, as the years went by, Theseus. Constance Benson played Titania. There may be no more telling witness to the long life of the Victorian traditions for the play than Constance Benson. In her autobiography, she wrote, "I must have spent months of my life on the bank."[152]

Ben Greet carried *A Midsummer Night's Dream* in his repertoire from English greens to America's Chautauqua circuits and from Oxford to Yale to midwestern universities over four decades. The play was a regular entry in his Old Vic seasons from 1914 to 1918.[153] Gordon Crosse saw Greet's "Pastoral Players" perform at Oxford in Worcester College's gardens in June 1892. Greet used a small stage, with audiences seated directly in front of it, and though he used little or no scenery, influenced by William Poel's ideas on Elizabethan staging, the productions were otherwise conventional. His promptbook, like Benson's, shows the familiar textual cuts.[154] Like Benson, Greet cultivated much young talent over the years: Robert Atkins (Oberon), who later would sustain the outdoor Shakespeare tradition with his own Regent's Park company, Sybil Thorndike (Hermia, Helena), Russell Thorndike (Snout), Leslie French (Puck), and Leo Carroll and Dudley Digges. Throughout the years, Greet played Bottom, performing the role as late as 1932, when he was a white-haired man of seventy-five.[155]

By the end of the first decade of the twentieth century, productions of the play were overripe with novelties. Nat Goodwin's 1903 production in the huge New Amsterdam theatre in New York featured luminous mushrooms, a festive procession of Dionysus in the last act, and Mendelssohn arranged by Victor Herbert. Odell reported that he and the play were "swallowed up in waves of melody."[156] In Otho Stuart's Christmas season productions of 1905 and 1906, Elizabeth Parkina, a Covent Garden opera soprano, delivered Horn's "I know a bank" with trills, flourishes, and encores. "No one knows what it is all about or why such warbling should be introduced," wrote Percy Fitzgerald, himself fond of Mendelssohn's score. Walter Hampden played Oberon, bringing "six foot of good American manhood to the role." The clowns were successful, but one reviewer commented, "The rest of the play is too romantic for our time as for our stage."[157] In Annie Russell's extravagant production in New York's new Astor Theatre in 1906, colored lights bobbed up in flowers when Puck (Russell) kissed them; an electric-eyed owl blinked from the trees; the forest included a brook practical enough for Quince and the others to tumble into when chased by Puck; and a pumpkin-faced actor named John Bunny, as Bottom, woke from his dream and tried to eat the hay he discovered in his pouch.[158] When Tree revived his production in 1911, golden leaves fell at the end of the first act, as if signaling the Indian summer of the painted stage. It was in this revival that Tree added the famous real rabbits that followed trails of bran around the stage, distracting audiences and actors. At one performance, Arthur Bourchier, playing Bottom, finally drove one rabbit from the stage. When he repented and carried it on for a curtain call, it bit him for his pains. *Punch* praised the rabbit troupe above all.[159]

Such productions were obviously sinking of their own literal weight. The pictorial stage was straining to provide comfortable illusions of fairies at the bottom of the garden. Similar infantalizing visions lie at the heart of James M. Barrie's *Peter Pan, or the Boy Who Would Not Grow Up*. In 1904, adult West End audiences were called on to revive the dying Tinker Bell: "Do you believe in fairies? Say quick that you believe! If you believe, clap your hands!"[160] Sir Arthur Conan Doyle, creator of Sherlock Holmes, the world's most scientific sleuth, published a book entitled *The Coming of the Fairies*, which offered photographs of fairies supposedly taken by two young girls. Doyle, who was an ardent spiritualist, was wholly convinced by these photographs, one of which seemed to show four scantily clad fairies about eight inches high, with butterfly wings, prancing in the air beneath the chin of one of the girls. But they were paper doll fairies, contrived by the girls.[161]

PLATE 1. Backdrop by W. Gordon for 1.1, Charles Kean's production, Princess's Theatre, London, 1856. Kean's promptbook describes the scene as "a Terrace adjoining the palace of Theseus, Overlooking the City of Athens." This and the other Kean production watercolors reproduced here were done by the scenic artists themselves in 1859. Trustees of the Victoria and Albert Museum.

PLATE 2. The meeting of Oberon and Titania, 2.1, Kean's production, 1856. F. Lloyds's setting included a backdrop by W. Gordon based on J. M. W. Turner's painting *The Golden Bough*. Fanny Ternan as Oberon (left), Ellen Terry as Puck (at Oberon's feet), and Charlotte Leclercq as Titania. Trustees of the Victoria and Albert Museum.

PLATE 3. Dance of fairies, 2.2, Kean's production, 1856. Scenery painted by F. Lloyds. The play's long association with the romantic ballet is caught here and in plate 5. It continued well into the twentieth century (see figs. 47 and 48). Trustees of the Victoria and Albert Museum.

PLATE 4. Interior of Theseus's palace, 5.1, Kean's production, 1856. The stage at center was used for *Pyramus and Thisbe*. This setting underwent a "transformation" to that in plate 5. Trustees of the Victoria and Albert Museum.

PLATE 5 . Fairy finale, 5.2, Kean's production, 1856. Scenery by F. Lloyds. All the fairies in this mid-Victorian production were played by women. Trustees of the Victoria and Albert Museum.

PLATES 6, 7 . Costume designs by Percy Anderson for Theseus and Puck, Sir Herbert Beerbohm Tree's production, 1900, Her Majesty's Theatre, London. Bristol University Theatre
Collection.

PLATES 8, 9, 10. Barker's golden fairies and Puck: Christine Silver as Titania, Dennis Neilson-Terry as Oberon, and Donald Calthrop as Puck. *Illustrated London News, Supplement,* 11 April 1914.

PLATE 11. Oberon (Powys Thomas) and Titania (Muriel Pavlow) as exotic birds, Shake-speare Memorial Theatre, Stratford-upon-Avon, 1954, directed by George Devine and de-signed by Motley. Thomas F. Holte, photographer. Shakespeare Centre Library.

PLATE 12. Forest setting, Royal Shakespeare Theatre, Stratford-upon-Avon, 1959, directed by Peter Hall and designed by Lila de Nobili, assisted by Henry Bardon. With changes in lighting and backdrops, this unit setting also served for Theseus's palace. Thomas F. Holte, photographer. Shakespeare Centre Library.

PLATE 13. Design for Titania's costume by Jim Dine for the San Francisco Actor's Work-shop production, 1966, directed by John Hancock. Museum of Modern Art, New York.

PLATE 14. The young lovers, Royal Shakespeare Company production, 1970, directed by Peter Brook. Frances de la Tour as Helena (left), Ben Kingsley as Demetrius (right), Mary Rutherford as Hermia, and Terence Tapin as Lysander. Thomas F. Holte, photographer. Shakespeare Centre Library.

PLATE 15. Alan Howard as Oberon (left) and John Kane as Puck, Royal Shakespeare Company production, 1970, directed by Peter Brook. Thomas F. Holte, photographer. Shakespeare Centre Library.

PLATE 16. Alan Howard as Oberon (left), Sara Kestelman as Titania, and John Kane as Puck, Royal Shakespeare Company production, 1970, directed by Peter Brook, designed by Sally Jacobs. Thomas F. Holte, photographer. Shakespeare Centre Library.

PLATE 17. Theseus's palace, Royal Shakespeare Theatre, Stratford-upon-Avon, 1982, directed by Ron Daniels, designed by Maria Bjornson. Thomas F. Holte, photographer. Shakespeare Centre Library.

Chapter seven

THE *DREAM* OF MODERNISM

THE "NEW HIEROGLYPHIC LANGUAGE OF SCENERY"

AND THE THEOLOGY OF THE TEXT

Starveling: All that I have to say is to tell you that the lantern is the moon, I the
man i'th moon, this thorn bush my thorn bush, and this dog my dog.

On 6 February 1914, only months before the start of World War I,
Harley Granville Barker staged *A Midsummer Night's Dream* in a radically new
scenic language. Seeking to put to rest the illusionistic and historical pictorialism
of Victorian Shakespeare in favor of a method he hoped would recover Shakespeare's poetry, he offered stylized, suggestive scenery and the famous gilded,
orientalized fairies that particularly shocked his audiences in both London and
New York. This and Barker's other two Shakespearean productions, *A Winter's
Tale* and *Twelfth Night*, created at the Savoy Theatre between 1912 and 1914,
have been rightly recognized for their remarkable break from moribund traditions. But in the process of the appreciation of Barker as a pioneer in modernist
theatre practice, these productions have been idealized and dehistoricized.[1]

For all of modernism's break from the dying gods of the nineteenth century,
it did not give up religion so much as seek it in art. Its artists saw themselves not
only as provocateurs but as prophets, and they viewed art as a liberator of the
spirit from the trappings of a spiritually mordant past. The new art was to create
new forms from a mystical aesthetic center and to symbolize transcendent essences with new purity. Modernism's first bright dreams were left in shreds by
the horrors of mechanized warfare. What remained when the center could not

hold became even more sacred: the dream of an aesthetic center, of art transcending the instabilities of history, assuring a permanent beauty.

A Midsummer Night's Dream was the last of Barker's three landmark Shakespearean productions, all of which revealed a bold new scenography. "There is no Shakespearean tradition," Barker wrote, seeking to dislodge the belief that Victorian pictorialism had some special sanction. "We have the text to guide us, half a dozen stage directions, and that is all. I abide by the text and the demands of the text, and beyond that I claim freedom."[2] If all vestiges of dead theatrical traditions were to be thrown off, a new theatrical vocabulary for Shakespeare had to be created ab ovo. Barker was astute about it: "To invent a new hieroglyphic language of scenery, that in a phrase, is the problem." He made these points in touching pleas for more patient critics and a more open-minded public in a letter to *Play Pictorial* after the stormy critical reception of his modernistic *Twelfth Night*.[3] His *A Midsummer Night's Dream* was even more controversial. This particular play had long been fondly bound up, of course, with Athenian grandeur, Warwickshire forests, and Mendelssohn's music. London audiences had seen Tree's rabbit redux only three years earlier. Now Barker jettisoned it all for nonrepresentational forests and oriental fairies, and they shocked viewers almost as much as Marcel Duchamp's *Nude Descending a Staircase* had shocked New York the year before.

Barker had meant to be wholly faithful to Shakespeare's text with his new scenic vocabulary, which he hoped would allow access to the timeless essence of the play. He was too theatrically sophisticated to believe, with William Poel, that Shakespeare could be recovered for the new century by playing the plays on a quasi-Elizabethan stage. "We shall not save our souls by being Elizabethan," he wrote.[4] But Barker's own investment in the Shakespearean text was, nonetheless, almost theological, for he saw the text as self-enclosed and timeless, much the way formalism was beginning to do, and he wrote of the "screeds of word music" in *A Midsummer Night's Dream*.[5] This investment would become characteristic of modernist theatre practice in the production of the classics: all authentic meaning was assumed to be inherent in the text; all elements of the production were to be unified and in its service, to be "naturalized to the text's internal dynamics," to borrow a phrase from W. B. Worthen.[6] The director was to be the master of this integration, and as is well known, Barker is important in the early development of this figure. (Edward Gordon Craig's dream of replacing actors with puppets is, while extreme, perfectly consistent with these idealist aesthetics and the authoritarian control they entailed.) By contrast, in the poststructuralist view of text in the late twentieth century, a Shakespearean performance is seen as a site of negotiations between the text and contemporary culture, in which the latter inevitably exerts its own strong claims. Both text and event may be resonant with many signifiers and many available, even conflicting, meanings. From this perspective, there is an inevitable paradox in Barker's earnest, imaginative quest for a twentieth-century theatrical voice that would not color the timeless essence of Shakespeare.

Barker often vowed his intention to be true to Shakespeare's text. In 1910, he had himself photographed intently absorbed in a copy of the First Folio, the image of the modernist director at one with the text, ostensibly with nothing between them.[7] Implicit in the photograph is a message similar to T. S. Eliot's comment about Shakespearean production. In his well-known 1924 essay, "Four Elizabethan Dramatists," Eliot wrote: "I know that I rebel against most performances of Shakespeare's plays because I want a direct relationship between the work of art and myself, and I want the performance to be such as will not interrupt or alter this relationship. . . . I would have a work of art such that it needs only to be completed and cannot be altered by each interpretation."[8] In his introduction to the collected prefaces, Barker closed with a "golden rule" for Shakespeare in the theatre: "Whether staging or costuming or cutting is in question . . . : Gain Shakespeare's effects by Shakespeare's means when you can; for plainly, this will be the better way. But gain Shakespeare's effects; and it is your business to discern them."[9] In his 1924 preface to *A Midsummer Night's Dream*, he wrote: "Let the producer first bring his work to completion on Shakespeare's own terms, . . . perfect the music of the poetry and the grace of the play's movement, [and] not so much else will need doing."[10] This is the recognizable vision of Barker the reformer, rejecting the pictorial stage for one of poetry. But a theatrical transaction on "Shakespeare's own terms" in 1914 was no more possible, of course, than it had been for Tree. Again, sophisticated man of the theatre though Barker was, his quest was at bottom not so different from that of formalist criticism's contemporary interest in developing verbal and structural analyses to evaluate the poem in and of itself, which ultimately tended to isolate the literary text from history and culture in the interest of establishing literature as a purely aesthetic object. In contrast to such literary aesthetics, the theatre's transactions with classical texts are always temporal and, far from being immune to contamination by contemporary culture, they thrive on the encounter.

For Barker and his designer for *A Midsummer Night's Dream*, Norman Wilkinson, the solution to the problem of providing a local habitation for Shakespeare's play in the modern world was symbolist scenery. Barker had been influenced by Poel's insistence on an Elizabethan-type stage that would allow the flow of Shakespeare's plays, but he rejected Poel's bare platform. Scenery, or in the phrase coming into use, scenic decor was wanted, decor that eschewed literal representation for suggestion, symbolism, and atmospheric ambience. Barker and his designers borrowed visually from every new direction but were specifically indebted to the pioneers in symbolist stage design, Edward Gordon Craig and Max Reinhardt and his designers in Berlin, who had been influenced by Craig.[11] Barker and Wilkinson believed their new symbolic scenic methods would function metaphorically, giving direct access to the essence of the play. On the occasion of the New York opening of *A Midsummer Night's Dream* in 1915, Wilkinson told an interviewer: "I have ignored time and place. . . . I firmly believe . . . that an imitation of reality on the stage can never pass for the real thing, whereas a symbol, if it makes no attempt to reproduce nature, can be a thing of beauty in itself. . . . With Shakespeare the decorations must be no more than an accompaniment to the play."[12] Of course, the new scenic methods would be "accompaniment" as value laden as Kean's Periclean palaces or Mendelssohn's score.

To be sure, Barker's actors spoke more of the play's text than had been heard since Shakespeare's day. His promptbook shows omissions of something less than three lines and the slight alteration of some five words,[13] compared to nineteenth-century reductions of from 17 to 40 percent.[14] He did add a song to the end of the play; the issue was a textual fine point. Barker believed, with many editors after Samuel Johnson, that the Folio was missing the lyrics for "The Song," indicated in an italicized heading before Oberon's "Now until the break of day" (5.2.31). Barker therefore inserted the wedding song that is sung for Theseus and Hippolyta at the beginning of *The Two Noble Kinsmen*, beginning "Roses, their sharp spines being gone" and including the lines "All dear nature's children sweet, / Lie fore bride and bridegroom's feet" (1.1.1–24). The lines were set by folk-music specialist Cecil Sharp.

Nor did Barker alter the order of the scenes as had been a common practice; the settings were conceived to allow scenes to flow, unencumbered by changes of heavy scenery. Wilkinson's settings involved the use of a forestage with the unusual depth of twelve feet, carpeted with a light gray ground cloth. (In the New York restaging, the stage boxes on either side of the proscenium were converted to forestage entrances.) Two steps spanning its width rose to a second level in front of a flat, modernistic proscenium frame (that masked the permanent proscenium). Painted curtains hung in folds across the frame, and these rose to expose two distinct scenic units. No footlights were used; the stage was

FIGURE 27. Theseus's court, 1.1, Barker's production, Savoy Theatre, 1914. Scenery and costumes designed by Norman Wilkinson. Baliol Holloway as Theseus, Evelyn Hope as Hippolyta. *Sketch*, 25 February 1914.

lit mostly in what the critic for *Punch* described as "pitiless" white light from the instruments hung in front of the balcony.[15]

Theseus met his court in Act 1 in an austere and symmetrical tableau in front of a gray-white curtain laced with frail green-and-gold grapevine patterns in the style of Art Nouveau (fig. 27). Theseus sat with Hippolyta on a severe black throne-bench on a dais, framed by staff-bearing Amazons. For the subsequent meeting of Peter Quince and his actors, the grapevine curtain rose to reveal a second curtain, in salmon pink, on which was suggestively sketched a cottage door, windows, trees, and city rooftops in the background. This curtain then went up to disclose a third curtain, painted green at the bottom and electric blue above, spangled with stars and a moon. The white lights dimmed slightly, and in this radically new forest, Oberon and Titania were met, with their fairy trains (fig. 28; plates 8–10).

"The fairies are the producer's test," said Barker in a preface to his 1914 edition of the play, and it was Barker's golden fairies that became the production's most controversial and remembered feature. They were clad entirely in gold, their faces and hands gilded from expensive, small sheets of gold leaf in

FIGURE 28. Moonlight meeting of Oberon and Titania in the forest, Barker's production, 1914. *Sketch*, 25 February 1914.

painstaking applications. Their hair hung "in gold curls like shavings from new yellow board," said American critic Walter Pritchard Eaton. Trying to offer an unalarmed, detailed review of the production, Eaton wrote of the fairies:

> They are undeniably strange and at once differentiated from anything mortal. It may very well be questioned if they are the fairies of Shakespeare's vision. They are not ethereal, but solid as gilt statues, and stiff like statues, too, moving with quaint, automatic motions. . . . These stiff gold fairies are better than the more conventional representations, even if they do rather orientalize a purely Elizabethan play.[16]

Times critic A. B. Walkley asked: "Is it Titania's Indian Boy that has given Mr. Barker his notion of Orientalizing Shakespeare's fairies? Or is it Bakst? Anyhow they look like Cambodian idols and posture like Nijinsky in *Le Dieu Bleu*."[17] Critic Desmond McCarthy described them as "ormolu fairies, looking as though they had been detached from some fantastic, bristling old clock" (fig. 29; plates 8–10).[18] One wore a scimitar and moved like a marionette out of *Petrouchka*, which had premiered in 1911 with designs by Aleksandr Benois. Another wore a waist-length beard; one carried a pen and scroll and another a

FIGURE 29. Fairy attendant to Titania, Barker's production, 1914. *Illustrated London News,*
11 April 1914.

book. A promptbook names some of them: the Major, the Doctor, and the Professor.[19] A New York critic described the golden creatures as "eighteen karats fine and twice as hard."[20] In the forest scenes, they stopped in frozen positions, invisible to the eyes of the human lovers who moved through and around them. They clearly had some debt to Léon Bakst's orientalized designs for the Sergey Diaghilev ballets for *The Firebird* or *Sheherazade*, recently seen in London.[21] Several reviewers were reminded of Max Reinhardt's orientalist *Sumurun* of 1912. Apparently behind Barker's appropriation of the Orient for his fairies was the assumption that audiences would find in this an analogue for Shakespeare's unworldly creatures.

Only Puck among the fairies went unorientalized and ungilded. Played by Donald Calthrop, he was suited in scarlet, with hints of Elizabethan style in his doublet, flounced at the waist, and puffy breeches with red tights and slippers. This was topped with a short wig of yellow hair, "streaming like a comet behind him" (plate 10).[22] The apparent intent was that Puck be a hobgoblin flash of English folklore, but such subtle cues seemed to have been lost on reviewers amid the other visual innovations.

Barker gave the fairies several pieces of stage business that would cut across any illusionistic expectations that audiences might retain. Oberon stood "unseen" at center stage with his arms crossed and Puck at his feet, watching the lovers' confusions, and it was left to the audience to imagine him invisible. After the sequence of the lovers' confusion was played on the forestage and Oberon had commanded Puck to overcast the night, Puck effected a scene change by motioning for the stage lights to dim and then bending down to raise the painted night forest curtain as it ascended.[23]

The mechanical golden fairies moved to old English folk tunes, in what was surely the most amazing juxtaposition of Barker's eclectic cultural borrowings. Mendelssohn was completely abandoned, together with all other familiar accretions, such as the nineteenth-century songs by Thomas Simpson Cooke and Charles Edward Horne, which had been heard as recently as Tree's revival. The English folk music was arranged by Cecil Sharp. Two trumpet fanfares, two minutes apart, replaced Mendelssohn's overture. Titania's call for "a roundel and a fairy song" (2.2.1) was answered by an English round, which led into selected folk melodies that fit the lullaby lyrics. "Greensleeves" was used for the bergamask dance, heretofore omitted, and the dance was an authentic folk dance known as the Wryesdale dance. For the fairy finale, Mendelssohn's mincing violins were replaced by several folk-dance tunes, including "Sellenger's Round."[24] (All the musical accompaniment was played offstage.) The *Times* suggested Stravinksy's music would have been more approriate under the circumstances.[25]

FIGURE 30. Titania asleep in the forest, with her fairy guard, Barker's production, 1914. This controversial forest consisted of a green knoll, backed by painted silk draperies in greens, blues, and purples. Private collection.

The single setting that caused most comment was the forest scene in which Titania is sung to sleep (2.2), for which a full-stage, literal forest was usual (fig. 30). The cottage curtain rose to expose a green knoll, backed by silken draperies painted in greens, blues, and purples. Above its center was a large wreath of grapes, from within which descended a slender tent of green diaphanous curtains for Titania's bower. Lighted from above by colored electric bulbs, these blew in the breeze. In 1914, this sophisticated "bank where the wild thyme blows" was suggestion with a vengeance.

Barker's final act opened on a severe, modernistic, black-and-white palace for Theseus (figs. 31 and 32), a vision of the age of Pericles touched by futurism.[26] Behind the white forestage, seven steps rose to a platform backed by seven staggered white pillars, striped in silver and black, backed by black curtains on which hung symmetrically placed stars. A wave motif ran along the bottom of the pil-

FIGURE 31. Theseus's palace and the performance of *Pyramus and Thisbe*, Barker's production, 1914. *Sketch*, 25 February 1914.

lars and the hems of the attendant's white costumes. Was this Minoan or Art Nouveau, reviewers wondered. On the forestage, the court reclined, Roman-style, on green-cushioned silver couches to watch *Pyramus and Thisbe*, played on the upper platform. With the court's departure, the golden fairies entered and, in a somewhat mechanized blessing dance, wove in and out of the seven pillars, dropping rose petals, then disappearing one by one as the lights dimmed (fig. 32). The curtain fell, and Puck gave his epilogue on the forestage, exiting on a final trumpet note.

When the production came to Manhattan in 1915, Barker explained to an interviewer his challenge to conventional pictorialism by saying, "What is really needed is a great white box. That's what our theatre really is."[27] Peter Brook probably knew nothing of Barker's comment, but Brook effectively restated that challenge to illusionistic theatre a half century later with Sally Jacobs's white box setting for his 1970 production of the play (plate 16).

In comparison to the scenery and costumes, Barker's actors received very little critical attention. They reportedly spoke relatively rapidly in all three of the Savoy Shakespeare productions and declaimed less than was customary. At the same time, they lacked any consistent, sure, alternative style, seeming, said one critic, to be "embarrassed by the very loveliness of the lines they have to speak."[28] Lillah McCarthy, then Barker's wife, was praised for her amusingly in-

FIGURE 32. Final scene of the fairy blessing of Theseus's palace, Barker's production, 1914. *Sketch*, 25 February 1914.

congruous dignity as Helena, and Laura Cowie's Hermia was singled out as "markedly modern" in a blue-green Greek-style dress, flecked with stars, which might have been worn on the street in 1914.[29] Barker's promptbook shows comic byplay for the young lovers' quarrels that gently mocked their ardor.[30] He cast Dennis Neilson-Terry in the role of Oberon, only the second time in seventy-four years that a male had played the role. (Neilson-Terry's mother, Julia, had played the role in Tree's 1900 production.)[31] The new masculinity of Oberon apparently made no mark, perhaps because of the golden encasements of the fairies, and reviewers were silent about any new sexual dimension in the fairy kingdom. Calthrop's Puck was a sharp departure from the custom of perky female Pucks, but he was too eccentric for critic William Archer and others.[32] Archer also found the intelligent, mercurial Nigel Playfair miscast as Bottom. Some reviewers thought the mechanicals relatively free of traditional business, but the reviews and promptbooks offer evidence of much that was traditional, as Trevor Griffiths has noted, from the fussy Quince to the timorous Starveling. The rose petals dropped by the fairies in Barker's ending seem a memory of Benson's last act.[33] One innovation went unnoticed by critics. Helena is referred to as "old Nedar's Helena" by Egeus (4.1.129), but Nedar (presumably Helena's father) never appears in the play. Barker had him present, silently, in the final court scene, a symmetrical counterpart to Egeus.

The production provoked a great critical debate on both sides of the Atlantic. Individual critics were often very mixed in their responses, as they tried to admire, but had difficulty assenting to, the sophisticated new visual language. A. B. Walkley, the *Times* critic who was startled by, and skeptical of, the golden fairies as Cambodian idols, also wrote fondly: "The mind goes back to the golden fairies, and one's memories of this production must always be golden memories."[34] Desmond McCarthy, a friend of Barker's, admitted going twice to adjust his sensibilities to the new vocabulary and recommended that his readers do likewise. McCarthy's final verdict that the fairies were "the most convincing fairies yet seen upon the stage" is not very convincing, for he still expressed doubts that they were best "for making the peculiar poetry of Shakespeare's fairies felt." He also thought the Savoy scenery got as much attention as the scenery ever had at Tree's His Majesty's.[35] The ten-year-old John Gielgud, who went to see his cousin, Dennis Neilson-Terry, as Oberon, remembered audiences being "slightly bewildered."[36] John Palmer of the London *Saturday Review*, usually a supporter of Barker, titled his review, "Shakespeare slaughtered to make an intellectual and post-Impressionist holiday." Palmer praised the ingenious scenery but concluded that the production, "though it be almost everything by turns, and nothing long, is never Shakespeare's 'Dream.'" He found the new vocabulary inconsistent, the production "more like a battlefield than a collaboration," with the metallic fairies out of place in Wilkinson's delicate settings, as was the "red puppet-box Puck."[37] Gordon Crosse remembered that Barker's departures from convention "stuck in some throats, including mine," but said these "did not seriously detract from our admiration for his achievement as a whole."[38] The *Nation*'s critic seemed to compliment "a new fairy convention" but then added: "Some blasting Nihilistic force of futurism has gone rioting among the elves. . . . The politics of fairyland are evidently an elaborate and complicated business."[39]

One looks in vain for evidence of any heartfelt surrender to the production. Palmer wrote of Barker's "perfect sanity" and the "sunlight" of an intelligence that cast no moonlight over the play. The *Athenaeum* detected an air of solemnity and earnestness about the work. William Archer, Barker's friend and frequent supporter, wrote him privately to say that "in attaining distinction you miss something of delightfulness."[40] An American critic made the cogent observation that Barker's production seemed to be "a world arbitrarily made."[41] Perhaps no one else in these years could have been as resourceful as Barker in the attempt at a new theatrical vocabulary for Shakespeare. The vision does seem to have been more of Apollo than Dionysus, as G. Wilson Knight once observed of Barker's theatre work in general, a case of a sophisticated intellect trying to do the work of an impassioned imagination.[42]

Unquestionably, the basic difficulty for audiences was seeing Shakespeare by the light of the new scenic language. This emerges even more clearly from the visit of Barker's *A Midsummer Night's Dream* to New York. In repertory with other plays that he directed for over two months, *A Midsummer Night's Dream* played only twenty-two times, half of these being matinee performances. Two of the other plays, which were also in the new stagecraft mode — Anatole France's *The Man Who Married a Dumb Wife*, designed by the American Robert Edmond Jones, and George Bernard Shaw's *Androcles and the Lion*, designed by Albert Rothenstein — together ran seventy-seven performances.[43] For two senior American critics, Shakespeare in the new scenic vocabulary was almost unholy. George C. D. Odell closed his postwar *Shakespeare from Betterton to Irving* by laying a wreath on Tree's tomb and giving a blistering sermon on Barker's *A Midsummer Night's Dream*. "I hope," he wrote, "that this silly and vulgar way of presenting Shakespeare died with all other vain, frivolous, unsimple things burnt up in the great war-conflagration." William Winter described the fairies as animated "steam radiators" and spent twenty-three pages of his *Shakespeare on the Stage* decrying Barker's "desecration" of the play.[44] For Odell and Winter, Barker's visual world clearly spoke much louder than any of his attentions to the text. That these two men could feel so disenfranchised reminds us that Barker's new scenic vocabulary had been appropriated from a sophisticated, cosmopolitan world of contemporary high art, and this for a fond play long accessible in popular, sentimental vocabulary.

Not long after this production of *A Midsummer Night's Dream*, Barker stopped directing. His self-exile from directing puzzled and dismayed his followers. William Bridges-Adams mourned the loss in his *Lost Leader* (1954), and Barker's biographer, C. B. Purdom, intently probed all possible reasons.[45] After the war, Barker campaigned for a national theatre and immersed himself in the writing of the prefaces for the illustrated collector's edition of the plays published by Ernest Benn in 1924. In them, he deals with the internal theatrical dynamics of the plays, advocates a departure from the practices of the illusionistic theatre, and offers general, suggestive directorial advice. Perhaps, as Dennis Kennedy suggests, Barker saw the prefaces as a continuation of his theatre work.[46] But the discourse of the prefaces and the so-called Player's edition reveal a different story. The front matter of each volume carefully explained that the texts were "printed literatum," although with modern "s's," and stressed that they were "illustrated by artists interested in the modern stage, whose object has been to aid in creating for the reader the atmosphere of an ideal dramatic representation." In short, in this large, handsome, limited edition of the plays and in Barker's prefaces, true texts and ideal productions are dreamed of, removed from actual theatrical production and the often complex cultural transactions it entails. Barker had been surprised and disappointed by the controversial reception of his Shakespearean productions. In his 1924 preface to *A Midsummer Night's Dream*, he never mentions his own 1914 production. He allows that the modern theatre must employ staging conventions that "yield spontaneous enjoyment" and observes that directors have the responsibility of tastefully discerning which conventions "have aesthetic validity and which have none." [47] While he acknowledges theatrical "conventions," the expectation is that theatrical representation should seek only Shakespeare's effects, without significant mediation: "Let the producer first bring his work to completion on Shakespeare's own terms." [48]

Barker's immediate successors were deeply influenced by his stress upon Shakespeare's poetry, the swifter delivery of the language, and the swifter movement of the play through the use of simplified scenery. His prefaces influenced the next two generations of directors. In 1957, when Henry Hewes, theatre critic for the *Saturday Review of Literature*, asked twenty-one Shakespearean directors which readings had been the most valuable to their work, the most frequently mentioned were Barker's prefaces. [49]

Barker's production was not the end of moonlight and Mendelssohn for *A Midsummer Night's Dream*. In the years after World War I in England and America, there were two general trends for staging the play: productions in the Victorian pictorial tradition and those touched by modernism in general in their less literal but very neoromantic theatrical vocabularies.

Heavily in the Victorian vein was Basil Dean's staging of the play at Christmas in 1924 at Drury Lane. As manager, his declared aim was to sustain Tree's policies "brought up to date." [50] Theseus's palace was "a garish affair like Alma-Tadema at his best — or worst," said critic James Agate. [51] Designer George Harris imported special electrical equipment to provide a new technological version of the prolonged sunrise in the forest over the sleeping lovers. In the last act, hydraulic lifts delivered dozens of child fairies up to levels behind enormous Grecian pillars, stuttering to a stop too soon and leaving the fairies to scramble their way over the edge and into the Mendelssohn dance finale. It was on this occasion that critic Herbert Farjeon wrote the inevitable line, "I can't see the dream for the trees"; he reprinted the omitted "forgeries of jealousy" speech in his review. [52] When Sydney Carroll began the Open Air Theatre in Regent's

Park in 1933, he did so with *A Midsummer Night's Dream*. Robert Atkins staged it and continued to do so, almost annually, throughout the 1950s. In the leafy, natural setting, Victorian traditions held, including Mendelssohn's music and the casting of women in the role of Oberon, especially during the years of World War II, when few men were available. Atkins in the role of Bottom was described as "a majestic Bottom-Pyramus, with a voice like a slow, rich cascade of treacle."[53] Atkins's companies, too, were nurseries for upcoming young actors, among them Francis L. Sullivan, who played Bottom, and Jessica Tandy, Fay Compton, and Elsa Lanchester, all of whom played Titania.

A Midsummer Night's Dream was not among the scenically radical productions of Terence Gray at Cambridge in the late 1920s, influenced by Vsevolod Meyerhold, nor among those of Theodore Kommisarzhevsky at Stratford in the 1930s, influenced by Russian constructivism. The first new staging strategy for this play after Barker was essentially neoromantic, placing it within the world of an Elizabethan or Jacobean court, playing on the associations of the play with a court wedding and Elizabeth I. This was not an attempt at Poel's bare-boards replica of an Elizabethan theatre. Nor was it Patrick Kirwan's literal Elizabethanism out at Stratford, where W. R. Beverley's act drop depicted a state procession of Elizabeth through Southwark to the Globe, like a frame from a D. W. Griffith film.[54] This was a modernist, suggestive, less literal dream of an eternal golden world. In retrospect, it seems an appropriate visual analogue to the modernist theological investment in Shakespeare's text.

This modernist rendering of the play as an Elizabethan or Jacobean court wedding masque begins with director Harcourt Williams's staging at the Old Vic in 1929. Williams, a Barker protégé, was pledged to the cause of restoring Shakespeare's poetry and gave copies of Barker's preface to the play to his company during rehearsals.[55] In his cast, he had John Gielgud as Oberon to sing the poetry. Gielgud, too, had been influenced by Barker.

Williams later said that his vision was inspired by a John Masefield book, probably *William Shakespeare* (1911), in which the Edwardian poet celebrates Shakespeare's Englishness.[56] "Shakespeare's heart always turned for quiet happiness to the country where he lived as a boy," begins the essay on *A Midsummer Night's Dream*. The theory that Shakespeare had composed the play for a court wedding at which Elizabeth was present had new currency in these years.[57] Williams also had bad memories of Augustin Daly's heavy barge and of too much Mendelssohn from his years acting with Benson's company.

Under the Old Vic's founder, Lilian Baylis, Williams had only about twenty pounds per production with which to conjure scenery. Gielgud was costly, contracted at twenty pounds per week.[58] But designer Paul Smyth evoked images of Kenilworth for Theseus's palace and drew on Paolo Veronese's paintings for the court lovers' costumes (which also were serving in a current Sadler's Wells opera). He imitated Inigo Jones's classically inspired designs for the fairy costumes, although Puck (Leslie French) was all in red — a memory of Barker's production. For the forest setting, Williams followed a suggestion of Edward Gordon Craig's son, using a horseshoe-shaped rostrum upstage, along which Puck could "fly." Behind it, bunched curtains simulated tree trunks, and Smyth provided a painted forest drop with a silver sky. In the forest there was a steep flight of steps, which Hermia and Helena clambered up in their elaborate farthingales. Audiences were not yet accustomed to symbolist forests with flights of steps in them, however.[59] James Agate longed for a Hawes Craven wood (Craven had painted for Sir Henry Irving and Tree) and campaigned for a return to Mendelssohn's score, instead of the "sober, four-square Christmas carols" arranged by Cecil Sharp that Williams had brought over from Barker's 1914 production. Baylis and some of the Old Vic company thought Williams had gone too far, but Agate, Ivor Brown, and other critics granted that the Elizabethan motif had at least rid the play of rabbits and fairies in tulle.[60] Williams also achieved his goal of getting rid of the traditional, slow, deliberate intoning of Shakespeare's verse. He stressed swift delivery, as well as swift changes of scenes; critics still were unaccustomed to both. His text was the Folio and was little altered.[61] Gielgud delivered Oberon's poetry with the patrician elegance that would become his trademark. By 1929, he was gaining the vocal command he wanted: "It gave me a wonderful sense of power that I was beginning to control the lovely language, which at rehearsals moved me so much that tears would spring to my eyes."[62] Creating a canticle of elegantly spoken language, and with the complete sexual neutrality thought appropriate for Shakespeare's fairy king, Gielgud offered an aloof and otherwordly Oberon.

William Bridges-Adams, a Barker disciple, often staged *A Midsummer Night's Dream* during his fifteen-year career at Stratford-upon-Avon. Stratford-upon-Avon in these years had become, thanks to the automobile, a point of summer pilgrimage for many visitors. Here, at his birthplace in the heart of Warwickshire, Shakespeare was fully institutionalized. By the 1920s, the ambitions of the theatre's board, especially its chairman, Archibald Flower, and Bridges-Adams, were international. A royal charter was secured in 1925. The destruction by fire of the old theatre was followed by the building of the present one in 1932. The campaign for the funds was not only national; a large influx came from wealthy Americans under the name of the American Shakespeare Foundation (many

Americans were already among Stratford's tourists).[63] The successful campaign assured Stratford's greater international visibility. Although not nationally subsidized, the Stratford theatre was the nearest thing to the English national theatre of which Barker and Archer had dreamed, notwithstanding the controversy that flamed around its new modernist theatre, designed by Elizabeth Scott.[64]

Bridges-Adams had been a stage manager for William Poel, but like Barker, he had rejected Poel's purism, calling it Elizabethan "Methodism." He began by offering nearly uncut texts, for which Ben Greet nicknamed him "Una-Bridges-Adams."[65] This purity, too, he later relinquished, as his own instincts prevailed. His promptbooks for *A Midsummer Night's Dream* show many interlinear cuttings, including Lysander's "So quick bright things come to confusion" (1.1.149).[66] He efficiently alternated fairly conventional full-stage sets with short scenes played in front of traverse curtains, which allowed swifter play. A critic of Bridges-Adams's 1921 production of *A Midsummer Night's Dream* wrote, "What I fear he will never do is give the world a beautiful production."[67] As Sally Beauman has shown, Bridges-Adams could not do much innovating at first under the constraints of the tight budget imposed by Flower and the assembly-line summer seasons in which a production had to be mounted in five days — four to six productions in six weeks. Little could be done under such circumstances to retrain actors or shed trite traditions.[68]

In 1932, for the opening season of the new theatre, Bridges-Adams teamed with Norman Wilkinson (Barker's designer) to create a production that critics did find scenically beautiful, both in the premiere and in later revivals.[69] Bridges-Adams wanted to strike the note of a joyful Elizabethan epithalamium. With a light hand, Wilkinson evoked an Elizabethan court world for the palace scenes. The lights came up on a curtain-in-folds act drop, upon which was sketched the exterior of a Palladian English mansion, modeled on nearby Charlecote Hall. This rose to disclose the interior of a great hall, with a fanciful, airy, three-arched Tudor screen (fig. 33). The court wore rich Elizabethan costumes in dove gray and white, with the women in pannier skirts and Hippolyta and Theseus in red or red-lined capes (fig. 34). The mechanicals met in 1.2 as usual in Peter Quince's shop (fig. 35). The fairies were descendants of the Barker-Wilkinson creations of 1914, somewhat tempered: "a silver-and-blue troupe of mannikins, whose keynote was unearthiness, quaint little people with grey faces, witches' hats, spangled garments, [and] chattering tongues, who served a dusky red-lipped queen."[70] Wilkinson's forest was now no Art Nouveau abstraction, but a neoromantic restatement of the wood. A dark backdrop of whimsically styled trees, as if taken from a children's book illustration, framed a knoll on which

FIGURE 33. Interior of Theseus's palace, modeled on Charlecote Hall, William Bridges-Adams's production, Shakespeare Memorial Theatre, Stratford-upon-Avon, 1932. Designed by Norman Wilkinson. Shakespeare Centre Library.

stood a hollow oak (fig. 36). Here Oberon was concealed and Titania slept; the fairies, various-sized children, mimed pulling the rolling "Duke's oak" from one side of the stage to the other, with an ineptness that annoyed even the home-town reviewer.[71] Bridges-Adams's inventive, atmospheric lighting used specially focused instruments to pick out Titania or Bottom against the dark background, giving them a luminous presence. In all, the forest sequence was "a moonlight nocturne," as one reviewer wrote, albeit a modernized recapitulation of the nineteenth-century romantic vision. Mendelssohn's score still accompanied it. The production almost was successful enough to redeem the season and subdue the criticism of the new Shakespeare Memorial Theatre as a "brickyard slab."

FIGURE 34. Theseus's palace, 5.1. Costumes and sets by Norman Wilkinson for the 1932 Bridges-Adams production used again here in 1937 at Stratford-upon-Avon. Left to right: Valerie Tudor, Hermia; Paul Stephenson, Lysander; Joyce Bland, Helena; Patrick Crean, Demetrius; C. Rivers Gadsby, Philostrate; Clement McCallin, Theseus; Mary Hignett, Hippolyta. Shakespeare Centre Library.

Wilkinson's settings and costumes continued to be used in Stratford revivals of the play as late as 1944.[72]

In England in these years, old and new styles of acting were sometimes juxtaposed. A new generation of actors was coming into its own, more comfortable with a swifter delivery of the language and sometimes bringing new dimensions to the characters. In Bridges-Adams's earlier Stratford productions, Baliol Holloway played Bottom, very probably in an older, demonstrative style, with the relatively traditional, slow delivery (notwithstanding the fact that he had played Theseus under Barker in 1914). When Holloway joined Williams's cast later at the Old Vic, after Ralph Richardson had played the role, the company was shocked at Holloway's slow pace and older style of delivery.[73] (Holloway played Bottom at Stratford as late as 1937.) At the Old Vic, the actors of a comparatively modern sensibility in Williams's production included Margaret Webster

FIGURE 35. Quince's workshop, designed by Norman Wilkinson for the 1932 Bridges-Adams production, used again here in 1937 at Stratford-upon-Avon. Left to right: Stanley Howlett, Snug; Randle Ayrton, Quince; Baliol Holloway, Bottom; Dennis Roberts, Snout; Gerald Kay Souper, Starveling; Richard Blatchely, Flute. Shakespeare Centre Library.

as Hermia, Leslie French as Puck, Gielgud as Oberon, and Martita Hunt as Helena. (Hunt was the Juliet, Portia, and Rosalind of these years.) The young Ralph Richardson was Bottom in Bridges-Adams's 1931 revival, fully engrossed with Master Mustardseed. Richardson shed the usual ass's head for a suggestive donkey's muzzle on his chin and a pair of ears. (He played the role again in the Tyrone Guthrie production of 1937.) Basil Dean's heavily Victorian production had a remarkably fresh cast that included Hay Petrie as a satyrlike Puck of infectious animal spirits, young Edith Evans as a richly comic Helena, Gwen Ffrangçon Davies as a remote, sadly smiling Titania, Frank Cellier as Quince, H. O. Nicholson as Starveling, and Miles Malleson as Snout.[74]

In England between the wars, the play remained, in all, a ubiquitous, popular favorite, with deep cultural associations. In these years, Sean O'Casey saw the boys at Sloane School perform the play under their teacher-director, Guy Boas. O'Casey was wholly captivated and thought it worth more attention than the

FIGURE 36. Forest setting by Norman Wilkinson for the 1932 Bridges-Adams production. Lighting by Bridges-Adams. Dorothy Francis as Titania and Roy Byford as Bottom. Shakespeare Centre Library.

capitalist London papers had given it. The boys, ranging from nine to nineteen years of age,

> caught hold of Shakespeare's skirts with the same assurance that children once caught hold of the skirts of Christ. Shakespeare's mighty name didn't frighten them. . . . They shamed the strutting professionals by giving a simple, high-minded, and graceful performance, grandly different from most of those which change Shakespeare's majesty and charm into the puffing pomp of a Lord Mayor's Show. If there be a God, and if Shakespeare be in Heaven, then God send him down to see the play performed by the London lads of Sloane School standing in Hortensia Road in the Borough of Chelsea.[75]

Chapter eight

THE *DREAM* OF MODERNISM

THE SACRED AND THE SECULAR

Oberon: How now, mad spirit?
  What nightrule now about this haunted grove?

The modernist and neoromantic variations on *A Midsummer Night's Dream* continue throughout the era between the two world wars. The prolific Austrian director Max Reinhardt staged the play in some thirteen variations between 1905 and 1934, and, with William Dieterle, directed the Warner Brothers film in 1935. In these productions, Reinhardt's vision remained fundamentally neoromantic, although, with the rise of Hitler, darker shadows fall across his last versions, including the film. In Hitler's Germany, a Nazi campaign all but erased the work and Jewish name of Felix Mendelssohn and sought to replace his score for the play with one by an Aryan composer. In New York City in the swing era, there was the promise, unfulfilled, of a uniquely American conception in *Swingin' the Dream*, with its jazz score and African American cast. In England, in the years before and following World War II, the Old Vic offered reiterations of the Victorian iconography, now half nostalgia, half metaphor. The neoromantic vocabulary for the play was extended still further by George Balanchine's ballet in 1962, inspired by Mendelssohn's score. The era of neoromantic and modernist variations on the play could be said to have ended with the elegantly cool twelve-tone opera of Benjamin Britten in 1960.

Of the twenty-two plays of Shakespeare that Reinhardt staged, *A Midsummer Night's Dream* was, by any account, the favorite and the hallmark of the Austrian director's career. Various productions of the play were in the repertoire of Reinhardt's Neues Theater or Deutsches Theater in Berlin during every season from 1905 to 1919; during those seasons, the play was performed 587 times. New or touring productions of the play directed by Reinhardt played in western European cities from London to Vienna and Stockholm to Florence. American audiences in six major cities saw Reinhardt productions of the play between 1927 and 1934.[1]

Reinhardt is, of course, a major reference point in any discussion of the development of the modernist theatre director. He became known as a magician of elaborate spectacle and a virtuoso of theatrical style. It is generally agreed that he established eclecticism as the norm for modern directing, selecting a scenic style or venue considered suitable for each play.[2] He directed a wide variety of classical and modern works, from Euripides through Calderón de la Barca to Strindberg and Pirandello. He staged Ibsen's *Ghosts* in the intimate Kammerspiele Theatre, which he constructed in the Deutsches Theater complex, and Hugo von Hofmannsthal's adaptation of the medieval *Everyman* in Salzburg's cathedral square. For his staging of *The Miracle*, a wordless, full-length religious pageant, he had the interiors of theatres in London and New York elaborately redecorated to resemble medieval cathedrals. During the making of the film of *A Midsummer Night's Dream*, the Hollywood movie colony came to refer to him as "Maximum Maxie."[3] Reinhardt was also known, especially to German-speaking audiences, for the strength of his casts, which over the years included Alexander Moissi, Paul Wegener, Albert Basserman, Else Heims, Helen Thimig, Max Pallenberg, Oscar Homolka, and Emil Jannings.

Reinhardt's successes with Shakespeare, together with his other achievements in his Berlin theatres, made him a popular figure in the Wilhelmine era. He was on the board of directors of Berlin's prestigious *Deutsche Gesellschaft*, an elite association that supported the Wilhelmine government. During the war years, as his son has pointed out, the foreign ministry sent Reinhardt and his company "as cultural propagandists to all neutral countries."[4]

In his Shakespearean productions, he was visually eclectic. Their scenic designs ranged within one three-year period from Gustav Knina's detailed neoromantic forest for *A Midsummer Night's Dream* (1905) to the radically modernist designs by Carl Czeschka for *King Lear* (1908). But modernist assumptions always prevailed; each production was to give direct access to the stable, universal meanings of the text. In addition, Reinhardt may be said to have been something of a populist at heart, his instincts and appetites in marked contrast with Barker's intellectual idealism. Reinhardt envisioned the theatre as a festive event, popularly accessible. A high degree of theatrical sophistication often sits side-by-side with showmanship and sentimentality in his productions, as is the case in his productions of *A Midsummer Night's Dream*.

His first production of the play opened at Berlin's Neues Theatre am Schiff-bauerdamm on 31 January 1905, when he was just emerging from nine years as an actor in the naturalistic productions of Otto Brahm. Hailed as a welcome neoromantic reaction to German naturalism, it launched his directing career, and Reinhardt was seen as the harbinger of a new era for German theatre. Respectful of the *tranche de vie* school though he was, Reinhardt had grown weary of its grim production style: "In those Naturalistic performances, something was almost always eaten on stage, usually dumplings and sauerkraut."[5] As early as 1901, Reinhardt was already articulate in his vision of a theatre "which gives people pleasure again. . . . I feel that people have had enough of always encountering their own misery in the theatre, that what they long for are brighter colors and an intensification of life. . . . I would like to show life from another side . . . one equally true and authentic in its serenity, filled with color and light."[6] For this theatre he wanted a small ensemble of the best actors. "I believe in a theatre which belongs to actors. The purely literary aspect should no longer be the sole deciding factor. That was the case because the authors dominated the theatre; I am an actor, I feel with actors, and for me the actor is the natural center of the theatre." To be sure, the classics, especially Shakespeare, were to be the center of the repertoire, but "one must stage the classics in a new way," Reinhardt insisted, "as if they were written by playwrights of today, as if their works were expressions of life today. One has to look at them with new eyes, approach them with the same fresh and carefree manner which one would bring to new works; one has to understand them from a present-day point of view." With such productions of the classics, the theatre would "once again become festive, which is its proper destiny. Theatre is richness and abundance."[7]

In his second season at the Neues Theater am Schiffbauerdamm (later the home of Brecht's Berliner Ensemble), he installed a revolving stage (recently developed in Germany by Karl Lautenschläger in the Munich Residenztheater and in use in Japanese Kabuki theatre since the eighteenth century). He also installed a fixed cyclorama and a new lighting system. "*Light* is the main thing! So: 'More light,'" he wrote in instructions to Berthold Held about renovations of the Neues Theater.[8]

He first made use of these innovations in his 1905 production of *A Midsummer Night's Dream*. It featured a revolving, shadowy, three-dimensional forest,

FIGURE 37. Forest scene on revolving stage for Max Reinhardt's production at the Deutsches Theater, Berlin, 1913. Setting by Ernst Stern. Reinhardt also had used a revolving setting for his first production of the play in 1905. Max Reinhardt-Forschungstätte, Salzburg.

created by set and lighting designer Gustav Knina, which was the wonder of the production for critics. The scene changes in the forest seemed to take the lovers and the fairies through the three-dimensional woodland, providing different views of giant trees, grassy inclines, winding paths, grottos, and a lake. Reinhardt's *Regiebuch* called for tall trees: "The tops begin high up, so that the elves appear very small. The tree-trunks must be as thick as possible. The roof of leaves is high up."[9] (Figure 37 shows a later version of a revolving set for Reinhardt by Ernst Stern.) "In the beginning was the wood," wrote Heinz Herald. For the whole play, "it is its nurse, its native soil; from it everything flows."[10] The fairies were costumed as woodsy elves of all shapes and sizes, with green hair and tights in colors of lilac, violet, greens, and blues; a light covering of iridescent gauzes was used to try to render them all somewhat less material. Some, played by children, were fitted with small quilted wings. Among Oberon's train were creatures out of German folk traditions: "trolls, dwarfs, gnomes, and pixies."[11] The operative term for the fairies throughout his *Regiebuch* is always *die elfen*, and overall, Reinhardt's wood belonged to Teutonic elves and Grimm's fairy tales rather than to fey creatures in Victorian tutus. The forest was constantly alive with their comings and goings: "It breathes, it is alive," wrote Herald; "their motion is music, like their speech."[12] Judging from the critics and the *Regiebuch*, a spirit of playfulness prevailed. The *Regiebuch* instructs: "Everything is alive [*lebendig*]. Everything is moving. Everyone skips, tumbles, jumps, runs and dances."[13] The fairies flew in and hovered in a silver cloud above Puck, who lay in the grass. Elves whispered and whistled from hiding places; they tickled the feet and noses of the sleeping lovers. Puffs of smoke blossomed out of the ground. At one point Titania hovered above the lake, and her fairies danced around her below. The promptbook calls frequently for the *Flügmaschine* and *Glüwürmchen*. The music here, as in all of Reinhardt's productions of the play, was Mendelssohn's. Simon Williams suggests that the playfulness extended to the humans; Theseus's ban on Hermia's love for Lysander was delivered in a jesting tone, as if it might not be inviolable.[14]

Oberon, played by Alexander Moissi (Reinhardt's Hamlet), was a central presence, a figure out of a Black Forest fairy tale. The *Regiebuch* hints at one point that he might make his first entrance into the moonlit wood riding a white stag with large antlers; the impression was to be mythic.[15] He did wear a lighted crown and, after the entrance, made his way down through the dark wood cautiously into the light. In some later Reinhardt productions, the Oberons wear a rather imposing rack of antlers; in the film, Oberon (Victor Jory) wears a crown of silver and antlerlike twigs and rides a black horse. Hugo von Hofmannsthal remembered Moissi: "As the Triton's horn captures the sound of the sea, so in him was the voice of the lovers. In his mind was . . . the sea. He was the whole wood."[16] The Puck of Gertrude Eysoldt was an earthy forest creature, broad faced and heavy hipped, with a suggestion of the satyr in her furry tights and furry feet, the animal skin around her shoulders, and the berries in her hair. This was a sharp break from English and German traditions of nimble, petite Pucks, but Siegfried Jacobsohn found her irritating, her humor forced.[17]

Clearly, Reinhardt orchestrated the forest world to such an extent that it became a text in itself, more of a presence than it had ever been in the painted scenic worlds of his predecessors. All the sources, together with the few surviving photographs of the production, suggest a sophisticated but very literal illusionism.[18] Looking back on the 1905 staging ten years later, Reinhardt himself was afraid that he had followed the path of the Duke of Saxe-Meiningen so far in creating visual illusion that "people came to look at the real trees on the stage; that . . . impressed them more than the art we were presenting."[19]

By 1925, at least one theatre critic was looking back on the 1905 staging as rather orthodox illusionism.[20] But at the time, Reinhardt's departure from conventional pictorialism was sufficient that many astute observers were sure they had found poetry in it. Journalist Maximilian Harden, known for his critical eye, wrote that the moss carpet and glowworms could have been seen at Tree's theatre or at Berlin's Hof Theater a few years before, but "not to these things was [Reinhardt's] success due; it would have come even without make-believe trees." Harden continued, "What I saw were childish things with a child's laughing joy." For him, "Never had *A Midsummer Night's Dream* been staged less pompously."[21] Another observer thought "the whole representation was not yet symbolic, but the mood was caught, and the public found itself transplanted, as if by a magician's wand, underneath the cool shadows of gigantic trees, and it opened eyes and hearts to receive the poet's message."[22]

The visible turning of the three-dimensional forest may have tempered the illusionism, allowing for an awareness of artifice, as Michael Patterson has suggested.[23] The lighting and sound, too, were major factors in creating both the forest atmosphere and allowing a sense of the poetic. In the first forest scene, the moon shone through scrims which were then raised as the lights were brought up gradually, revealing the scene. Moonlight fell from the open sky around the treetops (Reinhardt had done away with borders), through the leaves, mottling the forest floor.[24] Jacobsohn described the wood as a spiritual realm, "where moonlight shimmered, and the morning light dazzled. In the distance, terrestrial voices were heard. Here and there a glow-worm shone. Leaves rustled, and twigs cracked."[25] Scenes in the wood were lit from various directions, including offstage; the mechanicals came to Quince's cottage through the woods at night by lantern light, and once inside, a spotlight from the prompter's box threw their shadows on the walls of the hut. The final act opened with pageantry that recalls Tieck and Mendelssohn. Theseus and Hippolyta entered the palace in a torchlight procession with fifty-four servants, soldiers, and men and women of the court.[26] Harden noted that Reinhardt permitted "a corner of the starlit sky to look down upon the ample scene of wedding bliss and elfin pretense . . . this interplay of elemental spirits must not be mewed up, locking Nature out; . . . Nature here is paramount . . . those who embraced each other here in passionate dances must remain within the realism of Nature and must not be separated from her by solid walls."[27] Rudolf Kommer, later a Reinhardt publicist, wrote of the production as a whole:

It was a revelation. Berlin was jubilant. He had added not a word, he had not cut a line. And yet, it seemed a new play entirely. Full of life, color, music and joy, it had a message that did away in one evening with all the voluptuous pessimism and sordidness of the preceding fifteen or twenty years of Naturalism. . . . It inaugurated a new period in German literature; it opened the way for the neo-romanticists.[28]

The critics' experience, then, was that the staging allowed some space for the play of spectatorial imagination, an experience especially understandable in the context of naturalism and Victorian picture-book Shakespeare. Reinhardt's forest remained a romantic, reassuring world to be sure, where both nature and the supernatural were benevolent and intertwined and real fairies lay just behind the tall grass. Nothing dark prevailed here; the ambience was pleasantly seductive, designed to win the surrender of the senses. Reinhardt put a modified version of his 1905 production into the repertoire at the Deutsches Theater the next year, the first year of his management of the theatre that had been Otto Brahm's.

His productions of the play thereafter were characteristically eclectic. Four years later, he staged the play with designs by Karl Walser that reflected the new aesthetic in which the impressionistic replaced the literal and illusionistic. On the shallow "relief" stage of George Fuch's small Künstlertheater in Munich (a stage that itself reflected German experiments with a less illusionistic stage for Shakespeare), Walser created a lighter-weight forest with four gaily rendered beech trees on a low mound and framed the simple setting with flowered borders and hangings that were self-consciously decorative.[29] In 1913, Reinhardt returned to his revolving wood in a new production designed by Ernst Stern that was part of a Shakespeare cycle at the Deutsches Theater. The scale was larger, but the trees were somewhat less literal (see fig. 37).[30] Reinhardt had staged *Hamlet* in this theatre on a quasi-Elizabethan stage in 1910, but he never experimented with *A Midsummer Night's Dream* in this mode. Nor did he mount it in the radical modernist manner of his *Winter's Tale* (1906) and *King Lear* (1908), whose sets by Emil Orlik and Carl Czeschka, respectively, were influenced by Edward Gordon Craig.[31]

In 1921, Reinhardt staged *A Midsummer Night's Dream* in the cavernous Grosses Schauspielhaus. The theatre had been remodeled in 1918 by Hans Poelzig out of the old Circus Schumann, where Reinhardt had staged, among other classics, Aeschylus' *Oresteia*, Sophocles' *Oedipus Rex*, and Shakespeare's *Julius Caesar*. Under a vast dome supported by pillars dripping with stalactites, a horseshoe of embanked seats ringed an orchestra that was connected to a proscenium stage.[32] Although it seated 3,500 people, it was sometimes known as "the theatre of the 5,000." Reinhardt's avowed intention with the Schumann and its remodeled successor was to bring the actor out from the scenery and into closer contact with the audience, as actors had once been on classical stages. Reinhardt also hoped ultimately to offer admission prices that would make this theatre a people's theatre, accessible to a wider audience.[33]

For *A Midsummer Night's Dream*, the large area of the horseshoe orchestra was covered with a carpet of grass, and the proscenium stage behind served either as the wood or palace. The fairies danced through the wood behind, choreographed by Eugenie Edouardova, solo dancer of the St. Petersburg Ballet. But in the large, high-ceilinged theatre, the accoustics swallowed any subtleties of language.[34] Berlin critics were at best kind, and at worst called Reinhardt a circus showman and notoriety seeker.[35] Few plays proved appropriate for the huge theatre, Reinhardt did not reach his wider public, and he eventually counted the Schauspielhaus experiment a failure.

Enthusiasm for Reinhardt's neoromantic work was waning in Berlin.[36] Not only had the Schaulspielhaus failed, but a new generation of political-minded theatre artists was emerging in Berlin, which included Erwin Piscator, Leopold Jessner, and Bertolt Brecht. Reinhardt returned to Austria in 1920, where he established the Salzburg Festival with his staging of Hofmannsthal's *Everyman*, and in 1923 he undertook the artistic directorship of the theatre in the Josefstadt in Vienna. He staged *A Midsummer Night's Dream* in this intimate red-and-gold theatre in 1925, using a setting of relative simplicity. Otto Niedermoser's set consisted of a black, fluted canopy hanging above a green carpet into which were woven huge white blossoms. Tapestries flanked the sides of the stage, twisted and turned into a semblance of towering trees.[37] Tree branches and leaves were painted on downstage scrims, imparting a misty quality to scenery and actors (shades of Samuel Phelps). Pools of light defined acting areas and picked out principal actors in sharp relief against the darker backgrounds. A young American designer, Ernest de Weerth, costumed Oberon, Titania, and the fairies in silvery gauze, laced with branches. Actors outfitted in foliage created trees or bushes.[38] Mendelssohn's score, played by an orchestra behind the scenes, was carefully synchronized with actions and lines.

Perhaps Reinhardt's boldest scenic choice for the play came with his 1927 staging in the Salzburg Festspielhaus, which seated three thousand people. He and his designer, Oscar Strnad, created an Austrian baroque world for the play, almost certainly influenced by Reinhardt's concurrent renovations of his own fairy-tale palace of Leopoldskron. The playing area was set within a large oval baroque frame, with two huge lanterns above. For the palace scenes, various steps and levels, decorated with candelabra, rose toward two twisting baroque columns that framed a large palace door (fig. 38). Through it the night sky could be seen in the final scene. Ernest de Weerth's costumes were derived from Tie-

FIGURE 38. Theseus's palace in the final scene of Max Reinhardt's production at the Salzburg Festival, 1927. Setting by Oscar Strnad, costumes by Ernest de Weerth after Tiepolo. Reinhardt staged variations of this production in Vienna and New York in that year. Max Reinhardt-Forschungstätte, Salzburg.

polo paintings and featured heavily draped, puff-sleeved gowns, which were textured and ornamented, heavy breastplates, and flowing capes. Theseus and Hippolyta wore fantastic sculpted helmets, whose several plumes rose three feet above their heads. The staging of the final scene could be taken for the finale of a baroque opera (fig. 38). The forest scenes were staged on levels surrounded by a starlit cyclorama, with chiaroscuro lighting. An additional frame of leaves and flowers enhanced the effect of a dreamworld. Puffs of smoke came out of the ground, as they had in 1905, and Oberon and Puck entered from a trap, Oberon wearing a tall plume and accompanied by six tree-root-like creatures. The critics' accounts stress the constant movement of actors through space, surprising appearances out of darkness, and the effectiveness of the forest atmosphere in general.[39]

Reinhardt brought a variation of this version to New York City in November 1927 (two years after *The Miracle*), along with seven other of his productions. It was the first staging of the play New Yorkers had seen since Barker's, and it was better received, which is somewhat surprising considering that the performance was in German and not very long after World War I.[40] The play, which ran for twenty-three performances, featured the best of Reinhardt's now internationally famous company: Alexander Moissi as Oberon, Lily Darvas as Titania, Vladimir Skoloff as Puck, Paul Hartmann as Theseus, the Thimig brothers, Hans and Hermann, as Lysander and Demetrius, and Otto Walberg as Bottom. De Weerth's costumes were used but not the Salzburg setting.

At the Century Theatre, Strnad provided a large circular platform sloping toward the audience and ringed with eight fluted columns. Semicircular runways descended from it on either side, and wide stairs rose up through its center, broken by several low landings. Backed with a cyclorama and carefully lit with area lighting, the unit structure served for both palace and forest.[41] Reinhardt's visual orchestration of the action across this setting impressed critics and probably helped the production transcend any language barrier. On the terraced set "that seems to scale the stars," the *Commonweal* critic wrote, "the gnomes of fairyland cavort, swing, run and dance, now leaping from rock to rock, now disappearing into mysterious caverns . . . , now clear in shafts of moonlight, now obscured by wreaths of fog, until one is completely swept into the realm of fantasy and woodland magic."[42] At the beginning of the play and again in the last act, Theseus and Hippolyta rose from the orchestra pit in a candlelight procession to Mendelssohn, played by an orchestra located high in the second balcony. No one seems to have asked precisely what it meant to have Theseus's court in high baroque costumes. Harald Kreutzberg (a sprite) and Tilly Losch (First Fairy), prima ballerina with the Vienna State Opera, danced two ballet numbers in mists. Sokoloff, Pan-like in pointed ears and animal skins, virtually danced the role of Puck, "clinging to the earth as if he were some small thing native to it," wrote a dance critic.[43]

Brooks Atkinson in the *New York Times* insisted that the production "was without excrescent tricks or florid embellishment" and attributed the atmosphere chiefly to the actors,[44] while Joseph Wood Krutch, writing in the *Nation*, admired the powers of actors who could hold their own amid the effects. Krutch had strong reservations about the aesthetic principles underlying the staging. Reinhardt seemed

to ask of the audience as little, and to give them as much as possible; and it is the essence of his method rather to stun the senses than appeal to the imagination. . . . Reinhardt is content with nothing less than a complete realization of every all-but-impossible suggestion of the text. The enchanted wood must actually be filled with incredibly magic lights and shadows; fairies, appearing from nowhere, must dance with an agility hitherto existing only in Shakespeare's imagination; and, in short, the whole poem must be translated into visual terms. In Reinhardt's hands the play, ceasing to be merely a play, becomes an elaborate, highly synthetic spectacle, a thing of swelling music, shifting lights, gorgeous pageantry.[45]

Overall, as this survey of his productions of the play between 1905 and 1927 makes clear, Reinhardt's neoromantic vision of it had not changed fundamentally, only the stylistic surfaces. A world war had been fought in Europe, but not in these woods. Any darkness in them was there by virtue of a pantheistic elementalism, perhaps derived out of German folk culture, from which the Oberon of Moissi and the Pucks of Eysoldt and Sokoloff seem to have come. There was nothing so primitive here that Mendelssohn's score could have been replaced by Igor Stravinsky's *Rite of Spring* (1913). Nor had the sexual readings of dreams by Reinhardt's Viennese contemporary Sigmund Freud yet unloosed any of the eroticism in the text in these productions. In retrospect, the development from the literal, three-dimensional, revolving forests to the impressionistic baroque architecture and the choreography of light, movement, and Mendelssohn can be seen as modulations of a neoromantic symbolism. In the 1927 staging, these elements are still signaling some mystical, unnamed center. In the appropriation of the baroque style, the surfaces are smoothed for a generalized evocation of the exotic (just as Barker orientalized his fairies), avoiding cultural specificity. The strategy is characteristic of the visual eclecticism of modernist theatre practice.

Reinhardt's lavish outdoor productions of *A Midsummer Night's Dream* in Florence (1933), Oxford (1934), and Hollywood (1935) are spectacular variations on his neoromantic vision.[46] But some remarkable, darker images emerge in them. Hitler came to power in Berlin on 30 January 1933, and the Jewish-born Reinhardt left the city within a few months, never to return.[47] Soon after, Reinhardt lost his Berlin theatre properties to the Nazis. As did others at the time, he apparently had thought that in Salzburg and Vienna his art might be insulated from the growing Nazi power, that the brownshirts might not prevail if the civilizing forces of German culture were sustained. Reinhardt resorted to attempts at compromise and propitiation (trying at one point to negotiate the preservation of his lavish Leopoldskron), but to no avail.[48] Over the next three years, Reinhardt often directed outside the German-speaking world, and, by 1937, he was living in exile in Hollywood.

In 1933, at the invitation of the Italian government, he directed the play for a May festival in Florence, staging it with an Italian cast on the terraced levels of the Boboli Gardens, with the Pitti Palace in the background. He used the Austrian baroque costumes, torchlight processions, spotlights, and Mendelssohn. The Oxford University Drama Society (OUDS) invited him to stage the play at Oxford in June. This production became the source of many tales among the English about the great German spectacle-maker, including a story of Reinhardt's cablegram that preceded him to Oxford, requesting "eighty extras and a lake." But Oxford was pleased to have him. It had conferred an honorary doctorate on him in May.[49]

The site of the production was Headington Hill, near Magdalen Bridge, which offered a foreground meadow, with elms and beaches, backed with fields and woods. The playing area was vast, the stage management coordinated through field telephones. In the first scene, the court men and women, dressed in their baroque costumes, stepped out from behind the trees, where they had been hiding, to begin the play. The mechanicals entered from individual paths deep in the woods, their lanterns seen bobbing in the darkness before they converged on the playing area. Puck, running across the greensward, vanished instantly in an unseen pit, his arm reemerging to trip up the artisans as they entered. When Oberon climbed a tree to hear the lovers, the tree shimmered. The London *Times* thought the emphasis of the play had been altered; this was "a tale of sprites and goblins pursuing the natural life of their own dwelling-place, into which men and women have blindly wandered."[50] A pond was built, chiefly for some elaborate business for Bottom, played by OUDS president Felix Felton. After waking from his dream, Bottom felt for the missing ass's ears and then made a fifty-yard run across the vast acting space to the pond, where, seeing his own reflection, he screamed in relief and danced off through the trees.[51]

That Bottom was so relieved at being released from his dream is new and intriguing: the dreamworld could be terribly frightening. Philip Arnhold's Oberon was probably a darker king of shadows than had ever been seen in the stage history of the play. Details are scarce about his Oxford performance, but when Reinhardt brought Arnhold to America for the Hollywood Bowl production a year later, there were reports of the "weird effect" and "gentle malevolence" in his performance.[52] Perhaps there had been hints of this in Moissi's Oberon, but the suggestion of a slightly sinister Oberon in Arnhold's performance is unmistakable.

Another disturbing element in the Oxford production was unforgettable for Felton and the critics. At the end of her solo dance to Mendelssohn's nocturne, the petite Danish dancer Nini Theilade, as the First Fairy, was carried off into the dark forest on the shoulder of a strong male in black. Felton remembered "a slowly narrowing spotlight following the undulation of her hands to a pinpoint of light in the darkness" before she disappeared into the woods.[53] Derivative of romantic ballet though the moment might have been — and the dance was accompanied by the lightly romantic music of the nocturne — it hinted at a dark eroticism never seen before in connection with this play. In the 1935 film the dance became a feature: the diminuitive feminine dancer, floating in chiffons at the edge of the "haunted grove," is forcibly carried off into the dark by a powerful, faceless male figure in black. This image and those of the frightened Bottom and the somewhat sinister Oberon suggest that the dream could become a nightmare and that Reinhardt's vision was darkening.[54] After Hitler had been named Reich Chancellor early in 1933, Reinhardt had watched the Nazis disrupt and then close a production in his Deutsches Theater in which two Jews had key roles. When in March he himself had directed Calderón de la Barca's *The Great World Theatre* there, adapted by Hofmannsthal, both the Jewish dramatist and the Jewish director were the targets of Nazi anti-Semitic criticism in Joseph Goebbels's newspaper, *Der Angriff*.[55] It was at this point that Reinhardt left Berlin, and soon after his representatives failed to negotiate a renewal of the theatre's mortgage. In Oxford in June, while he was directing the play, he was trying to come to terms with the loss. He wrote to the "National Socialist Administration of Germany" to give up his Deutsches Theater properties, though by then Nazi control of them was a fait accompli.[56] While his outdoor productions of the play in this period are certainly romantic on the whole, the abduction of the fairy and the sinister Oberon are the first dark theatrical images in the performance history of the play. In this they belong to the troubled twentieth century.

In 1934, Reinhardt received an invitation from the California Festival Association to direct *A Midsummer Night's Dream* in three different venues. He responded enthusiastically to the possibilities of these "Californian *Dreams*," suggesting that they would advertise the California landscape and perhaps lead to the creation of a cultural festival like Salzburg's.[57] The sites for these were the Hollywood Bowl, the San Francisco War Memorial Opera House, and the University of California campus at Berkeley. In the last, the Faculty Glade was used

FIGURE 39. Entrance of Theseus and Hippolyta in the last act of Max Reinhardt's 1934 production in the Greek Theatre, University of California-Berkeley. Max Reinhardt-Forschungstätte, Salzburg.

for most of the production, and the audience was then led to the Greek Theatre for the last act (fig. 39).

In the Hollywood Bowl production in September, the scale was even more vast than in Florence or Oxford. The orchestra shell was removed, and a stage 250 feet wide and 100 feet deep was created. An artificial hill sloped downward to a flat playing area that was sodded and planted with bushes and fully grown trees and included Bottom's pond. A suspension bridge ran 350 feet down to the stage from an adjacent hill, down which court processions (with hundreds of extras) entered by torchlight in the first and final acts and down which the fairy trains also entered (including a ballet corps of sixty and children as fairies and gnomes), all to Mendelssohn. The score was played by the Los Angeles Philharmonic, hidden behind the playing area. Four thousand arc lights were used; fireflies were simulated by thirty thousand electric lights, strung throughout the stage area. The actors' voices were electrically amplified so as to be heard by the audience of twelve thousand, for which the seating area had been reconfigured.[58]

Among the cast were Mickey Rooney as Puck and Olivia de Havilland as Hermia (who played these roles in the film), Arnhold as Oberon, and Walter Connelly as Bottom. According to his son, Reinhardt had dreamed originally of a cast of Hollywood stars intriguing to imagine: John Barrymore as Oberon, Greta Garbo as Titania, Fred Astaire (or Eddie Cantor) as Puck, Charlie Chaplin as Bottom, Clark Gable as Demetrius, Gary Cooper as Lysander, Joan Crawford as Hermia, Myrna Loy as Helena, W. C. Fields as Flute/Thisby, Wallace Beery as Snug/Lion, and Walter Huston as Theseus.[59]

Amid the spectacle of the pageant in the Hollywood Bowl and an opening night audience of celebrities, including Mae West and Marlene Dietrich, there was, once again, the poignant image of dancer Nini Theilade as the First Fairy being carried off into darkness, a spotlight focusing on her undulating hands.[60] The effect of it, according to the *Los Angeles Times*, was "uncanny."[61] Philip Arnhold's darker Oberon was costumed by Max Ree in deep purple, with a menacing mask of makeup and the stag horn crown, and his train was in blue and purple.[62]

"The poetic word, pageantry, music and spectacle all mingled to create a spell that is unearthly and has the true quality of fairyland," wrote the *Los Angeles Times* critic; it was "a bewitching processional of romance and of comedy, conjured by a master hand and by an intuition remarkable."[63] Critics found fault with much of the acting, but the *New York Times* critic praised the Puck of Mickey Rooney, who "revealed a greater comprehension of his role than almost anyone in the cast."[64] The generally enthusiastic reception resulted in Warner Brothers giving Reinhardt a lucrative contract to direct a film of the play and promising two more films.[65]

The film followed within a year. Reinhardt was assisted by Warner Brothers director William Dieterle, who had once acted for him. Jack J. Jorgens offers a loving, detailed appreciation of it in his *Shakespeare on Film* (1977) as a remarkable early effort in creating a full-length movie (140 minutes), with sound, of a Shakespeare play.[66] Of interest here is the film's cultural context and its relation to Reinhardt's stage productions. It was made amid the Great Depression and a rising concern in America over Hitler's power. To a considerable extent, Reinhardt created it as a romantic escape. In his foreword to a 1935 edition of the play, illustrated with photographs from the film, he wrote, "When stark reality weighs too heavily upon us, an all-wise Providence provides deliverance. . . . *A Midsummer Night's Dream* is an invitation to escape reality, a plea for the glorious release to be found in sheer fantasy." [67] The film was seen by some critics in 1935 as a throwback to nineteenth-century romantic stage traditions for the play. The early motion pictures were the natural offspring of the nineteenth-century pictorial stage and its star system. [68] Hollywood built its empire on lavish, illusionistic spectacles and attractive personalities. But this film is somewhat more complex, offering several sequences in which there are disquieting moments. The film is also the natural successor to Reinhardt's own visually well-orchestrated stage productions.

In the film, the pictorial sequence receives top priority; the spoken text is trimmed to the barest essentials of plot exposition, and segments of scenes have been freely rearranged. [69] At the beginning, Theseus disembarks from his ship, and, while loyal Athenians sing a patriotic hymn, he is conducted in a triumphal pageant beneath a tassled canopy, together with the captive, sad Hippolyta. After announcing their forthcoming wedding, he and Hippolyta ride off in a chariot drawn by a team of white horses. Athens here looks a little more like Caesar's Rome; the palace hall for the final scenes is a Hollywood version of baroque Salzburg (fig. 44). The forest sequence opens with an elaborate ballet to Mendelssohn's scherzo, as the fairies are called to the forest by Rooney's Puck (fig. 42), described in later years by one wit as a son of Tarzan. [70] He awakes from a bed of grass to howl at the rising moon. A horned stag is seen against the moon, and a glimpse of a unicorn confirms that we are in an enchanted forest. The forest, created with sixty-seven truckloads of trees and shrubbery, included a transplanted redwood tree, a pond, and a stream, all arranged over sixty-six thousand square feet (figs. 41 and 43). [71] Much of this is redolent of the naturalistic forest visions of 1905 and 1913. Titania's fairies — adults and children in white, gauzy costumes of ribboned cellophane — sweep through what seem acres of trees, hills, and streams. They dance to the accompaniment of an orchestra of grotesque trolls (apparently actors of short stature in rubber masks). Titania and her tribe materialize in a moonbeam by means of innovative splicing, and another train of fairies dance up a stairway of vapory mists that winds upward around a giant tree and ends in the stars. Oberon appears through filters of spangled gauze. When Puck chases the frightened mechanicals through bush and brier, he is turned into a hound, a hog, and fire, in a sequence only described in the play (3.1.101–106). Little space is left in the mesmerizing sequences for the play of a spectator's imagination, so thorough is Reinhardt's control. One

FIGURE 40. Titania (Anita Louise) carries the Indian boy away from Oberon (Victor Jory), on horseback, with his bat-winged henchman of the night, in the 1935 film directed by Max Reinhardt and William Dieterle. Turner Entertainment Company.

thinks of the full-length Disney animations to come; *Snow White and the Seven Dwarfs* was made two years later.

The film amplifies further some of the relatively disturbing images that developed in Reinhardt's stagings of 1933 and 1934. When the lovers wake after their night in the forest, they are sure they have only dreamed (Olivia de Havilland as Hermia, Jean Muir as Helena, Dick Powell as Lysander, and Ross Alexander as Demetrius). They are, in fact, greatly relieved to find that they have

FIGURE 41. The mechanicals rehearse in the forest in the 1935 film. At right, James Cagney as Bottom and Joe E. Brown as Flute; at left, Frank McHugh as Quince, seated and holding book. Turner Entertainment Company.

only dreamed, and the film emphasizes that dreams can be terrifying. Bottom's translation is, again, a nightmare. When Bottom (James Cagney) first discovers he has an ass's head, he trembles violently, the camera panning slowly from his trembling head down to his shaking knees and back up. After Cagney sees his assified reflection in the pond, he cries against a tree. When he opens his eyes, however, he discovers the beautiful Titania (Anita Louise), a glamorous, blond fairy godmother, who comforts him Madonna-like, as Jorgens has noted.[72] Victor Jory's Oberon is a menacing, nearly Satanic figure in a black-sequined costume and antlers. Making his demand for the Indian boy, he is seated on a black

FIGURE 42. Mickey Rooney as Puck, above the sleeping Dick Powell as Lysander in the 1935 film. Turner Entertainment Company.

horse and accompanied by large, bat-winged men, all in black, bald, and masked (fig. 40).[73] His demand is at first rather easily resisted by Titania and her soft-fleshed train. But at the end of their quarrel, toward dawn, Oberon and his web-winged attendants shepherd the somnolent, yielding, female fairies beneath his immense, billowing black cape, and they follow him as in a dream as he moves through the forest in his glittering chariot. He is a powerful patriarchal personification of the night, both ominous and benign. Near the end of the sequence,

FIGURE 43. Titania's fairies in one of the ballet sequences in the forest in the 1935 film. Turner Entertainment Company.

the focus shifts to Titania gazing into Oberon's eyes in a stupor of loving surrender required by the male gaze of the camera, and they fly away together.

The abduction of the First Fairy occurs in this same sequence, now fully
developed, with Nini Theilade choreographed by Bronislawa Nijinska. As the
film's souvenir program describes it, the nocturnal ballet

> tells the story of the creatures of the wood who are happy only in the moon-
> light and wage war against the approach of darkness. The lovers are asleep

FIGURE 44. Theseus's palace, with wedding guests, in the 1935 film. Turner Entertainment Company.

in the wood when Puck appears, heralding the departure of the moonlight. Across the meadows comes the chariot of Oberon, and close to him are countless elves, fairies and night creatures.

Suddenly there appears a startling, iridescent creature. She dances wildly, finally taking refuge beside Titania. Then Darkness itself, an awesome creature, emerges from the wood and woos the dancer. She tries to flee, but . . . the fearsome being lifts her high and she is swallowed up in the blackness of night.[74]

Their dance is elegantly fluid, their bodies briefly touch suggestively, pelvis to pelvis, just before the powerful, masked figure lifts her and slowly carries her off. The camera lingers long on her undulating hands, gradually disappearing; stars fleck the darkness, and Mendelssohn's nocturne resolves peacefully on low tonic notes on the double bass. The image, like that of the powerful Oberon gathering the procession of trance-walking women fairies under his black cape of night, oscillates between the romantic and the ominous, light and shadow, sexual fantasy and a nightmare of domination. Near the end of the film, Reinhardt and Dieterle interpolated another disquieting sequence. When the artisans return after the play to dance their bergamask, they find the hall empty. The aristocrats have sneaked away, and the rustics register their disappointment at this callous treatment.[75] Theseus's court no longer seems benign.

On the occasion of the premiere, Reinhardt made statements embracing the new medium. Never one for small projects, he called for "a synthesis of theatre and film in order ultimately to create a *gesamtkunstwerk* for the masses."[76] But the masses did not respond to his film; it was not commercially successful. Although it won some critical praise, there were predictable detractors. For the British film critic Sydney Carroll, Shakespeare did not belong on film, any more than American actors belonged in the church of Shakespeare. He patronizingly compared Rooney to Tom Sawyer, Cagney to an American gangster, Titania's train to *Ziegfeld's Follies* girls, and the lovers to college coeds.[77] As a result of the film's lack of commercial success, together with the fact that its cost of $1.5 million was double the budget, Reinhardt was not contracted for further films.[78]

The play continued to be popular in Germany during the 1930s. But under the Nazi regime, the name and the works of Felix Mendelssohn began to be systematically erased from symphonic repertoires, theatrical productions, and scholarship. Felix, the grandson of the German Jewish philosopher Moses Mendelssohn, had been reared as a Christian (baptized as Lutheran). But Felix's father had written to him prophetically in 1829, "There can no more be a Christian Mendelssohn than there can be a Jewish Confucius. If Mendelssohn is your name you are *ipso facto*, a Jew." And, inseparable as the name Mendelssohn was from German romantic music and, in the case of *Ein Sommersnachstraum*, from German Shakespeare, the name was a Jewish name in the eyes of the Nazis, and that, as Fred K. Prieberg writes, was sufficient.[79]

Not long after Hitler came to power, the search began for a new score for the play that would be Aryan, whatever that meant. Theatres were under relentless pressure from operatives of the National Socialist Party and its press. Music from Purcell's *Fairy Queen* and Carl Maria von Weber's *Oberon* was used for major professional German productions of the play in 1934, and by 1935 non-Jewish German composers were providing new scores for stagings of it. In the 1938–1939 season, there were thirty-two productions of *A Midsummer Night's Dream* in major German cities; Mendelssohn's score was not used for a single one of these.[80] According to Prieberg, between 1933 and 1945 there were at least forty-four attempts to create "*juden reine*" (Jewish-pure) music for the play. At one point, a national competition was considered.[81] The most prominent composer to respond to the national call, and the most gifted, was Carl Orff, best known then and now for his *Carmina Burana* (1937). In 1938, Orff accepted a commission of five thousand marks to compose a new incidental score for the play.[82] Orff's score, influenced by Richard Strauss, premiered in a Frankfurt production on 14 October 1939, directed by Robert George and designed by Helmut Jürgens. In 1944, he composed a second score. Surveying all his work on the play in an article for the *Shakespear-Jahrbuch* in 1964, Orff viewed the scores of 1938 and 1944 as unsuccessful, and he withdrew them.[83] His subsequent scores for the play were used for productions at the Darmstadt Landestheater in 1952, in Bochum in 1954, at the Empire State Music Festival in Ellenville, New York, in 1963, and in Stuttgart in 1964.[84] In his later work, Orff created a fairy world that was elemental and somewhat sinister in nature, his music emphasizing the erotic and the frightening entanglements of the dark forest night and his characteristically percussive orchestration accompanying the supernatural figures.[85] For Bottom's ousel-cock song (3.1.118–121), Bottom summoned a double-bass player on stage to accompany him.[86]

The few significant professional stage productions of *A Midsummer Night's Dream* that Americans saw between 1914 and 1960 in New York or other major cities were those of Barker, Reinhardt, or the touring Old Vic. On America's Chautauqua circuit, the Victorian traditions continued under the old English master of the greensward, Ben Greet.

The one production in this period that had uniquely American promise was *Swingin' the Dream*, a musical adaptation by Gilbert Seldes and Erik Charell, with music by Jimmy Van Heusen and lyrics by Eddie de Lange. It opened at the Center Theatre in Manhattan's Rockefeller Center in 1939, in the golden years of the swing era. It featured the jazz bands of Benny Goodman and Bud Freeman on opposite sides of the stage, as well as a pit orchestra. Its cast included Louis Armstrong as Bottom, Butterfly McQueen as Puck, Maxine Sullivan as Titania, Juan Hernandez as Oberon, and the Dandridge sisters as three pixies. Agnes de Mille and Herbert White choreographed the dancers, among whom were African American fairies, twenty-six jitterbugs, and tap dancer Bill

Bailey. The score included works that became jazz classics, including "Jumpin' at the Woodside" and "Darn that Dream," as well as a swing version of Mendelssohn's "Wedding March."[87]

This spin on Shakespeare was inspired by the takeoffs on Gilbert and Sullivan in the previous season, when the Federal Theatre Project production of *The Swing Mikado* and Mike Todd's production of *The Hot Mikado* had competed head-to-head on Broadway. Seldes and Charell set their version in New Orleans in the 1890s. Challenged about the adaptation, Charell observed that, for most Americans, Shakespeare's play was in a foreign language.[88] Seldes's interest in the project probably followed from his campaign to give the popular arts (jazz, musical comedy, vaudeville, comic strips) the kind of critical attention the high arts enjoyed. His 1924 *The Seven Lively Arts* is a forerunner of works in today's field of cultural studies. The scenery was designed "after cartoons by Walt Disney" (perhaps the recent *Snow White*?) by Walter Jagemann and Herbert Andrews. Theseus's palace was the Louisiana governor's summer mansion, and the forest was a "voodoo wood" nearby. The mechanicals met in a swinging-door saloon. Titania made her first entry into the forest in a rolling guide chair, like those used at the 1939 World's Fair; Titania's bank was a bed in a hollow tree, judging from a rehearsal sketch by artist Don Freeman. She sang several sultry blues numbers, including "Darn that Dream," into a microphone disguised as a rearing caterpillar. Puck charmed the lovers to sleep with a flit-gun. Armstrong seems to have used his trumpet little, except when he played "Jeepers Creepers" instead of singing the ousel-cock song.[89] Reviewers found it all fun, if overcharged, for the first hour but too loyal to Shakespeare thereafter. Some compared the show unfavorably to George Abbott's recent *Boys from Syracuse*, a musical version of *The Comedy of Errors*, which they thought the better adaptation for being freer with Shakespeare.[90] Much of the spoken text was lost in the large Center Theatre. The Goodman sextet, which included Lionel Hampton, Fletcher Henderson, and Charlie Christian, seems to have delighted reviewers more than anything else in the production.

Like the versions of the Mikado with black casts and Marc Connelly's *Green Pastures* (1930), *Swingin' the Dream* was created by whites for a predominantly white Broadway audience. Viewed in retrospect, the production seems to have been all too ready to exploit racial stereotypes, even while showcasing remarkable African American talent. Armstrong as Bottom, rolling his eyes in fear in the forest and strongly influenced by the Hollywood film comic, Lincoln Perry (Stepin Fetchit), was not much removed from the stereotype of the ignorant, superstitious, ghost-haunted Negro.[91] Just three years before, Armstrong was featured in the film *Pennies from Heaven* as the leader of a band in Bing Crosby's

Haunted House Cafe, singing a musical number that exploited the same stereotype, entitled "Skeleton in My Closet."[92] While New York's white newspaper
critics praised the African American performers, they simultaneously characterized them in the patronizing racial terms commonly used in the era for black
entertainers, such as "dark-skinned steppers" and "the lighthearted colored
folks [who] are out there beaming and grinning and rolling their eyes and dancing."[93] The producers priced tickets low, in the worthy aim of making the show
accessible to a wide audience. But it ran only thirteen performances, and its
heavy costs meant a heavy loss of $100,000.[94]

In London, the Old Vic created two significant productions in the years just
before and after World War II, both of which revisited what had become a nos-
talgically remembered vocabulary. But hints of menace and a darker sexuality
are to be found amid the romantic fantasy, as they were in Reinhardt's late
productions.

In his 1937 staging at the Old Vic, Tyrone Guthrie and his designer, Oliver
Messel, sought to "make a union between the words of Shakespeare, the music
of Mendelssohn, and the architecture of the Old Vic."[95] Inside the gilded proscenium, an armored Theseus, guarded by Nubian slaves, held court among garlanded Grecian pillars. The young lovers quarreled in the expansive, melodra-
matic gestures of the nineteenth century. Ninette de Valois choreographed a
"corps de Sylphides," all in white tulle; the fairies flew on wires behind scrims
on which giant bell-like flowers were painted. In the final scene, lighted fairy
wands weaved through a darkened fairy palace to Mendelssohn's score. "You
can almost see our young Queen [Victoria] leaning forward in one of the
boxes," wrote critic Herbert Farjeon.[96] In fact, the young Princess Elizabeth was
brought by the queen mother to this, her first Shakespearean production.[97] Robert Helpmann played Oberon; Vivien Leigh, Titania, and Ralph Richardson,
Bottom. Helpmann's Oberon, in a closely fitted black and sequined costume,
with black wings and cape, a spiky crown, and green sequins on his eyelids,
clearly was influenced by Victory Jory's Oberon in Reinhardt's film. Harcourt
Williams remembered that Helpmann looked "like some strange, sinister stag-
beetle [and] was indeed a spirit of another sort . . . his speech and movement . . .
beautiful."[98] There can be little doubt that this otherworldliness flowed in some
part from the feline grace of Helpmann's movement and the sexual ambiguity of
his performance, although these qualities go unmentioned by critics. Androg-
yny marks the major Oberons from the 1930s through the 1950s, from Gielgud
through Helpmann to the countertenors for whom Benjamin Britten wrote

the role of Oberon in his 1960 opera (Russell Oberlin played the role in the premiere). Richardson, who as a young actor had played Bottom for Bridges-Adams in 1931, was now mature and memorable in his "naive and eager vanity." Old Vic historian Audrey Williamson, who saw him, wrote, "On that glowing, complacent moon-dial the expressions crossed like summer clouds" (fig. 45).[99]

In most post–World War II English productions, the scenic style for the play tended toward relatively suggestive, sophisticated representations of palace and forest (although, in the photographs, mainstream Shakespearean productions in this period look today like grand opera on a slightly reduced scale). James Bailey's first-act setting for Michael Benthall's 1949 production at Stratford-upon-Avon suggested a Veronese palace, with lightly brushed perspectives of classical architecture, tassled canopies, and swags of draperies. A sideboard display of opulent court dinnerware was added for the wedding scene. The palace was inhabited by high Renaissance heroic figures in brocaded gowns and capes, helmets with perfectly upright plumes, and velvet doublets and lace collars. The forest setting was symmetrically composed, featuring one carefully fallen classical pillar. But its foliage was exotic and dark and seemed to critic Harold Hobson like "a part of the garden of the House of Usher, a thing of sedgy brooks, and dank, overgrown tree trunks, making avenues of funereal blackness." Hermia's fear sent her screaming through this wood, her cries for Lysander answered only by echoes.[100]

This and other postwar productions are strongly marked with assertions of male control of conventional sexual relationships. At Stratford, Hippolyta was a captive war bride in leopard skin, wearing cowrie shells and heavy metal bracelets.[101] A bodyguard of black-garbed young men accompanied Oberon, who "hid behind trees and haunted the passer-by with twirling arms and forbidding gestures."[102] Titania's fairies were ballerinas in tulle, with bare shoulders and arms, low-cut bodices, and long, garlanded hair — their sexuality strongly emphasized. In the 1954 Old Vic production, in a classic image from the vocabulary of the romantic ballet, Titania poised on point under the fingertips of her controlling male partner in the climactic moment of her final dance with Oberon (see fig. 48). The souvenir program of that production carried one in the series of famous advertisements in this era by the Maidenform Brassiere Company. Captioned "I dreamed I danced a ballet in my Maidenform bra," it showed a young woman dancing on point in a tutu and bra.[103] In the 1949 Stratford-upon-Avon production, Diana Wynyard as Helena wore a delicately chiffoned, strapless, low-cut bodice in velvet, draped with beads, her featured bosom also emphasized by a suppressed waist (fig. 46). In this photograph by noted theatre and

FIGURE 45. Ralph Richardson as Bottom, Old Vic Theatre, 1937. Directed by Tyrone Guthrie, designed by Oliver Messel. Theatre Museum, Victoria and Albert Museum.

FIGURE 46. Diana Wynyard as Helena, Old Vic Theatre, 1949. Directed by Michael Ben-thall. Angus McBean's photograph, in its formal, high-fashion portrait style, captures the post–World War II trend toward elegant, neoromantic fantasy. Wynyard's Helena is in sharp contrast to the high-spirited, athletic Helenas of the 1960s and after. Harvard Theatre Collection.

fashion photographer Angus McBean, the highly formal composition at once displays and contains the female figure, cannily poised between being sexually available and imposingly respectable.

The English Theseuses in this era are wholly idealized in performances by Leon Quartermaine (Haymarket, 1945), Harry Andrews (Stratford-upon-Avon, 1949), Anthony Nicholls (Old Vic, 1954), and Keith Michell (Stratford-upon-Avon, 1954). Theseus is portrayed much as Una Ellis Fermor described him in 1944, as a kingly king anticipating Shakespeare's ideal monarch, Henry V, perhaps even a reflection of Elizabeth I. Of the Theseus who explains to Hippolyta that he has always "picked a welcome" from the stumbling efforts of the fearful, tongue-tied clerks sent to greet him on his visits, Ellis Fermor wrote glowingly that this was not Theseus "but the last and greatest of the Tudor monarchs." [104]

In these alternating images of heroic men and pliant women, and in the sometimes conflicting suggestions of thorny menace, noble authority, and soft erotic fantasy, these productions probably were playing out bourgeois postwar fantasies and apprehensions. The strong reinforcement of conventional gender roles and romantic relationships in these versions, together with the idealized Theseus, likely spoke to the longings for the return to a simpler past and domestic and state stability. But that past was receding quickly, and behind the foregrounded romantic fantasies, with their obligatory ballets to Mendelssohn, were questions about how to go forward.

The problem is evident in Nevill Coghill's staging at the Haymarket in January 1945, just before the end of the war. Coghill, like Harcourt Williams before him, struck the note of the Elizabethan-Jacobean masque. But John Gielgud appeared as a somewhat sinister Oberon (apparently derivative of Reinhardt's), with a spiky crown and his face made up in a greenish hue, gravely disturbing London critics. James Agate found him as terrifying as the ghost of Hamlet's father. [105] As a result of the criticism, Gielgud transformed his Oberon into a handsome, youthful, clean-shaven, golden-haired fairy king. [106] In the 1929 Old Vic production, Gielgud had reveled in the language of Oberon. Now, sixteen years later, he allowed himself to be carried away by the language, vocally and emotionally. Perhaps this was, as Ronald Hayman suggests, the compensatory effort of an actor who believed he was too old for the role (Gielgud was then forty). [107] But Gielgud's reverence for Shakespeare's language at this time might also be seen as the anxious, overfond evocation of a golden age of England. Olivier had just completed his chauvinistic film of *Henry V*. One critic described the masque motif of Coghill's production as an attempt at "turning Athens into Whitehall." [108] Coghill also replaced Mendelssohn with a quasi-Elizabethan masque score by Leslie Bridgewater. The choice promptly resulted in a "back-to-Mendelssohn" campaign by Agate, and the ensuing debate over whether the music should be Mendelssohn or Elizabethan was hardly more than a comfortable conversation among club members about canonical authenticity.[109]

Some productions did tentatively test cultural boundaries. When Guthrie returned to the play for the Old Vic in 1951, designer Tanya Moiseiwitsch created a cool, elegant grove of twisted bamboo for the forest, garnished with silver flowers and lighted in marine colors. It was backed with a very sketchy landscape with ancient Greek temples, albeit in the far distance.[110] ("I have rarely found Shakespearean Athens further off," wrote critic Ivor Brown.) Not only was Guthrie's Oberon (Kenneth Griffith) slightly sinister, but Titania (Jill Balcon) was no longer in tulle. Her face makeup was rather grotesque, and she wore a costume that reminded Brown of the witches in *Macbeth*.

In 1954, the year following Elizabeth II's coronation, which brought with it many prophecies of "a new Elizabethan age," the Old Vic invoked the Victorian vocabulary again, this time in grandiose proportions. In the postwar years, the company had built a reputation in England and America for its command of Shakespeare and for its talented stars, which included Gielgud, Richardson, Olivier, Claire Bloom, John Neville, Richard Burton, Alec Guinness, Peggy Ashcroft, and Rosemary Harris. Now, with American impresario and producer Sol Hurok, director Michael Benthall brought together the forces of the Old Vic, twenty-four dancers from the Sadler's Wells Ballet, an orchestra of sixty to play Mendelssohn's score, and thirteen tons of scenery, designed by Robin and Christopher Ironside, which included over a dozen painted drops, each fifty-one feet wide.[111] The production opened in Edinburgh's Empire Theatre in September and was then "airlifted" to New York and the old Metropolitan Opera House, both vast theatres and architecturally redolent of the turn of the century. It then toured major cities in the United States and Canada and was recorded and widely marketed on long-playing records by RCA Victor.

Robert Helpmann was the choreographer and again played Oberon as a slightly sinister king of shadows. He and his rather ominous train of all-male dancers wore gold-veined green armor, bristling with spiky wings and crowns (fig. 47). Titania was played by dancer Moira Shearer, known to British and American audiences for her recent appearances in the leading roles in *Sleeping Beauty*, *Swan Lake*, and the film *The Red Shoes*. She danced on point, with large, translucent wings arching above her back (fig. 48). (She and Helpmann had danced in the 1946 *Fairy Queen* at Covent Garden, he as Oberon and she in the role of Spring.)

These stars and the scenic spectacle drew record-breaking houses in New

FIGURES 47, 48. Robert Helpmann as Oberon (above), with his fairy train, and Helpmann with Moira Shearer as Titania (below), in the 1954 Old Vic production. Directed by Michael Benthall, scenery and costumes by Robin and Christopher Ironside. Bristol University Theatre Collection.

York,[112] but even mainstream critics, with few exceptions, found the production unsatisfying and unsuccessful, even on its own terms.[113] "Everything is in the best taste of a departed era," wrote Brooks Atkinson of the *New York Times*. The dances of Helpmann and Shearer were "gravely beautiful" but dutiful contributions to a monumental art enterprise. Walter Kerr found the production more than an anachronism. Benthall had "unearthed not only the garish and literal scenery of an earlier tradition," wrote Kerr, "but the empty gestures, the chilling rhetoric, and the marble postures as well. He has been lavish about it."[114] Kerr's memorable characterization makes clear just how tired and vacuous the too-familiar Victorian vocabulary now seemed:

> There are slow and languid fade-ins through greenish gauze to slow and languid figures uncurling theselves from tree-trunks. Acres and acres of receding arches, in the best ruined classic manner, rise stodgily into the heavens. Trumpeters in gold hoist their trumpets, fairies in gossamer flutter their hands, kneeling maidens toss actual rose petals as Titania and Oberon mark off Mendelssohn's "Wedding March." The boys wear laurel wreaths, the girls tiaras; when Bottom puts on his donkey's head, it has pronounced eye-lashes, ears that prick up, and lips that would do credit to Francis the Mule. An elaborate love-chase is staged behind a scrim of spiders' webs, with the wily Puck nestling neatly at the center of one.[115]

Titania reentered with her rose-garlanded Bottom in a sort of gondola, and when Bottom woke from his dream he discovered not the traditional hay in his pouch but a rose in his hair. Theseus's palace in the last act was an impressionistic, but still grandiose, baroque fantasy in the spirit of a Bibiena design. Oberon and Titania, seated on the thrones of Theseus and Hippolyta during the fairy revels, were flown off as the final curtain fell. As in Victorian productions, the actors in the roles of the rustics, including Stanley Holloway's Bottom, seem to have asserted themselves in broad terms, as if in competition with the spectacular palaces and forests (figs. 49 and 50). With the exception of Helpmann, the actors spoke the words with no distinction; Shearer could not be heard, even with amplification. The text, or most of it, was reverently reproduced in the lavish souvenir booklet.[116]

The cultural fatigue of this vocabulary was evident. The 1954 Old Vic production marks the end of the resort to Victorian staging traditions for the play. Mendelssohn's score went out of use in major productions of the play proper thereafter. The move away from the proscenium stage for Shakespeare was already under way in the Stratford, Ontario, Shakespeare Festival, where, in 1953, Tyrone Guthrie and Tanya Moiseiwitsch had created a thrust stage in their tent

FIGURES 49, 50. Stanley Holloway as Bottom (above) and Eliot Makeham as Quince (below) in the 1954 Old Vic production. Bristol University Theatre Collection.

theatre, which was incorporated in the permanent Shakespeare Festival Theatre a few years later. A far more profound attack on the illusionistic stage had developed in East Berlin and would soon influence the West. Bertolt Brecht's anti-Aristotelian dramaturgy and his anti-illusionistic staging of his plays with the Berliner Ensemble were defining a new postwar theatre of social criticism that would wither the roots of neoromantic Shakespeare.

In the meantime, the search for an alternative to the exhausted tradition often ended in cultural sterility. At Stratford-upon-Avon, in George Devine's production, the fairies were conceived as birds and insects in a forest of metallic trees. Oberon (Powys Thomas) and Titania (Muriel Pavlow) were elaborately beaked and feathered birds, in exotic blue-and-red-feathered headdresses. Titania's face was painted with "broad white eye-streaks from crown to bill that gave her the air, light, bright and ferocious, of a falcon," wrote Richard David (plate 11).[117] Puck was toadlike. Overall, the production seemed to critics to be cold, autumnal, and lacking enchantment. "There was an odd feeling of dead leaves in the air," wrote one critic.[118] If something dark was intended, the stage language offered little more than its own stylistic eccentricity.

America's relatively new Shakespeare festival in Stratford, Connecticut, staged the first major American production of the play in over half a century in 1958. Lightly neoromantic, it offered little new and nothing profound, but it was popular and belongs to what Roberta Kerensky Cooper has called the golden age of Stratford, which was its years under artistic director John Houseman.[119] Director Jack Landau was clearly borrowing from the British tradition of the Elizabethan epithalamium, begun in Harcourt Williams's Old Vic staging in 1929.[120] For the season, designer Rouben Ter-Aruturian modified the huge proscenium stage with the suggestion of a thrust stage in the hope of combining the Elizabethan platform stage with the visual virtues of the proscenium stage. (The influence of Ontario's thrust stage surely was felt here.) It was backed with hangings of horizontal wooden crating strips, like Venetian blinds. David Hays created a graceful upstage gallery structure, which spanned the proscenium and was flanked by wide staircases descending toward the audience right and left; it was used for all the Shakespeare plays during this season. For *A Midsummer Night's Dream*, the lower level was fitted out with five slender Tudor arches on rolling platforms, which were moved (by winches) from beneath the gallery into downstage positions, serving as mobile bowers. In the forest scenes, the blinds opened to reveal a translucent blue-green drop behind, painted with delicately stylized trees. The costumes were in high Elizabethan-Jacobean style, and Marc Blitzstein provided similarly styled music, some of which was sung by countertenor Russell Oberlin.[121]

The Oberon and Titania of Richard Waring and film star June Havoc were in the mold of the Old Vic productions, with Waring, the much more competent of the two in verse delivery, costumed in the black-sequined manner of Victor Jory and Robert Helpmann. The highly spirited young lovers evoked a stern rebuke from the *Shakespeare Quarterly* critic for their "distasteful roughhouse" in the Hermia-Helena quarrel.[122] Amid the derivative style of the Elizabethan masque, the American production had fresh authenticity in its mechanicals, each distinctly individual, and they pleased the critics most: Hiram Sherman as Bottom, Will Geer as Snout, Morris Carnovsky as Quince, and Ellis Rabb as Starveling. When the production toured in 1960–1961, the popular comedian Bert Lahr was cast as Bottom in a deliberate attempt to appeal to a wide audience.[123]

In the early 1960s, the traditions of Mendelssohn and moonlight, roses and tulle, were brought over into the classical ballet. Two different works were choreographed within two years by George Balanchine (1962) and Sir Frederick Ashton (1964). Working under Robert Helpmann, Ashton had choreographed the dance for Mendelssohn's nocturne for the 1954 Old Vic production. His ballet was created for the four-hundredth anniversary of Shakespeare's birth and was first performed at Covent Garden on 2 April 1964 by the Royal Ballet, of which Ashton was the artistic director.[124] Using Mendelssohn's music, it compresses the play's action into one act, ending with Bottom restored to himself but puzzled by memories of his dream.[125] Balanchine had choreographed the fairy dances for the 1958 production at Stratford, Connecticut. His inspiration to create the ballet when he was fifty came not from the play but from Mendelssohn's score, although the play had been a favorite since childhood, when he had danced as an elf in a production in St. Petersburg around 1912.[126] Its arrangement of two acts and six scenes followed Shakespeare's plot closely; portions of five other Mendelssohn works were incorporated to provide accompaniment for the extensive dance action of the play.[127]

Act 1 opens in the wood with the quarrel of Oberon and Titania, includes the confusions of the young lovers, and closes on their discovery, asleep, by Theseus. Act 2 begins with a processional of the court to the "Wedding March" into a pavilion in the forest for the nuptial festivities. A series of divertissements are danced for the guests, after which the court retires, and the forest becomes the domain of the fairies again. The New York City Ballet premiered the work at the City Center in New York on 17 January 1962, with Edward Villella as Oberon, Melissa Hayden as Titania, and African American dancer Arthur Mitchell as Puck. Its popular success has made the piece a staple in the company's repertoire ever since. Dan Eriksen directed a Columbia Pictures film of the ballet in 1967, with Villella, Mitchell, and Suzanne Farrell (as Titania).[128] On the occasion of the company's revival of the ballet in the summer of 1995, Anna Kisselgoff, the *New York Times* dance critic, characterized it as "the New York City Ballet's mini-Nutcracker."[129] One of its few critics was Igor Stravinsky, who thought the Mendelssohn score "ought to be used only for Schlegel's version of the play, the production of which should then be clothed in the provincial German court style of the period."[130]

The crossover of the play into ballet is not surprising. Elaborate dances had been incorporated into productions since Vestris and Kean, and fairy ballets were prominent in productions a century later, in the 1950s. The crossover may even seem late, coming as it did in the 1960s, at the point when productions of the play proper were about to jettison all Victorian traditions. It was timely for the expansion of ballet and the growing audience for dance in general. I will leave to dance historians full explanations of this and detailed analyses of these two ballets, but it must be noted here that in music, scenery, and glossary of movement, both ballets were variations on the neoromantic idiom for the play as represented in the mid-1950s, that idiom itself only one remove from the Victorian vocabulary. In the 1960s, Shakespeare's play began to have a very different life, or rather, many varied lives. The popular success of the Balanchine ballet has meant that there has been a continuum of the quasi-Victorian image of the play down through the closing years of this century, running parallel to the very diverse approaches to the play over those three decades.

The long era of neoromantic and modernist productions of the play may be said to have a final coda in Benjamin Britten's twelve-tone opera in 1960, with its libretto by Peter Pears.[131] Sometimes characterized as a chamber opera, the composition is an aesthetically rarified work, modernist in its twelve-tone vocabulary and its taut, overdetermined musical unity.[132] It was created for the elite Aldeburgh Festival, which Britten had helped found in the east Suffolk fishing village on the North Sea and with which his work has long been associated. The opera was conceived for the small stage of the relatively intimate Jubilee Hall (capacity 316) and for a small orchestra and special instrumentation. Notable among its many unique features, the role of Oberon is written for countertenor, in range and quality an echo of the castrati voices of the Renaissance and the baroque period. Puck is written as a nonsinging, speaking role; dancer Leonide Massine II played it in the premiere. Boys are required for the roles of the other fairies. Subtle but unmistakable in the opera is the homoerotic coloring of the character or Oberon and his relationship with Puck.

At the Aldeburgh premiere, many critics complimented the composer on succeeding in making an opera of the play "while retaining a tone and emphasis that are recognizably Shakespearean," as one scholar put it.[133] When it premiered at Covent Garden, Philip Hope-Wallace of the *Guardian* declared that, whatever its problems, "the work cannot be faulted for lack of a true feeling for Shakespeare," a *New York Times* critic wrote that the opera was "a captivating blend of Shakespeare's moonlit lyricism and a modern composer's delicate songfulness," and there were the inevitable comparisons with Verdi's Shakespearean successes.[134] In addition, librettist Peter Pears has been praised for preserving as much as possible of the text (about half of the text was cut — the norm for Shakespearean operas) and Britten for achieving musical equivalencies of it.[135] Given the mixture of Britten's Schoenbergian twelve-tone scales, his distilled modernist instrumentation, his choice of a countertenor for Oberon, and the neoromantic settings in which the opera opened in Aldeburgh and London, the whole "Shakespearean" test of fidelity seems to strain anxiously after canonical legitimacy. Peter Evans's 1979 assessments on this point, then, are particularly welcome: "Whatever the magnificence of the verbal stuff on which a composer works, the worlds of feeling through which we move in an opera are those conjured up by the music, and Britten's 'Dream' creates an atmosphere which . . . cannot be mistaken for Shakespeare's."[136]

Britten's unifying musical concept is that of the forest fairy world as a kind of primeval presence. The three-act opera is set entirely in the forest, opening with the quarrel of Oberon and Tytania (Pears preferred the Quarto spelling),[137] which precipitates all the action. Theseus and Hippolyta do not appear until the last act — their introduction at that late point being somewhat awkward. Britten creates the strong presence of the night forest with a spellbinding passage in which soft, tremulous strings (marked "slow and mysterious") play twelve major triadic chords, beginning with a D-flat triad, in semitonal oppositions, joined by long glissandi. Act 2 opens with four equally spellbinding chords that symbolize sleep. The fairy voicings are all high, the better to be nonhuman. Tytania is scored for a coloratura, boy trebles sing the roles of the four named fairies, and either boy trebles (seven in the Covent Garden premiere) or women serve in the fairy chorus.

For each set of characters, Britten provides distinct musical idioms and instrumentation, using (in the original Aldeburgh score) a unique twenty-eight-piece orchestra. Strings (twelve) and woodwinds (six) represent the lovers; two harps, celeste, harpsichord, and light percussion accompany the fairies (including drum taps for Puck and wood blocks, which the fairies themselves play on stage). Bottom and company are accompanied by low bass and brass, with staccato woodwinds. A slide trombone gives low comedy embellishments to the performances of Pyramus and Lion, and a bassoon is heard behind the mechanicals' rehearsal in an echo of Mendelssohn. Horns wake the lovers and later bring on the scenic transformation to Theseus's court in the last act.[138] All is done with great delicacy and sophistication.

By most critical accounts, Britten's twelve-tone composition works best for his forest fairy world and the fairy songs. These create, for ears accustomed to conventional Western harmonies, an eerie, supernatural musical ground, albeit one that is kept relatively accessible by Britten's conservative, kid-gloves handling of this vocabulary. Critic Philip Hope-Wallace wrote: "All that is concerned with the supernatural elements, all the music of sleep and dreams and woods bewitched, is quite marvelously successful."[139] Christina Burridge, in her musicological analysis, observed, "One mark of Britten's achievement in setting the play is that it is precisely those passages that in the original are most 'poetic,' the most rich in verbal music — the fairies' songs, Tytania's and Oberon's set pieces — that are the most successful in the opera."[140] By many accounts, the most sublime music in the opera is the song for the final fairy blessing. The twelve-tone vocabulary seems, at best, a neutral medium for Theseus and Hippolyta (bass and contralto) and a very cool and formal one for the young lovers (a conventional quartet), though its dissonances serve their forest love dilemmas.

Oberon, as played by countertenors, has been apt to be more than countered by the coloraturas in the role of Tytania, except in studio recordings. The viability of this delicate voice quality has been especially at issue in performances in large opera houses. Russell Oberlin's Oberon in the Covent Garden premiere, while much praised (and more so than Alfred Deller's at Aldeburgh), was, said one critic, "vocally routed" by Joan Carlyle's regal Tytania.[141] Peter Evans is skeptical about possible musical success in the Oberon-Tytania quarrel, observing that, in the nature of things it "is likely to be won by Tytania's sheer superiority of vocal power."[142]

The countertenor Oberon, by virtue of his vocal range and quality, his relationship with the virile, younger Puck, and his desire for the Indian boy, becomes a singularly haunting central figure. His desire for revenge on Tytania is dark, and he is capricious in his use of power over Puck, at one point musically seductive as he sends Puck to bring back the magic love-flower and, at another, dragging him on stage by the ear when Puck errs in dispensing the love-juice. This Oberon could be said to be a further development in the tradition of previous androgynous Oberons, particularly those of John Gielgud and Robert Helpmann. But this Oberon's relationship to Puck and his desire for the Indian boy are echoes of disturbing motifs in several other Britten operas, notably *Peter*

Grimes and *The Turn of the Screw*, in which an older man is sexually attracted to a very young boy. In late 1996, the Metropolitan Opera was mounting a production of Britten's *A Midsummer Night's Dream*, its first staging of the work, and *New York Times* critic Anthony Tommasini wrote of both the opera's "thinly veiled pederasty" and of the "homoerotic undertones" in the conception of Oberon, suggesting that Britten "did not have to contort Shakespeare much to uncover this implicit [homosexual] theme."[143] Tommasini's interview with Tim Albery, director of the Metropolitan's production, made clear that Albery had considered these issues, though to what extent they might surface in the production remained to be seen. Not in the history of the play or of this opera in particular had an overt homosexual reading of Oberon been thinkable until this time; in the 1990s, after a decade of increasing public awareness of homosexuality in the wake of the AIDS epidemic, it was, perhaps, inevitable. As to pederasty, it is likely that the scores of stories in the press had sensitized the public to the covert sexual abuse of children and made the Indian boy sadly problematic.

The compelling musical unity that Britten achieves comes at the cost of the play's complexity. As Peter Evans observes, Britten "has chosen to employ means of intra-musical unity that inevitably have the effect of subsuming the specific incidents, as though offering a view that embraces all."[144] William Godsalve and others argue that there are compensations in the complex music.[145] But we miss any erotic dimensions of the four young lovers' relationships and of Titania's dalliance with Bottom. Egeus is cut, which diminishes the young lovers' difficulties and some of the conflict. Significantly, the libretto omits Theseus's and Hippolyta's exchange about the lovers' strange stories of the night (5.1.1–27); any reflection on the ways in which we construct narratives of our experiences is inimical to Britten's tight modernist controls. Finally, in a much-criticized choice, Britten renders *Pyramus and Thisby* as a parody on opera conventions (Pears preferred "Thisby" to "Thisbe"). It includes a special glance at Donizetti in the aria for Thisby's death-scene aria and at Schoenberg in the *Sprechtstimme* for Wall. In the premiere, Pears played Flute/Thisby and reportedly parodied Joan Sutherland's recent performance in *Lucia di Lammermoor*.[146] Among its fourteen numbers, the tempos of which are indicated in Italian, are Pyramus's "O grim-looked night" ("*Moderato ma tenebroso*"), a duet for Pyramus and Thisby on "My love thou art" ("*Allegro brilliante*"), Thisby's "These lily lips" ("*lento*"), and the prologue, "Gentles, perchance you wonder at this show," which Britten marks "*Andante pesante*." As Burridge notes, the parody makes the mechanicals self-conscious in a way they are not in the play.[147] An audience's laughter at, and admiration for, Quince and company gets displaced by a self-congratulatory amusement at the inside musical joke.

These issues not withstanding, Britten's opera has been regarded generally as the best Shakespearean opera by a modern composer and has been revived rather often in major venues in Europe and the United States.[148] Presumably, it will become part of the regular repertoire of the Metropolitan Opera. In the postmodern, post-1960s world, the Britten opera, the Balanchine ballet, and productions of the play itself that are relatively radical would be seen regularly, side by side by side.

Chapter nine

POSTMODERNISM

"THE FIERCE VEXATION OF A DREAM"

Oberon: May all to Athens back again repair,
    And think no more of this night's accidents
    But as the fierce vexation of a dream.

In the aftermath of World War II, a darker view of the human condition increasingly affected most transactions with Shakespeare's plays, including his fairy play. Long one of the fond touchstones of Western literature and one which had acquired nationalistic dimensions, *A Midsummer Night's Dream* emerged in the mid-1960s in productions that envisioned most of its characters as sexually vexed. There could be no repairing back to Athens after Freud. Productions were, and still are, marked by explorations of repressed dreams, the unconscious, and the irrational — whether as a supposed source of authenticity or as dehumanizing. Such interests are likely to have been influenced by works ranging from Freud's *Civilization and Its Discontents* (1930) to those of such revisionists of Freud as R. D. Laing (*The Divided Self*, 1961) and Herbert Marcuse (*Eros and Civilization*, 1955). "The truce between civilization and the instincts is simply that — a truce. It can be broken at any moment," said Mark Lamos, the director of a production in the 1980s.[1] Perhaps the only other constant in theatrical approaches to the play from the 1960s through the mid-1990s is diversity. The play comes to the stage as an anthology of gender and class wars, as a critique of state oppression, as a celebration of Third-World cultures, and as an exploration of the Victorian or Edwardian past in postmodern angst. Such productions have been, of course, only a part of the revolution in Shakespearean production — the self-conscious contemporizing of the plays — which accompanied the rapid social changes in the latter half of the twentieth century. But this particular play has been remarkably responsive to the cultural negotiations of these decades. One production of this play was, and still is, seen as signaling and symbolizing that revolution: the Royal Shakespeare Company's (RSC) *A Midsummer Night's Dream* of 1970, directed by Peter Brook. For many, this production made the case that Shakespeare's plays in the theatre could be made to speak directly from and to contemporary sensibilities. Brook's own 1962 production of *King Lear* had been widely seen and discussed, but it did not make the case as irrevocably as did his bright, celebrative *A Midsummer Night's Dream*. With a North American tour in 1971 and a world tour in 1972–1973, which included thirty-five cities from Adelaide to Zagreb, Chicago to Osaka, the RSC production was an international phenomenon, probably seen by more theatre audiences than any single theatrical production of a Shakespearean play before or since.[2] It was indisputably the most influential Shakespearean production in the latter half of the twentieth century and the most discussed.

The discussions of the proper aims of Shakespearean production that followed in its wake were often cast in terms of how much interpretive freedom a director should have.[3] Both its admirers and its critics dealt with it at the time as "Brook's *Dream*," without much attention to the cultural forces that drove it. The extent to which Shakespearean productions have always been culturally contingent transactions with a text by contemporary artists and audiences was little acknowledged. In 1970, few were as perceptive about this fundamental cultural issue as the East German scholar Robert Weimann, who had begun to make the case that there were bound to be tensions between a Shakespearean play's Renaissance origins and values and the effects of that play in the present. Weimann explained that to try to equate "past significance and present meaning" was reductive of Shakespeare's plays to some "classical" ideology, whereas what they had offered their own audiences was a complex blend of politics and play, in which dominant discourses were at once subverted and reinforced. Moreover, he pointed out that the plays in performance, with their interactions between actor and spectator, whether in Shakespeare's theatre or ours, are bound to generate new meanings.[4] Before turning to the 1970 RSC production, we need to consider some developments in theatre theory and Shakespearean staging that preceded it.

Tyrone Guthrie, in his autobiography in 1959, observed: "What we of the twentieth century have inherited is not a Shakespearean tradition, it is merely a legacy of nineteenth-century theatrical conventions."[5] Barker had tried to deal with the legacy a half century before. In the 1950s, Guthrie and designer Tanya Moiseiwitsch were pioneers in the development of the open stage. They sought to break from nineteenth-century illusionism and create a stage that would offer the fluidity of the permanent, architectural Elizabethan stage, one that would bring the spectator into greater physical proximity to the stage and into a more active imaginative engagement with language and actor, both of which would be freed of scenic encumberments. Guthrie believed that such a stage would theatricalize the dramatic event. The Shakespeare Festival Theatre at Stratford, Ontario, designed by Guthrie and Moiseiwitsch, which evolved from a tent in 1953 to a permanent theatre by 1957, featured a dark, polished wood platform stage projecting into a large auditorium that wrapped around it in a manner modeled on the theatre at Epidaurus. The platform was backed by a handsome, permanent wooden facade, with entrances, stairways, and a prowlike second level. Stratford's theatre spawned other thrust stages, such as those of the Guthrie Theatre in Minneapolis, the Chichester Festival Stage, and the Olivier Theatre in the Royal National Theatre complex in London.[6]

In retrospect, the open stage can be seen as a product of late modernism. With its emphasis on the recovery of Shakespeare's language and on such factors as the proximity of actors to the audience, the project at the new-world Stratford seemed to suggest the possibility of a fresh, unmediated representation of the text, of the seamless transfer of the plays into the twentieth century. Writing in praise of the use of quasi-Elizabethan costumes in Douglas Campbell's 1960 production of *A Midsummer Night's Dream* in Ontario's Festival Theatre, Herbert Whittaker of the *Toronto Globe and Mail* commented, "The choice brings us closer to Shakespeare. We get the illusion time and time again that we are witnessing a performance contemporary with its author."[7] The agenda of the Ontario festival was to achieve international prestige; this bucolic Stratford, too, could provide world-class productions of the universal Shakespeare, icon of high culture. The result was a comfortable, idealizing representation of the plays, with a high degree of modernist sophistication, visually and musically. By 1962, artistic director Michael Langham, Guthrie's successor, was, he confessed, feeling out of touch with contemporary culture and theatre; his subsequent attempts at relating the festival's work to contemporary life encountered resistance from "both the press and the middle-aged public of Ontario . . . [though] not at all [from] our young audiences. . . . I already had the impression that in Establishment Ontario the twentieth century was culturally invalid."[8] But by then the Ontario open-stage style, which was almost inimical to taking frank, contemporary possession of the plays, was becoming an influential model for a Shakespearean production style that was ostensibly as timeless as the plays — Shakespeare without tense.

While the Ontario festival was rooted in a conservative, modernist neutrality, the founding of the RSC in Stratford-upon-Avon in 1960 was rooted in a desire to inform Shakespeare's work with the spirit of contemporary culture. The RSC's new royal charter notwithstanding, it was born on the eve of the 1960s with a leftist social consciousness that was, in some part, due to the influence of Bertolt Brecht and his Berliner Ensemble productions.

Peter Hall's 1959 production of *A Midsummer Night's Dream* on Stratford-upon-Avon's main stage (not quite yet the Royal Shakespeare Theatre) is a transition piece, both for the developing RSC and for the play, bridging the 1950s and 1960s. At first controversial, it evolved through revivals over a four-year period, until by 1963, mainstream critics were finding it wholly congenial, having become accustomed to leaving Victorian conventions behind. An NBC televised version of it was shown in the United States in 1959, and it was revived as an RSC production on Stratford's main stage in 1962 and at London's Aldwych Theatre in 1963, performed in both proscenium theatres on modified Ontario-influenced thrust stages. In 1969, Hall directed an RSC film of the play derivative of it.

Hall, twenty-eight in 1959, had been a Stratford protégé of Glen Byam Shaw, known for his high-power star casts. But Hall had also been influenced by Brecht's Berliner Ensemble in its London visit in 1956, and he and his fellow directors, including Peter Brook, soon moved away from Stratford's textual orthodoxy and star-power orientation toward more contemporary readings and the creation of an ensemble of younger actors. At the RSC, a new generation of actors gradually began to inform Shakespeare with the spirit of contemporary culture, with sensibilities formed in what Hall in 1963 characterized as "our world of contradictions." In an essay that year on "Shakespeare and the Modern Director," Hall stressed the dependence of the theatre and its metaphors upon "a nation's vocabulary, its whole culture." For him, "the means of expressing Shakespeare's intentions must vary with these developments" (a premise that he seemed to abandon later in his National Theatre years). New directorial interpretations were "not a sin but a necessity because the accretions of time have to be stripped away."[9]

Hall's 1959 *A Midsummer Night's Dream* did suggest a contradictory and somewhat uneasy world. It abandoned the Victorian vocabulary and instead sought, however tentatively, some conversation between the play's Elizabethan origins and the present. In 1959, critics noted first the departures from tradition: "Titania Without the Ballet," headlined the *Daily Telegraph* review, and it was, indeed, without chiffon and Mendelssohn.[10] The setting of Lila de Nobili and Henry Bardon offered the attributes of an Elizabethan stage. Simple wooden steps descended from a balustraded gallery; the space beneath the gallery served for Titania's sleep; and the stage was strewn with rushes. No act curtain was used (plate 12). Ontario's theatre was an influence, but Hall expressed doubts about the limitations of its bare stage, saying, "Nor do I think that the words of the play should carry all the burden of creating the illusion in theatre."[11] The Elizabethanesque unit setting was combined with romantic but lightly theatrical pictures. For the palace scenes, this unit was backed by a painted drop representing a Tudor hall facade and lit in warm ambers. For the wood scenes, it was dressed with shrubbery and flowers brought on by the actors and backed by projections of a glowing green forest (plate 12). The design offered, then, a kind of unstable compromise between a return to Elizabethan authenticity and illusionistic elements. As such, it proved congenial to a recurring motif in the production that the irrational forest fairy world was just beneath the surface of the decorous court. De Nobili costumed the courtiers in high Elizabethan style, patterned on Hilliard miniatures, thought critic John Russell Brown.[12] Oberon (Ian Richardson) and Puck (Ian Holm) wore court dress, too, but below their starched ruffs they were barefoot and bare-legged — "an inexplicable lack of taste," declared critic Muriel St. Clare Byrne (fig. 51).[13] Puck erupted unceremoniously through numerous traps from beneath the stage. The fairies were impish urchins rather than languorous ballet dancers; they were eclectically costumed, some in remnants of classical armor, some as country maids, some as gowned court women.[14] A soft touch of tinkling bells signaled their appearance. Titania's attendant fairy made a weary complaint of having to "hang a pearl in *every* cowslip's ear."[15] Judi Dench's Titania (1962), costumed as a sensuous, undersea queen, finned, barefoot, and crowned with wild white hair, was nature's child, a kind of Shakespearean Ondine, whose fondness for Bottom was sexually playful.[16] The fairy world was not one of theatrical artifice, nor was it so much a supernatural realm as a natural liminal one, an irrepressible, irrational force that could not and should not be denied.

Charles Laughton was Bottom in the 1959 premiere, weighing in heavily in the Stratford star tradition of the 1950s. Kenneth Tynan characterized him in the role as "a rapscallion uncle dressed up to entertain the children at a Christmas party."[17] But Albert Finney and Vanessa Redgrave brought the sensibilities of a new generation of actors to the young lovers, making them more anxious and coltish than courtly. Redgrave was a gawky, comic Helena, subject to

FIGURE 51. Ian Richardson as Oberon (left) and Ian Holm as Puck in the Royal Shakespeare Company production, 1959–1962. Directed by Peter Hall, designed by Lila de Nobili, assisted by Henry Bardon. Shakespeare Centre Library.

thumping falls. Muriel St. Clare Byrne, reviewing the play in the *Shakespeare Quarterly*, indicated her displeasure that the quartet had been encouraged to "galumph" through their woodland confusions and complained that "these hobble-dehoys and hoydens are out of place in the concluding court scene."[18] Tynan objected that too many people "fell unfunnily down."[19] Critics also complained of the inept speaking of the poetry by the lovers. (This was a concern of critics throughout the four-year life of the production.)[20] Such departures from the form and grace in movement and the pleasing melodies of speech that had been traditionally associated with Shakespearean acting were violations of an upper-class decorum thought appropriate to the classics. Franco Zeffirelli's *Romeo and Juliet* at the Old Vic in 1960 also broke from those traditions. (It could be argued that Leonard Bernstein's 1957 *West Side Story*, with its rival gangs, had already breached the class barriers.) In Hall's 1969 film of the play, a close relative of his 1959 staging, the young lovers (with Diana Rigg as Helena) became increasingly mud spattered and confused in their forest chase, and the fairies were controversial because they all had dirty faces.[21] By the time of the 1962 stage revival, Hall had refined the impression of confused young lovers, who were now more sympathetically seen as "lost, helpless young people who find themselves shocked by each new action as they take it. Their self-confidence is steadily and ludicrously turned inside out."[22] There seemed to be little ease in the discordant spheres of the mortal lovers and the fairy royalty, but Bottom and friends appeared to be content with their lives. Their experiences seem to have been more integral to the play as they functioned more as individuals and less as generic class inferiors and clowns. (It is worth noting that Hall was the first artistic director at Stratford to come from a working-class family.)[23] With the casting of Paul Hardwick as Bottom in 1962 (fig. 52), the playing of *Pyramus and Thisbe* became simpler and more innocent, his Pyramus proving to be a rather touching amateur actor.[24] During the artisans' forest rehearsal, Snug (John Nettleton in 1963) wandered off to smell a flower until the accusing silence of the others brought him back.[25] The translated Bottom wore no ass's head, only hooves on his hands and a pair of donkey's ears, which left his face fully visible. In all, the innovative attributes of Hall's staging — its marked departure from scenic and costuming conventions for this play; its interest in the irrational, including sexual desire, just beneath the surfaces of the rational world; its interest in individualizing all the characters, especially the lovers and the mechanicals; and its less decorous acting of Shakespeare — link it with productions to come.

The spirit of liberation of the early 1960s touched even Ontario, where acting styles were relatively traditional, the young lovers (including Kate Reid as

FIGURE 52. Paul Hardwick as Bottom and Judi Dench as Titania in the Royal Shakespeare Company production, 1962. Shakespeare Centre Library.

Helena, Leo Ciceri as Lysander, and Peter Donat as Demetrius) were prominent, and they and the fairies (especially Bruno Gerussi's Oberon) were athletic. Mendelssohn and balletic fairies were gone, and the production was "more
like a track meet than a shimmering fairy story," wrote Brooks Atkinson, who
with other critics lamented the poorly spoken poetry.[26] Stratford's idealized
Elizabethanism was still the prevailing mode overall, however, with quasi-
Elizabethan guitar music composed and played on stage by Canadian composer
Harry Somers ("a terrible let-down from Mendelssohn," wrote one reviewer).[27]
There was even an echo of Charles Kean in the Maypole dance of the fairies in
the finale, many of whom were children.[28]

At the Old Vic in 1960, Michael Langham opened his production with a hy-
meneal chant and Dionysian dance in preparation for the entrance of Hippolyta
in manacles. Kenneth Tynan complained of Langham's view that "all life as well
as all nature has been set a-jangling."[29] At the Royal Court Theatre in London,
home of the English Stage Company and the drama of a new generation of playwrights — notably John Osborne, John Arden, and Arnold Wesker — director
Tony Richardson drew on the new generation of actors to do *A Midsummer
Night's Dream* in 1962. Rita Tushingham played Hermia, Samantha Eggar was
Titania, Lynn Redgrave was Helena, Nicol Williamson was Flute, and David
Warner played Snout. The results distressed critics, who complained of the
poor speech of the young actors who had never played Shakespeare, one critic
saying they spoke the poetry "flatfootedly," without much music, rushing and
chopping the verse.[30] Richardson said he chose his young cast for their "freshness and youth," but clearly they also brought to Shakespeare manners and sensibilities to which critics were unaccustomed.[31] Colin Blakely's Bottom seems to
have sought an authentic, common touch for Bottom by making him an Ulster-
man. In the Regent's Park production in the summer of 1962, the young lovers
also shattered decorum, quarreling like children in the forest.[32] In New York in
1964, the young lovers were popular in Joseph Papp's mobile theatre production
that, with an integrated cast, toured the city's five boroughs in the summer and
its high schools in the fall. Lysander drew great laughter with the lines, "You
have her father's love, Demetrius; / Let me have Hermia's. Do you marry him"
(1.1.93–94).[33] Papp's attempt to make Shakespeare less highbrow and more accessible had mixed results, but middle- and upper-class ownership of Shakespeare was being challenged.[34]

In this cultural climate it is not entirely surprising, then, to find the Beatles
entering the performance life of the play. The rock group from Liverpool, happily assaulting musical, class, and even national barriers, performed *Pyramus and
Thisbe* in a 1964 television special entitled "Around the Beatles." Produced by

the British company Rediffusion, the special was seen in England and in the United States. The show, which included some of the group's most famous songs, opened with a spoof. Paul McCartney was Pyramus, wearing an odd helmet and a doublet on which was a large "P," with an olive branch running through it; John Lennon was Thisbe in a bonnet and a dress with a large "T" on the chest; George Harrison was Moonshine in a nightcap and a nightgown with a crescent moon on it; and Ringo Starr was Lion in a furry headpiece and a doublet with a large "L" on it. As a curtain raiser, John, Paul, and George mimed a trumpet fanfare, and Ringo hoisted a flag and set off a cannon.[35] It apparently was a parodic contribution to the nearly worldwide celebration in 1964 of the four-hundredth anniversary of Shakespeare's birth. In America, an inane musical spoof of the play by Rick Besoyan, entitled *Babes in the Woods*, opened in New York late that year.[36] The following year Fleetwood Films produced an odd, animated adaptation of the play, with the cartoon character Mr. Magoo as Puck.

By the time of the quadricentennial of Shakespeare's birth and observances reverent and irreverent, Western Shakespearean production and criticism had begun to reflect the postwar cultural changes. In the early 1960s, the works of three theatre figures on the Continent had a profound influence on the way Shakespeare was read and played: Antonin Artaud's *The Theatre and Its Double* (first published in 1938 and translated into English in 1958), Jan Kott's *Shakespeare Our Contemporary* (published in Polish and French in 1962 and in English in 1964), and Bertolt Brecht's Berliner Ensemble productions, along with his manifesto, *Short Organum for the Theatre* (first published in German in 1949 and in English in 1964). Together they triangulated the ground on which the Western classical tradition stood. Artaud critiqued Western theatre's logocentric preoccupations with texts and the repetition of masterpieces that gave no access to or release of what he suggested were the dark forces at the heart of the human condition. In an impassioned rhetoric that evoked images of the bodily suffering of actor and spectator, he called for a "theatre of cruelty" that would return spectators to a primordial unconscious, to a reuniting of the long disassociated physical and metaphysical.[37] Kott offered existential, absurdist readings of the plays, in a radical appropriation of Shakespeare to represent a dark, postwar vision of the human condition as absurd and futile.[38] Brecht sought to dismantle Aristotelian structure, illusionistic staging, and romantic aesthetics in the interest of awakening the spectator to question and change the social conditions left unaddressed and unchallenged in traditional Western theatre, the "culinary" theatre.[39] The changes in Shakespearean production that began in the 1960s were the result of complex social changes, of course, but the influences of Artaud, Kott, and Brecht were profound. Their works were congenial to the cultural changes. Because Artaud's and Kott's ideas had an especially direct impact on productions of *A Midsummer Night's Dream*, I want to review them here.[40]

Artaud saw in Western culture an absence of "everything that used to sustain our lives," and in the opening pages of *The Theatre and Its Double* he wrote of a deep "rupture between things and words," a cleavage between spirit and body and between civilized culture and the mysterious, dangerous forces at the dark heart of life, to which the theatre should give access.[41] He called for a theatre that would "break through language in order to touch life," for the re-creation of a theatre that would sever itself from the Western reverence for texts, from Aristotelian storytelling and the mere mirroring of daily reality. A "theatre of cruelty" was necessary to liberate Western audiences from dead masterpieces, from a decadent theatre of detached art, whose only purpose is to distract us in our leisure. "Shakespeare himself is responsible for this abberation and decline," he wrote in his famous chapter "No More Masterpieces."[42] Drawing on Balinese dance theatre, Artaud theorized a theatre reaching beyond discursive language, key-hole realism, and psychology, a theatre in which the spectator would be enveloped in spectacle, sound, music, dance, and gesture. Theatre should provide a release from the cosmic cruelty repressed in modern Western culture, draining "the abscesses" that otherwise lead to hatred and violence. Theatre should return audiences to the primordial, to the experience of the original undivided spirit before matter and materialization, to the unity prior to dissociation. In this theatre, the actor would be an athlete of the passions, the actor's body a graphic text in itself, a concept that Polish director Jerzy Grotowski (*Towards a Poor Theatre*, 1968) sought to bring into practical training and performance. Artaud's rebellion was against the pre–World War II French theatre, but his vision influenced directors in the 1960s, such as Peter Brook and Ariane Mnouchkine, who sought alternatives to a logocentric theatre and Stanislavskian realism in highly theatrical productions that sometimes evoked ancient rites or appropriated Eastern myths or oriental theatrical modes. In their productions in the 1990s, such as Brook's *Mahabharata* and Mnouchkine's *Richard II*, *Le Nuit des rois*, and *Les Atrides*, spoken dialogue was subsumed in theatrically elaborated productions of epic proportions. These productions were developed by companies working collectively over long periods and involved dance, music, ritualized movement, stylized acting and makeup, and opulent, exotic costumes, often influenced in all of these elements by ancient Indian or Japanese theatre.[43]

Kott's most famous chapter of *Shakespeare Our Contemporary* aligned Shakespeare and Beckett in a comparison of *King Lear* with *Endgame* and *Waiting for Godot*. It had an immediate impact on Brook's bleak staging of *King Lear* in 1962. No small part of Kott's success was his theatrical as well as his existential reading of the staging dynamics of Gloucester's suicide "leap." But Kott's chapter on *A Midsummer Night's Dream* was also widely influential. His influence may be apparent as early as 1966 in the staging of the play by John Hancock at the Actor's Workshop in San Francisco, and the productions of Mnouchkine in Paris in 1968 and Brook in 1970 were both touched by Kott. Director John Hirsch flirted lightly with Kott's reading at Stratford, Ontario, in 1968 and again at the Guthrie Theatre in 1972 and 1984. Kott was certainly behind the dark productions of Konrad Swinarski in Krakow in 1970, in which silent, secret police spied for the nobility throughout the play, and he helped shape the productions of directors Christoph Schroth in Halle in 1971 and Alexander Lang and Thomas Langhoff in East Berlin in 1980.[44] Kott's direct influence is not always possible to establish firmly, but it is hard to imagine several American productions of the 1970s and 1980s without Kott: Alvin Epstein's at the Yale Repertory Theatre in 1975, Liviu Ciulei's at the Guthrie Theatre in 1985, and Mark Lamos's at the Hartford Stage Company in 1988.

Kott's reading of *A Midsummer Night's Dream* reflects his general vision of the bleak condition of humankind in a cruel, inscrutable world, void of any metaphysical design and meaning, subject to the terrors of the state and the "Grand Mechanism" of a continuingly corrupted human history. Kott characterizes Puck as a manipulator, akin to the devil and to Ariel in *The Tempest*, whom Kott compares to a Soviet KGB agent. He argues that the suddenness of desire in the young lovers and the absence of individuality in them reduces them to mere sexual partners, making the play brutally erotic and very modern. Kott sees in the play a veritable bestiary of animal eroticism, with sexually symbolic images that range from fawning spaniels to worms to snakes to bulls. "From antiquity up to the Renaissance the ass was credited with the strongest sexual potency and among all the quadrapeds was supposed to have the longest and hardest phallus," writes Kott.[45] Promiscuity abounds in the fairy world. He imagines Titania's court as consisting of "old men and women toothless and shaking, their mouths wet with saliva, who sniggering[ly] procure a monster for their mistress."[46] Five pages of his essay are devoted to detailed descriptions of deformed humanity, bestial acts, and scatalogical images in Goya's *Caprichos*, from which Kott then moves to picture Titania caressing the ass's head, an image he thinks more akin to Bosch than to Chagall. Alien or excessive as some readers found Kott's readings, others found in them a liberation of the plays from traditional, romantic views. For them, Kott not only "deprived Shakespeare of the comfortable status of a tamed classic," as Dennis Kennedy put it, he also provided a powerful model of contemporary intervention, implacably driven by twentieth-century experience.[47]

Shadows had crept into some productions of the play before — Reinhardt's slightly menacing Oberon and his trembling Bottom, Hall's anxious young lovers, and Langham's manacled Hippolyta — but these were slight compared to those to come. A radically antiromantic production was created in 1966 by John Hancock, the new twenty-two-year-old artistic director of the San Francisco Actor's Workshop. He staged it later that year at the Pittsburgh Playhouse's Craft Avenue Theatre and again in June 1967 at the off-Broadway Theatre De Lys.[48] The sets and costumes were designed by Robert LaVigne after drawings by Jim Dine, an important figure in the pop art movement in which artists such as Claes Oldenburg and Red Grooms took images of American popular culture as their iconic and ironic subjects. Dine visually coded characters with pop images — the comic book Wonder Woman was the source for Titania's costume (plate 13) — and Hancock offered a Jean Genet-like vision of perverted power and exhausted romantic traditions.

The setting consisted of a long, curving, planked ramp that began upstage left and wound down to the orchestra pit at center. It circled a revolving stage with a few real trees, whose pots were covered with oriental floral rugs, and the stage was backed by black vinyl sheeting. Framing the set was a rainbow proscenium, striped in shiny Red Devil house-paint enamels. (Rainbow stripes were a frequent motif in Dine paintings.) At one end of the rainbow sat a 1940 Wurlitzer jukebox, glowing and bubbling in neon colors and blaring forth Mendelssohn's "Wedding March" at any moment that was sexually suggestive and playing Gustav Mahler's *Song of the Earth* at other times.[49]

The performance opened with two doctors in white wheeling a cart full of corpses, plague victims, down the circular ramp. Members of the court breathed through cloths to protect themselves from the unmentioned plague. (Was this a refence to the war in Vietnam?) Theseus (Alvin Epstein in New York) planned his nuptials in defiance of the morbid atmosphere and reveled in his captured bride. Hippolyta was an African American woman in leopard skins (Gloria Foster in New York), brooding in a black bamboo cage. Theseus applied the law of Athens harshly to Hermia. Sexual perversion was rampant in the courts of both the Athenian and fairy worlds. "The decadence is palpable," wrote Michael Smith in the *Village Voice*.[50] Epstein and Foster doubled as Oberon and Titania, suggesting a thoroughly nightmarish universe. (The first occasion of the doubling of these roles, to my knowledge, was in a New York production of the Shakespearewrights company in 1956.)[51]

In the forest, the fairies were puppet insects, hairy bats, cobwebs, and dolls with wings, operated on strings from poles ("by Zombies," Hancock recalled), all painted with Dayglo colors, phosphorescent under ultraviolet lights.[52] (Czechoslovakian director Jiri Trnka had used puppets in his 1959 animated film of the play, re-released in 1961 with narration by Richard Burton, but they were charming puppets.)[53] Puck was played by the muscular, scantily clad Barton Heyman, who had recently played Stanley Kowalski in Hancock's Pittsburgh production of *A Streetcar Named Desire*. His body was horizontally banded in rainbow colors, and he made his entrance swinging on an overstuffed red satin heart on a chain, an amour-weary Puck with artificial peonies stuck behind his ears.[54] Titania's Wonder Woman costume consisted of blue-spangled shorts, a halter with breast cups target-striped in rainbow colors, and high, shiny, red boots. Dine's original design for Titania (plate 13) shows her equipped with slender, battery-powered light bulbs placed over her genitals ("let wires show; let batteries show!" instructs Dine's handwritten note). But ultimately it was Demetrius who was wired with an electric codpiece that flashed on to register his sexual passions.[55] Helena was performed in drag by the six-foot-four-inch Robert Benson in a blond wig, putting Helena's relationship with the other three lovers in a new light and disrupting the conventional romantic symmetry of the quartet.[56] Oberon (Alvin Epstein) was a headless, faceless, menacing spirit, whom Hancock himself described as "an empty shroud — a silver lamé shroud, with, as far as you can see, nobody inside it. But with a hand — a rainbow hand — that worked magic. The other hand was a dead stick."[57] This somewhat sadistic Oberon put the lovers through an agonized, slow motion chase on the forest turntable. It was while enjoying their torment that Puck delivered his "What fools these mortals be!"[58]

The original costume designs for the mechanicals were in some part derivative of hippie culture, although changes were made, and ultimately critics were sure they saw something Brechtian in them. Peter Quince appeared barechested in a burlap vest, with burlap pants; the tools that were to hang in loops on his vest and pants proved impractical in action, as did the pots and pans that were to hang on Snout's coat.[59] In a remarkable scene after their play, the artisans clamored to be paid, and the court set its steel-helmeted guards on them to drive them up the ramp and out of the palace while decadent courtiers cavorted to bed.

The production baffled most critics, and some rejected it angrily; "A Midsummer Nightmare," was *Newsday*'s headline, and "Opium Dream" was the *New York Times*'s. *Variety*'s critic found it "campy," the *Shakespeare Quarterly* critic damned it as a wearisome attempt to improve on a great writer; and several reviewers complained that Kott's book was probably behind its bleak vision of a diseased society.[60] The *New York Times*'s Dan Sullivan, complaining that Hancock had "given us a comment on a play instead of the play itself," revealed the fundamental modernist assumptions still in play in 1966: texts were stable, and the proper work of the director was the noninterventional servicing of a text's universality.[61] Also evident in his response was the prevailing modernist dependence on the avant-garde artist as the visionary provider of tomorrow's mainstream art.[62] By the mid-1960s, however, this one-track model was being supplanted in the theatre by the work of groups seeking alternative theatrical forms and lifestyles that did not lead back to the mainstream, groups such as La Mama, the Open Theatre, the Living Theatre, and Mabou Mines.[63] To the *New York Times* critic and others, the Hancock production seemed, at best, a failed send-up.

But satire is not an adequate characterization here, anymore than it was for the Mabou Mines's *Lear* in 1990, a production that similarly confused and dismayed mainstream critics with its grandmotherly woman as Lear, ruling over her farm in rural Georgia, and her transvestite Fool, carrying a dildo and flaunting his unorthodox sexuality.[64] Hancock's production was neither an avant-garde interpretation of *A Midsummer Night's Dream* nor a satire, in any conventional sense of those terms, nor even camp (Susan Sontag's "Notes on 'Camp'" was published in 1964).[65] Rather, it may be said to have staged, however crudely, a critique of the play's conventional theatrical readings and trappings together with an exploration of what Louis Montrose has described as the play's fascination with unstable hierarchies and gender categories.[66] The production in effect overturned every normative expectation audiences had of the play: expectations of benevolent state power, conventional gender roles, romantic love, white magic, the orderly continuation of the kingdom, and the beneficence of high art in general. It also demystified the text, suggesting with its headless, faceless Oberon the problem of representing any metaphysical presence behind the signifiers, critiquing the conventional dream of that presence. The real subject here was that absent center to which all the sophisticated symbolism in the staging of Reinhardt and other modernist directors had been referring spectators.[67] It is probably for this reason that Michael Smith of the *Village Voice* thought he saw in Hancock's staging "not a bunch of flashy ideas but a complete conception, not a flourish of theatrical tricks but a fully realized production, with an original coherent style and point of view. Hancock's work is enormously impressive."[68] No wonder some critics accused it of being influenced by Kott's book, which had been widely reviewed and discussed by this time. The production could be taken as the refutation of a whole history of romantic and modernist interpretations of the play and the replacement of those views by a bleak vision of the human condition. But the Hancock production, with its rainbow proscenium, also exuded a lively, witty faith in an artistic process of critiquing a legacy of tired illusions, a faith that finally seems more American than European, influenced though the production may have been by Artaud and possibly Kott. It may be described as early postmodern; the term seems especially appropriate given Jim Dine's scenic contribution. As Andreas Huyssen has suggested, the theoretical notion of the postmodern first took shape in the context of pop art.[69]

Shakespeare scholar Allan Lewis tried to win tolerance for Hancock's production and what he took to be its Kottian vision: "It does make Shakespeare a modern Polish intellectual with French leanings, but it is defensible. Much of *A Midsummer Night's Dream* is based on Ovid's *Epistles* and *The Golden Ass* of Apuleius, neither models of Puritan morality."[70] Lewis's better argument was that a traditionally romantic production of the play, playing concurrently at Stratford, Connecticut, was equally challengeable. Stratford's 1967 production was staged by Cyril Ritchard with a corps de ballet reminiscent of productions of the late 1940s. With strips of gaily colored cloth hung from the flies, silver foil added for forest scenes, and Titania flown in on a tinsel-covered bower, the set suggested Christmas decorations to some critics. Ritchard, in a star turn, doubled as Oberon and Bottom. The only interest the production had for most critics was in how this novel trick was done.[71]

A spirit akin to Artaud was in play in Ariane Mnouchkine's staging of *A Midsummer Night's Dream* in February 1968, in the formative years of her now famous Théâtre du Soleil. From her beginnings in the early 1960s, Mnouchkine envisioned a people's theatre, as had Jean Vilar with his Théâtre Nationale Populaire, one of several key influences on her. Among other theatrical sources, Mnouchkine has drawn on the theories of Vsevolod Meyerhold as well as Artaud; upon the work and ideas of Jacques Copeau, including the open stage of his Théâtre du Vieux-Colombier; on the commedia dell'arte and Indian dance theatre; and on her training with mime Jacques Lecoq, with its emphasis on the physical expression of emotion.[72] She eschews Western, Stanislavskian acting, with its focus on individual psychology, and reaches instead for an epic, metaphoric choreography, hoping to tap archetypal energies. She and her company create their productions collectively, as a community of artists working together on each production over a long period of time in their home in the Cartoucherie on the outskirts of Paris. The idealistic spirit extends to the communal sharing of meals in this micro-utopia. At lengthy performances, such as those of *Les Atrides*, simple meals, international in flavor, are provided for audiences at intermissions, where one is apt to encounter Mnouchkine herself serving. While a leftist ideology and disenchantment with the spiritual impoverishment of the West run deep in her, Mnouchkine's is not an austere, poor theatre. Her long suit has been a highly theatricalized theatre of heightened imagery, physicalized emotion, dance, music, and sound. Her productions are elaborate, often appropriating costume, dance, and masks from oriental cultures with a high order of aesthetic discrimination, and Mnouchkine has received some government subsidies for them.[73]

Mnouchkine's *Le Songe d'une nuit d'été* was the company's fourth production and its first Shakespearean one. It was the unlikely sequel to her theatrical, cruel rendering of Arnold Wesker's naturalistic *The Kitchen* (*La Cuisine*), which had been the highlight of the Paris theatre season of 1967.[74] *Le Songe d'une nuit d'été* was developed in a space that had been the circus ring in a building once the home of the Cirque Medrano in Montmartre. Mnouchkine's vision of the play certainly was touched by the spirits of Artaud and Kott (the differences notwithstanding for the moment):

> the most savage, the most violent play that you could dream of. A fabulous bestiary with depths which concern nothing less that the "savage god" which sleeps in the heart of men; corrosive anguish, terror. . . . It is also the accidental, the unexpected, the breakdown of the natural order of things, the transgressing of taboos.[75]

A translation by Jules Supervielle was reworked by Phillipe Léotard (who played Bottom) to "strip the text of its prettiness," according to Adrian Kiernander.[76] For the setting, designer Roberto Moscoso covered the steeply raked floor of the wide, semicircular playing area with beige goatskins, the furry pelts laid end to end. The floor was backed with a high, gaunt cyclorama of driftwood planks, through the holes in which a huge, strangely luminous full moon was seen at center, flanked by smaller moons. Other moons of wood and metal hung on the wooden curtain.[77] Oberon, Puck, and other fairies were satyrlike, wearing denim or leather trousers with their chests bared and painted with large red spots (suggesting blood?). For the meeting of Oberon and Titania by the strange moonlight, some of the fairies wore floor-length purple robes, white, African-influenced masks featuring elongated noses to their waists, and huge furry headpieces, which made them look like some fantastic high priests of the moon. The vast goatskin stage, which looked like a lunar landscape in the yellow light of the night scenes, was athletically used by the cast of twenty-six. Puck (René Patrignani) tumbled across it, acrobatic but grotesque; Oberon and Titania, played by Germinal Casado and Ursula Kubler from Maurice Béjart's contemporary dance company, glided across it, he in jeans and a leather vest and she in a flowing silk cape and leather pants and halter. Françoise Tournafond costumed the entire court in trousers and knee-length tunics, East Indian in style, giving the court a formal, ceremonial presence. On-stage musicians in Indian costume provided the music, largely percussive, composed by Jacques Lasry.[78]

Oberon was a disturbingly malevolent creature who apparently strangled one of Titania's attendants and raped Hermia.[79] Puck took pleasure in the torment of the young lovers, reminding critic Henri Gouhier of August Strindberg's comments on some dark elements of the play. Strindberg disliked Puck, seeing in him "not a figure of light but of evil," who rejoiced in the suffering of the innocent.[80] Gouhier wrote of Mnouchkine's Puck as lubricious and demonic; another critic thought him nearer to Mephisto than to elves.[81] Gouhier described Mnouchkine's conception as wholly Dionysian, while Shakespeare's play is his "most Apollonian." In her vision, "the dream is entirely a nightmare," Gouhier wrote; "c'est une nuit sans clair de lune."[82]

The mechanicals were the production's only realistic element. Conceived as clowns, they were dressed in brightly colored, nineteenth-century working-class costumes and were given to knockabout clown business. In the lunar landscape, they were the most problematic and least successful element of the production. The performance ended with an athletic round dance in which the full company — fairies, mechanicals, and courtiers — all joined hands.[83]

With its combination of rich theatrical imagery and its dark vision, the production seems to have invoked both the spirit of Artaud's prayers for a return to the primordial and Kott's fable of a terminally deformed world.[84] Its dialectic between desire and despair recalls Artaud and Nietzsche. Like many of Mnouchkine's productions to come, it seems to have been an attempt to create a mythological, archetypal theatre, to access the ineffable with an iconography of the exotic, with borrowings in this case from Africa and India.[85] Her intent goes far beyond the orientalized golden fairies that Barker hoped would serve Shakespeare's text. Mnouchkine's archetypal imagery reaches for some metaphysical plenitude (to borrow from Derrida's analysis of Artaud) behind and beyond the text, the Artaudian point where primordial presence, text, and performance might become one in a theatre of pure presence, of unity prior to dissociation.[86] Yet Mnouchkine's production also suggests a deconstructive vision of the play, haunted by absences; there was nothing divine or benevolent beneath these moons. The multiple moons, gaunt masks, and blooded fairies seem hollowed out signifiers. The production staged a compelling dialectic between the hallowing and the hollowing, between presence and absence, between the Artaudian goatskin floor and the Derridean moons. In such a context, the chief difficulty, understandably, was in defining the ever social mechanicals.

Mnouchkine's theatre was filled nightly for the production, and it helped establish the company.[87] Invitations to tour *Le Songe* and other works in the company's repertoire came from several French cities, Italy, and the Soviet Union. But the company was soon drawn into the political upheavals of the spring of 1968. The run of *Le Songe* was cut short in favor of a tour of *La Cuisine* to workers in factories, many of whom, according to Kiernander, expressed regret that they could not see *Le Songe* instead.[88]

By the late 1960s, a number of productions in England, the United States, and Canada were boasting contemporary features, many quite superficial. In an Edinburgh production, jazz singer Cleo Laine doubled as Titania and Hippolyta, and Bottom wore a leather motorcyle jacket and a crash helmet.[89] Overt eroticism among the fairies became the trend, reflecting the increasing sexual freedoms of the era. In Peter Hall's 1969 film version of the play, Judi Dench's Titania was a sensuous sea queen, all but bare-bosomed in netting over a nearly transparent body stocking. Suggestions of sexual decadence or corrupted power at court also appeared, but these finally amounted to little more than political chic. In his Ontario production of 1968, director John Hirsch, a Hungarian émigré, was obviously flirting with Kott's reading, although Hirsch's program notes nowhere acknowledged it. Nor do his pre-production working notes, which called for the court to be "a dead frozen world. The court in uniform. Everything is buttoned, concealing warped bodies. A general corseting." This "society of fossils" was dressed in high Victorian dress uniforms; Theseus (Kenneth Pogue) was an elderly, doddering, corseted general, with a ravenous sexual appetite, and his bride, Hippolyta, wore a black riding habit and boots and carried a riding crop. Hirsch notes described the fairies as "children of the free loins of Night, moon-ripened and moon-governed. They lead a life of total sexual experience."[90] Martha Henry was an erotic Titania, husky voiced and sensuous in a gossamer body stocking. "Never was Bottom more lovingly stroked," wrote Arnold Edinborough in the *Shakespeare Quarterly*.[91] The Indian boy was an attractive young African American man in his late teens, for whom, it was implied, both Titania and Oberon had some erotic longing. Enrage some critics though these particular elements did, they led nowhere; the production remained conventionally romantic in all other ways. The *New York Times*'s Dan

Sullivan observed that "Hirsch's direction begins audaciously, but pulls away from the logical result of his audacity when the moment of truth arrives," much as did Stanley Silverman's score, which opened with an ironic reference to Mendelssohn "but respectfully knuckled under to 'The Wedding March' in the traditional manner."[92] By the end of the production, Theseus and Hippolyta were harmless lovebirds, like the young couples.[93]

For Peter Brook, no contemporary Shakespearean performance practice could begin within what he called "the deadly theatre," which was the product of conventional, commercial theatre practices in which productions had to be packaged in about three weeks. In his 1968 book, *The Empty Space*, Brook, influenced by Artaud and Grotowski, called for "a holy theatre." The bright circus theatricalism of his 1970 *A Midsummer Night's Dream* is best understood in the light of this holy quest.[94] In some part, it can be seen as akin to the quest for sincerity and authenticity in the era, terms that, as Lionel Trilling explained at the time, had almost become code words for the idea that truth and the source of a renewed society might lie in some pre-rational holy madness.[95] In *The Empty Space*, Brook wrote: "Once, the theatre could begin as magic: magic at the sacred festival, or magic as the footlights came up. Today, it is the other way round. . . . We cannot assume that the audience will assemble devoutly and attentively. It is up to us to capture its attention and compel its belief. To do so we must prove that there will be no trickery. We must open our empty hands and show that really there is nothing up our sleeves. Only then can we begin."[96]

To Brook, Mnouchkine, and others, it seemed necessary and possible in the 1960s that the theatre should take upon itself nothing less than the tasks of recapturing the sacred and creating a new community of faith as an alternative to a soulless Western capitalist society. Making this possible began with a process of retraining the actor to avoid any imitations of traditional (false) acting style and "to discover by himself what exists in himself."[97] It was necessary to engage each actor in each role in a contemporary transaction with the text to discover what Brook liked to call "the hidden play." "It's from the hidden inner life of the performer that the magic, the unfolding possibilities of the play, must emerge." Brook sought, he said, "an essential area" in the Shakespeare play, "where meaning between actor and audience can be shared again. This form of intensity makes all question of the play's relation to the past unimportant. . . . All theatre begins when it is alive — all other theatre is dead."[98] Brook worked collaboratively with his relatively young cast and staff, which included assistant director Michael Bogdanov. He developed further the new methods of training used in his previous productions of *The Balcony*, *Marat/Sade*, and *US*. A six-month preparation period included company exercises in improvisation, concentration, spontaneous encounters with portions of the text, and stick exercises reminiscent of aikido. "As we passed the sticks from hand to hand, to the rhythm of drums, over long distances, or from great heights, so we were to learn to handle words and speeches, sharing and experiencing them as a united group," wrote John Kane, who played Puck. The actual rehearsal period, eight weeks in length, then followed. Kane remembers that the studio "filled up with trapezes, ropes, plastic rods, spinning plates, tennis-balls, hoops, paper string, and a variety of musical instruments," with which the company exercised daily before coming to the text.[99] In the trapeze work, the actors learned to concentrate on close coordination with each other. Sally Jacobs introduced Kane to the costume for Puck, a luminous yellow, blousy jumpsuit with a blue skullcap, inspired by the costumes of acrobats in a Chinese circus she and Brook had seen in Paris.[100] Brook decided that several roles should be doubled; he wanted a small company, believing that the quality of actor involvement would be better and that the foregrounding of a performance by a small ensemble would heighten the sense of theatrical metaphor.[101] Alan Howard doubled as Theseus/Oberon, Sara Kestelman as Hippolyta/Titania, John Kane as Philostrate/Puck, and Philip Locke as Egeus/Quince. Brook also liked the possibilities of dreamlike associations of doubling.

Brook and his company thus sought to do nothing less than invent a new theatrical vocabulary for the play on the tabula rasa of designer Jacobs's white box stage (not unlike Barker). Jacobs's trapezoidal white box consisted of three walls, each about four inches thick, with two swinging doors set flush in the upstage wall and a raked stage (fig. 53; plate 16). It was in some part an offspring of the all-white permanent unit setting of the RSC at Stratford in the 1969–1970 season, notably seen in Trevor Nunn's staging of *The Winter's Tale*.[102] Black masking drapes originally hung behind the white box, but Brook removed them in Paris during the world tour, consistent with his idea that "there is really nothing up our sleeves," thus allowing all the devices to be seen, including the two thirty-two-foot towers supporting the high bridge from which all suspensions hung.[103] Four white swings hung a few feet forward of the back wall, and two trapeze bars, their cables running up to traveling pulleys, hung at left and right. Around the top of the walls ran a metal catwalk. Ladders led to it at down right and left and at the slots in the side walls.[104] Stage managers, lighting board operators, and drummers were visible on the catwalk, and the fairies often observed the action from it. From there they threw blue foil "lightning bolts" when Oberon and Titania made their first entrances and lowered large metal coils (resembling Slinky toys) over the lovers in the forest to simulate the fright-

FIGURE 53. The mechanicals meet (1.2) on Sally Jacobs's white box setting for Peter Brook's Royal Shakespeare Company production, 1970. Thomas F. Holte, photographer. Shakespeare Centre Library.

ening, confusing wood (plate 14).[105] The intention, overall, was to move the play into the heightened realm of metaphor and away from realism and illusionism.

The production opened with a blaze of Brechtian white light and jazz-rock drums as the company ran onto the white setting in satin capes lined in silver and gold, tumbling, juggling, scampering up the ladders, and circling the stage, "aerialists pronouncing the circus begun," wrote one New York critic.[106] The entire production pulsed with kinetic energy. Oberon, in a purple satin gown and slippered feet, stood at ease on his trapeze bar high above the confused young lovers in the forest, a concerned love god. When Puck returned to him with the love potion (2.1), Puck sailed to Oberon's side on his own trapeze and, some fifteen feet above the stage, Puck passed the "potion" to Oberon — a silver plate spinning on a slender, clear Lucite rod, from Puck's rod to Oberon's — with an acrobatic skill and concentration that hushed and then delighted the audience (plate 15). When Puck returned to report the results of Oberon's love drug on Titania, he entered swinging out from the catwalk on a rope to his midair trapeze bar, Oberon greeting him with "Here comes my messenger. How now, mad spirit?" (3.2.4). The two then swayed side to side on their bars, lustily singing, "so it came to pass, / Titania waked and straightway loved an ass" (3.2.33–34). Puck appeared on stilts at another point to confuse the lovers in the forest.[107] Some critics thought they saw influences of Meyerhold in all the gymnastics.

The young lovers, the men in their tie-dyed shirts and the women in ankle-length white dresses (plate 14), pursued their quarrels athletically in 3.2 and with a lack of inhibition that audiences cheered. When Puck charmed Lysander with the love juice, Lysander (Christopher Gable or Terence Taplin) woke too instantly and reached for Puck's crotch. In pursuit of Demetrius (Ben Kingsley), Frances de la Tour's Helena brought him down with a rugby tackle, pinned him to the ground, and sat astraddle his chest. As Hermia, tiny Mary Rutherford managed to throw herself horizontally across an upstage door to bar Lysander's way. Lysander then hung her from a nearby trapeze which ascended, leaving her in midair hanging by her hands and kicking her feet as Helena described her as a puppet. Such strategies seemed artificial only to a few critics. Most spoke of the earnestness and dexterity of the actors, and most were agreed on the clarity and freshness in the handling of the text. Irving Wardle of the London *Times* wrote, "I have never heard it spoken with more scrupulous attention to sense and music."[108] A few thought the staging overwhelmed the poetry, leaving the subtleties of Shakespeare's play "scanted in the scurry," as Walter Kerr put it.[109] One Shakespearean scholar reportedly closed his eyes during the Stratford performance, loving the way it was spoken, hating the way it was presented.[110] There were occasional odd readings, such as Helena's broadly mock-heroic delivery of lines on her friendship with Hermia ("O, is all quite forgot? / All schooldays' friendship, childhood innocence? / We, Hermia, like two artificial gods . . ." (3.2.202–220). But my own experience was that the language was not only spoken clearly but with less artifice and more spontaneity than I had ever heard consistently throughout a Shakespearean production.

The fairies — four young, full-bodied men and women in long, full-sleeved tunic tops and white slacks — were always present, suspended on their swings or on the ladders and catwalk; their entrances and exits were punctuated with hand harps, cymbals, and drums in Richard Peaslee's "scoring" of the production with interpolated sounds. At the opening of the forest scene (2.1), they thrust whirling, whistling lengths of orange or green plastic tubing (toys known as Free-Kas) through the swinging doors ahead of them. One of them tossed out an almanac for Quince to check for moonshine on the night of the mechanicals' performance, and another thrust an alarm clock through one of the vertical slots in the side walls to wake Bottom from his dream after the court had left. Suspended on their swings, the four sang Titania to sleep with something like an Indian Vedic chant. Titania slept in an enormous red feather bower, which, after Oberon had charmed her, rose to the humming incantations of the fairies, carrying the green-robed fairy queen upward to sleep in midair until awakened by Bottom's song (plate 16).

The first of the two acts ended with a Dionysian scene that left the most lasting impression of the production and was characteristic of its broad, and sometimes crude, brush. Titania was clearly sexually enamored with Bottom (David Waller). (That Oberon and Titania were sexually active fairies was clear in Oberon's groping of her breasts and genitals during the moonlight quarrel.) When the awakened Titania said to Bottom, "I am a spirit of no common rate: / The summer still doth tend upon my state; / And I do love thee" (3.2.146–148), she jumped on his back, legs around his waist. With Mendelssohn's "Wedding March" blaring from loudspeakers and colored streamers and confetti showering down from the catwalks, Bottom was then carried off to Titania's bower on the shoulders of her fairies, one of whom thrust an arm between Bottom's legs to simulate a huge erection, which throbbed to the "Wedding March" music (fig. 54). There was little doubt about what would happen in the bower. Brook acknowledged the influence of Kott's stress on the eroticism of the play and spoke in Kottian terms of the phallus and sexual potency of the ass. Brook also found a Strindbergian sexual situation in this, saying, "Oberon's deliberate cool intention is to degrade Titania as a woman," and the ass was the perfect legendary animal for her sexual humiliation. "Titania tries to invest her love under all the forms of spiritual romance at her disposal — Oberon destroys her illusions totally. . . . Yet there's no cynicism in Oberon's action — he isn't a sadist. The play is about something very mysterious, and only to be understood by the complexity of human love."[112] In an interview with Margaret Croyden, he said: "It is as though . . . a husband secured the largest truckdriver for his wife to sleep with to smash her illusions about sex and to alleviate the difficulties in their marriage."[113] John Russell Brown complained in his review, "The director has here left the text far behind."[114] Croyden, caught up in the spirit of liberation in the production, found Freud in the interpretation, saying that with the doubling, the conjuring up of the ass for Hippolyta/Titania is Theseus/Oberon's attempt

FIGURE 54. Bottom (David Waller) rides on the shoulders of the fairies, while Titania (Sarah Kestelman) dances around them in the ribald sexual celebration to Mendelssohn's "Wedding March" that ended the first half of Peter Brook's Royal Shakespeare Company production, 1970. David Farrell, photographer. Shakespeare Centre Library.

to awake her sexuality: "acting out through dreams what real life forbids insures a conjugal reconciliation."[115] I suspect that for many in the audience, the moment of Bottom's transport was read in the general spirit of the 1960s as a celebration of liberated sexuality and as a release from Shakespearean stuffiness.

Important to the production as was this interest in the potency of an irrational dreamworld, in performance its young lovers became the emotional center. Fully contemporary in manner and sensibility, they were the liberated, idealistic, and anxious youth of the 1960s, flower children in love in a fragile world in which quick, bright things could easily come to confusion.[116] In the United States in the 1960s, that world included the war in Vietnam, the source of profound alienation among many of the young people in this first generation to come of age after World War II. On campuses from Berkeley to Columbia, they had protested this war of "the establishment," and some had fled to San Francisco's Haight-Ashbury or to communes, seeking an alternative lifestyle.

The opening scene of Hermia's confrontation with her father and Theseus was played with formal, authoritarian severity, the lines almost intoned, as if ritualizing a centuries-old conflict between the young-in-love and their parents. Theseus was especially severe, circling Hermia menacingly as he gave her the options of death or becoming a nun if she refused to obey her father. After the exit of the court, a musician entered at right to play a flamenco guitar plaintively beneath the scene between Lysander and Hermia on the course of true love: "Or if there were a sympathy in choice, / War, death, or sickness did lay seige to it, / Making it momentary as a sound, / Swift as a shadow, short as any dream" (1.1.141–144). Lysander said his simple good-bye to Helena at the end of this scene not perfunctorily but with expansive compassion: "Helena, adieu. / As you on him, Demetrius dote on you" (1.1.224–225). Not surprisingly, this company noticed, and exploited for the first time in the play's performance history, the fact that the Quarto text indicates no explicit reconciliation between Hermia and her father, Egeus.[117] After the hunting party discovers the young lovers asleep in the wood and the Duke intervenes ("Egeus, I will overbear your will, / For in the temple by and by with us / These couples shall eternally be knit" [4.1.178–180]), Egeus is given no reply, nor is there any stage direction to suggest his response or Hermia's to him. He is then absent from the last act. In this production, after Theseus had announced the marriage plan, Egeus moved sharply down right away from the royal party, his back to the Duke. As Theseus went on to cancel the hunt, Egeus exited alone, very visibly, before the departure of the court and in a different direction.[118] Egeus (Philip Locke) did not return in the final act; Brook did not adopt the Folio text and have Egeus replace Philostrate. The choice clearly suggested that the division between father and daughter was deep and would continue. (Because Philip Locke doubled as Egeus and Quince, it was a bit confusing when Quince/Egeus came on in the final act to deliver the prologue for *Pyramus and Thisbe*.) No production thereafter could neglect the matter, but other directors have chosen differently. Elijah Moshinsky, for example, in his 1981 BBC Television production, has Hermia move toward her father and embrace him, and before he exits, he kisses Hermia's hand.

The mechanicals' rehearsal and performance of their play were of great interest to Brook and the company from the beginning because of the issues of authenticity that were raised. Brook told an interviewer:

> We have dropped all pretence of making magic by bluff, through stage tricks. . . . We present all elements with which we are going to work in the open. This is related to one of the key lines in the play when the question arises about whether the man who is going to play the lion should be a real lion or only pretend to be real. Out of this academic and very Brechtian discussion comes the formulation that the actor should say to the audience, "I am a man as other men are." That is the necessary beginning for a play about the spirit world — the actors must present themselves as men who are like all other men. It's from the hidden inner life of the performer that the magic, the unfolding possibilities of the play must emerge. The core of the *Dream* is the Pyramus and Thisbe play, which doesn't come at the end of a highly organized work just for comic relief. The actor's art is truly celebrated in this episode — it becomes a mysterious interplay of invisible elements, the joy, the magic of the *Dream*.[119]

So it was that David Waller as Bottom made an earnest effort to instruct Snug in how to play the lion: "Nay, you must name his name, and half his face must be seen through the lion's neck, and he himself must speak through, saying thus . . . 'If you think I come hither as a lion, it were pity of my life. No, I am no such thing. I am a man, as other men are'" (3.1.33–38). When Snug got carried away by roaring in the actual performance, he apologized to his audience. And Bottom delivered with utmost sincerity Shakespeare's parodying bombast in which Pyramus discovers Thisbe dead: "What dreadful dole is here? . . . O fates, come, come, / Cut thread and thrum, / Quail, crush, conclude, and quell" (5.1.273–282). Theseus took great pains to understand Philostrate's description of *Pyramus and Thisbe* as "tragical mirth" and "tedious and brief," and he watched intently to be sure the players' performances were not mocked by the giddy courtiers. "The nineteenth-century tradition assumes that because people are workmen they are comic and empty-headed and they're to be laughed at, [but] . . . there is nothing in the text that suggests they are stage-yokels from the country," said Brook.[120] The actors attempted to bring a contemporary blue-collar ethos to the mechanicals. Bottom wore a nylon mesh undershirt, fatigue pants, and workboots (see fig. 54). As they made their first entrance, there was much pounding on the pipes of the catwalk above, as if to simulate construction sounds, and at one point in the American tour, the artisans sang a tune from a familiar American beer commercial as they entered down the orchestra aisles.[121] Bottom drew laughs from his mates when he did a bit of belly dancing as he demonstrated how he could act the role of Thisbe. Bottom's translation left him not with an ass's head, but only a red ball nose and a cap with earlike points — the image of a theatrical clown (and reminiscent of Bert Lahr). Later, when the group was bemoaning the loss of Bottom for their play ("O sweet bully Bottom! Thus hath he lost sixpence a day during his life" [4.2.19–20]), the group concluded their plaint by singing in barbershop harmony the lines, "O sweet bully Bottom, sixpence a day."[122]

After *Pyramus and Thisbe* and the exit of the court, the company entered and faced the audience while Alan Howard, who played both Theseus and Oberon, delivered somberly and directly to the audience, "Now until the break of day / Through this house each fairy stray . . . ," (5.2.31–52), as the house lights gradually came up. With Puck's final lines, "Give me your hands, if we be friends / And Robin shall restore amends" (Epilogue, 15–16), the actors left the stage to an explosion of drums to come into the auditorium and shake hands with the audience. The moment, in performances in both England and the United States, was something of a lovefest, "a feast of friendship," as one British critic described the response at Stratford-upon-Avon, in which, wrote another, the audience "eagerly clutched the cast's hands as they burst up the aisles."[123] The response was identical everywhere. It seemed as if audiences were, in effect, eager to carry the young love-world of the production away with them into the world outside.

Most critics were ebullient, from Stratford to New York, but there were dissenters. A brief sampling will suffice to illustrate the issues. Harold Hobson in the *Sunday Times* wrote of it as "more than refreshing, magnificent, the sort of thing one sees only once in a lifetime, and then only from a man of genius." Jack Kroll of *Newsweek* thought it "one of the most beautiful Shakespearean productions of our lifetime." Clive Barnes called it "the most important work yet of the world's most imaginative and inventive director," a radiant production which rendered the play "an allegory of sensual love, and a magic playground of lost innocence and hidden fears. Love in Shakespeare comes as suddenly as death." Barnes expected that it would reshape future Shakespearean production.[124] For many critics, the production's departure from the moonlight and Mendelssohn traditions was foremost; for some that was all there was. Stanley Kauffmann wrote that Brook "spends the whole evening stripping away [the traditions]. . . . The point here seems only a series of points." For Kauffmann, the production was "an unresolved figure in dialectics" in which the actors sounded traditional and "the antithesis is the anti-traditional look; but the synthesis?"[125] Walter Kerr was not caught up in it: "I accepted what was given me without ever quite seeing the sense of it." Kerr thought the lyrical dream had been turned into "a thing of bumps and bruises," the comedy coarsened, and the characters over-simplified, and he wondered if someone who did not know the play would have been able to follow it.[126] There were other dissenting critics, more Americans than British, who were too distracted by the novel staging to be enchanted. Benedict Nightingale wrote in the *New Statesman* that Brook had "remolded" the play "with the help of Billy Smart, Walt Disney, J. G. Ballard and . . . his own sleeping, hallucinating self."[127] Douglas Watt ended his mixed review in the *Daily News* with the comment, "when it is good it is very good, and when it is not it is precious."[128] John Simon, one of the only critics to note the influence of Kott and Artaud on Brook, found no virtues in it. "Brook systematically de-poeticizes the play," wrote Simon. "The actors seem all chosen for their below-average to bad looks, their lower class accents." While no text was cut, said Simon (and this the promptbook verifies), the poetry was not felt.[129] "We are merely tickled by the strange discords, the cunning weirdness, the *dépaysement* of it all. And instead of being allowed to savor Shakespeare's genius, we are forced to admire Brook's cleverness."[130] For Simon, like Hazlitt, author and text had been displaced (his review was entitled "Bardicide"); against Brook's ag-gressively contemporary vision of the play Simon silently posited the possibility of an ideal, unmediated vision and offered no inquiry into the cultural formation of this or any prior production. John Russell Brown, like Simon, was alarmed at the transgression of the text and criticized especially the handling of Titania and Bottom. He pointed out that Oberon does not plan for her fornication with an ass with a giant phallus; Oberon does not know what Titania will "dote on" when she wakes. Simon observed that, according to Oberon, the first thing the charmed Titania will see when she awakes, "she shall pursue it with the soul of love." "I would not have thought," wrote Simon, "that the 'soul of love' was instant intercourse."[131] In the production's sometimes broad eroticism, Kott's dark view of Titania and Bottom was actually converted into an occasion for a sexual fantasy appropriate to an adolescent male.

But such discriminations were swept away in the popular appeals of the pro-duction: its radical, bright departure from the tired staging traditions for this play, its celebrative theatrical energy and overt sexuality, and its investment in the confusions and hopes of its earnest young lovers, so contemporary in spirit. While the production was born more of Brook's utopian idealism and theatrical aesthetics than of any direct social activism, it had immediate relevance for younger audiences. Not so long before this production, the antiwar protestor Jerry Rubin had advised his contemporaries not to trust anyone over thirty, and the term "generation gap" had developed. In New York, the opening in 1971 came only eight months after the tragedy at Kent State University, when young Americans in the Ohio National Guard had fired, fatally, on young Americans protesting the Vietnam war. The tragedy compounded the nation's pain over the loss of young Americans in the war itself and was still a fresh wound in the American psyche in 1971. The RSC production's appeal lay largely in its celebration of its own youthful, aggressive contemporary engagement with Shakespeare and the possibility of *communitas*, which it promised in its curtain call lovefest. Without question, its ethos was sentimental, in a new way for a play with a long history of sentimentality in performance, and it was reductive of the play's complexities. But this aggressive exploration of the play on contemporary terms had a profound impact on Shakespearean production long after the era of the flower children had faded.

The Hancock, Mnouchkine, and Brook productions all bear the attributes of the early stages of the postmodernist Weltanschauung. These directors at once stage the text and their problematic relationship to it, simultaneously occupying and displacing it, each offering this dialectic as the only assurance of authenticity. Where Mnouchkine offered a dark dialectic between desire and despair, Brook sought a new order of authenticity in exuberant young love, uninhibited eroticism, and a frank theatricality that eschewed all older forms of illusion. While an antiauthoritarian spirit prevailed in all three productions, manifest in such elements as suspicious depictions of the state, rejection of formal decorum, and an insistence on overt sexuality, these stagings were not explicitly political. Issues of feminism, cultural diversity, and the repressive power of the state did not yet inform them as they would productions of the play in the decades to come. When Titania was made a sexual toy again, it would be in order to critique that very cultural construction of her. In some future productions, the eroticism would be dark and violent, the state indifferently oppressive, and innocence a thing more longed for than recovered.

Brook's production was something of a preemptive strike, as Jonathan Miller once noted.[132] But not only did it become the reference point for Shakespearean performance practice in general over the next decade, *A Midsummer Night's*

Dream itself, once a fond piece for all occasions, became, as the critic William Henry III observed in the mid-1980s, "a summit that virtually every world-class director seeks to scale."[133] The burden of reinventing the play now fell heavily on every director. In the twenty-five years since Brook's staging, the diversity of approaches is staggering to review, with directors, designers, and musicians borrowing from every possible cultural bank. In the pursuit of new vocabularies for the fairy world, for example, productions have appropriated cultures of emerging minority populations or of cultures historically subordinated to Western interests. Multicultural casting was especially congenial to Joseph Papp's agenda for accessible Shakespeare. As early as 1961, James Earl Jones played a "silver-tongued, satanic Oberon" to Kathleen Widdoes's Titania in Central Park.[134] In the RSC's 1977 production, directed by John Barton, Patrick Stewart's Oberon was a near-nude, muscular, bronze, Aztec chieftain (fig. 55). In the Arena Stage production in Washington, D.C., in 1981, African American actor Avery Brooks was the athletic Oberon to Kathleen Turner's Titania, who lounged around a suburban-looking swimming pool. In the New York Shakespeare Festival in 1988, director A. J. Antoon offered an Afro-Brazilian fairy world of bossa nova dances and voodoo spells, set in turn-of-the-century Brazil. In 1991, the festival featured a production by Brazil's Teatro Ornitorrinco, directed by Cacá Rosset. Titania was queen of the Amazon, presiding over reptilian fairies amid a defoliated rain forest. Theseus presided over a Spanish colonial court. Given the context of the Columbus quincentennial, some postcolonial parable of conquest may have been intended, but this was never made explicit. The production seems simply to have exploited the exotic effects of the carnivalesque (a procession of captive Amazons on stilts) and the primitive (nude nymphs bathing Titania in a rite of nature).[135] While such productions probably challenged the expectations of audiences accustomed to canonical, Caucasian Shakespeare, some were also susceptible to criticism as opportunistic appropriations of the exotic.

The diversity of theatrical approaches is also evidence of a Western culture not so much inclusive as criss-crossed with hundreds of fracture lines. The four-hundred-year-old play has come to our theatres elaboratedly staged in both neo-romantic and darkly antiromantic veins, explored as an anthology of gender and class wars, and dressed in Victorian and Edwardian vocabularies as if to try on the vestments of lost religions. In the Communist satellite countries in Eastern Europe, it was used, until the fall of the Berlin Wall, to critique the illusions of a harmonious society in those oppressive states. Western stagings often have emphasized troubling, anxious relationships between all the pairs of lovers and have continued to underscore the play with an eroticism unthinkable only three

FIGURE 55. Final scene, Royal Shakespeare Theatre, 1977. Directed by John Barton. Marjorie Bland as Titania and Patrick Stewart as Oberon; behind them, Carmen Du Sautoy as Hippolyta and Richard Durden as Theseus. Photograph, Joe Cocks Studio. Shakespeare Centre Library.

decades ago. They have called out every possible musical and visual vocabulary, from Elizabethan to baroque to Victorian, sometimes all in one production, sometimes staging self-consciously the postmodern problem of creating unifying strategies. Some have been bravura explorations of the dissonances in the play; the gentler productions have mingled a sense of a loss of innocence with longings for authenticity and reconciliation. In contrast to the last decade of the nineteenth century, at the end of the twentieth century no single vision, no singular production, can be said to represent a norm.

The play has been darkest in the hands of Eastern European directors. In East Germany, several productions in the 1970s turned away from the romantic illusionism of Max Reinhardt, which still prevailed, and were informed by contemporary social issues, antiromantic visions of love apparently colored by Kott's essay, and theatricalizations apparently derivative of Artaud and his disciple, Jerzy Grotowski. In Halle in 1971, director Christopher Schroth rejected any notion of the play as a celebration of social and romantic harmony. Productions of Shakespeare in the Soviet satellite nations often offered veiled, subversive critiques of the state, and Schroth emphasized the struggle of the young for individual freedom amid a rigid, oppressive society. This theme was a common one in East German Shakespearean productions in general in the 1980s, according to Lawrence Guntner.[136] The forest, a menacing jungle of tree trunks, was a distorted mirror of the court (Schroth doubled Theseus/Oberon and Hippolyta/Titania to this end), and in it the young lovers were terribly confused by their passions. Oberon had to intervene to prevent Lysander and Demetrius from killing each other. Maik Hamburger did the new translation but wrote of being interested less in the fine points of Shakespeare's language than in his theatrical *gestus* (Brecht's much debated term); the emphasis was on helping actors physicalize emotional relationships and social situations.[137] There was great interest in the portrait of a fully developed, complex Bottom, who had a great capacity for love. But there was no resolve into harmony in the last act. Theseus's court cruelly mocked the artisans' amateur performance of *Pyramus and Thisbe*, for Schroth the only true love story in the play. Guntner reports that the young lovers, fully assimilated into the oppressive Athenian order, now laughed at notions of equality and freedom of choice in the matters of love once so important to them. He reads this element of the production as "not only a criticism of how the state was treating its young people but . . . also a sad commentary on the official treatment of theatre by the East German government."[138]

In 1980, in what was still East Berlin, Alexander Lang's long-running production of the play at the Deutsches Theater, once Reinhardt's, offered an even more polemical indictment of the state and the disparities between social reality and government versions of it. Informed by a strong vision of a male-dominated society of brutal sexual relations in which women were always victims, it presented a social critique as relevant to the capitalistic West. In the first scene, Theseus sat Hippolyta on his knee and fondled her breast, which she endured, slumped in her ermine cape, defeated and vacant-eyed. Egeus carried a screaming Hermia in over his shoulder, dumped her on the floor in front of Theseus, and held a knife to her throat.[139] In the forest, manipulations of the state seemed to be behind the uses of the love potion. Oberon and Puck forcibly drugged Lysander and Demetrius, whose passions then ran to lust and aggression. Demetrius nearly raped Hermia, and he and Lysander traded karate blows in their fight. But ultimately the four lovers (all in contemporary dress) seemed anesthetized, helplessly drugged, only to wake up to be led into conventional, male-dominated marriages. Martin Linzer, a theatre critic for *Theater der Zeit*, reported that Lang had found significance in the fact that the court women are entirely silent in Shakespeare's fifth act and in the apparent ready adjustment to the establishment by the young men, who ridicule the artisans' play.[140] Titania, asserting her independence in the style of a Hollywood vamp in a fitted off-the-shoulder dress, high heels, and a feather boa, seemed to be a sexual threat to Oberon, in part because she found happiness in the arms of Bottom (whose erection was once again simulated by the arm of a fairy). When awakened, writes Guntner, "she cried and clung so tightly to her animal lover that Oberon and Puck had to extract her focibly from his arms."[141] Theseus's hunting party was in pursuit of Hippolyta, who turned out to be lesbian. Lang doubled Theseus/Oberon and Hippolyta/Titania, perhaps to reinforce the image of these brutalizing relationships. The mechanicals played their play nervously to an official audience that had no interest in art. Gero Troike's setting was a simple, anti-illusionistic, three-sided box of red paper.

Thomas Langhoff's production at the Maxim Gorki Theatre in Berlin later that year, while also thoroughly contemporized, was more celebratory.[142] It was characterized by youthful exuberance, the power of love driving the young lovers to defy parent and state and break through the paper walls of the palace into the forest. But once there, they encountered an aberrant and unstable world. The forest floor was a trampoline on which they bounced, tripped, and staggered, propelled by changing emotions. Titania was a moody, despotic queen, bald, with tiny bells on her ankles, and her court included a giant woman in a black negligee, a winged dwarf with a plastic penis, and a muscular man with antlers growing from his thighs.[143] Titania and Oberon swung over the stage on ropes, and she slept in a fabric swing. Oberon was a lustful Pan and Puck a gnome, seen behind the bushes with a nymph. The young lovers experienced the potion not as a manipulative, paralyzing tool of Oberon but as if it were their first marijuana high, which released inhibitions and from which they awoke with giggles. The artisans, arriving with a bicycle and a case of beer, tried to perform *Pyramus and Thisbe* amid the court's rude interruptions. Their performance became more and more passionate and convincing, finally silencing their audience.[144] But Theseus interrupted the mechanicals' bergamask dance and called for a song to disperse winter, and the court then tore down the paper walls of the set and went off to bed.[145] The influences of Kott's dark reading and Brook's production are obvious here, but clearly the social critiques did not partake of Kott's bleak, existential despair, nor did these productions share Brook's utopian dream.[146]

In the English-speaking theatre, productions have not been so polemical or grim, even when Kott-influenced, with the notable exceptions of those in the United States by the Romanian-born director Liviu Ciulei. In Ciulei's production at the Guthrie Theatre in 1985, the sixty-two-year-old director saw the play as being about struggles for power in a patriarchal society.[147] Beni Montresor's setting consisted of reflective Chinese-red vinyl flooring and red walls that framed a large black square at upstage center, in the middle of which glowed a luminous orange full moon, all as sharply etched and mesmerizing as a De Chirico painting. Up center, a square Plexiglass platform was raised and lowered on cables to create Titania's bed or the mechanicals' stage. Philip Glass's hypnotic, mournful "Music in Twelve Parts" was used for the score.[148] All the lovers' relationships were delineated in sharp, antagonistic terms. The opening scene set the tone for the production. A captive, defiant Hippolyta, a tall African woman with spiky hair (Lorraine Toussaint), was led on by Theseus's court women and men. They stripped her of her black guerrilla fatigues, throwing them on the brazier in front of her, and dressed her in white robes like theirs, enacting a ritual replacement of Hippolyta's self-defined womanhood with a conquered, compliant femininity.[149] But she snarled sarcastically her reply to the white Theseus (Gary Reinecke), "Four days will quickly steep themselves in night" (1.1.7) and remained defiant throughout most of the play, not seeming to come to a complete reconciliation even by the fifth-act nuptials.[150] Said Ciulei of his Hippolyta: "She is a beautiful black forced to marry a doddering white. From the outset, Shakespeare dramatizes the viciousness of the patriarchy, dissembling its savagery in verbal politeness."[151] Given this color code, it is not clear, then, how audiences were to read the relationship between the cruel, black Oberon (Peter Francis-James) and the victimized, white Titania (Harriet Harris). In any case, their opening marital quarrel took place at a long dinner table at which the angry Titania knocked over a decanter of wine, staining the white cloth. When Oberon administered the potion to Titania, he did so cruelly, "as a terrorist chloroforming a kidnap victim," said Minneapolis critic Mike Steele. When Titania waked from her drugged state to discover she had loved an ass, she gave a piercing scream of humiliation and collapsed to the ground. And it was clear, said Robert Brustein, that "the wounds don't heal."[152] Lysander and Demetrius came into the forest with switchblades and seemed willing at one point to kill Hermia. When the lovers slept after their chase, they all arose to enact a troubling dream of their forest night encounters within a voluminous, billowing transparent fabric managed by the fairies. In the dream, Titania cavorted with Bottom, who lifted his ass's head to reveal himself to be Oberon. The four young lovers eyed one another uneasily after awakening, and, in the curtain call, the pairs came out mismatched again, exchanging partners in confusion at the bow. A female Puck delivered with disgust, "the man shall have his mare again, and all shall be . . . well — ," ending with a dismissive gesture and a shrug.[153] In the last act, the court guests hooted at the artisans' play and, hearing the clock strike, left before the bergamask. When the mechanicals entered singing and dancing, they found no one there.[154]

The production won wide coverage and much admiration in the national press, although Brustein found the details of interpretation vivid but absent any unifying metaphor.[155] To the regret of these critics, Ciulei's *A Midsummer Night's Dream* was his finale as the Guthrie's artistic director. His dark, contemporary, Eastern European visions of Shakespeare's plays, which also had included in this season a strong postcolonial staging of *The Tempest*, were not congenial to audiences in the midwestern Twin Cities served by the Guthrie. One local radio critic said, "I for one am tired of going to that theatre and seeing Eastern European intellectualism passed off as high art."[156] To accusations that Ciulei was being unfaithful to Shakespeare's play, he said, "When we stage it, even in the moment when we read it, we become interpreters. We transform it with our minds. We betray it. So the most ambitiously faithful production of the play would still be a betrayal."[157] Ciulei was invited to stage variations on this production at the Pepsico Summerfare at the State University of New York-Purchase in 1986, and at Arena Stage in Washington, D.C., in 1989, in both instances to mixed reviews. Hap Erstein of the *Washington Times* admired the memorable stage images but was skeptical of the "bitter darkness" that had replaced "the play's sense of playfulness." David Richards of the *Washington Post* tried to emphasize the visual magic of the production but said so little of Ciulei's dark vision that one can only assume he was trying not to frighten conservative Washington audiences away.[158] Frank Rich of the *New York Times* criticized the production for being dry and cerebral, comparable in this regard to Ciulei's recent staging of *Hamlet* with Kevin Kline in New York. Rich was critical of both Ciulei and Mark Lamos, who had recently directed a chilly version at the Hartford Stage Company, for turning actors into cogs to serve their concepts: "Leading directors are no less capable than leading Hollywood actors of turning Shakespeare's plays into self-absorbed star turns."[159]

The Yale Repertory Theatre also staged a dark, ironic conception in 1975, Artaud- and Kott-influenced. The director, Alvin Epstein, had been Oberon in the Hancock production of 1966. Epstein's production was regarded as one of the better in the Yale Repertory years under artistic director Robert Brustein and was revived in 1980 at Brustein's American Repertory Theatre. In both, Epstein used music from Purcell's *Fairy Queen*, and both were designed by Tony Straiges. The court scenes were played against a backdrop out of Paolo Uccello, showing plumed knights astride massive horses clashing with lances, perhaps an echo of the sexual conflicts. But the primary emphasis was on creating an eerie fairy world and an earthy eroticism. Oberon and the grotesque fairies slithered, lizardlike, across a barren lunar landscape and down a steel slide; above, the moon itself was a silver globe amid blue-green heavens. In the Yale staging, the handsome Oberon and Titania were Christopher Lloyd and African American dancer-actress Carmen de Lavallade, "tall, chiseled creatures in flesh-toned tights, glorifications of the body in motion," wrote Arthur Holmberg. Epstein, who had studied with Martha Graham, was intent upon physicalizing emotions, and, according to Holmberg, "the beauty of [Oberon and Titania's] sexual love, expressed through movement, finally triumphed over the anger, jealousy, and aggression that had separated them."[160] But there was no doubt of the sexual consummation between Titania and Bottom, given the positions in which they awakened. Epstein used Purcell's score to counterpoint the sexual conflicts and the grotesque. Played by the Yale Symphony Orchestra conducted by Otto-Werner Mueller, its vocal portions were sung by a chorus in silver masks, looking, said Mel Gussow, "like a sculptured ensemble of moon men."[161] "Love in the play unleashes destructive forces," said Epstein, but "on the other hand, the lovers yearn for harmony and order. Purcell's music counterpointed the cruelty of my production."[162] Such a juxtaposition is a postmodern strategy, and, in this case, the sublime Purcell score in live performance seems to have provided a very strong, even redeeming, antithesis to the stark, erotic reading. There were also gratuitously ludicrous things in this production, characteristic of the obligatory irreverence of the Yale Rep in this era. Jeremy Geidt, a short, stocky, broadly comic white actor, played Theseus to the Hippolyta of the handsome black actress Franchelle Stewart Dorn, imposing of voice and bosom, whom he tried repeatedly, in gross horseplay, to bed. The young lovers seemed not to have registered strongly in this production, with the exception of the Helena of the young Meryl Streep.[163]

Endangering erotic forces surged through Mark Lamos's production at the Hartford Stage Company. "The truce between civilization and the instincts is simply that — a truce. It can be broken at any moment," said the director. "I wanted to destabilize the end to dramatize the persistence of sexual tensions after marriage."[164] So, during a final dance, Demetrius and Lysander switched partners, flirting with the wrong women. A jealous quarrel broke out into violence but was interrupted by Mendelssohn's "Wedding March," and the couples paired off correctly, if unpromisingly. The fairies' costumes by Jess Goldstein were an eclectic assortment of Elizabethan ruffs, satin britches, tattered gauze and commedia dell'arte caps and masks, intended to "suggest the role of costume in sexual fantasy — sexual role-playing as masquerade," said Goldstein.[165] "These fairies might be East Village sylphs straggling home sexually exhausted from a Halloween party in Soho," wrote an admiring Arthur Holmberg.[166] Michael Yeargan's setting featured a Greek pediment upside down, its fluted pillars still attached, thrust like legs at an unsettling angle toward the moon.

In the midst of such productions, Robin Phillips's staging at Stratford, Ontario, in the 1976 and 1977 seasons, which sought to make the play Queen Elizabeth's dream, must be described as conservative. The Ontario Festival Theatre operation needed to prove its Canadianness at the time. Phillips's attempt to capitalize on all the associations of the play with Elizabeth I and a court wedding came in the year of Elizabeth II's silver jubilee, during which she visited her former colonies in North America. The festival souvenir program of 1976 bore the first Elizabeth's portrait on the cover, floating in a half-concealing mist of mystery. The epithalamium motif has a long history in productions of the play, as we have seen. Phillips took the idea a step further and attempted to make the whole play Elizabeth's dream. "It would have been natural for the leading poet of the age to cap the wedding festivities with a play doing homage to the Queen as the wellspring of passion and romantic devotion," said a note in the 1977 program. In this theory, Elizabeth was actually Shakespeare's inspiration for the play:

> The Queen was essentially a mystery to her people. . . . Standing always in the light, she cast ominous shadows. Her mind travelled to dark wooded places to which no other mortal had access. She was steadfast and capricious; compassionate and imperious; compounded of flesh and blood and of iron and air. She was a young girl flirting with love and great Queen demanding it. She was Gloriana and she was a faded, ageing woman, desperately lonely.[167]

The production opened with Hippolyta alone in a spotlight, the image of the red-haired Gloriana out of a Nicholas Hilliard portrait in an elaborate lace ruff and pearl-encrusted dress (the costumes were by Susan Benson), while a woman's voice was heard singing Bottom's "I have had a most rare vision. I have had a dream past the wit of man to say what dream it was" (4.1.202–203). The lights came up on the quasi-Elizabethan thrust stage, which quickly filled with gallants and court ladies in lavish Elizabethan costumes in somber black and gold, surrounding their queen, all framed by large candlesticks suggestive of a great hall. "The whole stage was a dazzling vision of black and gold Elizabethan court splendour," wrote an enthusiastic Roger Warren.[168] Hippolyta and Titania were played by the same actress (Jessica Tandy in 1976 and Maggie Smith in 1977), suggesting two aspects of the queen's personality. Theseus (Jeremy Brett in 1976 and Barry MacGregor in 1977) was played to suggest the kind of dominating male that might have made Elizabeth avoid marriage and escape to fantasies of love. After the mechanicals' entertainment, Theseus stalked off the stage to bed without waiting for Hippolyta/Titania to accompany him.[169] Hermia and Helena were younger, mirror images of Elizabeth, perhaps in her younger follies of love, and the fairies around Titania were variations on courtiers.[170] Philostrate became Puck in the 1977 casting. Hippolyta/Elizabeth, not Theseus, gave the lines on "the lunatic, the lover, and the poet," which, in the context, seemed a meditation on fantasy appropriate to her, thought the *Shakespeare Quarterly* critic, Ralph Berry.[171] When Maggie Smith took over the figuring of Hippolyta/Elizabeth/Titania in 1977, the conceit shifted slightly to the dream of a younger queen. Elizabeth's tight red curls gave way to Smith's honey-colored hair let down to her waist and, as Titania, she floated in a diaphanous gown, radiant with backlighting, and brought an airy sensuousness to Titania's affections for Bottom (Alan Scarfe). Smith brought her familiar, comic feminine trademarks to the performance, the "charming air of vagueness" and the "airy movement of hands that always seem to be trying to escape from the rest of her," with "one hand forever fluttering to her forehead or nape."[172] The image of her in a circle of moonlight doting on the man in the giant ass's head had "a breathtaking beauty to it," wrote *New York Times* critic Richard Eder.[173]

A few critics, such as Kevin Kelly of the *Boston Globe*, shared Roger Warren's enthusiasm for Phillips's conceit of the play as Elizabeth's dream.[174] But many more found it esoteric, cold, or simply muddled. Eder said Phillips had made the playful play "a late autumn nightmare from the court of Elizabeth" and "impaled the play upon an icy conceit." Others objected to the pervading gloom of the somber court costumes and lighting. Canadian critic Ronald Bryden, arguing that the 1977 season had vindicated Phillips as the new artistic director, said the "weakness of premise" in Phillips's 1976 production "scarcely mattered" in the 1977 revival, and this seems in large part to have been due to the comic finesse of Smith's performance.[175] The worlds of the fairies and mechanicals were somewhat lost in this dream of power. Hume Cronyn's Bottom in 1976 offered an earnest querulousness and donkey ears that he wiggled shamelessly with a wire control in his pocket, which apparently made him a sentimental favorite.[176]

RSC director Ron Daniels returned to the past with a postmodern difference in 1981. Daniels found "melancholic longings" for reconciliation in the play, and his production for the main house in Stratford-upon-Avon suggested a plaintive dialogue between a fading past and an apprehensive present.[177] The staging was far from Brook's bright, erotic circus of a decade before. In Maria Bjornson's setting, Daniels's young lovers inhabited a high Victorian court of red-velvet swag curtains and potted palms, hoop skirts and crinolines, fitted frock coats, dove gray spats, and chin-high collars. (The RSC had just enjoyed enormous success with its adaptation of Charles Dickens's *Nicholas Nickleby*.) Mendelssohn's music drifted in from another room, and Stephen Oliver provided a romantic score that nodded to Mendelssohn's with its passages of music beneath certain speeches in the play. The forest world to which the lovers fled was a nineteenth-century backstage world of muslin flats and wicker prop trunks, dimly luminous under gas-lamp footlights. The fairies who haunted it were Victorian doll puppets, china doll spectres, some cracked, sans eyes, sans hair, sans clothing. The Oberon and Titania they served were king and queen of a tinsel world of nineteenth-century pantomime and romantic ballet. Among the relics of ancient belief-making, a light seemed in danger of dying out; the question, felt with urgency, was how it was to be burning.

The production was susceptible to nostalgic readings seeking the old, familiar play among fond Victorian trappings, but the grotesque puppets provoked puzzlement and suspicion. Michael Billington of the *Guardian* was offended by them: "I began to feel like Ben Jonson's Zeal-of-the-land Busy, bursting in on a puppet show crying, 'I will no longer endure your profanations.'"[178] But Robert Cushman of the *Observer*, more representative of the general critical response, thought Daniels was "actually playing very straight with us," returning to the "full panoply of Victoriana." If the puppets distressed some critics, much else charmed, including Bjornson's setting for the court, "a blown-up Pollock [toy-theatre] print."[179] Michael Coveney was the more exploring of the morning-after reviewers, sensing a movement toward reconciliation underlying the production.[180] Daniels himself said in a discussion at the Shakespeare Institute that he had approached rehearsals feeling the play was "filled with unease," even made a passing comparison to *Timon of Athens*, which he had recently directed at Stratford's Other Place, and ventured that Shakespeare had been both thrilled and frightened by the possibilities of his dream play. In a letter responding to a sympathetic review I had written in which I had stressed the "apprehensions" and "dark shapes" in the production, Daniels emphasized the reconciliation theme and ultimately

the unbounded joy of the work, a joy that stems not only from the humor in the piece but also from the very heart of the play and what it is attempting to do. . . . It seems to me that the play does start with a whole series of opposites, unreconcilables, ranging from the most obvious ones of city and wood, night and day, man and woman, fancy and will, reason and imagination, dream and waking to even the conflicting acting styles of the piece — the literate and academic versifying of the lovers and the vulgar popular comedy of the mechanicals, and so forth. There is in the play I think an attempt to reconcile these opposites, and the most clear expression of this view comes right at the end of the play [with Puck's epilogue]. . . . I think that however uneasily, Shakespeare is . . . proposing that the movement of our lives should be one towards reconciling opposites, towards being whole and not toward being exclusive or fearful or dogmatic.[181]

By the end of the play, he noted, the woodland fairies have invaded the world of the city.

Theseus and Hippolyta at the beginning . . . are half people; by the end they have grown not only into each other but in themselves. . . . What I do find wonderful is that Shakespeare is anxious about this reconciliation. It is not a happy ending, except in imagination. His own internal conflicts and ours, whether personal or political in a wider sense, are not resolved in the theatre. But in our lives and in our world.[182]

Theseus's palace (plate 17) did, indeed, suggest a Pollock toy-theatre version of a Charles Kean setting, but not a charming miniature. Theseus interrogated Hermia in a monumental Victorian court, with an imposing central arch hung with a gold-fringed portiere, all framed by wing sets, pillars, painted architraves, and potted ferns, and over which loomed baroque clouds in violets and blues. Males paraded women in vast bustles and trains and sat them picturesquely on a black-tufted, leather divan. Much in the text was alive to this Victorian climate: Egeus's list of indictments against Lysander, who "hath bewitched the bosom of my child . . . With . . . verses of feigning love, . . . bracelets of thy hair, rings, gauds, . . . nosegays" (1.1.27–34); all the talk of lovestruck males and the chaste females who must not chase them, of virginity, maiden pilgrimages, primrose beds, dowager aunts, and roses fading on the cheek; and all the establishment rhetoric, festooned with sententiae.

The forest of the lovers' confusion was the backstage of a Victorian theatre, Theseus's palace turned inside-out, with the machines and props of theatrical illusion in dusty disarray. One could lose one's way between illusion and reality here. (When the production moved to the Barbican, Bjornson added an elaborate golden Victorian proscenium arch.) In the lovers' chase, a cutout tree flew

FIGURE 56. Joseph Marcell as Puck, with fairy puppets, including his look-alike at right, Royal Shakespeare Theatre, Stratford-upon-Avon, 1981. Directed by Ron Daniels, designed by Maria Bjornson. Photograph, Joe Cocks Studio. Shakespeare Centre Library.

in up left to land askew, and another flew in backward, showing "Act I. Sc. 3" lettered on its backside. Lysander and Demetrius, led by Puck in their pursuit of one another, floundered beneath a billowing sky canvas, lowered from stage-wide battens. Oberon, in a suit of glittering golds and purples out of a toy-theatre *Aladdin*, entered like a demon king in a pantomime, riding on an iron spiral staircase that emerged through a trap amid theatrical smoke and blue lights. Puck, played by a black actor (Joseph Marcell) as symmetrically proportioned as a jack-in-the-box puppet, had a small black look-alike among the puppet fairies (fig. 56). At one point he descended riding a stage counterweight. The costumes for *Pyramus and Thisbe* had a touch of the Sicilian puppet theatre about them. Critic Roger Warren, who admired Peter Hall's concurrent staging of Britten's opera at Glyndebourne as a variation on Hall's 1959 vision of the play in a country manor house and who had praised Robin Phillips's dream of Elizabeth at the 1976 Ontario festival, predictably found only ugly haphazardness and contradictions in Daniels's staging. He detested the "nasty" doll fairies, "beloved of the makers of horror films." [183]

Designer Maria Bjornson's puppet fairies first emerged from the wicker prop basket, rod-manipulated by Bunraku-like operators in black, with veiled or smudged faces. The strange assortment of china-head dolls, two to three feet high and rod-manipulated, were in various stages of decay. Moved by the operators in large sweeping motions amid the vast stage, against the black cyclorama they seemed like small macabre souls, darting through the dark void. They scattered in the winds at Oberon's first entrance and hovered anxiously around the quarreling fairy king and queen, shifting and darting, their puppet limbs clacking quietly in the silences like bones. Daniels came to see them as "the neglected children of a parental quarrel," the quarrel between the archetypal male and female, from whose dissension issues "a progeny of evils," including alterations of the seasons. (Given Titania's description of the weather, Daniels had the mechanicals enter in sou'westers.) "We are their parents and original," says Titania (2.1.117). These spectral fairies seemed to hover in limbo, waiting for the mending of a world long broken, haunting relics of belief or souls no longer prayed for, within an inch of vanishing irrecoverably on the night wind. They attacked Oberon when he came to work his charm on Titania, and audiences gasped when he struck one of the puppet fairies' brittle heads fiercely, sending dust and sequins flying. By the end of the play, Oberon sought to make his peace with them, and the black puppet Puck, at first unsure, took his offered hand.

Mike Gwilym as Oberon offered no romantic countenance or rolling vowels and no humor. With small eyes set low in his skull beneath a high forehead, he was a disquieting figure, absorbed in the negotiations of the night. Juliet Stevenson's Titania was solidly pretty, warm, and maternal, a perfect fairy queen for a hometown children's theatre. Her dress was that of romantic ballet but overspangled with blue and green sequins, and the skirt was cut away to show the hoop structure supporting the illusion. Oberon and Titania's dance of reconciliation was a key moment in the production (fig. 57). After Oberon had wakened her, he showed her Bottom in the ass's head — quite ugly for once — as if to say, kindly, "You see on what thin ground we stand." Daniels spoke of the "existential sense" behind the play: "I am how you look at me. Look at me with love and I am loveable. Look at me with hate, and that is how I shall appear — ugly."[184] Their dance — a slow classical pas de deux in which she twirled figures around him — was not so beautifully danced (they were not Moira Shearer and Robert Helpmann). It even seemed a tentative, precarious memory of a romantic past, and it ended in their close, anxious embrace, as if this might be the one dance left to dance on the edge of a vanishing enchantment. They were a fairy king and queen of deeper shadows and their dance one that longed for reconciliation without quite believing in that possibility. Gwilym and Stevenson

FIGURE 57. Juliet Stevenson as Titania and Mike Gwilym as Oberon in their reconciliation dance before dawn, Royal Shakespeare Theatre, Stratford-upon-Avon, 1981. Bottom (Geoffrey Hutchings) sleeps in the background. Photograph, Joe Cocks Studio. Shakespeare Centre Library.

doubled as Theseus and Hippolyta, but this seems not to have registered meaningfully on critics. Daniels sought one final image of reconciliation in Puck's epilogue: Oberon and the black puppet shook hands, with the full company on stage behind them. The moment also offered an unmistakable, topical suggestion of racial reconciliation. Overall, the production suggested that poets and lovers, actors and spectators, can, with imagination, probably re-create faith in a world of faded faiths, but it is a precarious dance. In retrospect, there is some irony in the fact that this uneasy RSC production was mounted in the summer of the ill-fated wedding of Prince Charles and Lady Diana.[185]

Most major productions thereafter in the 1980s and 1990s created a romanticized past — Victorian, Edwardian, Cavalier, or eclectic — and more in nostalgia than postmodern angst, with reconciliation often a strong motif. Late in 1982, in the first production of the play at the National Theatre of Great Britain, Paul Scofield was a grizzled, ancient Oberon amid centuries-old Elizabethan fairies. In director Bill Bryden's wistful vision, they dwelled in the wood around a country manor, perhaps, as critic Michael Coveney suggested, the spirits of former servants in the big house, now inhabited by an Edwardian summer community in white suits and long dresses.[186] The ancient fairies haunted this Brideshead comfortingly and benevolently. Bob Crowley's set consisted of a scrim facade of trees and moonlight, with one solid, noble doorway. Susan Fleetwood as Titania wore an Elizabethan gown that was a frayed and patched memory of a lost age, and this and the costumes of all the fairies (designed by Deirdre Clancy) were the faded colors of the leaves and petals that covered the stage. But she and other fairies were ageless spirits, Titania with wild, long hair and Scofield "an eerie wizard with the aspect of a suprised cockatoo," both suggesting some persistent "earth magic from age to age," wrote Irving Wardle, "a force lying in wait behind all the changing civilized surfaces."[187] Reviewers found little magic or sexuality in the production, but Bryden had orchestrated a careful progression from dissension to harmony, not only between Oberon and Titania but between the mortals and fairies. Both Oberon and Titania were concerned for the disorder proceeding from their quarrel. Scofield's Oberon, a sonorous and benevolent magus, was passionately concerned to put everything right, watching the lovers' confusions with paternal concern or gently disentangling Titania from her asinine lover.[188] Oberon watched the lovers' quarrels from the fifth row of the auditorium, and other fairies watched the mortals from everywhere, including the balconies, as if to suggest their presence among today's audiences. Oberon and Titania came face-to-face with an unseeing Theseus (Edward de Souza) and Hippolyta (Marsha Hunt), "a more powerful moment than can be produced by the now orthodox doubling of the roles," thought Robert Cushman of the *Observer*.[189] In the forest, the fairies intently watched the mechanicals rehearse, and in the final court scene, solicitous fairies brought out lanterns to mark the acting area for *Pyramus and Thisbe*. The polite young lovers made no exceptional mark, except Karl Johnson's Lysander, a priggish young man lecturing on love and arranging flowers on his pillow before sleeping in the forest. The mechanicals won high praise for humor that arose from well-developed individual characters: Derek Newark as a burley, quietly self-confident Bottom; J. G. Devlin's Peter Quince as an unusually bossy and boring amateur thespian; and Tony Hayworth's Snout, who as Wall tottered under the weight of his brick cothurni. The mechanicals first gathered around an accordion to sing a fraternal song, and their bergamask was a four-man British music hall sand-dance.[190] The motif of harmony extended to Puck's "Give me your hands, if we be friends" (Epilogue, 14), taken as a cue for concluding handshakes between the company and the audience, a device redolent of Brook's production, which reviewers now found cloying.

In the United States, James Lapine's production for the New York Shake-speare Festival also offered a neoromantic Edwardian fantasy. It featured a nineteenth-century sylvan setting under the stars in the outdoor Delacorte Theatre in Central Park, landscaped by scene designer Heidi Landesman. The broad playing space at the foot of the amphitheatre was converted into grassy slopes with flowering shrubs, a pond with a statue of cupid, grotto entrances, and a tree-enclosed bower for Titania. The young lovers in Edwardian dress included Christine Baranski's Helena in white gloves and a broad-brimmed picture hat, who was as fair as Hermia and delighted critics with her blend of "distraught despair and lady-like fretfulness." [191] In a strategy congenial with Papp's people's Shakespeare, the young Lapine wanted fairies "from every culture and kind of myth," so Oberon (William Hurt) appeared to be a Senecan Indian; [192] Titania was played by African American actress Michele Shay, costumed in sequins and veils; one of the fairies was created in the image of a bad-tempered, folk-tale figure called the Blue Hag (Angela Pietropinto); and Puck was played by a woman (Marcell Rosenblatt). While none of these offered distinguished performances, critics declared the production a pleasant summer diversion, and Emile Ardolino later directed an adaptation of it for television. [193]

Victorian images marked Richard Sewall's production at the Theatre of Monmouth, Maine, in 1982, with Lysander as a young Tennyson, jotting down love verses, and a Titania with wings out of a Paul Konewka silhouette. [194] Woody Allen's film *A Midsummer Night's Sex Comedy*, inspired by the play and by Ingmar Bergman's *Smiles of a Summer Night*, featured a changing dance of partners among three couples at an elegant country summer house in upstate New York in the early 1900s. Strains of Mendelssohn were heard at the opening of the soft-focus 1981 film. The characters, dressed in Edwardian costumes, were ancestors of Allen's identity-anxious urban Americans of the late twentieth century. They came to believe in the Tinker Bell–like spirits that appeared in their midst. [195] The domesticated magic is reminiscent of James M. Barrie's sentimental *Dear Brutus* of 1917. [196] The fairies emerged from a large Victorian wardrobe out of C. S. Lewis in Sheila Hancock's 1983 production, designed by Bob Crowley, in the RSC's Other Place. But they were grotesque fairies, "as a Victorian child might have seen them in a nightmare," wrote Roger Warren, who observed that it made little sense for them to sing a lullaby to protect Titania against bizarre creatures. [197] The mechanicals were Victorian costermongers (with Daniel Day Lewis as Flute/Thisbe). Amanda Root's Hermia was one of the strengths of an uneven production, dragging a large Gladstone bag through her forest travails.

Elija Moshinsky chose to do his film of the play for BBC Television's

Shakespeare series in seventeenth-century Cavalier style, with designs by David Myerscough-Jones. Settings, costuming, lighting, and camera angles re-create the feel of the Dutch masters in a dense, neoromantic realism. The acting is intimate and low key. Theseus (Nigel Davenport) interrogates the quartet of young lovers in his great house library as they sit stiffly at a library table, surrounded by implements of science and reason, a massive clock ticking in the background. Helena (Cherith Mellor), a homely spinster in wire-rim glasses, does her "How happy some o'er other some can be" (1.1.226) against a background of pillars of a somber great hall, from which we hear the echoing screeches of a caged bird. The mechanicals meet in a pub in a scene out of Frans Hals; the mechanicals with their tankards are crowded into a booth, over the back of which sits Flute, smoking a clay pipe. The forest suggests a nineteenth-century Claude Lorrain landscape, with a Charles Kean moon in a sky that is clearly painted. The muddy pool through which the lovers wade and through which Puck drags Flute seems gratuitously real. Bottom sees his ass's head in it, as Cagney did, but not his recovered form. The lovers' quarrels at poolside are grim and damp, the foursome becoming as muddy as those in Peter Hall's film. The fairies seem vaguely Celtic, a wild band of changeling children from a tinker's caravan. Oberon — Peter McEnery, dark-skinned and handsome in long black hair — first appears bareback on a black horse (reminiscent of Reinhardt's film, which influenced Moshinsky). Helen Mirren, in white gown and long blond hair, brings to Titania her compellingly intense presence, in which quick intelligence and warm feminine desire coalesce. The imagery for Titania in her bower — for the fairy lullaby and her night with Bottom — was taken from Rembrandt's golden *Danaë*, in which the naked Danaë in her bed awaits Jupiter who, in the myth, comes to her in a shower of gold.[198] Amid such connoiseurial imagery and conservatism, it is jarring when Bottom (Brian Glover), lying on top of Titania with a fairy scratching his donkey back, so explicitly experiences sexual orgasm and relief. Titania's reconciliation with Oberon is managed with her quick surrender to his sensuous kisses. Hippolyta has a fierce opening face-off with Theseus in the beginning of the film, with lines delivered in low, hostile tones. But thereafter, as Nicholas Shrimpton pointed out, Hippolyta appears as "a bubblingly enthusiastic fiancée."[199]

Behind the realism and the conservatism of this film for television are several contributory factors. The BBC series producer, Jonathan Miller, has said that he sees Shakespeare as an essentially "domestic" playwright in general and Oberon and Titania as behaving like ordinary people.[200] Whether or not this was cynical opportunism, the television medium itself is a domesticating one, in which the particularities of personality and prosaic emotion fill the small screen, and metaphor and metonym are often lost among the kitchen drama realism. Market forces also shaped the vocabularies of this production and the BBC Television series in general. American support of the production came from its cosponsor, Time/Life, with the stipulation that the plays be set in or near Shakespeare's time or in the "appropriate" historical period. Further, because the tapes would be widely used for teaching Shakespeare to school audiences, productions had to be governed by some contemporary normative standards. While these were never articulated, Time/Life required that assurances about these standards be written into the contract.[201] This protectionism ran counter to the direction in which Shakespearean performance practices had been moving in the previous decade. Many major directors now believed that any vital theatrical realization of the plays involved an open conversation between the canon and contemporary culture. There could be no such thing as unmediated Shakespeare. Shakespearean performance practices also were acknowledging the perception of increasing tension between the culture that produced Shakespeare's plays and the culture of the late twentieth century. Moreover, by 1980, a new generation of Shakespearean scholars was emerging who began to show that not even the texts of Shakespeare's plays were as stable as former editors had claimed.[202] The attempt of Time/Life to stabilize Shakespearean performance practices to ensure some kind of canonical correctness was ironic at this juncture and no less political than the practices that it sought to suppress. Predictably, the restrictions could not entirely erase late-twentieth-century culture from the series.

Theatrical productions of the play in the late 1980s and early 1990s came in a resolutely eclectic mix of vernacular vocabularies. Bill Alexander's 1986 production for the RSC placed the lovers in the 1930s and the mechanicals in the 1950s — seeking in both eras the strong male chauvinism that he apparently wanted to play against and some nostalgia quotient. Setting Shakespeare's plays in the near past had by this time become the trend, and for the overexposed *A Midsummer Night's Dream* (four productions in eight years by the RSC alone), directors new and old were straining at inventiveness.[202] Janet McTeer doubled in the roles of Hippolyta and Titania, and her Hippolyta, being bored with her worldly, lawyerlike Theseus (Richard Easton), fantasized another world in which she could enjoy a virile fairy king (Gerard Murphy, who had *not* doubled as Theseus) and a delightful Bottom. The device was a variation on Robin Phillips's concept of Elizabeth's dream. Bottom (Pete Postlethwaite) was therefore portrayed as a gentle man, more bohemian poet than blue-collar weaver, strangely beautiful in his translated state, an alternative to ordinary males. In the closing, Hippolyta/Titania left Theseus's side to sing the fairy blessing with Oberon.[204] William Dudley's elaborate forest setting was impressive in itself but seemed to many critics to be utterly unconnected to the play. A gigantic spider-web hovered above huge vegetation — oversize leaves, tree trunks, and toad-stools — in which Titania slept. Dudley was influenced by the famous drawings of Arthur Rackham, Henry Fuseli, and Richard Dadd, but critics found only a sterile, shop-window prettiness in it.[205] This forest was not the world of disorder that Titania describes and which the lovers experience.[206] Alexander himself later expressed regret over the choice of "a trivialized aesthetic," and the forest setting was greatly simplified when the production moved to the Barbican.[207]

John Caird's 1989 production for the RSC, with a largely new young company, juxtaposed an Edwardian court and Victorian tutus with post–punk rock. Sue Blane's set was, wrote Nicholas de Jongh, "a ruined adventure playground," inhabited by fairies who were "a crew of urchins and schoolchildren, little girls in pantomime wings, tu-tus, and mismatching black boots." Forming the background was a nostalgic scrap heap of bicycles, bathtubs, piano skeletons, brass beds, and chamber pots. (Caird was Trevor Nunn's assistant on *Nicholas Nickleby*.) Puck (Richard McCabe), a bad boy in a school tie and knickers, put on goggles to navigate his girdle around the earth. The fairies' wings were strapped on; Oberon woke from a nap and put his wings on "with the prosaic weariness of someone slipping his dentures back in," said one critic.[208] A rock subversion of Mendelssohn's score was played before the production, and with Oberon's command to his queen to "rock the ground whereon these sleepers be" (4.1.85), "the stage exploded in a post-punk mélange (by Michael Tubbs) of *Come Dancing* and Prokofiev's *Romeo and Juliet* suite." Many critics delighted in the production's irreverences.[209] The performances of John Carlisle as Theseus/Oberon and Clare Higgins as Hippolyta/Titania helped sustain the balance between parody and poetry. Among the company's fresher achievements was the mechanicals' performance of *Pyramus and Thisbe*, rendered in such a way as to be a comic reflection of the plights of Hermia, Lysander, Demetrius, and Helena.[210]

The Ontario festival imported the Abbey Theatre's former artistic director, Joe Dowling, to provide his youth-oriented production for the Festival Theatre in 1993. Dowling's pop-culture approach had been developed in his previous productions of the play with the Acting Company in New York in 1991 and at the Abbey earlier in 1993. The Ontario festival was anxiously trying to reach all markets after two deficit seasons, and the offerings in their three theatres mined popular and classical canons from *Gypsy*, *The Mikado*, and *The Importance of Being Earnest* to Shakespeare's *King John* and Euripides' *Bacchae*.[211] The *New York Times*'s Ben Brantley described Dowling's production as "a pop-Freudian 'Dream,' staged amid Hayden Griffen's rock-show forest of inflatable phallic trees and borrowing liberally from such topical adolescent fare as 'A Nightmare on Elm Street' and MTV videos."[212] Oberon was a Freddy Krueger figure who manipulated the young lovers "like a demonic puppeteer," according to Brantley, and Titania was a sexy, feline figure from the musical *Cats*, in an orange spandex suit with black stripes.[213] Puck delivered verse with a touch of rap, and the fairies' lullaby to Titania was done as a Shirelles doo-wop number. Keith Thomas's score often simulated the music of Madonna and Prince. Dowling spoke of exploring the eroticism in the play and of being influenced by Kott, but the production was obviously a lightweight family affair. The feline Titania's red hair was meticulously coiffed, and in the bower with Bottom, she lounged in his arms in lipstick, mascara, and morning gown. The mechanicals wore comfortable sweaters (Robin Starveling was played as a matronly woman by Barbara Byrne), and the playbill carried G. K. Chesterton's essay on the play from his *The Common Man*, which included this Edwardian sentiment: "If ever the son of man in his wanderings was at home and drinking by the fireside, he is at home in the house of Theseus."[214] Brantley saw the show with an audience "mostly middle-aged or older" and observed that the audience "lapped up all the teen-age references and gave the play the only standing ovation I witnessed at Stratford."[215]

Amid such pandering superficiality and the thin variations on the Edwardian vocabulary, Robert Lepage's 1992 staging of the play in a muddy bank around a pool in the Olivier Theatre could be taken in earnest. In the first scene, Philostrate punted a hospital bed around the pool, bearing Theseus and Hippolyta and the young lovers — dreaming, apparently, beneath the single bare lightbulb that hung above the set. The pool later became Titania's bower. The young lovers' quarrels in the forest turned into "mud wrestling and group sex" on the muddy bank, according to critic George L. Geckle, who characterized the production as "a mudsummer nightmare."[216] Audiences in the first few rows were given raincoats to protect them from the splatter. The fairies were dressed in black, with blue faces. Puck, played by contortionist Angela Laurier, scuttled about the stage on her hands, with her legs folded over her shoulders. She and one of the blue fairies coupled sexually in the mud. Clinging to Bottom's back, this Puck provided his ass's ears with her legs. The fairies provided the rest of the "forest" by placing chairs in the pool. At the end of the forest sequence, the lovers showered off their mud and dressed in dry white clothes, ostensibly cleansed of their dream. The cast was ethnically diverse; an Indonesian gamelan and other exotic, primitive instruments provided the music.[217]

The program carried notes from Freud, Jung, and Kott. Lepage said the company developed its approach in workshops, and the actors ultimately were interested in identifying certain recurrences in dreams:

"The main thing was water and the ideas of traps and danger zones," said the young, Canadian-born director. "We decided it would be a watery dream, a dark dream, a very muddy, slippery environment . . . a dangerous place, like in those dreams when you want to run away and you can't because your feet are stuck. And there is also the idea that you have these white, innocent, pristine teenagers going into this very dirty and sleazy world and coming out of it stained by their own dreams, their own sexuality, their own darkness. That's the thing about adolescent sexuality, it's an extraordinary moment of your life, but it's also a very spooky one. It's full of traps, and it's very compromising with wet dreams and menstruation and so on."[218]

The production also seems to have much in common with the ideas of Artaud and Grotowski. But Lepage's quest for "theatricality" has not the roar of the old prophets; one can hardly critique it as a quest for some metaphysical plenitude that is not there. Beneath the bare lightbulb, the empty space seems much diminished here.

Karin Beier's production for the Düsseldorf Schauspielhaus in 1995–1996 used the play to stage a vision of a postmodern Babel developing amid the efforts to shape the European Union. Her company of fourteen actors from different nations performed the play in nine languages, mining every possibility in the text and the conceit to explore cultural dissonance and disempowerment. (In Beier's earlier production of *Romeo and Juliet* [1992–1994], the Montagues spoke English and the Capulets French.) When the characters were not caught up in language confusions and cultural differences, they seemed to be subjects in the thrall of a cruel sexuality, as has been the case in a number of postmodern productions. Staging the play simply, with a hodgepodge of street-theatre costumes and properties and with the usual doubling in the roles of Theseus/Oberon and Hippolyta/Titania, the youthful company was inventive and winning but, given the conceit, seldom subtle.

Beier's *A Midsummer Night's Dream* grew out of her idea for a *Europäisher Shakespeare*, which in turn was the result of a 1995 directors' workshop organized by the new Union of European Theatres.[219] The production opened with a striking image of Hippolyta as a black Amazon (Josette Bushell-Mingo, who doubled as Titania), bending her golden bow. We next saw her as Theseus's captive, nude and terrified. As she was reclothed in Western dress by court attendants, Theseus, a suave Italian clad in morning coat and striped pants with a gold chain of office around his neck (Paolo Calabresi from Milan, who also played Oberon), taught her how to speak her new language, prompting her so that Hippolyta's lines were now delivered in poignant subservience: "Four days will quickly steep themselves in night, / Four nights will quickly dream away the time; / And then the moon, like to a silver bow / New bent in heaven, shall behold the night / Of our solemnities" (1.1.7–11). In the forest, the Jewish, Hebrew-speaking Lysander (Michael Teplitzsky from Tel Aviv) and the English-speaking Hermia (Penny Needler, a British actress delivering the lines with an American accent) tried to communicate about the course of true love, resorting to pantomime. To Hermia's "I swear to thee by Cupid's strongest bow," he queried, "Cupit?" which she tried to clarify by flapping her arms, winglike.[220] Shakespeare did not seem to be the common currency in this intercultural realm, although Helena (Giorgia Senesi from Milan) tried to outdo Hermia's English by reciting in heavily Italian-inflected English Shakespeare's sonnet eighteen, "Shall I compare thee to a summer's day?" Trying to tempt Demetrius (Gergö Kaszás from Budapest), Helena did a striptease, ending on the floor, thrusting her pelvis up at him. Fortunately, the sequence ended only in a tango. *Pyramus and Thisbe* was the comic highlight of the polyglot performance, as the actors offered advice on playing the roles in their respective national styles. Petra Squenz (Margherita di Rauso from Milan) directed in operatic style, Flute (Jost Grix from Düsseldorf) demonstrated a Brechtian alienation effect, Starveling cited from Stanislavski and ended a tearful speech with "V Mosva, V Mosva," and Bottom (Jacek Poniedzialek from Cracow) offered a lesson in Grotowskian techniques, ending as a quivering figure that may have been a parody of the acting in Grotowski's famous *The Constant Prince*. The mechanicals' final performance was, wrote Marvin Carlson, "a hopeless melange of styles" that delighted the audience.[221] Some of the cultural stereotyping seemed theatrically opportunistic, however, and some brought severe criticism. Daniel Mufson wrote:

> Beier's overall project has an ugly superficiality at its core. "Fucking Jew," spits out the Hungarian Demetrius at the Israeli Lysander, who spits back "Fucking Gypsy," and the audience laughs merrily along at . . . what? Perhaps at the way both utter internationally recognized epithets . . . perhaps at the scene of two historically scorned minorities scorning one another? . . . Rather than critique or undermine national stereotypes, the most Beier hopes for as she reinforces these mythical and dangerous identities is that one can enjoy them for all their humorous diversity, a proposition as politically questionable as it is aesthetically spineless.[222]

The lavish aestheticism of Adrian Noble's production with the RSC in 1994–1995 was a hollow alternative in the 1990s, although not all critics agreed with that opinion. The visually stunning production, created in the main house in

Stratford, toured San Francisco, Chicago, Washington, D.C., and New York. Noble and his designers, Anthony Ward (setting and costumes) and Chris Parry (lighting), floated a large, fuschia-colored umbrella upside down amid a blue-black heaven hung with bare lightbulbs. Titania and Bottom floated upward in this velvet-lined umbrella, and Puck and the first fairy entered floating down (a little like Mary Poppins) to the red-dappled floor on smaller ones. This defining image of the production apparently derived from Titania's speech on the weather and the umbrellas of René Magritte.[223] But the RSC's umbrellas were hardly those of the Magritte who ironically and wittily subverts our expectations of a link between signs and essences, representation and presence.[224] These beautiful, romantic umbrellas offered the comforting protection of an extravagant, self-referential theatricality. The staging flirted with the idea of the surreal, seeking to blur the lines between the fairy and mortal worlds. At the opening of the play, Hippolyta swung on a swing within the brownish drab walls of a boxlike room with one door — apparently the court. For the forest, the walls evaporated easily in washes of red light substantial enough to float on, and a line of mist-shrouded doors appeared across the upstage. Opening simultaneously, they revealed, in shadowing shafts of light, the puzzled lovers. (Such doors have become almost international theatrical analogues of the poststructural idea of subjectivity. They may be indebted to the setting for Meyerhold's 1926 production of Gogol's *Inspector General*.)[225] Alex Jennings and Lindsay Duncan doubled as Theseus/Oberon and Hippolyta/Titania, the distinctions made by a change of a cape for him and a robe for her. Two freestanding doors emerged from traps in the forest to provide perches from which Oberon and Puck watched the mortals. The only disturbingly surreal moment came when Puck (Barry Lynch) wrapped the sleeping lovers in grommeted canvases and hung them on sky hooks, suspending them in midair like floating larvae.

The program notes claimed that Noble's production "explicitly honored" Peter Brook's.[226] Perhaps a few distant echoes were discernable: Hippolyta on her swing, Puck in his baggy yellow trousers; the act break coming as Titania and Bottom ascended toward consummation in the umbrella. But Noble's production was glibly sophisticated and without any of the urgency and cultural immediacy of Brook's. In concept, staging, and acting, it was satisfied to be self-enclosed. The language was beautifully enunciated, especially by Jennings and Duncan, British t's crossed and all vowels and gestures perfectly rounded in an artificial high-fashion comedy style. Oberon and Titania, who sometimes seemed to be quarreling stars from the Ice Capades, easily reconciled in a passionless dance. The production missed — or avoided — many opportunities for engaging issues of contemporary interest. The Egeus-Hermia question was not broached; Egeus simply left the stage quietly after Theseus overruled him. Hippolyta, the Amazon, was no advocate for the young lovers nor a voice for feminism. But Hermia decked the males in the forest fight with fierce black-belt prowess. Such contemporary byplay as there was, sexual and otherwise, seemed gratuitous, unconnected, even cynical, as if to say, one of my students observed, "this is the kind of thing we do now." Titania caressed Bottom's crotch with her bare foot, and Bottom (Desmond Barrit) emerged from the bower with his fly open and shirttail protruding. The level of humor is characteristic of Barrit, a television comedian who recently had done a broad star turn as both of the Antipholuses for the RSC's *Comedy of Errors*. The fairies, an otherwise indeterminate group, comically mocked him with phallic sticks erect between their legs. When Puck kissed Oberon fully and sensually on the mouth before "I fly . . . ," the audience was surely being tantalized with a suggestion of gay sexual behavior, and what this might mean within the context of a production so safe otherwise was not disclosed.

Lacking an honest center, Noble's suave production finally was simply cunning. Created to please mainstream audiences and to be exported, it tacitly but deliberately eschewed anything that, in the conservative mid-1990s and amid jeopardized funding for the arts, might be construed as politically troublesome or deconstructed Shakespeare. It apparently succeeded. The souvenir program carried a full-page color photo of the notably conservative Prince Charles, president of the RSC, and a text with his blessing on "this elegant and witty production, which I and my children have much enjoyed." In the United States, the production was advertised on radio in Churchillian tones, with the accent on the *Royal* Shakespeare Company, and the souvenir program notes prominently displayed the theory that the play had been composed for a wedding in a noble family.

Epilogue

Theseus: No epilogue, I pray you; for your play needs no excuse.

To the reader who has followed these four hundred years of the play's performance history, the epilogue will be self-evident, at least in part: we do not go to definitive theatres; we go to the theatres of our times. But the matter is much more complicated than the old history truism that the theatre reflects its times or the new history truism that dominant ideologies inscribe themselves upon it. Through the play, imaginative theatre artists have created representations of their culture that are of considerable complexity. Catherine Belsey has observed that the drama thrives on conflict and is seldom homiletic; theatrical productions are no more singleminded.[1] Productions of this play have often simultaneously affirmed and challenged cultural practices of the social mainstream. True, we have seen productions that, by and large, seek to reinforce dominant cultural practices; one thinks of Ludwig Tieck's or Sir Herbert Beerbohm Tree's. But, laggard though the theatre is among the arts — it follows rather than leads, perhaps because it is dependent on quickly accessible vocabularies — it also thrives on, and gives testimony to, contradictory social energies, staging them, not resolving them. Purcell's opera of 1692 was designed in part as a tribute to the marriage of William and Mary, but that elegant stage engine was parented by absolutist masque traditions and by an era straining toward relatively less hierarchical rule. The story of David Garrick's three tries at this play in the next century is a microcosm of Garrick's championing of a universal, transcendent Shakespeare while at the same time he was naturalizing him for mid-eighteenth-century London audiences. Barker's remarkable 1914 production virtually staged a paradox central to modernist theatre practice: the quest for a new, twentieth-century scenic vocabulary that would speak eternal Shakespeare. The productions of John Hancock, Ariane Mnouchkine, and Peter Brook at once stage Shakespeare's four-hundred-year-old text and their problematic relationship to it, simultaneously occupying and displacing it, each offering this self-conscious dialectic as an assurance of authenticity.

Productions in the last third of the twentieth century have been intent on probing the play's erotic dimensions, but over the last decade they have been equally interested in tracing the gender conflicts in the play's patriarchal frame. Theatre artists have been intrigued with the captive Hippolyta ("I wooed thee with my sword" [1.1.16]) and Oberon's jealousy ("And with the juice of this I'll streak her eyes, / And make her full of hateful fantasies" [2.1.257–258]). This development would seem to mine that originary unease about gender and power within Elizabethan patriarchy that Louis Montrose believes is at the heart of the play, a play he describes as "a cultural fantasia upon Nature's universal theme."[2] We also have had a corollary, feminist interest in Titania's delicate description of the womanly bond between her and the pregnant mother of the Indian boy ("When we have laughed to see the sails conceive, / And grow big-bellied with the wanton wind" [2.1.128–129]). In addition, when theatre artists have sought vocabularies for the play's four levels of characters — the young lovers, mechanicals, aristocratic rulers, and fairies — they have engaged or complex negotiations of class structure, race, and national identity. Sometimes a cruel and indifferent aristocracy has been set up in contrast with the simplicity and powerlessness of the mechanicals ("O sweet bully Bottom! Thus hath he lost sixpence a day during his life" [4.2.18–19]). Productions also have caught us sifting the Victorian and Edwardian past for some threadbare vestiges of belief in the supernatural. Taking us through all the play's dialectics and their points of contact with our culture, most recent productions have not brought us to any resting point of final domestic tranquility at the play's end but to a kind of midsummer night's amnesty, not letting us forget the precariousness of our condition.

It is fitting that Bottom should have the last word about the theatre and our dreams. He has complete faith in the theatre's ability to represent them. Waking at dawn in the forest and reflecting on his dream, which has been both terrifying and delightful, he knows that there can be no rational representation of his experience. "The eye of man hath not heard, the ear of man hath not seen, man's hand is not able to taste, his tongue to conceive, nor his heart to report what my dream was," he says (4.1.208–211), strenuously garbling St. Paul.[3] The best way to capture his complex dream, he determines, will be to have Quince write a ballad of it. And Bottom proposes to sing this ballad of desire and mortality at the most important moment of the play, in the "latter end," at the death of Pyramus's beloved Thisbe. Bottom does not get to sing the ballad, nor is it necessary. But his instinct is profoundly right: his world will inform his performance of the play.

APPENDIX: WEDDING STUDIES

This appendix lists, in a form less cumbersome than notes, the weddings proposed for which *A Midsummer Night's Dream* was ostensibly written, together with the twentieth-century scholarship surrounding the issue. Most of this literature is referred to and assessed in chapter 1.

The weddings proposed are, in chronological order: (1) Robert Devereux, Earl of Essex, to Frances Sidney (Sir Philip's widow), April or May 1590; (2) Robert Carey, Earl of Monmouth-to-be, to Elizabeth Trevannion, 1592; (3) Sir Thomas Heneage to Countess Mary of Southampton, 2 May 1594; (4) Henry Percy, Earl of Northumberland, to Lady Dorothy Devereux, May 1595(?); (5) William Stanley, Earl of Derby, to Elizabeth Vere, 26(?) January 1595; (6) Edward Russell, Earl of Bedford, to Lucy Harrington, 1595; (7) Sir Thomas Berkeley, Lord Hunsdon-to-be, to Elizabeth Carey, 19 February 1596; (8) Henry Guildford and William Petrie to the daughters of the Earl of Worcester, Elizabeth and Catherine, 8 November 1596 (for which Edmund Spenser wrote *Prothalamion*); (9) Henry Wriothesley, Earl of Southampton, to Elizabeth Vernon, February or August 1598; (10) Roger Manners, Earl of Rutland, to Elizabeth Sidney (daughter of Sir Philip), 1599; and (11) Henry, Lord Herbert, to Anne Russell, 16 June 1600.

A summary of nineteenth-century conjectures on weddings 1, 5, 6, and 9 will be found in Horace Howard Furness, ed. *A Midsummer Night's Dream* (New York: J. B. Lippincott, 1895; reprint, 1963), 259–264. Influential discussions of weddings 1, 3, 5, 6, and 7 will be found in Sir E. K. Chambers, "The Occasion of *A Midsummer Night's Dream*," in *A Book of Homage to Shakespeare*, ed. I. Gollanz (Oxford, 1916), 154–160 (reprinted in E. K. Chambers, *Shakespearean Gleanings* [Oxford: Clarendon Press, 1944], 61–67) (weddings 5 and 7); E. K. Chambers, *The Elizabethan Stage* (Oxford: Clarendon Press, 1923), 4:109 and 2:194 (weddings 5 and 7); E. K. Chambers, *William Shakespeare, A Study of Facts and Problems* (Oxford: Clarendon Press, 1930), 1:358–363; and Harold Brooks, ed., *A Midsummer Night's Dream* (London: Methuen, 1979), liii–lxxxviii. Also on weddings 1, 3, 5, and 7, see Eva Turner Clark, *Hidden Allusions in Shakespeare's Plays* (New York, 1931; reprint, 3d ed., ed. Ruth Loyd Miller, Port Washington, Wash.: Kennikat Press, 1974), 613–626 (wedding 5); Peter Alexander, *Shakespeare's Life and Art* (London: James Nisbet & Sons, 1939), 105–106; John H. Long, *Shakespeare's Use of Music* (Gainesville: University Press of

Florida, 1955), 82–94; A. W. Rowse, *William Shakespeare, a Biography* (London: Macmillian, 1963), 202–211 (wedding 3); and Marion A. Taylor, *Bottom, Thou Art Translated* (Amsterdam: Rodopi NV, 1973), 221–223 (wedding 3). On wedding 8, see Burns Martin, "*A Midsummer Night's Dream*," *Times Literary Supplement*, 24 January 1935, 48; Giles Dawson, "A Gentleman's Purse," *Yale Review* 39 (June 1950), 631–646; and Maureen Duffy, *The Erotic World of Faery* (London: Hodder and Stoughton, 1972), chapter 8, passim. On wedding 9, see Sir Arthur Quiller-Couch and John Dover Wilson, eds., *A Midsummer Night's Dream* (Cambridge: Cambridge University Press, 1924), ix–x, xx–xxi, 87–92.

Several scholars have argued that there are numerous topical, allegorical allusions in the play, wedding related or not. Edith Rickert, in "Political Propaganda and Satire in *A Midsummer Night's Dream*," *Modern Philology* (August 1923), 53–57, and (November 1923), 133–154, sees Titania as Elizabeth and Bottom as King James of Scotland. Eva Turner Clark (*Hidden Allusions*) erects the case that the play was written by the Earl of Oxford about 1583 and was first produced before Elizabeth in 1584 and that it contains allusions to the unrealized match between Elizabeth and François, Duke of Alençon. Steven W. May sees many allusions appropos of wedding 7 in "*A Midsummer Night's Dream* and the Carey-Berkeley Wedding," in *Renaissance Papers 1983*, ed. A. Leigh Deneef and M. Thomas Hester (Raleigh, N.C.: Southeastern Renaissance Conference, 1984), 43–52. See also David Wiles, *Shakespeare's Almanac, A Midsummer Night's Dream, Marriage and the Elizabethan Calendar* (Cambridge: D. S. Brewer, 1993).

For other scholarship on the wedding issue, see D. Allen Carroll and Gary Jay Williams, *A Midsummer Night's Dream, An Annotated Bibliography* (New York: Garland, 1986), under "occasion" in the index, plus entry 476a. A. L. Rowse made the unsupported statement that the play premiered at wedding 4 in the introduction to his 1984 edition of the play (Lanham, Md.: University Press of America, 1984). Important works since are W. B. Hunter, "The Date and Occasion for *A Midsummer Night's Dream*," in *Milton's Comus: Family Piece* (Troy, N.Y., 1983); W. B. Hunter, "The First Performance of *A Midsummer Night's Dream*," *Notes and Queries*, 230 (1985), 45–47 (weddings 3 and 7); E. A. J. Honigmann, *Shakespeare: The "Lost Years"* (Manchester, 1985), appendix C, 150–154 (wedding 5); Marion Colthorpe, "Queen Elizabeth I and *A Midsummer Night's Dream*," *Notes and Queries*, 232 (June 1987), 206–207 (wedding 7); and Wiles, *Shakespeare's Almanac*. Wiles reviews all the arguments and advances his own for wedding 7, together with arguments for multiple family allusions.

Very few scholars have questioned the wedding premiere idea. Henry Cunningham, in his 1905 Arden edition of the play (Heath, 1905), thought the play ultimately celebrated a noble marriage (wedding 5) but suggested without further explanation that this was not so "in the first instance." He said, "Marriage or no marriage, we should have had *A Midsummer Night's Dream*, though, perhaps not exactly in its present form" (xxix). The only serious arguments against a wedding premiere heretofore have been those offered by Stanley Wells, ed., *A Midsummer Night's Dream* (Harmondsworth, Middlesex: Penguin, 1967), 13–14; see also Stanley Wells and Gary Taylor, eds., *William Shakespeare, a Textual Companion* (Oxford: Clarendon Press, 1987), 118. Peter Holland's edition of the play (Oxford: Clarendon Press, 1994) also rejects the wedding premiere idea.

ILLUSTRATION CREDITS

Every attempt has been made to secure permission for all illustrations. I am grateful to the following: Bristol University Theatre Collection: plates 6–7, figs. 47–50; British Museum: fig. 9; Devonshire Collection, Trustees of the Chatsworth Settlement: figs. 1, 2; Folger Shakespeare Library: figs. 3–6, 11, 15; Goethe Collection, Stiftung Weimarer Klassik, Weimar: fig. 14; Harvard Theatre Collection: figs. 12, 46; *Illustrated London News*, *Supplement*, 11 April 1914: plates 8–10, fig. 29; Musée des Beaux-Arts, Bordeaux: fig. 8; Museum of Modern Art, New York: plate 13; Max Reinhardt-Forschungstätte, Salzburg: figs. 37–39; Billy Rose Theatre Collection, New York Public Library for the Performing Arts, Astor, Lenox and Tilden Foundations: figs. 16–21; Shakespeare Centre Library Trustees, Stratford-upon-Avon: figs. 55–57, Joe Cocks Studio; fig. 54, David Farrell, photographer; plates 11, 12, 14–17, fig. 53, Thomas F. Holte, photographer; and figs. 33–36, 51, 52; *Sketch*, 25 February 1914: figs. 27, 28, 31, 32; Theatre Museum, National Museum of the Performing Arts, Victoria and Albert Museum Trustees: figs. 23–26, 45; Turner Entertainment Company: figs. 40–44, stills from the Reinhardt-Dieterle film, copyright 1935, Turner Entertainment Company, all rights reserved; Victoria and Albert Museum Trustees: plates 1–5, fig. 7; Yale-Rockefeller Collection of Theatrical Prints, Yale School of Drama Library: fig. 10.

NOTES

1. The Wedding-play Myth and the *Dream* in Full Play

1. Jacques Lacan, *Ecrits*, trans. Alan Sheridan (London: Tavistock, 1977), 65.

2. Samuel Schoenbaum, *William Shakespeare, a Documentary Life* (New York: Oxford University Press, with Scolar Press, 1975), 138.

3. Roland Barthes, "Myth Today," in *Mythologies*, trans. Annette Lavers (London: Paladin, 1973), 155–156.

4. Louis Adrian Montrose, "'Shaping Fantasies': Figurations of Gender and Power in Elizabethan Culture," *Representations* 1 (1983), 61–94; I cite from the essay as published in *Representing the English Renaissance*, ed. Stephen Greenblatt, (Berkeley: University of California Press, 1988), 31–64; Louis Adrian Montrose, "A Kingdom of Shadows," and Penry James, "Shakespeare's *A Midsummer Night's Dream*, Social Tensions Contained," both in *The Theatrical City*, ed. David L. Smith, Richard Strier, and David Bevington (Cambridge: Cambridge University Press, 1995), 69–86 and 55–67, respectively. See also Shirley Nelson Garner's ahistorical feminist analysis of the play as affirming patriarchal order in "Jack shall have Jill; / Nought shall go ill," *Women's Studies* 9 (1981), 47–63.

5. Nicholas Rowe, *Life of Shakespear* (London: Jacob Tonson, 1709), 1:viii.

6. William Shakspear, *Der Sommernachstrom*, in *Shakspear's Dramatische Werke*, üebersetzung von August Wilhelm von Schlegel, erganzt und erläutert von Ludwig Tieck, Dritter Teil (Berlin: Reimer, 1830), 353.

7. René Wellek, *A History of Modern Criticism: 1750–1950* (New Haven, Conn.: Yale University Press, 1955), 2:95–96.

8. F. L. Fleay was as serious as any about the theory, arguing in his *A Chronicle of the Life and Work of William Shakespeare* (London: J. C. Nimmu, 1886) for the Russell-Harrington wedding (181) and then in his *A Chronicle of the English Drama, 1559–1642* (London: Reeves and Turner, 1891) for the Southhampton-Vernon wedding (2:194). Edward Dowden, in his *Shakspere: A Critical Study of His Mind and Art* (London: Henry S. King, 1873), wanted a court-wedding premiere (67), and Sir Sidney Lee, in his 1898 *A Life of Shakespeare*, could not resist the Russell-Harrington wedding (161–162). See Horace Howard Furness's 1895 edition of the play for summaries of these (except Lee) and others, (New York: J. B. Lippincott, 1895; reprint 1963), 259–264.

9. John Masefield, *William Shakespeare* (New York: Henry Holt, 1911 [Home University Library of Modern Knowledge]), 66–67.

10. See, for example, the poem by W. J. Courthope ("C.B., Litt. D., F. B. A., formerly Professor of Poetry in the University of Oxford . . . ") in which he assures readers that "a free-born Empire patriot's consciousness, / Tuned the Music of our Shakespeare's tongue" (*A Book of Homage to Shakespeare*, ed. I. Gollanz [Oxford, 1916], 142). The copy in the Folger Shakespeare Library, bound in white leather, is a special edition; it was also issued in conventional covers.

11. Sir Arthur Quiller-Couch and John Dover Wilson, eds., *A Midsummer Night's Dream*, (Cambridge: Cambridge University Press, 1924), ix–x, xx–xxi, 87–92.

12. Cited in Stanley Wells, "Tales from Shakespeare," *Proceedings of the British Academy* 73 (1987), 140–141.

13. E. K. Chambers, *William Shakespeare, a Study of Facts and Problems* (Oxford: Clarendon Press, 1930), 1:361.

14. Quiller-Couch and Dover Wilson, 87–92; Fleay, *A Chronicle of the English Drama*, 2:194. Dover Wilson's acute analysis of mislining in the 1600 Quarto led him to suspect two or three stages of revision (80–86).

15. Chambers, 1:361.

16. E. K. Chambers, "The Occasion of *A Midsummer Night's Dream*," in Gollanz, 154; E. K. Chambers, *The Elizabethan Stage* (Oxford: Clarendon Press, 1944), 4:109, note 11. Stowe is the source of the date and place. Chambers and other advocates of this wedding also point out that Shakespeare may have belonged to a company of the groom's late brother, Ferdinando, a company that had performed some of Shakespeare's earliest plays in 1592 (see Chambers, *The Elizabethan Stage*, 2:118–134, especially 130). It is a considerable leap from this circumstance to a Shakespeare play made-to-order for the 1595 wedding. Edmund Spenser's *Tears of the Muses* was dedicated to Ferdinando's wife in 1591, and Warburton suggested in his edition (1747) that Shakespeare was referring to the death of Spenser in poverty in the lines he gives Philostrate to describe one of the proposed wedding entertainments: "The thrice-three muses mourning for the death / of learning, late deceased in beggary" (5.1.52–53). Lines alluding to Spenser's death in poverty seem unlikely to have been put before the family of Spenser's patron at a family wedding. Today it is more widely thought that the lines borrow Spenser's title but refer to Robert Greene's death.

17. Chambers, "The Occasion," 154–160; Chambers, *The Elizabethan Stage*, 4:109 and 2:194.

18. Eva Turner Clark, *Hidden Allusions in Shakespeare's Plays* (New York, 1931; reprint, 3d. ed., ed. Ruth Loyd Miller, Port Washington, Wash.: Kennikat Press, 1974), 613–626; Eva Turner Clark, *The Man Who Was Shakespeare* (New York: Richard Smith, 1937), 136, 176–177. Clark indicates that a number of particular lines allude to the courtship. For example, Titania says, "The moon methinks, looks with a wat'ry eye, / And when she weeps, weeps every little flower, / Lamenting some enforcèd chastity" (3.1.190–192). Clark suggests that this refers to tears shed by Elizabeth's maids of honor when she announced her intended betrothal to Alençon.

19. Marion A. Taylor, *Bottom, Thou Art Translated* (Amsterdam: Rodopi NV, 1973), 198–200 and chapters 5 and 6, passim. Snout is supposedly named for an envoy named Du Bex (Bec in French meaning beak, bill).

20. Chambers, "The Occasion," 159–160.

21. Leslie Hotson, *Shakespeare versus Shallow* (Boston: Little, Brown, 1931), 111–122. Harold Brooks, in his edition of *A Midsummer Night's Dream* (London: Methuen, 1979), finds Hotson's argument congenial to his argument for the Carey-Berkeley wedding (lvii). H. J. Oliver, editor of the New Arden *Merry Wives of Windsor* (London: Methuen, 1971), finds Hotson's theory plausible but is more circumspect (xliv–lii). T. W. Craik, editor of the Oxford edition of the play (*The Merry Wives of Windsor* [Oxford: Clarendon Press, 1989]), infers that the first performance was in some way connected with the Order of the Garter (1–6).

22. Chambers, *The Elizabethan Stage*, 2:194–195, 4:110.

23. David Wiles, *Shakespeare's Almanac* (Cambridge: D. S. Brewer, 1993), 156–170.

24. William B. Hunter, *Milton's Comus* (Troy, N.Y.: Whitson, 1983), appendix, 95–101. John Draper finds a convenient conjunction of the new moon and Venus in May 1595 and thus places the play's premiere on the date of the 1595 court wedding of Henry Percy and Lady Dorothy Devereux ("The Queen Makes a Match and Shakespeare a Comedy," *Yearbook of English Studies* 2 [1972], 61–67).

25. Wiles, 163 and chapter 10, passim.

26. Chambers, "The Occasion," 154–160; Chambers, *The Elizabethan Stage*, 4:109, note 10, and 4:164–165. In the latter, he lists John Stow's *Annales*, in which the wedding is noted but with no mention of Chamberlain's company (768); he also cites the Chamber Accounts, but no performance by the company on 26 January 1595 is recorded in his listing of Chamber Accounts, (4:165). Chambers himself had said in his 1916 essay (154) that the Treasurer of the Chamber made no payment for a court performance on 26 January 1595.

27. Chambers, *The Elizabethan Stage*, 1:168, note 1. Throgmorton planned to lie prostrate before the queen during a song, and a muse was to present the queen with a wedding ring, set with diamonds and a heart-shaped ruby in a coronet and inscribed "Elizabeth potest." Wiles (151) provides a concise summary of the Raleigh connection.

28. John Stow, *Annales, or a General Chronicle of England*, augmented by Edmond Howe (London: Thomas Adams, 1615), 768.

29. Masques and plays were often prepared together for one occasion, as Chambers observes (*The Elizabethan Stage*, 1:207). The Kenilworth progress is one such instance (see 1:123). But no play is mentioned in the case of the Vere-Stanley wedding festivities.

30. Wells first noted this in the introduction to the 1967 New Penguin edition of the play, 14; see also Stanley Wells and Gary Taylor, eds., *William Shakespeare, a Textual Companion* (Oxford: Clarendon Press, 1987), 118–119.

31. Reproduced in color in G. Blakemore Evans, ed., *The Riverside Shakespeare* (Boston: Houghton Mifflin, 1974), plate 4, following 46.

32. Chambers, *The Elizabethan Stage*, 4:77–116, Court Calendar, 1558–1603; Wiles (141) cites a late 1594 record of payment to players for performing a play at the marriage of Henry, Earl of Northumberland, and Dorothy Devereux (another nominee for the occasion of Shakespeare's play). As Wiles points out, the ceremony apparently did not actually take place until sometime in 1595.

33. Chambers, *The Elizabethan Stage*, 1:169.

34. For a full description of the festivities, see Roy Strong, *The Cult of Elizabeth* (Wallop, Hampshire: Thames & Hudson, 1977), 28–30. Chambers's Court Calendar shows only three exceptions to the wedding masque custom recorded between 1558 and 1616. Of these, on one occasion in 1614, a play (unidentified) was given for a court wedding along with two masques; another exception was Samuel Daniel's *Hymen's Triumph*, given for a court wedding a month later. Daniel's work, entitled a pastoral, is the first "play" known with certainty to have been written for such an occasion. Daniel, unlike Shakespeare, is the author of three court masques.

35. Andrew Gurr, *The Shakespearean Stage, 1574–1642*, 2d ed. rev. (Cambridge: Cambridge University Press, 1980), 25–26.

36. See, for example, Enid Welsford, *The Court Masque* (Cambridge: Cambridge University Press, 1927), 331–332; Francis Fergusson and C. J. Sisson, eds., *A Midsummer Night's Dream* (New York: Dell, 1960), 6 (reprinted in Fergusson's *Shakespeare: The Pattern in His Carpet* [New York: Delacorte Press, 1970]); and Wolfgang Clemen, ed., *A Midsummer Night's Dream* (New York: New American Library, 1963), introduction.

37. Chambers, "The Occasion," 154–160; Chambers, *The Elizabethan Stage*, 4:109, note 11.

38. Marion Colthorpe, "Queen Elizabeth I and *A Midsummer Night's Dream*," *Notes and Queries* 232 (June 1987), 206–207.

39. John Smyth, "The Berkeley Manuscripts," in *The Lives of the Berkeleys*, ed. J. Maclean (Gloucester: John Bellows, 1883), 2:395.

40. Colthorpe, 206.

41. Ibid.

42. Smyth, 2:394.

43. Wiles, 156–157.

44. Phyllis I. H. Naylor, *Astrology, an Historical Examination* (London, 1967), 82; Bernard Capp, *English Almanacs, 1500–1800* (Ithaca, N.Y.: Cornell University Press, 1979), chapter 2, 23–66, passim.

45. Wiles, 154–155. See also Capp.

46. Capp, 31; Naylor, 90–91; Don Cameron Allen, *The Star-Crossed Renaissance* (Durham, N.C.: Duke University Press, 1941), 148.

47. See Capp, chapter 2.

48. Allen, 185–189.

49. Sonnet fourteen, in Blakemore Evans, 1752.

50. A close comparison of Oberon's speech with the accounts of Robert Langham and George Gascoigne was worked out by N. J. Halpin in 1843 and is cited at length in Furness's Variorum edition, 80–87. As Chambers noted, there is a generic quality to such pageants (*William Shakespeare*, 1:358).

51. Wiles, 170.

52. J. Thomas Looney, *"Shakespeare" Identified* (New York: Duell, Sloan, and Pearce [1920]); Charlton Ogburn, *The Mysterious William Shakespeare* (New York: Dodd, Mead, 1984), 731.

53. Steven W. May, "*A Midsummer Night's Dream* and the Carey-Berkeley Wedding," in *Renaissance Papers 1983*, ed. A. Leigh Deneef and M. Thomas Hester (Raleigh, N.C.: Southeastern Renaissance Conference, 1984), 43–52. May also suggests that the young lovers' confusions refer to the breakup of a match between Elizabeth Carey and William Herbert that preceded the speedy courtship of Elizabeth and Thomas Berkeley.

54. Wiles, 171.

55. G. R. Hibbard, "Love, Marriage and Money in Shakespeare's Theatre and Shakespeare's England," in *The Elizabethan Theatre VI*, ed. G. R. Hibbard (Toronto: University of Waterloo and Macmillan, 1975), 134–135. Andrew Gurr has suggested that treatments of the marriage issue may have distinguished the repertoire of Shakespeare's company from that of other companies ("Inter-textuality at Windsor," *Shakespeare Quarterly* 38 [1987], 195, 200).

56. Wiles, 174–175.

57. The indenture for the transfer of this property from Sir William More to James Burbage, on 4 February 1596, describes it as being "all those seven great upper rooms as they are now divided, being all upon one floor and sometime being one great and entire room." It is unlikely that this structurally divided space was altered into a theatre within two weeks. Irwin Smith, *Shakespeare's Blackfriars Playhouse* (New York: New York University Press, 1964), 161; Glynne Wickham, *Early English Stages* (London: Routledge and Kegan Paul, 1972), 2:130.

58. Smith, 72–73.

59. Wells and Taylor, 120, 340–341; they date the play at 1598, still finding it likely that it was commissioned.

60. Rowe, 1:viii–ix.

61. Craik, 1–13.

62. Quiller-Couch and Dover Wilson, 103; 105 and notes to 1.1.72–78; 116 and notes to 2.2.148–187; 124 and notes to 3.1.145–146.

63. There is the specific instance of Lord Hunsdon requesting a performance for the Flemish ambassador in 1600, for which the company did *1 Henry IV*, a play already in the company's repertoire. Wells and Taylor, 117–118; Chambers, *The Elizabethan Stage*, 1:220.

64. Stanley Wells, ed., *A Midsummer Night's Dream* (Harmondsworth, Middlesex: Pen-

guin, 1967), 13. R. A. Foakes agrees with Wells (*A Midsummer Night's Dream* [Cambridge, 1984], 2.1.158n).

65. Brooks, lv.

66. This seems to have been the average court payment under Elizabeth; see Chambers, *The Elizabethan Stage*, 1:217–218. This might have been comparable to a very good day's take at the public playhouse. Samuel Kiechel, a merchant from Ulm who visited London in 1584, wrote, "It may well be that [the theatres] take as much as from 50 to 60 dollars [£10 to £12], at once, especially when they act anything new . . . and double prices are charged" (Chambers, *The Elizabethan Stage*, 2:358). In 1612–1613, the King's Men were paid £153 6s. 8d. for performing fourteen plays at court (Schoenbaum, 224), which would be approximately £10 per performance, allowing for a 10 percent tip.

67. Chambers, *The Elizabethan Stage*, 4:108–115, Court Calendar.

68. My general argument here runs counter to Wickham's suggestion that plays were written with the court stage in mind (Wickham, 2:148–150; see also 158–161 and chapter 14, passim). Wickham also seems to suggest the court was the more appreciative and satisfying audience when he says, "The roofed hall, candlelight and ceremonial occasions [were] the alpha and omega of the professional actor's status and environment, . . . notwithstanding notable and extensive sallies into less sophisticated places of public recreation" (2:150).

69. Chambers, *William Shakespeare*, 2:342.

70. Stephen Orgel, ed., *The Tempest* (Oxford: Clarendon Press, 1987), 1.

71. Brooks, liii, note 2.

72. To give a specific example, the turn-of-the-century Oxbridge efforts to put Shakespeare in the academic canon required such validations; see Terry Eagleton's tracing of the rise of English studies in *Literary Theory: An Introduction* (Minneapolis: University of Minnesota Press, 1983), chapter 1, passim. See also Gary Taylor, *Reinventing Shakespeare* (New York: Weidenfeld and Nicholson, 1989), chapter 4, 193–196, and chapter 5, passim.

73. Gerald Eades Bentley, *The Profession of Dramatist in Shakespeare's Time, 1590–1642* (Princeton, N. J.: Princeton University Press, 1971), 8.

74. Paradoxically, the argument also supposes an unlikely mix of common players with boys from aristocratic families.

75. See, for example, W. W. Greg, *Shakespeare's First Folio* (Oxford: Clarendon Press, 1955), 242; Brooks, xli–xlii; Foakes, 137–138; Wells and Taylor, 279. See also Robert K. Turner Jr., "Printing Methods and Textual Problems in *A Midsummer Night's Dream*, Q1," *Studies in Bibliography* 15 (1962), 33–55. For a discussion of Shakespearean textual problems in general and in this play's Act 5 in particular, see Gary Taylor, "Revising Shakespeare," *Text* 3 (1987), 285–304.

76. Wells, *A Midsummer Night's Dream*, 12–13.

77. Brooks suggests (and Wiles follows) that the line in Puck's epilogue, "We will make amends ere long," shows that the epilogue was designed exclusively for a regular playhouse audience who would return (Brooks, note to 5.1.416; Wiles, 121). But this seems an overly literal reading of a pro forma line.

78. Paul N. Siegel, "*A Midsummer Night's Dream* and the Wedding Guests," *Shakespeare Quarterly* 4 (1953), 139–144.

79. Paul A. Olson, "*A Midsummer Night's Dream* and the Meaning of Court Marriage" *ELH* 24 (1957), 95–119.

80. Smith, 61–162. The "stews" refer to the brothels that neighbored the theatres on the Southbank. Not all scholars have been so exclusivist. G. K. Hunter, in his study of John Lyly and his influence, views *A Midsummer Night's Dream* and *Love's Labour's Lost* as more Lylian

than earlier Shakespeare, possibly "because the occasion of these plays is aristocratic rather than popular." But he demonstrates such accessible appeals of *A Midsummer Night's Dream* as its narrative speed and shows the differences between Lyly and Shakespeare, concluding that, in this play, Shakespeare "remains true to himself" (*John Lyly: The Humanist as Courtier* [London: Routledge and Kegan Paul, 1962], 318–323).

81. Alfred Harbage, *Shakespeare's Audience* (Cambridge: Harvard University Press, 1941), 90, 158–164, and chapters 3, 6, and 7, passim. Harbage subsequently made in full the corresponding case that it was the tastes of the private theatre audiences, an urbane, decadent Jacobean court elite, that led playwrights away from the public theatre audiences and so to the drama's decline (*Shakespeare and the Rival Traditions* [New York: Macmillan, 1952], part 1, chapters 3 and 4; part 2, chapter 6, passim).

82. Ann Jennalie Cook, "The Audience of Shakespeare's Plays: A Reconsideration," *Shakespeare Studies* 7 (1974), 283–305; Ann Jennalie Cook, *The Privileged Playgoers of Shakespeare's London, 1576–1642* (Princeton, N.J.: Princeton University Press, 1981), 272–275.

83. Andrew Gurr, *Playgoing in Shakespeare's London* (Cambridge: Cambridge University Press, 1987), 1–12. Gurr also makes the good point that there is reason to be cautious about generalizations because of the span of years involved and the social changes during them.

84. Ibid., 167, 169.

85. R. W. Dent, "Imagination in *A Midsummer Night's Dream*," *Shakespeare Quarterly* 15 (1964), 118. See also Terry Eagleton's discussion of the issue of the precariousness of identity in his *William Shakespeare* (Oxford: Basil Blackwell, 1986), 20–26.

86. Egeus complains to Theseus that Lysander "hath bewitched the bosom of my child" with "rings, gauds, conceits, / Knacks, trifles, nosegays, [and] sweetmeats," (1.1.27, 33–34).

87. See the discussion of this in Robert Weimann's *Shakespeare and the Popular Tradition in the Theater: Studies in the Social Dimension of Dramatic Form and Function*, ed. Robert Schwartz (Baltimore: Johns Hopkins University Press, 1987), 216 f.

88. See, for example, Roy Strong's *Splendor at Court* (Boston, 1973).

89. Barbara Freedman, *Staging the Gaze: Postmodernism, Psychoanalysis, and Shakespearean Comedy* (Ithaca, N.Y.: Cornell University Press, 1991), chapters 3–6.

90. Montrose, 53.

91. Ibid., 41.

92. Ibid., 41–42; Montrose goes on to draw upon the prevailing ideas of procreation in Aristotle and Galen and shows briefly this male concern in other of Shakespeare's plays.

93. Ibid., 35.

94. Ibid., 49, 48–51.

95. For a summary of the discussions of the place of reason and imagination in the play and of Renaissance views on the subject, see Foakes, 37–38.

96. Ibid., 37.

97. See the discussion of the 1981 RSC production, directed by Ron Daniels, in chapter 9.

98. Jan Kott, *Shakespeare Our Contemporary*, trans. Boleslaw Taborski (Garden City, N.Y.: Doubleday, 1964), 207–228.

99. Brooks, cxxx.

100. David P. Young, *Something of Great Constancy: The Art of* A Midsummer Night's Dream (New Haven, Conn.: Yale University Press, 1966), 160.

101. Foakes, 39; see also 40.

102. Bernard Beckerman, *Shakespeare at the Globe, 1599–1609* (New York, 1962), 106.

103. For a discussion of the relation of these two plays and their dating, see Amy J. Riess and George Walton Williams, "Tragical Mirth": From *Romeo* to *Dream*," *Shakespeare Quarterly* 43 (1992), 214–218.

104. Titania's "young squire" is almost certainly a small boy, perhaps played by a child rather than by one of the boy actors.

105. Edmund Spenser, *The Faerie Queene*, ed. P. C. Bayley (Oxford: Oxford University Press, 1965), 230, 2.10.76.

106. See chapter 4.

107. Homer Swander, "Editors vs. a Text: The Scripted Geography of *A Midsummer Night's Dream*," *Studies in Philology* 37 (1990), 83–108.

108. See the discussion of Vestris's production in chapter 4.

109. For an extensive discussion of the evidence for act division and intervals in performance, the implications for meaning, and the general relationship between the practice and the printing of plays, see Gary Taylor, "The Structure of Performance: Act-Intervals in the London Theatres, 1576–1642," in *Shakespeare Reshaped, 1606–1623*, ed. Gary Taylor and John Jowett (Oxford: Clarendon Press, 1993), 3–50. For the alternative case that this stage direction was a necessary reminder to the stage manager that the lovers remain onstage during the ensuing scenes, see Foakes, 141–143.

110. See Andrew Gurr's discussion of continuous playing in his *The Shakespearean Stage*, 3d ed. (Cambridge: Cambridge University Press, 1992), 176–178.

111. Andrew Sabol, ed., *Four Hundred Songs and Dances from the Stuart Masque* (Providence, R. I.: Brown University Press, 1978), 594.

112. Skiles Howard, "Hands, Feet, and Bottoms: Decentering the Cosmic Dance in *A Midsummer Night's Dream*," *Shakespeare Quarterly* 44 (1993), 336.

113. Brooks, cxxiv; he draws for support on Olson, 115, and John H. Long, *Shakespeare's Use of Music* (Gainesville: University Press of Florida, 1955), 93.

114. Quiller-Couch and Dover Wilson, 151, 5.1.389–390n.

115. See 2.2.68–70, and the first Quarto stage directions at 3.5.42, 68.

116. For a discussion of the issue, see Furness, 239n; Brooks, cxxiii–cxxivn; Foakes, 132n; and Wells and Taylor, 286n. Richmond Noble suggested that Oberon may have commenced solo and then was joined by the fairies at the third line (*Shakespeare's Use of Song* [Oxford: Oxford University Press, 1923], 56). Long (98–99) disagreed and placed the beginning of the singing at Oberon's entrance lines.

117. King James VI, *Daemonologie* (Edinburgh, 1599), 143, cited in Katherine M. Briggs, *The Anatomy of Puck* (London, 1959).

118. Reginald Scot, *The Discoveries of Witchcraft* (London, 1584), 408–409.

119. R. A. Foakes and R. T. Rickert, eds., *Henslowe's Diary* (Cambridge: Cambridge University Press, 1961), 325.

120. Stephen Orgel and Roy Strong, *The Theatre of the Stuart Court* (London: Sotheby Park Bernet; Berkeley: University of California Press, 1973), 1:203.

121. King James VI, 65, cited in Briggs, 24.

122. *Robin Goodfellow, His Mad Pranks and Merry Jests* (London: F. Grove, 1628); Maureen Duffy reproduces the frontispiece from the 1639 edition in her *The Erotic World of Faery* (London: Hodder and Stoughten, 1972), plate 12, opposite 152. See also Lewis Spence, *The Fairy Tradition in Britain* (New York: Rider, 1948), 18–21.

123. William Haughton, *Grim, the Collier of Croydon*, in *A Choice Ternary of English Plays, Gratiae Theatrales*, ed. William M. Baillie (Binghamton, N.Y.: Medieval and Renaissance Texts Studies, 1984), 12, 241, opening stage direction for 4.1.

124. See Weimann's discussion of Puck, 193–196.

125. Foakes, 1.2.2n.

126. Ibid., 3.1.46n and 5.1.134n.

127. W. W. Greg, *The Shakespeare First Folio* (Oxford: Clarendon Press, 1955), 115–116.

128. T. W. Baldwin, in *The Organization and Personnel of the Shakespearean Company* (Princeton, N.J.: Princeton University Press, 1927), chart 2, opposite 26, casts Burbage as Demetrius and Robert Goffe as Oberon.

129. Foakes, 7.

130. Briggs, 13–24. Briggs shows that Elizabethan and Jacobean notions of fairies varied from horseback-trooping fairies to the child-sized Huon of Bordeaux, and she argues that Shakespeare was a literary pioneer in his diminutive fairies. She then automatically assumes that they were played by child actors.

131. In *Much Ado*, Kemp's name appears in the Quarto and Folio speech headings for the part in 4.2.

132. W. W. Greg, *A Bibliography of the English Printed Drama to the Restoration, I: Stationers' Records of Plays to 1616* (London: Oxford University Press, 1939), entry 56, 133–136. The dramatis personae for *Enough Is as Good as a Feast* (1565–1770) indicates the doubling arrangement for eighteen roles with the heading, "Seven may easely play this Enterlude." Further examples of doubling listings may be found in entries 24, 41, 48, 50, 52, 53, 59, 69, 70 (1576), 78 (1581), and 242 (1607). David M. Bevington, *From Mankind to Marlowe* (Cambridge: Harvard University Press, 1962), provides the cast lists of these and other plays.

133. Plots were skeletal outlines of plays, posted backstage for actors to consult just before or during performances.

134. Bevington, chapter 7, passim.

135. Scott McMillin, *The Elizabethan Theatre and* The Book of Sir Thomas More (Ithaca, N.Y.: Cornell University Press, 1987), 79 and chapter 4, passim. McMillin also shows the doubling possibilities for other plays of the Admiral's/Prince Henry's Men.

136. Gary Taylor, "We Happy Few: The 1600 Abridgement," in *Three Studies in the Text of* Henry V (Oxford: Clarendon Press, 1979), 83–84, passim. One example would be the assignment of the Dauphin's speeches in two scenes to Bourbon. Arthur Colby Sprague's brief *The Doubling of Parts in Shakespeare's Plays* (London: Society for Theatre Research, 1966) provides the only discussion of modern production practices in regard to doubling; we need a fuller one.

137. William A. Ringler Jr., "The Number of Actors in Shakespeare's Early Plays," in *The Seventeenth Century Stage: A Collection of Critical Essays*, ed. Gerald Eades Bentley (Chicago: University of Chicago Press, 1968), 130–134.

138. Ringler notes that these two sets of four characters are never on stage together; that between the exit of one group and the entrance of the other, there are intervals of lines by other characters sufficient to allow for costume changes; and that Puck's allegedly extraneous epilogue would have provided an interval for the costume change that would be necessary between the exit of the four doubling mechanicals after their bergamask dance (5.1.355) and their reentry as fairies.

Relevant to this casting issue, there is a problematic stage direction in the Folio itself at the beginning of 3.1: "Enter Peaseblossm, Cobweb, Moth, Mustardseed, and four fairies." This would give Titania eight fairies, which is never matched by any speech headings. The Folio stage direction seems to be a printer's error: in the Quarto, the four names fall at the end of Titania's speech, where she is calling her retinue, and the names are italicized; the Folio compositor took this as a stage direction and combined the names with the italicized Quarto stage direction, "Enter four fairies."

139. T. J. King, *Casting Shakespeare's Plays* (Cambridge: Cambridge University Press, 1992), 6, and tables 46 (Quarto) and 47 (Folio), 179–182.

140. King rejects Ringler's doubling of four fairies and four mechanicals, accepting the traditional argument that boys played these roles.

141. Francis Kirkman, ed., "The Merry Conceited Humors of Bottom the Weaver," in *The Wits, or, Sport upon Sport*, part 2 (London: Printed for Francis Kirkman, 1673), 141.

142. There are speech headings for Egeus (only once) and for a first and second lord. But the entry stage direction at the beginning of the scene (Kirkman, 32) calls for two lords only, together with the Duke and Duchess. The first lord may be Egeus, but it is not possible to be sure.

143. The doubling of the roles of Theseus/Oberon and Hippolyta/Titania would have broken the so-called reentry rule and presented a slight difficulty of an unusually fast costume change. After 4.1.101, Theseus and Hippolyta must reenter after Oberon and Titania exit. But in the modern theatre, costume changes of something less than fifteen seconds are not uncommon; when I saw these roles doubled in the RSC productions of 1970 and 1982, the changes were minimal and accomplished in less time. I doubt that this problem or the reentry rule would have prevented the Elizabethan company from doubling these roles, had it been necessary or desirable. But it probably was neither, as I argue in the next paragraph.

144. Director John Hancock doubled the roles in his 1966 San Francisco production, as did Peter Brook in 1970. See chapter 9.

145. Stephen Booth, "Speculations on Doubling in Shakespeare's Plays," in *Shakespeare: The Theatrical Dimension*, ed. Philip C. McGuire and David A. Samuelson (New York: AMS, 1979), 107. The essay was republished in Booth's *King Lear, Macbeth, Indefinition and Tragedy* (New Haven, Conn.: Yale University Press, 1983), 129–155.

146. James L. Calderwood, "Anamorphism and Theseus' Dream," *Shakespeare Quarterly* 42 (1991), 409–430.

147. Graham Bradshaw, *Shakespeare's Scepticism* (London: Harvester Press, 1983), 69.

148. Barbara Hodgdon, "Gaining a Father: The Role of Egeus in the Quarto and the Folio," *Review of English Studies* new series 37 (1986), 534–542. See also Philip C. McGuire, "Egeus and the Implications of Silence," in *Shakespeare and the Sense of Performance*, ed. Marvin and Ruth Thompson (Newark: University of Delaware Press, 1989), 103–115; and the review of the issue in Peter Holland, ed., *A Midsummer Night's Dream* (Oxford: Clarendon Press, 1993), 265–268.

149. Hodgdon, 539.

150. Francis Meres, *Palladis Tamia: Wit's Treasury*, in Chambers, *The Elizabethan Stage*, 4:246.

151. Chambers, *The Elizabethan Stage*, 3:279–280, letter of 15 January 1604 from Dudley Carleton to John Chamberlain. In *A Midsummer Night's Dream*, "Robin" is used as much as "Puck" in the lines and speech prefixes, however, and in those few contemporary allusions to the play that we have, it is not Robin for whom the play is remembered.

152. Edward Sharpham, *The Fleire* (London: Printed by F. B. . . . , 1607), E₁ verso.

153. Chambers, *The Elizabethan Stage*, 2:345; Gerald Eades Bentley, *The Jacobean and Caroline Stage* (London: Oxford University Press, 1941), 2:590.

154. John Munro, *The Shakspere Allusion Book, a Collection of Allusions to Shakspere from 1591–1700* (London: Oxford University Press, 1932), 1:291.

155. Manuscript, Folger Shakespeare Library; Bentley, *The Jacobean and Caroline Stage*, 1:26–28; the manuscript is reproduced in Wickham, 2, plate 22, no. 23 (note 247).

156. Ernest Law, *The History of Hampton Court Palace* (London: George Bell & Sons, 1890), 1:318–319.

157. Chambers, *William Shakespeare*, 2:348–352; Chambers provides the full documentation of the case, including the 1631 court decree.

158. James Shirley, *The Triumph of Beauty*, in *The Dramatic Works and Poems of James Shir-*

ley, ed. Rev. Alexander Dyce (London: John Murray, 1833), 6:319–325; first noted by Gerard Langbaine, *An Account of the English Dramatik Poets* (Oxford, 1691), 485.

159. Quiller-Couch and Dover Wilson, 160.

2. Shakespeare Absolute: Fairies, Gods, and Oranges in Purcell's *Fairy Queen*

1. Kirkman, preface.

2. The issue of 22–29 June 1653 of the royalist newsbook, *Mercurius Democritus*, relates an incident in which droll actor Robert Cox was betrayed to soldiers "and so abused many of the Gentry that formerly had been their Benefactors, who were forced to pay to the souldiers 5s. a piece for their coming out, as well as for their going in" (cited in Hyder E. Rollins, "Contributions to the History of the English Commonwealth Drama," *Studies in Philology* 18 [1921], 311).

3. It was first issued singly in a quarto in 1661 by Kirkman and Henry Marsh under the title *The Merry Conceited Humors of Bottom the Weaver. As it hath been often publikely acted by some of his Majesties comedians, and lately, privately, presented by several apprentices for their harmless recreation, with great applause* (Folger Shakespeare Library copy, S2937). *The Wits* is available in John James Elson's edition, *Cornell Studies in English*, 18 (Ithaca, N.Y.: Cornell University Press, 1932).

4. Kirkman boasts that strolling players at Charing Cross, at Bartholomew Fair, at country fairs, on mountebank stages, and in halls and taverns had performed the plays he was publishing. In 1691, Gerard Langbaine probably drew his conclusion that *Bottom the weaver* had been performed by strollers at fairs from Kirkman's 1673 title page (Langbaine, *An Account of the English Dramatick Poets* [Oxford, 1691; reprint, Los Angeles: William Clark Memorial Library, University of California, 1971], 2:460).

5. Chambers, *The Elizabethan Stage*, 2:270–292; Ernest Brennecke, with Henry Brennecke, *Shakespeare in Germany, 1590–1700, with Translations of Five Early Plays* (Chicago: University of Chicago Press, 1964), chapter 1, passim.

6. Two accounts also survive. Johannes Balthasar Schupp alluded in 1648 to a performance in years past in Nurnberg in which the lion was played by Master Hans, a furrier (Brennecke, 55–56). English comedians had played in Nurnberg many times between 1596 and 1623. Johannes von Rist gave a detailed account, printed in Frankfurt in 1666, of an elaborate, Germanized version of the play performed by English actors, probably in Hamburg between 1625 and 1650. Brennecke publishes a long excerpt (57–68).

7. Andreas Gryphius, *Absurda comica; oder, Herr Peter Squentz, Schimpff-Spiel*, in Brennecke, 73, 81. All references to this play hereafter are to this translation.

8. Brennecke, 101. Shakespeare's play suggests some ribald business with double entendres of Thisbe's "I kiss the wall's hole, not your lips at all" (5.1.200) and "My cherry lips have often kissed thy stones, / Thy stones with lime and hair knit up in thee" (5.1.189–190). But cruder humor is called for by Gryphius. Squentz, considering how to construct the wall, explains that "Thisbe must pull Pyramus's love-shaft out through the hole" (77). Pyramus, complaining of his love pains, is told by Thisbe to come to the wall: "Approach the hole, come night / Upraise your bottom well on high. / My dear, my dear it is the shaft" (91).

9. The play was in that half of Shakespeare's canon that had been assigned to Thomas Killigrew when Charles II gave patents to him and to William Davenant in 1660.

10. Samuel Pepys, *The Diary of Samuel Pepys*, ed. Robert Latham and William Matthews (Berkeley: University of California Press, 1970), 3:208.

11. Two surviving Restoration promptbooks suggest that managers thought it necessary to alter this play to accommodate audience tastes. One, which G. Blakemore Evans believes belonged to Killigrew's "Nursery," the King's Company training theatre for young actors, appears to be a working draft. It consists of three acts of the play, made up of First Folio pages, with textual cuts. If something like this version was staged, Titania would have been eliminated, Bottom's transformation cut, and the young lovers' exchanges much curtailed. No songs are indicated. The promptbook's few scenic notes, while not proof of performance, prescribe some stock sets: a "palace" for 1.1 and, for the meeting of the mechanicals in 1.2, the "baudy house" (G. Blakemore Evans, ed., *Shakespearean Promptbooks of the Seventeenth Century* [Charlottesville: University of Virginia Press, 1964], 3:1–8, 27–29; Charles H. Shattuck, ed., *The Shakespeare Promptbooks: A Descriptive Catalogue, A Midsummer Night's Dream*, catalog No. 2 [Urbana: University of Illinois Press, 1965]). (The promptbook entries in Shattuck's catalog are hereafter cited as "Shattuck *MND*.") Another promptbook, perhaps associated with Joseph Ashbury's series of Shakespearean productions at Dublin's Smock Alley Theatre in the 1670s, shows 611 lines cut, including most of the lyrical language; the mechanicals survive (Evans, 27–29). As to scenery, the Dublin promptbook only prescribes a "forest" for the wood scenes.

12. By contrast, he later described the musical adaptation of *The Tempest* in detail and taught himself a song from its score (Pepys, 9:48, 195: entries for 3 February and 11 May 1668).

13. In an anonymous play of 1690, there is a reference to "the woman in Shakespeare kissing the fellow with the ass's head," but this is probably not a reference to a performance (George Winchester Stone Jr., "*A Midsummer Night's Dream* in the Hands of Garrick and Colman," *PMLA* 54, [June 1939], 467n). In 1694, Shakespeare adapter Charles Gildon, born in 1665, wrote that *A Midsummer Night's Dream* and *Richard II* "are and have been on the stage in our memory," but he was almost certainly thinking of Purcell's *Fairy Queen* of 1692. (Gildon, "Reflections on Mr. Rymer's Short View of Tragedy, and an Attempt at a Vindication of Shakespear," in Gildon, *Miscellaneous Letters* [London: Benjamin Bragg, 1694], 113).

14. Narcissus Lutrell, *A Brief Relation of State Affairs, September 1678 to April 1714* (Oxford: Oxford University Press, 1857), 2:435, 28 April 1692; William Van Lennep, ed., *The London Stage 1660–1800*, Part 1: 1660–1700 (Carbondale: Southern Illinois University Press, 1962), 1:408–409.

15. For a discussion of the score's recovery and bibliographical problems, see the introduction and new preface to Anthony Lewis, ed., *The Works of Henry Purcell*, rev. ed. (London: Novello), 13:vii–ix. See also D. Allen Carroll and Gary Jay Williams, *A Midsummer Night's Dream, an Annotated Bibliography* (New York: Garland, 1986), entry T1129a and index listings under Henry Purcell.

16. Versions staged include: Cambridge University, 1920; Covent Garden, 1946; Nottingham University, 1960 (for the Purcell tercentenary); Edinburgh University, 1972; University Theatre, Newcastle-upon-Tyne, 1973; and Pennsylvania Opera Theatre, Philadelphia, 1988.

17. Furness, xx, 340–343.

18. George C. D. Odell, *Shakespeare from Betterton to Irving* (New York: Charles Scribner's Sons, 1920), 1:71–72, 192–195.

19. Hazelton Spencer, *Shakespeare Improved: The Restoration Versions in Quarto and On the Stage* (Cambridge: Harvard University Press, 1927; reprint; 1963), 42, 318–324.

20. Constant Lambert in Edward Mandinian et al., *Purcell's "The Fairy Queen" as Presented by the Sadler's Wells' Ballet and the Covent Garden Opera* (London: John Lehmann, 1948), 20.

21. W. Moelwyn Merchant, *Shakespeare and the Artist* (London: Oxford University Press, 1959), 26.

22. Robert Etheridge Moore, *Henry Purcell and the Restoration Theatre* (Cambridge: Harvard University Press, 1961), chapter 4, passim; Roger Savage, "The Shakespeare-Purcell Fairy Queen, a Defence and Recommendation," *Early Music* 1 (1973), 201–221; Curtis Alexander Price, *Henry Purcell and the London Stage* (Cambridge: Cambridge University Press, 1984), chapter 8, passim.

23. Moore, 104, 111, 107, respectively.

24. Eric Walter White, *A History of English Opera* (London: Faber and Faber, 1983), 121–124; Price, 5.

25. Stephen Orgel and Roy Strong, *The Theatre of the Stuart Court* (London: Sotheby Park Bernet, 1973), 1:13.

26. Moore, 29–31 and chapter 4, passim.

27. Stephen Baxter, *William III and the Defense of European Liberty, 1650–1702* (New York: Harcourt Brace & World, 1966), 48.

28. Franklin B. Zimmerman, *Henry Purcell, His Life and Times* (Philadelphia: University of Pennsylvania Press, 1983), 174, 180.

29. Samuel Johnson, "Preface to *Shakespeare*," in *Criticism*, ed. Charles Kaplan (San Francisco: Chandler, [1963]), 251: "We need not wonder to find Hector quoting Aristotle, when we see the loves of Theseus and Hippolyta combined with the Gothick mythology of fairies."

30. *The Fairy-Queen: An Opera. Represented at the Queen's Theatre By Their Majesties Servants* (London: Printed for Jacob Tonson, at the Judges-Head, in Chancery Lane, 1692) (Folger Shakespeare Library, S2681). All lines cited in the text hereafter are from this edition.

31. For a good account of the debate, one that takes this question of national identity into account, see Todd A. Gilman, "Augustan Criticism and Changing Conceptions of English Opera," *Theatre Survey* 36 (1995), 1–35. For other discussions of English opera form, see Moore, chapter 1, especially 29–31; and Eugene Haun, *But Hark! More Harmony: The Libretti in English of the Restoration Opera* (Ypsilanti: Eastern Michigan University Press, 1971), chapter 1.

32. Cited in Moore, 30–31.

33. *Gentleman's Journal*, January 1692, 5.

34. Nicholas Kenyon, "When Britain Ruled the Musical Waves under Purcell's Flag," *New York Times*, 1 January 1995.

35. The direction cited occurs in Act 1 in another issue of the first edition, dated 1692 (Folger Shakespeare Library S2681C, Copy 1). The title page of this issue advertises its "alterations, editions, and several new songs." The changes resulted in a radical alteration of the B gathering, including some expansion of text at the end of Act 1 to fill the gathering. This could account for the adding of these stage directions, but I take these directions to describe stage business in the original production. For a bibliographical analysis, see Paul Dunkin, "Issues of The Fairy Queen," *Library* 26 (1946), 297–304.

36. The descriptions are roughly evocative of two 1695 engravings of the east and south fronts of William's new palace at Hampton Court, reproduced in Ernest Law, *History of Hampton Court, Orange and Guelp Times* (London: G. Bell and Sons, 1924), 3:42 f, 44 f. W. Moelwyn Merchant insisted that this set was a copy of Giacomo Torelli's design for Act 2 of Corneille's *Andromeda*, produced at the Petit Bourbon in 1650, but it is simply generic (Merchant, 28–31; Merchant, "*A Midsummer Night's Dream*: A Visual Re-creation," in *Early Shakespeare, Stratford-upon-Avon Studies 3*, ed. John Russell Brown and Bernard Harris [London: Edward Arnold, 1961], 166–168). Merchant's claim in *Shakespeare and the Artist* that an

identical ground plan served for *The Fairy Queen* and *The Tempest*, one that was "a modified form of the Palladian Teatro Olimpico," is very doubtful and not supported.

37. Moore, 111.

38. Franklin B. Zimmerman, "The Court Music of Henry Purcell," in *The Age of William III and Mary II, Power, Politics, and Patronage 1688–1702*, ed. Robert P. Maccubbin and Martha Hamilton-Phillips (Williamsburg, Va.: College of William and Mary, the Grolier Club, and the Folger Shakespeare Library, 1989), 312–313. See also Zimmerman, *Henry Purcell*, 197–198.

39. Anthony Lewis, album notes for the recording of *The Fairy Queen*, with the Boyd Neel Orchestra, conducted by Anthony Lewis, Editions de l'Oiseau-Lyre OL 5 121–23, ca. 1971.

40. *The Fairy Queen* (1692), 30.

41. Its popularity is attested to in an odd story relating to Elkanah Settle, in Gilbert D. McEwen, *The Oracle of the Coffee House, John Dunton's Athenian Mercury* (San Marino, Calif.: Huntington Library, 1972), 76–84.

42. There has been confusion over this song's assignment. It is not assigned in *Some Select Songs, As They are Sung in the Fairy Queen* (London: J. Carr and Henry Playford, 1692). It is assigned to Reading and Ayliff in the publication of Purcell's songs entitled *Orpheus and Britannicus* (London: Henry Playford, 1698). An edition of this song alone, published in 1693 by Thomas Cross, includes in its heading the information that it was sung by "Mr. Reading and (Mr. Pate in Woman's Habit)." The opening parenthesis probably should have been placed after Pate's name. In any case, Reading and Pate were not both in women's clothes, given the context of the song, though that is the way the heading is interpreted by Shedlock (1888) and by Franklin B. Zimmerman, *Henry Purcell, 1659–1695, an Analytical Catalogue of His Music* (New York: St. Martin's Press, 1963). Pate, who was probably an Italian tenor or countertenor (see Pepys, May 1698), would have sung Mopsa, dressed in a woman's habit.

43. Savage, 213.

44. Ronald Paulson, *Emblem and Expression, Meaning in English Art of the Eighteenth Century* (Cambridge: Harvard University Press, 1975), 16–17.

45. James G. McManaway cites contemporary hydraulic entertainments at Bartholomew and Smithfield fairs in connection with this stage direction ("The Renaissance Heritage of English Staging [1642–1700]," in *Studies in Shakespeare, Bibliography, and Theatre*, ed. Richard Hosley, Arthur C. Kirsch, and John W. Velz [New York: Shakespeare Association of America, 1969], 237).

46. Franklin B. Zimmerman, *Henry Purcell, 1659–1695*, 2d. ed. rev. (Philadelphia: University of Pennsylvania Press, 1983), 173–174.

47. All except Price, who acknowledges it in a footnote, 347n.

48. G. E. Briscoe Eyre and Charles Robert Rivington, *A Transcript of the Stationers' Registers, 1640–1708 A.D.* (London: Privately printed, 1914), 2:393.

49. Zimmerman, *Henry Purcell, 1659–1695*, 173–174.

50. Odell, 1:73.

51. Wylie Sypher writes that the baroque "is able to win assent from the spirit through its power over the sensorium alone," effecting "a mighty katharsis by spectacle, by an expressive power" (*Four Stages of Renaissance Style, Transformations in Art and Literature, 1400–1700* [Garden City, N.Y.: Doubleday, 1955], 185).

52. See B. S. Allen, *Tides in English Taste* (Cambridge, 1937).

53. Edward Croft-Murray, "An English Painter of Chinoiseries," *Country Life Annual* 1955, cited in Eric Walter White, "Early Theatrical Performances of Purcell's Operas with a Calendar of Recorded Performances, 1690–1710," *Theatre Notebook* 13 (1958/59), 47; for examples of Robinson's painting, see Moore, 128–129 and plates 3 and 4.

54. The print was reproduced together with many others relevant to this discussion in the catalog of the Folger Shakespeare Library exhibit (Rachel Doggett, ed., *New World of Wonders, European Images of the Americas, 1492–1700* [Washington, D.C.: Folger Shakespeare Library, 1992], 161). On the feathers, see *Aphra Behn*, The Rover *and Other Plays* (Oxford: Oxford University Press, 1995), viii.

55. Nesca A. Robb, *William of Orange, a Personal Portrait* (New York: St. Martin's Press, 1966), 161–162.

56. *Oxford English Dictionary* (Oxford: Oxford University Press, 1971), 2001–2002, entry for "orange."

57. I am indebted to David Dyregrov for the suggestion that these orange trees might have been functioning in some way emblematic of William III.

58. Elizabeth Hamilton. *William's Mary* (New York: Taplinger, 1972); the painting is reproduced between pp. 146 and 147.

59. Ibid., 286.

60. A mezzotint of the arch is reproduced in Kneeth H. D. Haley, "International Affairs," in Maccubbin and Hamilton-Phillips, 39.

61. J. Govert Bildoo, *Komste van zyne Majesteit Willem III*. Koning van Groot Britanje, enz. in Holland . . . (Ims Graavenhaague: Arnould Leers, 1691), plate following 80. Another account by J. Beeck was published in London by Henry Rhodes and John Harris in 1692, with derivative engravings.

62. Moore, 145–146.

63. Allardyce Nicoll, *A History of Restoration Drama, 1660–1700* (Cambridge: Cambridge University Press, 1928), 319.

64. Lewis, album notes.

65. Zimmerman, *Henry Purcell, 1659–1695*, 198–199.

66. Lutrell, 2:435, 28 April 1692 and entries following.

67. Ibid., 2:301–302.

68. Given the evocation of the model royal marriage, one might suspect that the opera was associated with some court wedding in this year. But there is no evidence to link the opera to any one of the numerous weddings in noble families that Lutrell records between November 1691 and May 1692. (Ibid., 2:287, 303, 307, 340).

69. Ibid., 2:435. On the huge sums the duke's company invested in the mounting of its operas, see Judith Milhous, "The Multimedia Spectacular on the Restoration Stage," in *British Theatre and the Other Arts, 1660–1800*, ed. Shirley Strum Kenny (Washington, D.C.: Folger Books, 1984), 41–66.

70. John Downes, *Roscius Anglicanus*, ed. Judith Milhous and Robert D. Hume (London: Society for Theatre Research, 1987), 89. I suspect the expensive costumes would have been in the style of those designed by Henry Gissey for *Psyché*. See Jerome de La Gorce, "Les Costumes d'Henry Gissey pour les représentations de "Psyché," *Revue d'Art* (1984), 39–51; and Steven Dock, *Costume and Fashion in the Plays of Jean Baptiste Poquelin Molière* (Geneva: Editions Slatkin, 1992).

71. Jeremy Collier, *A Short View of the Immorality and Profaneness of the English Stage* (London: Printed for S. Keble et al., 1698), 188–195.

72. See Judith Milhous, *Thomas Betterton and the Management of Lincoln's Inn Fields, 1695–1708* (Carbondale: Southern Illinois University Press, 1979); and Robert D. Hume, "The Sponsorship of Opera in London, 1704–1720," *Modern Philology* 85 (1988), 420–432.

73. White, "Early Theatrical Performances," 51.

74. Ibid., 51, 45.

75. F. C. Brown, *Elkanah Settle, His Life and Work* (Chicago: University of Chicago Press,

1910), 96–97. Montague Summers, Allardyce Nicoll, and others passed Brown's attribution on, though seasoned with skepticism, and it was repeated by many others thereafter (Summers, *The Restoration Theatre* [London: Kegan Paul, Trench, Trubner, 1934], 235; Nicoll, 12, 150, 372, and 380n; Donald Wing, *Short Title Catalogue of Books Printed in England . . . 1641–1700* [New York: Columbia University Press, 1951], 3:232, #2681; Alfred Harbage, *Annals of English Drama 975-1000*, rev. by S. Schoenbaum [London: Methuen, 1964], 190; Van Lennep, *LS* 1, 1:108). The absence of any solid evidence led Judith Milhous and Robert D. Hume to urge that the adaptation be expunged from the list of Settle's works and classified as an anonymous work ("Attribution Problems in English Drama, 1660–1700," *Harvard Library Bulletin* 31 [Winter 1983], 15).

76. David Dyregrov, "Jo. Haines as Librettist for Purcell's *Fairy Queen*," *Restoration and 18th Century Theatre Research* 7 (1992), 29–54.

77. Savage, 206.

78. Milhous and Hume, "Attribution Problems," 15, note 18.

79. Zimmerman, *Henry Purcell 1659–1695*, Entry 629, 326–327.

3. "Signor Shakespearelli"

1. Emmett L. Avery, ed., *The London Stage 1600–1800*, Part 2: 1700–1729, 2 vols. (Carbondale: Southern Illinois University Press, 1960), 1:397.

2. See, for example, *Tatler* 14 (18 April 1709); and *Spectator* 13, 14, 22, 29, and 31 (March and April 1711).

3. A crotchet was the English term for a quick note that was half the value of a minim, symbolized by a stemmed black head; gamut refers to the entire range of recognized musical notes (*Oxford English Dictionary*).

4. *The Comick Masque of Pyramus and Thisbe As it is Perform'd at the theatre in Lincoln's Inn Fields* (London: W. Mears, 1716; facsimile, London: Cornmarket Press, 1969); John Genest, *Some Account of the English Stage from the Restoration in 1660 to 1830* (Bath, 1832), 4:604–605.

5. Charles Beecher Hogan, *Shakespeare in the Theatre, 1701–1800* (Oxford: Clarendon Press, 1952), 1:349; only nine performances are listed in Avery, *LS*, 2, 1.

6. *Pyramus and Thisbe: A Mock Opera, Written by Shakespeare. Set to Musick by Mr. Lampe. Perform'd at the Theatre Royal in Covent Garden . . . 1745* (London: H. Woodfall, 1745); Genest, 4:157; Hogan, 1:339.

7. It premiered on 25 January 1745, and its last performance of record was on 2 May 1754; see Arthur H. Scouten, ed., *The London Stage 1660–1800*, Part 3: 1729–1747, 2 vols. (Carbondale: Southern Illinois University Press, 1961), 2; and George Winchester Stone Jr., ed., *The London Stage 1660–1800*, Part 4: 1747–1776, 3 vols. (Carbondale: Southern Illinois University Press, 1962), 4, on these dates; Hogan, 1:339. For more detailed discussions of the Leveridge and Lampe texts, see Jack L. Jorgens, "Studies in the Criticism and Stage History of *A Midsummer Night's Dream*" (Ph.D. diss., New York University, 1970), 192–200, 202–204.

8. Odell, 1:244–247.

9. For readings of the cultural forces at work in these editions and their marketing, see Jonathan Bate, *Shakespearean Constitutions, Politics, Theatre, Criticism, 1730–1830* (London: Oxford University Press, 1989), 22–25; and Gary Taylor, *Reinventing Shakespeare* (New York: Weidenfeld and Nicolson, 1989), 69–99.

10. Prologue to Joseph Addison's *Cato*, in Frederick Tupper and James W. Tupper, *Repre-*

sentative English Dramas from Dryden to Sheridan (New York: Oxford University Press, 1914), 200–201.

11. *The Works of Samuel Johnson*, ed. Arthur Sherbo (New Haven, Conn.: Yale University Press, 1968), 7:160.

12. Elizabeth Griffith, *The Morality of Shakespeare's Drama Illustrated* (London: T. Cadell, 1775; reprint, New York: Augustus M. Kelly, 1971), 2, 15. Other such commentaries on the play, moral and poetical, occur in the notes to the 1776 edition of the play in *Bell's British Theatre*, 142, 144, 147, 157, and 180.

13. George Winchester Stone Jr. especially sought to vindicate Garrick in a series of articles on Garrick's handling of Shakespeare's plays, particularly in his "*A Midsummer Night's Dream* in the Hands of Garrick and Colman," *PMLA* 54 (1939), 467–482. For Stone's other articles, see the bibliography in Kalmin A. Burnim, *David Garrick, Director* (Carbondale: Southern Illinois University Press, 1961), 222–223.

14. Michael Dobson, *The Making of the National Poet, Shakespeare, Adaptation, and Authorship, 1660–1769* (Oxford: Clarendon Press, 1992), 8 and chapters 4 and 5. See also Linda Colley, *Britons, Forging the Nation 1707–1837* (New Haven, Conn.: Yale University Press, 1992).

15. Kalman A. Burnim, "Looking upon His Like Again: Garrick and the Artist," in *British Theatre and the Other Arts, 1660–1800*, ed. Shirley Strum Kenny (Washington, D.C.: Folger Shakespeare Library, 1984), 185. The listing of Garrick portraits in the *British Museum Catalogue of Engraved British Portraits* is exceeded only by those of Queen Victoria, Burnim reports in his survey of Garrick portraits. For an iconography, see the entry on Garrick in Philip H. Highfill Jr., Kalman A. Burnim, and Edward A. Langhans, eds., *A Biographical Dictionary of Actors, Actresses, Musicians, Dancers, Managers, and Other Stage Personnel in London, 1660–1800*, (Carbondale: Southern Illinois University Press, 1973).

16. Keith Thomas, "How Britain Made It," *New York Review of Books* (19 November 1992), 35.

17. Stone, *LS*, 4, 1:clix.

18. My figures on his Shakespearean productions and performances are derived from Harry William Pedicord and Fredrick Louis Bergmann, eds., *The Plays of David Garrick, Garrick's Adaptations of Shakespeare, 1744–1756* (Carbondale: Southern Illinois University Press, 1981), 3:xiv. The reference to the house of Shakespeare occurs in Garrick's letter to Somerset Draper, 1751, in David M. Little, George M. Kahrl, and Phoebe deK. Wilson, eds., *The Letters of David Garrick* (Cambridge: Harvard University Press, 1963), 1:172. My discussion here crosses paths with and is in part indebted to Bate, 22–60, and Dobson, chapter 4.

19. See Dobson's discussion of this, 179–180.

20. See Ibid., chapter 5.

21. Cited in George Winchester Stone Jr. and George M. Kahrl, *David Garrick, a Critical Biography* (Carbondale: Southern Illinois University Press, 1979), 648.

22. For an analysis of Garrick's adaptation of *The Country Wife*, see Harry William Pedicord, *The Theatrical Public in the Time of Garrick* (Carbondale: Southern Illinois University Press, 1954), 106–116; for an analysis of Garrick's *Hamlet*, see Burnim, *David Garrick*, 152–155.

23. See Dobson's analysis of Garrick's adaptation of these two plays, 187–198.

24. *Collection of Prints, from Pictures Painted for the Purpose of Illustrate the Dramatic Works of Shakspeare, by the Artisits of Great-Britain* (London: John and Josiah Boydell, 1803). A proposal of a national edition of the plays, ornamented with works by English artists, was, in fact, put to Garrick during the Stratford Jubilee by a Mr. Nicoll, cited by Josiah Boydell in his preface to the collected prints. Ultimately, that was realized in George Steevens's edition.

25. *The Fairies, An Opera. Taken from A Midsummer Night's Dream, Written by Shakespear. As it is Perform'd at the Theatre-Royal in Drury Lane. The Songs from Shakespear, Milton, Waller, Dryden, Lansdown, Hammond, & C. The Music composed by Mr. Smith*, 2d ed. (London: J. and R. Tonson and S. Draper, 1755). This "second edition" is actually the second issue of the first edition (also 1755) and adds Garrick's prologue and a song change. See G. Blakemore Evans, "Garrick's 'The Fairies' 1755: Two Editions," *Notes and Queries* n.s. 6 (1959), 410–411. My discussion hereafter is based on the Folger copy of this text and the Folger copy of the score (cited later). Date and casts are given in Genest, 4:407; and Hogan, 468–469. See also Odell, 1:358–359.

26. *The Fairies, An Opera. The Words taken from Shakespear & c. Set to Music by Mr. Smith.* (London: I. Walsh, [ca. 1755]), the score of the opera.

27. *The Fairies*, 2d ed., [A₃].

28. Roger Fiske, *English Theatre Music in the Eighteenth Century* (London: Oxford University Press, 1973), 205; Pedicord and Bergmann, 3:438–439.

29. Paget Toynbee, ed., *The Letters of Horace Walpole* (Oxford, 1903), 3:288, letter to Richard Bentley, 23 February 1755.

30. *The Fairies*, 2d ed., 49; Pedicord and Bergmann, 3:186.

31. *The Fairies*, 2d ed., [A₂].

32. The emendation of "suck" to "lurk" in *The Tempest*, 5.1.88, was Theobald's.

33. Stone identified these and other lyrics by Lansdowne, Waller, and Hammond in "*A Midsummer Night's Dream*," 471–472; see also the glosses of Pedicord and Bergmann, 3:158 ff.

34. Fiske, 244.

35. Theophilus Cibber, *Two Dissertations on the Theatres* (London: Griffiths, 1756), 36, 39.

36. Arthur Murphy, *Life of Garrick* (London: J. Wright, 1801), 1:269.

37. Little, Kahrl, and Wilson, 1:256, letter to French, 7 December 1756.

38. Genest, 4:407, 3 February.

39. Stone, "*A Midsummer Night's Dream*," 470.

40. Ibid., 470, 469, note 7. In their edition of Garrick's adaptations, Pedicord and Bergmann (3:438–439) express confidence that Garrick was the adaptor of *The Fairies*.

41. Dates and receipts are given by Stone in *LS*, 4, 1:467–472, and 4, 2:503, 505, which he derived from the Richard Cross manuscript, Folger Shakespeare Library. *The Fairies* brought in £200 the first night and a total of £1,720 over the eleven performances. Stone notes (*LS*, 4, 1:liii) that in the 1760s, a good house would bring £120. The average daily receipts in the 1758–1759 season are estimated to have been £151 (Pedicord, 15). *The Fairies* did not achieve popularity comparable to that of the adaptation of *The Tempest*, however, which played seventy-nine performances (Pedicord, 199).

42. Tate Wilkinson, *Memoirs of His Own Life* (York: Wilson, Spence, et al., 1790), 4:202.

43. Fiske, 638.

44. The cast lists in the editions include Master Reinhold as Oberon, Master Moore as Puck, and Master Evans as Fairy. Walpole in his 1755 letter mentions "two Italians and a French girl, and the chapel boys." The Cross diaries also mention the chapel boys.

45. Stone, *LS*, 4, 2:474; a bill for an oratorio on 14 March 1755 notes, "This day publish'd at 4s. Songs in the New English Opera Call'd *The Fairies*. Composed by Mr. Smith. Printed for I. Walsh." William Coxe, *Anecdotes of George Frideric Handel and John Christopher Smith* (London, 1799), 46–47.

46. *Books in Print* for 1994–1995 listed seven editions of Lambs' *Tales*; Wells, "Tales from Shakespeare," 131, noted that ten editions were in print in 1987.

47. The Tonson edition of the play, 1734, and manuscripts, Folger Shakespeare Library; see Shattuck, *MND*, Nos. 3 and 4.

48. Little, Kahrl, and Wilson, 1 : 386–388.

49. *A Midsummer Night's Dream. Written by Shakespeare. With Alterations and Additions and Several New Songs. As it is Performed at the Theatre-Royal in Drury Lane* (London: J. and R. Tonson, 1763). All references in the ensuing discussion are to the Folger Shakespeare Library copy of this edition, which contains a table of songs and composers.

50. Stone, *LS*, 4, 2 : 1021–1022.

51. *St. James Chronicle*, 24 November 1763. These passages and the ode are also cited in Stone, *"A Midsummer Night's Dream,"* 480–481.

52. Richard Cross and William Hopkins, manuscript, Folger Shakespeare Library, cited in Stone, *LS*, 4, 2 : 1021–1022, 1005; Dougald MacMillan, *Drury Lane Calendar, 1747–1776* (Oxford, 1938), 100.

53. In *"Midsummer Night's Dream* Music in 1763," *Theatre Notebook* 1 (1946), 23–26, Alfred Loewenberg reported on his examination of a copy of the play in the British Museum, which also included the rare table of thirty-three songs, and he speculated on Burney's additional contribution as compiler. None of Burney's music has survived, he reported, and to my knowledge, the complete score has still not surfaced. There may be some differences among texts; the text of the opera at the Folger Shakespeare Library shows no song assigned to Puck, while Loewenberg reported one. The role of Puck was noticeably reduced by Colman; many of his lines are reassigned, perhaps reflecting the inadequacies of the Master Cape who played him. Also, in the Folger copy, it seems to be the First Fairy who sings "Kingcup, daffodil, and rose" and thus has four not three solos, as Loewenberg reported.

54. The Garrick manuscripts at the Folger Shakespeare Library relating to the 1763 production include a song for a fairy in Capell's hand (Shattuck *MND*, No. 4).

55. In Garrick's version of *A Winter's Tale* a year later, the women characters were similarly weakened; see Irene G. Dash, "A Penchant for Perdita on the Eighteenth-Century English Stage," in *The Woman's Part, Feminist Criticism of Shakespeare* (Urbana: University of Illinois Press, 1980), 271–284.

56. Stone, *"A Midsummer Night's Dream,"* 473–480.

57. Colman's comments on Garrick's cutting, contained in four and a half manuscript pages that are keyed to Garrick's annotated copy of the play (Shattuck *MND*, No. 4).

58. *A Midsummer Night's Dream* (1763), 15.

59. William Hopkins's diary, as cited in Stone, *LS*, 2, 4 : 1021; see also MacMillan, 100.

60. Stone, *LS*, 4, 2 : 1022; Hopkins's diary, as cited in MacMillan, 100.

61. Hopkins's diary, as cited in MacMillan, 100. Discrepancies between the diary and its later transcriptions onto Drury Lane playbills are discussed in Stone, *LS*, 4, 2 : 1005.

62. *A Fairy Tale. In Two Acts. Taken from Shakespeare. As it is Performed at the Theatre-Royal in Drury Lane* (London: J. and R. Tonson, 1763); Hogan, 467.

63. MacMillan, 100; Stone, *LS*, 4, 2, calendars for the three seasons, 1763–1767; Hogan, 467.

64. *A Fairy Tale. As it is Performed at the Theatre Royal in the Haymarket* (London, 1777); Hogan, 467; Stone, *LS*, 5, 1 : 94.

65. When *A Fairy Tale* was revived at the Haymarket on 18 July 1777, a stock "Garrett chamber Flat" was used for the first meeting of the mechanicals in "Quince's house" (1.2) (Shattuck *MND*, No. 6; Genest, 8 : 549).

66. Garrick's preparation copy, 40, Shattuck, *MND*, No. 4.

67. Garrick letter to Sir William Young, cited in Stone, *LS*, 4, 1 : cxiv–cxv.

68. The engraving of Barsanti in figure 5 appeared in the *Bell's British Theatre* edition

of the play, 1 March 1776; a different engraving, less elaborate, appeared in the edition of the play published by J. Wenman in 1778. We may take Barsanti's costume as generally instructive, but she may never have played this role. She was with Colman's company in the summer of 1777, when Colman's *Fairy Tale* was done at the Haymarket (Genest, 5:91; Charles Beecher Hogan, ed., *The London Stage 1660–1800*, Part 5: 1776–1800, 3 vols. [Carbondale: Southern Illinois University Press, 1958], 1:89), but Helena and the other young lovers do not appear in that adaptation. No other version of the play was done during Barsanti's career (see the entry for Barsanti in Highfill, Burnim, and Langhans, 1:359–363).

69. At least five full-fledged operas have been derived from the play since: Franz von Suppé's *Sommernachtstraum* (1844), Georges Hüe's *Titania* (1903), Luigi Mancinelli's *Il sogno di una notte d'estate* (1917, never produced), Marcel Delannoy's *Puck* (1949), and Benjamin Britten's *A Midsummer Night's Dream* (1960) (*Grove's Dictionary of Music and Musicians*, ed. Eric Blom, 5th ed. [London, 1954], see under Shakespeare and under the name of each composer). For listings of scores of related operas, as well as incidental music for the play, see Bryan W. S. Gooch and David Thatcher, eds., *A Shakespeare Music Catalogue*, (Oxford: Clarendon Press, 1991), 2:969–1134. See also Carroll and Williams, entries 1001A and T1324.

4. The Scenic Language of Empire

1. August Wilhelm von Schlegel, "Lectures on Dramatic Art and Literature," in *Dramatic Theory and Criticism*, ed. Bernard F. Dukore (New York: Holt, Rinehart and Winston, 1974), 512, 509; René Wellek, *A History of Modern Criticism: 1750–1950*, vol. 2 (New Haven, Conn.: Yale University Press, 1975), chapter 2, passim.

2. Michael R. Booth, *Victorian Spectacular Theatre 1850–1910* (Boston: Routledge and Kegan Paul, 1981), 35–36.

3. As Jonathan Bate has reported (28, 184, and chapter 3), Shakespeare's history plays were sometimes revived for patriotic occasions. *Henry VIII* was staged at coronation time in 1761; *Henry V* was performed during the Seven Years War; and 2 *Henry IV* was revived on the occasion of the 1821 coronation.

4. Genest, 8:545–549, entry for 17 January 1816; Covent Garden playbill, 17 January 1816, Harvard Theatre Collection. The playbill for 15 February 1817 (Folger Shakespeare Library), reproduced in figure 6, is nearly identical to the bill for the production's opening date, 17 January 1816, as far as the information on *A Midsummer Night's Dream* is concerned.

5. Frederick Reynolds, *A Midsummer Night's Dream, Written by Shakespeare: With Alterations, Additions, and New Songs; as it is performed at the Theatre Royal, Covent Garden* (London: John Miller, 1816). Reynolds acknowledges his debt in the preface (iii–iv), and this is reinforced by a heavily annotated copy of the 1763 text in the Folger Shakespeare Library (Shattuck *MND*, No. 7) that appears to be Reynolds's preparation copy for the 1816 version. It does not agree in all points with the final printed text of the 1816 opera, but many of the lyrics are the same, and its provisional cast list is nearly that of the 1816 production.

6. Michael R. Booth (chapter 8) provides a survey of the development of the ideas of elaborate, historically correct scenery and costumes for Shakespeare's plays.

7. *Examiner*, 20 January 1816.

8. Genest, 8:545–549.

9. *Theatrical Inquisitor and Monthly Mirror*, 3 (January 1816), 73–74. However, Reynolds's published text was chastised later in the same journal (3 [June 1816], 446). Clearly, a manager or adapter could add "the pomp and magnificence of scenery," which was not seen as mediating Shakespeare's text, but it was not acceptable to omit any of Shakespeare's words.

10. Eluned Brown, ed., *The London Theatre 1811–1866, Selections from the Diary of Henry Crabbe Robinson* (London, 1966), 69, entry for 7 February 1816.

11. Genest, 8:545–549, reported eighteen performances; in his autobiography, Reynolds claimed the opera had twenty performances overall (*The Life and Times of Frederick Reynolds*, 2d ed. [London, 1827], 1:405). I have been able to find playbills testifying to fifteen performances (insofar as playbills are reliable evidence of actual performances). A playbill for 9 February 1816 (Billy Rose Theatre Collection, New York Public Library [NYPL]) advertises performances eleven through thirteen. A playbill for 26 June 1816 (Billy Rose Theatre Collection, NYPL) advertises the production for that date "with curtailments," and the Folger bill for 15 February 1817 indicates a revival date in the following season.

12. Reynolds, *The Life and Times*, 1:411. Odell (2:131–143) characterizes them, critically.

13. Odell, 2:111–114, 131; 1:72. Odell's chronological account of staged Shakespeare was, of course, a progressive history, working toward what he regarded as the ideal of Shakespearean staging in Irving and Tree, an agenda about which he was explicit. See, for example, 2:197.

14. Covent Garden playbill, 17 January 1816, Harvard Theatre Collection; Genest, 8:547.

15. Reynolds, *A Midsummer Night's Dream*, iii–iv; Reynolds, *The Life and Times*, 405. Garrick's 1755 version had eleven performances, and his 1763 version, which Reynolds borrowed on, had only one. Reynolds claimed twenty performances overall; see note 11.

16. The sources for the information on the songs and the composer credits are the 1816 text and the playbill's list of composers — neither of which seems to be complete or reliable. One can only estimate how much of the music was brought over from the 1763 opera and how much was newly composed. The problem, which is complicated by the loss of Charles Burney's 1763 music, is broached but not wholly solved by Loewenberg, 25–26; and in Gary Jay Williams, "'The Concord of this Discord': Music in the Stage History of *A Midsummer Night's Dream*," *Theater* (1973), 48–51.

17. Reynolds, *A Midsummer Night's Dream*, 10, 34, 36, 23–24, 22, 27.

18. Genest (8:546) comments that, in Act 2, "the dialogue between the lovers is properly curtailed, as a great part of it is written in a manner unworthy of Shakespeare."

19. *Examiner*, 20 January 1816.

20. Reynolds, *A Midsummer Night's Dream*, 18.

21. Ibid., 56.

22. Covent Garden playbill, 17 January 1816, Harvard Theatre Collection.

23. W. R. Connor, "Theseus in Classic Athens," in *The Quest for Theseus*, Anne G. Ward, W. R. Connor, Ruth B. Edwards, and Simon Tidworth, contributors (New York: Praeger, 1970), 143–174; W. den Boer, "Theseus: The Growth of Myth in History," *Greece and Rome* 16 (1969), 1–13.

24. Simon Tidworth, "From the Renaissance to Romanticism," in Ward et al., 226; Wellek, 2:325–326.

25. Cited in Tidworth, 226.

26. Ibid., 226–228. Barye's *Theseus* is in the Musée des Beaux-Arts, Bordeaux; his *Theseus Slays the Centaur, Bianor* is in the Hirschhorn Museum, Washington, D.C.

27. Felicia Hemans, *The Poetical Works of Mrs. Felicia Hemans* (Philadelphia, 1854), 34.

28. Douglas Bush, *Mythology and the Romantic Tradition in English Poetry* (Cambridge: Harvard University Press, 1969), 179–180, 219.

29. T. F. Dillon and Stephen Tucker, eds., *The Extravaganzas of J. R. Planché, Esq., 1825–1877* (London: Samuel French, 1879), 2:225–260.

30. Hugh Honour, "The Battle over Post-Modern Buildings," *New York Review of Books* 35 (29 September 1988), 32.

31. A full account of the Elgin operation and of the investigation of it in 1816 by the House of Commons committee, which wholly absolved Elgin, can be found in Jeannette Greenfield, *The Return of the Cultural Treasures* (New York: Cambridge University Press, 1989), 47–105. Greenfield places the Elgin affair in the context of other such appropriations and in the context of the international moral and legal issues involved. Much smaller fragments from the Athenian Parthenon are currently in museums in Copenhagen, Vienna, Heidelberg, Palermo, and the Vatican.

32. George Gordon, Lord Byron, *The Poetical Works of Lord Byron* (London: Oxford University Press, 1967), 143.

33. Cited in Greenfield, 62.

34. Cited in Ibid., 72. The Stuart and Revett volumes were published between 1762 and 1830; Greenfield does not cite the specific volume, and I have not had access to a copy of the nineteenth-century volumes.

35. Ibid., 62–72.

36. Tidworth, 226.

37. Ibid.

38. John Keats, "On Seeing the Elgin Marbles for the First Time," in *The Norton Anthology of English Literature*, ed. M. H. Abrams, et al. (New York: Norton, 1962), 1675, lines 11–12.

39. Samuel Johnson, "*Preface* to Shakespeare," in *Critical Theory since Plato*, ed. Hazard Adams (New York: Harcourt Brace Jovanovich, 1971), 329.

40. The only surviving visual evidence of the production is the engraving of John Duruset as Oberon (see fig. 10).

41. Reynolds, *A Midsummer Night's Dream*, 40–41.

42. Linda Colley, *Britons, Forging a Nation 1707–1837* (New Haven, Conn.: Yale University Press, 1992), 169–170.

43. *The Cambridge Modern History* (New York: Macmillan, 1909), 6:584, 551–585; 9:715, 733; G. M. Trevelyan, *History of England*, new illus. ed. (London: Longman, 1973), 702; and G. M. Trevelyan, *A Shortened History of England* (New York: Penguin, 1987), 440. As Trevelyan, in his patriarchal absolution of colonial privilege, expresses it, Hastings "saved British rule in India in spite of all, but not without making the kind of mistakes a strong man is like to make in difficult emergencies."

44. *The Cambridge Modern History*, 6:584, 551–585; 9:715, 733.

45. I am indebted here, of course, to Edward Said's *Orientalism* (London: Routledge, 1978), and also to Paul Brown's essay, "'This thing of darkness I acknowledge mine': *The Tempest* and the Discourse of Colonialism," in *Political Shakespeare*, ed. Jonathan Dollimore and Alan Sinfield (Ithaca, N.Y.: Cornell University Press, 1985), 48–71.

46. Reynolds, *A Midsummer Night's Dream*, 56.

47. Ibid., 49.

48. Ibid., 55.

49. "*The Scenery, Machinery, Dresses, and Decorations are entirely new. The Scenery painted by Mss. Phillips, Whitmore, Pugh, Grieve, Hollogan, Hodgins, and their assistants. The Machinery by Mr. SAUL. The Decorations by Mr. BRADWELL. The Dresses by Mr. Flower & Miss Egan*" (Covent Garden playbill, 17 January 1816, Harvard Theatre Collection). The identical credit appears on the playbill reproduced in figure 6. For examples of slightly earlier playbill descriptions of scenery, with scene painter credits, see Odell (2:109–110) on the 1814 *Richard III* and *Macbeth* at Drury Lane, with Edmund Kean.

50. Reynolds, *A Midsummer Night's Dream*, 5, 53.

51. John Ripley, Julius Caesar *on Stage in England and America, 1599–1973* (London:

Cambridge University Press, 1980), 55–56; James Robinson Planché, *Recollections and Reflections of J. R. Planché* (London: Tinsley Brothers, 1872), 1:54. I am grateful to Nicholas Brooke for bringing this to my attention. Kemble was in ill health; Reynolds's autobiography does not mention Kemble's name in relation to the production of *A Midsummer Night's Dream* but speaks only of an agreement between himself and Kemble's business manager, Henry Harris, to the effect that the Garrick-Colman opera would, "with certain alterations and additions," be an "effective revival" (Reynolds, *The Life and Times*, 1:404). The playbills I have examined do not carry Kemble's name, and Kemble's pretentious biographer, James Boaden, passes over this production, probably regarding it as beneath Kemble, "one of the most correct of our Shakespeareans" (James Boaden, Esq., *Memoirs of the Life of John Philip Kemble, Esq.* [London: Longman, Hurst, Rees, Orme, Brown, and Green, 1825], 2:165).

52. Kemble promptbook, (Shattuck *MND*, No. 8). The promptbook has notes in Kemble's hand and is made up from the published text of Reynolds's version (1816). Kemble made only a few minor changes in the Reynolds text.

53. Their names are listed on both the 17 January 1816 Covent Garden playbill, Harvard Theatre Collection, and the 15 February 1817 playbill in figure 6.

54. Reynolds, *A Midsummer Night's Dream*, 52.

55. Among the Covent Garden painters named on the playbill is John Henderson Grieve (1770–1845). With his two sons, Thomas and William, Grieve later painted for Vestris's 1840 production. Thomas then heads the scenic staff for Charles Kean's production in 1856, and Thomas and his son, Walford, paint for Charles Calvert's revival in 1865. Documentation for the Vestris and Kean productions will be found in chapter 5. My source for Calvert's production is an advertisement in the *Manchester Guardian*, 2 September 1865.

56. Odell suspected as much in his spirited account of the play on the New York stage, "*A Midsummer Night's Dream* on the New York Stage," in *Shaksperian Studies*, ed. Brander Matthews and A. H. Thorndike (New York, 1916), 121–126 (hereafter cited as Odell, "*MND*"); see also Odell, *Annals of the New York Stage* (New York: Columbia University Press, 1928), 3:236–237.

57. *New York American*, 9 November 1826. Other clues also point to this as the Reynolds opera. At the time, the Park was being managed by Stephen Price and English actor Edmund Simpson. When Simpson produced the play at the Park again in 1841, the version was probably Reynolds's. New York reviewers then noted that Helena was never told in Act 1 of Hermia's planned elopement, a sure mark of Reynolds's text (*The Spirit of the Times*, 4 September 1841; and a fugitive clipping entitled "The Theatrical World" from a New York newspaper, 4 September 1841, in Joseph Norton Ireland scrapbooks, Beinecke Library, Yale University).

58. *Evening Post*, 10 November 1826.

59. Bunn advertised the piece for at least six performances in the 1833–1834 season, always as the second half of the evening's bill, though it may have played only twice (playbills for 30 November and 10, 18, and 21 December, 1833; and for 19 April and 30 May 1834, Crawford Theatre Collection, Sterling Library, Yale University [hereafter cited as Crawford Theatre Collection, Yale University]). But in his autobiography, Bunn cites only two performances of the production in his proud list of Shakespearean productions (*The Stage, Both Before and Behind the Curtain* (London: Richard Bentley, 1840), 3:231.

60. Promptbook, University Library, University of Michigan, Ann Arbor; Shattuck *MND*, No. 9N, in Shattuck, "Supplement," *Theatre Notebook* 24 (1969).

61. Mendelssohn created his full incidental score, which became so integral to the Victorian theatrical vocabulary for the play, for the production of Ludwig Tieck, described in the next chapter. The history of Mendelssohn's music in connection with the play has been inaccurately treated in places too numerous to mention, including the Penguin edition of the

play (1959) and Oscar J. Campbell and Edward G. Quin, eds., *The Shakespeare Encyclopedia*. (New York, 1966).

5. "These Antique Fables . . . These Fairy Toys"

1. Vestris's production was long neglected compared to Shakespearean productions of the nineteenth-century's major male managers, but that has been remedied in recent scholarship. See Jorgens; Gary Jay Williams, "Madame Vestris's *A Midsummer Night's Dream* and the Web of Victorian Tradition," *Theatre Survey* 18 (November 1977), 1–22; and Trevor Griffiths, "A Neglected Pioneer Production: Madame Vestris's *A Midsummer Night's Dream* at Covent Garden, 1840," *Shakespeare Quarterly* 30 (1979), 386–396.

2. Based on contemporary playbills or reviews cited throughout chapters 4–6, the Oberons of major nineteenth-century English and American productions after Vestris's were: Park Theatre, 1841 — Charlotte Cushman; Princess's Theatre, 1847 — Sarah Flower; Grecian Theatre, London, 1851 — Julia Harland; Theatre Royal, Dublin, 1852 — Miss Lanza; Sadler's Wells, 1853 — Miss Hickson; Burton's Theatre, 1853 — Miss Raymond; Broadway Theatre, 1853 — Mme Poinisi; Boston Theatre, 1856 — Mrs. Barrow; Princess's Theatre (Kean), 1856 — Miss F. Ternan; Laura Keene's, 1859 — Marian McCarthy; Park Theatre, Brooklyn, 1865 — Mrs. Conway; Prince's, Manchester, 1865 — Pauline Markham; Olympic, 1865 — Fanny Stockton; Stadt Theatre, New York (German Company), 1868 — Olga von Plittersdorf; Selwyn's, Boston, 1869 — Miss Athena; Queen's, 1875 — Miss Sidney Cowell; Grand Opera House, New York, 1873 — Annie Kemp Bowler; Sadler's Wells (Edward Saker), 1880 — Laura Lawson; Daly's, New York, 1888 — Alice Hood; Star Theatre (John Albaugh), Chicago, 1888 — Carrie Daniels; Daly's, London, 1895 — Sybil Carlisle; Her Majesty's (Herbert Beerbohm Tree), 1900 — Julia Nielson.

After Vestris, Otho Stuart was the century's one exception, in Benson's 1889 London production. Walter Hampden played Oberon in 1905. John Duruset was Oberon in the 1816 opera, and a Mr. Richings played the role in the 1826 New York staging. While the tradition was set by Vestris's success, she was not the first woman to take the role; a Miss Rogers had played Oberon in the 1763 Garrick-Colman version, and a Miss Taylor played Oberon in Bunn's version in 1833. The tradition of a woman fairy king effectively ended with the 1914 production of Barker, but women were playing Oberon in Regent's Park productions as late as 1936 and 1942 (Phyllis Neilson Terry and Helen Cherry, respectively). Benjamin Britten wrote the role for a countertenor in his 1960 opera.

3. See Chapter 1.

4. See Nina Auerbach, *Woman and the Demon: The Life of a Victorian Myth* (Cambridge: Harvard University Press, 1982), 186, 188. Victorians were not, of course, the first to identify women with nature and the irrational and to make them mediators for men between nature and culture. See Helene P. Foley, "The Conception of Women in Athenian Drama," in *Reflections of Women in Antiquity*, ed. Helene P. Foley (New York: Gordon and Breach, 1981), 140 ff; and Sherry Ortner, "Is Female to Male as Nature Is to Culture?" in *Women, Culture, and Society*, ed. M. Rosaldo and L. Lamphere (Stanford, Calif.: Stanford University Press, 1981), 67–88.

5. *Pall Mall Gazette*, 11 January 1900.

6. Charles Molloy W[estmacott], *Memoirs of the Life, Public and Private Adventures of Madame Vestris* (London, 1939). Other biographies include Charles Pearce, *Madame Vestris and Her Times* (London, [1923]); Leo Waitzkin, *The Witch of Wych Street* (Cambridge: Harvard University Press, 1933); and William Appleton, *Madame Vestris and the London Stage* (New

York, 1974), which, while the best documented, is not at all shaped by feminist considerations. An early modern appreciation of her contribution as a manager is Ernest Bradlee Watson's, in his *Sheridan to Robertson* (Cambridge: Harvard University Press, 1926), chapter 9. See also note 1 in this chapter. A new feminist biography of Vestris is much needed.

7. John Coleman, *Plays and Playwrights I Have Known* (Philadelphia, 1890), 1:245; the plaster cast report is from Thomas H. Duncombe, *The Life and Correspondence of Thomas S. Duncombe* (London, 1868), 2:179.

8. *Spirit of the Times*, 23 April 1859. Marian McCarthy was Oberon in Laura Keene's production in her theatre in New York.

9. *New York Herald*, 14 November 1867.

10. Kathy Fletcher, "Planché, Vestris, and the Transvestite Role: Sexuality and Gender in Victorian Popular Theatre," *Nineteenth Century Theatre* 15 (1987), 21. Fletcher does much to explain the complex, interesting place of sexuality and Vestris's transvestite roles in the extravaganzas she created with Planché at the Olympic.

11. The fairy boom is outlined by Michael R. Booth, 35–37.

12. Appleton, 129.

13. Royal Archives, Windsor Castle, Victoria's journal for 5 February 1841, cited in George Rowell, *Queen Victoria Goes to the Theatre* (London, 1979?), 40.

14. James Orchard Halliwell, *An Introduction to Shakespeare's Midsummer Night's Dream* (London, 1841), 45. Halliwell issued a pamphlet entitled *The Management of Covent Garden Theatre Vindicated from the attack of an Anonymous Critic in a letter to the Editor of the Cambridge Advertiser* (London, 1841). There he vigorously defends Vestris's management of Covent Garden in general and Planché's rendering of the text of this play in particular.

15. A rare copy of an edition of the play (in the Folger Shakespeare Library) that was derived from Vestris's promptbook shows interlinear cutting of some 358 lines, and Halliwell, who saw the production, reported a few other omissions (Halliwell, *An Introduction*, 51–52): the prologue to *Pyramus and Thisbe* (26 lines) and Hermia's speech upon awakening alone in the forest (6 lines), giving a total of 290. *A Midsummer Night's Dream, As Revived at the Theatre Royal, Covent Garden, November 16, 1840, correctly printed from the prompt copy, with exits, entrances, etc. And for the First time that any Dramatic Work has possessed the same advantages in publication, Plots of the Scenery, Properties, Calls, copy of the original bill, incidents, etc.* (London: James Pattie [1840–1841] [hereafter cited as the Pattie edition]). In his 1970 dissertation, Jorgens was the first to recognize the importance of the Pattie edition in his discussion of Vestris's production.

16. Samuel Phelps cut 372 lines for his 1853 production but also had, for the first time, the virtue of no additional song-settings. William Burton, for his New York production in 1853, omitted 366 lines. In 1856, Charles Kean cut 828 lines. American actress-manager Laura Keene followed Kean's edition but cut even more in her 1859 staging. Augustin Daly cut 558 lines for his 1888 revival, and Sir Herbert Beerbohm Tree omitted 410 lines in his end-of-the-century production. The promptbook sources of these alterations are given in my discussions of each of these productions in chapter 6.

17. The promptbook sources of these alterations are given in my discussions of each of these productions in chapter 6. For further analysis, see Williams, "Madame Vestris's *A Midsummer Night's Dream*," 1–22.

18. Cited in Rowell, 40.

19. *John Bull*, 21 November 1840.

20. *The Town*, 21 November 1840; *Theatrical Journal*, 23 January 1840. Horn's duet was used, for example, in the productions of Thomas Barry (New York, 1854), Daly (New York, 1888), Sir Frank Benson (London, 1889), Tree (London, 1900), and Otho Stuart-Oscar Asche

(1905). The lines were still being sung as late as 1936 in Regent's Park but to Mendelssohn's "On Wings of Song."

21. Stage direction, Pattie edition.

22. *Spectator*, 21 November 1840.

23. Kean's backdrop was painted by William Gordon, who had painted for Vestris at the Olympic (Sybil Rosenfeld, *A Short History of Scene Design in Great Britain* [Oxford, 1973], 113); Gordon's name is not among those listed on Vestris's *A Midsummer Night's Dream* playbill, however.

24. *Theatrical Journal*, 1 May 1841.

25. Costume list, Pattie edition.

26. *Comedies*, (1839), 1:333.

27. It was by this device or the rearrangement of Shakespeare's scene sequence (which Vestris does later in the play) that the pictorial stage dealt with plays written for a stage on which continuous, fluid action had been possible.

28. The panorama, cousin to the dioramas Louis Daguerre had pioneered, was first used for a stage production by the Grieves in an 1820 Christmas pantomime (Rosenfeld, 107). The Grieves later painted a forest panorama for the Kean production; a foldout miniature watercolor of it survives in the Kean promptbook in the Harvard Theatre Collection.

29. *Theatrical Journal*, 1 May 1841. The machines were handled by E. W. Bradwell, who had created the "decorations" for Reynolds's opera and who had engineered flying fairies for Planché's *The Sleeping Beauty* (Covent Garden playbill, 17 January 1816, Harvard Theatre Collection; transcription of Covent Garden playbill, 16 November 1840, *Lacy's Acting Plays*, 28 [London, n.d.]).

30. *Times*, 17 November 1840.

31. *Spectator*, 21 November 1840. The Pattie edition gives the setting as follows: "Moonlight-transparent wood — platform, coloured as rising ground, crossing from the back R. —water piece, joining it, and running off, L. — large tree center."

32. *Spectator* and *John Bull*, 21 November 1840.

33. See Richard Foulkes, "Samuel Phelps's *A Midsummer Night's Dream*, Sadler's Wells — October 8, 1853," *Theatre Notebook* 23 (1968/69), 57–59.

34. Costume list, Pattie edition; and Vestris playbill for 16 November 1840, reproduced in *Lacy's Acting Plays*, 28. The playbill lists fifty-two fairy attendants in general, in addition to eight named and four unnamed fairies, plus three fauns, six satyrs, and a wood nymph.

35. *Literary Gazette*, 21 November 1840.

36. Moore promptbook for Burton's production, Shattuck *MND*, No. 10. Moore's notes suggest that he probably witnessed Vestris's production.

37. *Spectator*, 21 September 1840.

38. *Times*, 17 November 1840. The stage direction in the Pattie edition reads, with interpolated phrases from his list of scenes and properties: "The Scene glides away, part of it ascending, other parts descending and going off R.2.E. The [raised] Stage forms a flight of steps [and a platform center] — large flights of steps, R. and L. — platform and gallery [running along the back] from R. to L. Fairies all discovered with Torches of various coloured fires."

39. *Literary Gazette*, 21 November 1840.

40. *Athenaeum*, 21 November 1840, *Times*, 17 November 1840.

41. *Athenaeum*, 21 November 1840. Three of the women — Marshall (Puck), Cooper (Helena), and Lacy (Titania) — labored to project, and John Cooper (Theseus) reportedly declaimed (*Spectator*, 21 November 1840; *Times*, 17 November 1840).

42. Fred Belton, *Random Recollections of an Old Actor* (London, 1880), 151; *Spectator*, 21 November 1840.

43. In 1847, the Princess's Theatre in London offered the pantomime for the Easter holiday season, featuring "plenty of glitter and show" and scenery by William Roxby Beverly, who later painted for pantomimes at the Lyceum. It followed Vestris's model, though her production, the *Times* (6 April 1847) allowed, had been the more "tasteful."

44. Charles Dickens, ed., *The Life of Charles James Mathews, Chiefly Autobiographical* (London, 1879), 2:321–322. Macready's successful *The Tempest* of 1838 had a total of fifty-five performances.

45. Ibid., 2:91–93. On the playbill (reproduced in *Lacy's Acting Plays*), there is a listing of unspecified fairies that numbers fifty-two.

46. *The Lyre, Musical and Theatrical Gazette*, 21 May 1842; Dickens, 2:321–322.

47. Eric Blom, ed., *Grove's Dictionary of Music and Musicians*, 5th ed. (London, 1954), 5:744. On the score's dedication, I am grateful to Mendelssohn specialist, R. Larry Todd of Duke University.

48. See, for example, Alois Nagler on Tieck, in *Shakespeare's Stage* (New Haven, Conn.: Yale University Press, 1958) 26–30, 62; Julius Petersen, "Ludwig Tiecks *Sommernachtstraum* Inszenierung, mit 6 Ubbildungen," *Neues Archiv für Theatergeschichte*, II, herausgegeben von Max Hermann, in *Schriften der Gesellschaft für Theatergeschichte* (Berlin, 1930), 41:163–198.

49. Schlegel's translation of *A Midsummer Night's Dream* appeared in 1798. For details on the translation history, see Simon Williams, *Shakespeare on the German Stage, Volume I: 1586–1914* (Cambridge: Cambridge University Press, 1990), 51–52, 150–151.

50. At age seventeen, Tieck wrote a short play, *Sommersnacht*, in which Shakespeare as a boy falls asleep in the forest and, discovered by Titania and Oberon, is blessed by Oberon, at Titania's behest, with magic flower juices, "to consecrate him to the minstrel art" (*Sommersnacht*, trans. Mary C. Rumsy [London, 1854]).

51. Tieck's fullest discussion of the Elizabethan theatre was in an introductory essay in an 1811 volume of Elizabethan plays, in Tieck, *Kritische Schriften* (Leipzig, 1880); see also his 1820 *Die Buch über Shakspear*, ed. Henry Lüdecke (Halle, 1920).

52. The Tieck–Semper Fortune plans are reproduced in Simon Williams, 177.

53. Petersen, 174–175.

54. Edwin H. Zeydel, *Ludwig Tieck* (Princeton, N.J.: Princeton University Press, 1935), 328.

55. Eduard Devrient, "Meine Erinnerungen an Felix Mendelssohn-Bartholdy," in *Dramatische und Dramaturgische Schriften von Eduard Devrient* (Leipzig, 1869), 10:238 ff. In the intermission that followed, the king took tea and received guests in the royal box, and this continued during the introduction to the third act, to the distress of the composer (Eric Werner, *Mendelssohn*, trans. Dika Newlin [London: Collier Macmillan, 1963], 378).

56. Stanley Wells once asked, "What modern producer would permit a stage procession lasting as long as this passage of music does?" (Wells, *A Midsummer Night's Dream*, 8); see also Taylor, *Reinventing Shakespeare*, 217–218.

57. Feodor Wehl, *Didaskalien* (Leipzig, 1867), cited in Furness, 330.

58. Taylor, *Reinventing Shakespeare*, 217 and chapter 3, passim.

59. See Carol Duncan, "Art Museums and the Ritual of Citizenship," in *Exhibiting Cultures: The Poetics and Politics of Museum Display*, ed. Ivan Karp and Steven D. Lavine (Washington, D.C.: Smithsonian Institution Press, 1991), 88–90.

60. Ernst Leopold Stahl, *Shakespeare un das deutsche Theater* (Stuttgart, 1947), 287.

61. Will and Ariel Durant, *The Story of Civilization*, vol. 7, *The Age of Reason Begins* (New York: Simon and Schuster, 1961), 92.

6. The National and Natural Dream

1. J. Moyr Smith, editor and illustrator, *A Midsummer Night's Dreame* (London, 1892), xii.

2. In the introducton to his 1892 edition of the play, J. Moyr Smith (xiii) cites a written recollection from Fenton, who in 1892 was painting scenery for the Crystal Palace Theatre.

3. I draw here and elsewhere in my discussion on the promptbook at the Folger Shakespeare Library, Shattuck *MND*, No. 19, made for Phelps's final, 1861 revival of the play at Sadler's Wells. Although some new scenery by Charles Lewis was used, the promptbook's instructions agree repeatedly with descriptions of the 1853 critics.

4. *Lloyd's Weekly London News*, cited in full in May Phelps and J. Forbes Robertson, *The Life and Work of Samuel Phelps* (London: Sampson Low, et al., 1886), 131–133.

5. Fenton, cited by J. Moyr Smith, xiii.

6. *Spectator*, 15 October 1853; Henry Morley, *The Journal of a London Playgoer, from 1851 to 1866* (London: George Routledge and Sons, 1891), 60; *Athenaeum*, 15 October 1853.

7. *Punch*, 2 November 1861. Every critic praised Phelps's delivery of this speech.

8. Morley, 61.

9. Fenton, cited in J. Moyr Smith, xiii–xiv; playbill cast list, 8–13 October 1853, Theatre Museum, London.

10. Playbill for the 1861 revival, 19 and 21 October, Theatre Museum, London; no composer credit is given on the 1853 playbills I have seen or on those for the performances in the 1855–1856 season (Theatre Museum), but I suspect Phelps used Mendelssohn from the first.

11. *Lloyds Weekly Journal*, cited in Phelps and Robertson, 132.

12. Morley, 58, 61, 57, 59.

13. Ibid., 56, 57.

14. Based on the promptbook in Shattuck *MND*, No. 19.

15. Odell (*Shakespeare*, 2:297–298) assigned the step into illusionism to Kean, not Phelps, and saw Kean as the forerunner of Irving and Tree. He described the whole pictorial system as one in which almost perfect reproductions of locales were transplanted to the stage — "a canal in Venice, the forum of ancient Rome, a room in an English palace . . . the scene passed from resemblance into reality." Odell thought the result "was frequently of surpassing beauty" and objected only that the time necessary for scene changing meant that portions of Shakespeare's text had to be cut. He did not view the scenery as another text, and, even though he noted the evolution of scenery's function "from resemblance into reality," it did not occur to him that this visual language produced differences in meaning.

16. Roland Barthes, *Mythologies* (London: Paladin, 1973), 29–30.

17. Samuel Taylor Coleridge, *Biographia Literaria*, chapter 14, in *Criticism, Twenty Major Statements*, ed. Charles Kaplan (San Francisco: Chandler, n.d.), 304. While the famous phrase occurs in his discussion in *Lyrical Ballads* of the poem reader, Coleridge used similar phrases in his 1818 essay, "Progress of the Drama." As in other points, he may have been indebted to Schegel's idea of the "waking dream" in Schegel's "Lectures on Dramatic Art and Literature," 509.

18. Douglas Jerrold, *Punch*, 8 October 1853; Dennis Arundell, *The Story of Sadler's Wells, 1683–1964* (London, 1965), 153. Victoria never did visit Sadler's Wells in support of Phelps nor did she have his *A Midsummer Night's Dream* brought to Windsor castle, though she did see his *Romeo and Juliet* there in 1859.

19. Dutton Cook, *Nights at the Play*, 2 vols. (London, 1883), 2:62–65; Clement Scott, *The Drama of Yesterday and Today* (London, 1899), 1:62; Barton Baker, *History of the London Stage and Its Famous Players (1576–1903)* (London, 1904), 373.

20. Foulkes, 60; and notes by Shirley Allen, *Theatre Notebook* 24 (1968/69), 45–46. Foulkes,

who was the first to fully reconstruct the production, wrote, "Certainly not before, and probably not since has *A Midsummer Night's Dream* received such a fine and appropriate staging" (60).

21. Odell hoped it was better ("*MND*," 128). But one review reports the cutting of the necessary exposition on the elopement in the conference between Hermia and Helena in 1.1, a hallmark of Reynolds's text (fugitive clipping from a New York newspaper, 4 September 1841, in Ireland scrapbooks, Beinecke Library, Yale University).

22. *New York American*, 31 August 1841; *New York Evening Post*, 31 August, 8 September 1841. The production was advertised in the *Evening Post* for five nights.

23. William Burton's production opened on 3 February and Barry's on 6 February; Burton closed on 6 March and Barry on 11 March. Odell reproduces the opening day advertisements in "*MND*," 130–131; Thomas Alston Brown, *A History of the New York Stage* (New York, 1903) 1:397.

24. Odell, *Annals*, 5:429–430.

25. William Keese, *William E. Burton, Actor, Author, and Manager, a Sketch of His Career* (New York, 1885), passim; Thomas Alston Brown, 1:346 ff; Odell, "*MND*," 130; William Keese, *William E. Burton, a Sketch of His Career Other Than That of an Actor* (New York, 1891), 28.

26. Reynolds's operatic versions had been the basis of the previous two New York productions. Burton did trim the play by 366 lines (based on Burton's promptbook in Shattuck *MND*, No. 10) and with a hand less sensitive than Planché's. But, like Phelps, Burton used no extraneous songs.

27. Barry was listed as Simpson's stage manager in an advertisement in the *New York Evening Post*, 30 August 1841; Barry had staged the play at the Tremont Theatre in Boston in 1839 (transcribed copies of Tremont Theatre playbills in the Crawford Theatre Collection, Yale University) and again in Boston in 1856 and 1859 (playbills, Boston Theatre, 11 September 1856 and Selwyn's Theatre, 30 December 1869, Harvard Theatre Collection).

28. Odell, "*MND*," 130. Based on the promptbook prepared by Barry's stage manager, John B. Wright (Shattuck *MND*, No. 12 [hereafter cited as Barry promptbook]), Barry cut only 250 lines, but with much less discretion than Planché, Phelps, or Burton. Titania's "forgeries of jealousy" speech lost 20 lines; only a single line remained of Puck's "For night's swift dragons cut the clouds full fast," and nothing remained of his evocation of midnight, screech owls, and gaping graves. The young lovers lost 138 lines, and throughout, individual passages of poetry were uncarefully cut and the splicing through the omitted passages barely serviceable.

29. Barry promptbook. A few details of my description of Barry's staging derive from an undated Samuel French acting edition of the play, which advertises that the play is based on the Broadway Theatre production. It clearly was based, in large part, on Wright's promptbook.

30. Chambers Street Theatre playbill, 10 February 1853, Crawford Theatre Collection, Yale University.

31. The pamphlet and two playbills are pasted into the promptbook of Burton's production prepared by his stage manager, John Moore, Shattuck *MND*, No. 10 (hereafter cited as Burton pamphlet; Burton playbill; and Moore promptbook).

32. Burton playbill, 10 February 1853; Burton pamphlet.

33. Moore promptbook, scene plot: "Terrace and river beyond . . . aquaducts are painted in flat — Set porticos — Temples — Arches — Working fountain. Statues." *Daily Times*, 6 February 1854.

34. Kean's *King John* was derived from Macready's, and Macready's promptbook is repro-

duced in fascimile, together with pictures of the settings of both productions, in Charles H. Shattuck, ed., *William Charles Macready's* King John (Urbana: University of Illinois Press, 1962).

35. *New York Sunday Dispatch*, 5 February 1854.

36. *Albion*, 11 February 1854.

37. Moore promptbook; Barry promptbook. The cars probably derive from the 1816 Reynolds opera, which in turn may have borrowed the idea from Juno's peacock-borne entrance in *The Fairy Queen*.

38. *New York Herald*, 8 February 1854.

39. Moore promptbook; Barry promptbook.

40. Chamber's Street Theatre playbill, 10 February 1853, Crawford Theatre Collection, Yale University. Moore's promptbook contains many detailed allusions to textual cuts and scenic devices of Vestris's production, and Burton credited Moore with having "materially aided" him as a stage director. The practice of stage managers annotating personal promptbooks with notes from many productions of a Shakespeare play was common; it made managers the more valuable and accounts for many Shakespearean stage traditions.

41. All the features described in this paragraph are drawn from the Burton and Barry promptbooks and the French edition based on Barry's production.

42. Bunn and Vestris had used the overture. To my knowledge, the earliest use of the full incidental score with an English-speaking production was by the Theatre Royal, Dublin, which advertised "the whole of Mendelssohn's music" in November 1852 (playbill, Theatre Royal, Dublin, 18 November 1852, Crawford Theatre Collection, Yale University). Shattuck incorrectly followed Burton's claim in *Shakespeare on the American Stage from the Hallams to Edwin Booth* (Washington, D.C., 1976), 112–113.

43. *Albion*, 11 February 1854; Keese, *Burton, Actor, Author*, 172; Burton promptbook. Unfortunately, Burton had no Jerrold or Morley to record him.

44. *New York Daily Times* and *New York Herald*, 8 February 1854; William Davidge, *Footlight Flashes* (New York, 1866), 126; Thomas Alston Brown, 1:382.

45. *New York Tribune*, 7 February 1854.

46. On Harley, see *Spectator*, 21 November 1840; see the discussion of Tree's performance later in this chapter.

47. *Spectator*, 21 November 1840; the *Times*, 17 November 1840, expressed a similar opinion.

48. Phelps promptbook, Shattuck *MND*, No. 19.

49. Arthur Colby Sprague, *Shakespeare and the Actors, the Stage Business in His Plays 1660–1905* (New York: Russell and Russell, 1963), 364, note 185. Sprague (50–55) offers many examples of stage business in *A Midsummer Night's Dream*.

50. Tree promptbook, Shattuck *MND*, No. 30.

51. Burton promptbook.

52. Fugitive clipping (*New York Tribune*?), Ireland scrapbooks, 1872–1874, 23, pt. 2, Beinecke Library, Yale University.

53. Costume list, Pattie edition.

54. Barry promptbook.

55. John William Cole, *The Life and Theatrical Times of Charles Kean, F.S.A.* (London: Richard Bentley, 1895), 2:228, 169, 222, 209–210.

56. *Punch*, 28 March 1857.

57. Henry Morley often criticized Kean for allowing spectacle to displace Shakespeare's text, as he did on the occasion of Kean's *A Midsummer Night's Dream* (*Journal*, 132–135). A lengthy, unsigned article, entitled "The Drama versus Upholstery," appeared in the *Literary*

Gazette, 1 November 1856, complaining of Kean's emphasis on scenic spectacle at the Princess's Theatre.

58. Cole, 2:379.

59. Ibid., 382.

60. Charles Kean, ed., *A Midsummer Night's Dream arranged for representation at the Princess's Theatre, with Historical and Explanatory Notes by Charles Kean*, 3d ed. (London: John Chapman [1857?]), 5–6 (hereafter cited as Kean acting edition).

61. *Illustrated London News*, 18 October 1856.

62. Kean acting edition, 12.

63. Watercolor of the act curtain in the souvenir promptbook of Kean's production, assembled in 1859 by his prompter, T. W. Edmonds, with eleven watercolors of the scenes, Harvard Theatre Collection, Shattuck *MND*, No. 15a, in Shattuck, "Supplement" (hereafter cited as Edmonds promptbook).

64. Watercolor of the Act 2 entrance of Oberon and Titania, Victoria and Albert Museum, signed "F. Lloyds, 1859." A separate watercolor reproduces the backdrop alone — obviously a point of pride, signed by W. Gordon, labeled "Act II. Sc. 1. A Wood Near Athens. Moonlight." The human figures in Turner's foreground have been omitted. These are among four hundred watercolors of the scenery and accoutrements of Kean's productions given to the museum by Kean's niece, Mrs. F. M. Paget. All are set in large mats, and most are signed by the scene painter. See F. Strange, *Magazine of Art* 26 (1906), 454 ff. W. Moelwyn Merchant was incorrect to place this drop at the end of the panorama, which was used following this scene (*Shakespeare and the Artist*, 108). Martin Meisel comments on the paradisiacal quality of the scene in his *Realizations: Pictorial and Theatrical Arts in Nineteenth Century England* (Princeton, N.J.: Princeton University Press, 1983), 186–187.

65. Edmonds promptbook.

66. Among the critics who mentioned it were Morley, *Journal*, 133, and *Illustrated London News*, 18 October 1856. A miniature foldout of the panorama is contained in the Edmonds promptbook.

67. Morley, *Journal*, 133.

68. Ibid., 134; *Literary Gazette*, 18 October 1856; Theodor Fontane, *Die Londoner Theater*, in *Samtliche Werke, Dritter Teil* (München, 1967), 22:62–63.

69. Playbill, 4 March 1857, Crawford Theatre Collection, Yale University.

70. Victoria's diary, 17 February 1857, cited in Rowell, 71.

71. Unsigned essay on Kean's production in John M'Gilchrist, *Peripatetic Papers, Being a Volume of Miscellanies by the Members of a Literary Society* (London: James Blackwood, 1857), 304.

72. Fontane, 62–63.

73. Blocking diagram indicating each fairy's placement, Edmonds promptbook.

74. Herman Charles Merivale, *Bar, Stage, and Platform, Autobiographic Memories* (London: Chatto and Windus, 1902), 122–123.

75. Among the critics generally praising the production were those for the *Athenaeum*, *Spectator*, and *Illustrated London News*, 18 October 1856. Complaints were included in the reviews of Morley, *Journal*, 134, and *Literary Gazette*, 18 October 1856.

76. *Literary Gazette*, 18 October 1856; Fontane, 65.

77. Based on the Edmonds promptbook.

78. Advertisement, *Manchester Guardian*, 2 September 1865; review, *Manchester Guardian*, 4 September 1865; *A Midsummer Night's Dream. As Arranged for representation at the Prince's Theatre, Manchester, by Charles Calvert. As first performed on Saturday, 2nd September, 1865* (Manchester, n.d.).

79. Review by Austin Brereton, *The Theatre* (August 1880), 110–113; Edward Saker's acting edition (Liverpool, 1880), Sterling Library, Yale University; Russell Jackson, "Shakespeare in Liverpool, Edward Saker's Revivals, 1876–81," *Theatre Notebook* 32 (1978), 100–109.

80. She acknowledged Kean in the preface to her acting edition (New York: Samuel French, 1863).

81. Joseph Jefferson, *The Autobiography of Joseph Jefferson* (New York: Century, 1889), 205.

82. *New York Daily Tribune*, 19 April 1859.

83. Taylor, *Reinventing Shakespeare*, 199.

84. Ibid., 184.

85. Keene clearly exceeded Charles Kean's omission of 838 lines, based on the acting edition printed from her promptbook in French's Standard Drama (1859). Her promptbook (Billy Rose Theatre Collection, NYPL) is made up of pages of Thomas Barry's edition of the play, which already omitted 250 lines. Keene followed most of Kean's cuts and alterations and added some of her own. For example, Kean cut 90 lines from 1.1, and Keene, while restoring 13 of these, cut another 64 that he had left intact.

86. *New York Herald*, 17 April 1859. Keene also used excerpts from reviews in her advertisements, praising her production, in the *Herald*, 25 May 1859. She may be the orginator of this practice.

87. An adult woman as Puck was not uncommon in the nineteenth century. Reynolds, Bunn, and Vestris cast women in the role; Phelps used a young boy in 1853 but in later revivals used women, as did Augustin Daly (1873 and 1888) and Sir Herbert Beerbohm Tree (1900), according to playbills for these productions.

88. *New York Daily Tribune*, 19 April 1859; other reviews consulted include those in *Spirit of the Times*, *Daily News*, and *New York Times*, 22 April 1859.

89. Odell, *Annals*, 7:108–149.

90. *New York Times*, 22 April 1859.

91. *New York Herald*, 6 November 1867.

92. Kean's text was used, according to William Winter's review (*New York Daily Tribune*, 30 October 1867), and the Olympic playbill's scene synopsis follows Kean's five-act arrangment (Olympic playbill, 3 December 1867, Crawford Theatre Collection, Yale University).

93. Jefferson (396–397) discusses the public appetite at this time for spectacle; pieces of the story of Jefferson and Telbin's panorama are found in William Winter, *The Jeffersons* (Boston, 1881), 190–191; in William Winter, *Shakespeare on the Stage*, 3d series (New York, 1916), 265–266; and in Odell, *Annals*, 8:279.

94. *New York Daily Tribune*, 14 November 1867.

95. Olympic playbill, 3 December 1867, Crawford Theatre Collection, Yale University.

96. Fugitive review (William Winter, *New York Tribune*?) of the 1873 Daly production, in which the writer favorably recalls the 1867 production (Ireland scrapbooks [1872–1874] #23, part 2, Beinecke Library, Yale University).

97. Odell, *Annals*, 8:280–281.

98. Laurence Senelick, *The Age and Stage of George L. Fox* (Hanover, N.H.: University Press of New England, 1988), 136.

99. Daly also produced the play in 1873 but much less lavishly. George Heister, who had painted for the 1854 Broadway Theatre production, painted Daly's 1873 scenery.

100. Tree, in the souvenir program for his *The Tempest*, cited in Mrs. George Cran, *Herbert Beerbohm Tree* (London, 1907), 75–85.

101. *Saturday Review*, 13 November 1897.

102. Odell, *"MND,"* 151–152; Odell, *Annals*, 8:414, 418.

103. Odell, "*MND*," 152; Odell, *Annals*, 8:418.

104. Daly promptbook, 1888, Shattuck *MND*, No. 23. The trick was done with a mattress on springs that carried him up into the palanquin's canopy. The promptbook uses Daly's own edition of the play, with his stage directions printed. Daly's stage manager, John Moore, who was also Burton's, kept a composite promptbook of his own on this play, in which he provided the explanatory note on this mechanism (Burton promptbook).

105. Isadora Duncan, *My Life* (London, 1928), 44–45.

106. Odell, "*MND*," 152; *Cosmopolitan*, April 1888, 100. Montgomery was formerly the critic for the *New York Times*.

107. Odell, "*MND*," 152.

108. Playbill for Daly's production, 6 March 1888, Billy Rose Theatre Collection, NYPL. In the Reynolds opera, these lines were transposed to follow Oberon's promise, after reconciling with Titania, to bless Theseus's house (5.2.21).

109. Rehan's recent successes had included Kate in *The Taming of the Shrew*, and she would soon create a long-remembered Rosalind.

110. *New York Daily Tribune*, 1 February 1888.

111. *New York Herald*, 1 February 1888.

112. William Winter, *Ada Rehan* (New York, 1898), 35; William Winter, *New York Daily Tribune*, 1 February 1888.

113. George Bernard Shaw, *Dramatic Opinions and Essays* (London, 1906), 1:174. Shaw found Rehan a relief from the "mechanical intoning" of Sarah Bernhardt.

114. William Winter, *New York Daily Tribune*, 1 February 1888; Odell, *Annals*, 8:418.

115. The printed editions of the promptbooks of Daly, Vestris, and Kean all show this alteration.

116. Daly promptbook, Shattuck *MND*, No. 25, 11–12; Daly promptbook, Shattuck *MND*, No. 23.

117. *New York Herald*, 1 February 1888; *Freund's Music and Drama*, 11 February 1888.

118. *New York Times*, 3 July 1888 and 30 October 1888; *New York Herald*, 30 October 1888; *Freund's Music and Drama*, 3 November 1888; Star Theatre playbill, Brooklyn, 1888, Billy Rose Theatre Collection, NYPL.

119. The figure is based on the promptbook in Shattuck *MND*, No. 23. Shaw, 1:171; William Archer, *The Theatrical World of 1895* (London, 1896), 250. Contrary to Marvin Felheim's account, Daly did rearrange the scene sequence of the play, ending his fourth act not with Bottom's awakening but with Theseus's discovery of the lovers, which climaxes the act with the barge panorama. Daly omitted completely the scene of the mechanicals' reunion with Bottom (Marvin Felheim, *The Theatre of Augustin Daly* [Cambridge: Harvard University Press, 1956], 244). The order of lines was also occasionally rearranged in several scenes. I suspect from the correspondence between Daly and Winter at the Folger Shakespeare Library that it was Daly, not Winter, as Felheim has suggested, who edited the text and then submitted it to Winter for his blessing and preface.

120. Shaw, 1:177.

121. Herbert Farjeon, *The Shakespearean Scene* (London, n.d.), 127; H. Chance Newton, *Cues and Curtain Calls* (London, 1927), 149.

122. Gordon Crosse, *Shakespeare Playgoing 1890–1952* (London: A. R. Mowberry, 1953), 39.

123. The figure is based on the promptbook in Shattuck *MND*, No. 31. Another thirty-seven lines were cut if one follows the promptbook now in the Bristol University Theatre Collection, Shattuck *MND*, No. 29, in which the reunion of the artisans is cut.

124. Note in the souvenir program for the fiftieth performance of Tree's *The Tempest*. The

figure comes from Tree's address to the Oxford Debating Society, 28 May 1900, cited in Lynton Hudson, *The English Stage 1850–1950* (London, 1951), 138; Tree later cited these figures in *Thoughts and Afterthoughts* (London: Cassell, 1913), 46. See also Michael R. Booth's (127–130) account of Tree's staging.

125. Tree, 51.

126. Ibid., 65.

127. Hesketh Pearson, *Beerbohm Tree: His Life and Laughter* (London, 1956), 101; Crosse, 39.

128. George Rowell, "Tree's Shakespeare Festivals (1905–1913)," *Theatre Notebook* 29 (1975), 74–81; Ralph Berry, "The Aesthetics of Beerbohm Tree's Shakespeare Festivals," *Nineteenth Century Theatre Research* 9 (1981), 23–51 (with nine photographs).

129. Barbara Tuchman, *The Proud Tower* (New York, 1971), 67, 64–69.

130. Tree promptbook, Bristol University Theatre Collection, Shattuck *MND*, No. 30. Crosse (37) remembered scene-change intervals as long as forty-five minutes, in Tree's *Much Ado About Nothing*.

131. *Punch*, 24 January 1900.

132. Cited in Wells, "Tales from Shakespeare," 143.

133. *Times*, 11 January 1900.

134. Papers relating to Tree's *A Midsummer Night's Dream*, Bristol University Theatre Collection.

135. *Vanity Fair*, 18 January 1900; *Athenaeum*, 20 January 1900; Tree promptbook, Shattuck *MND*, No. 31.

136. *Pall Mall Gazette*, 11 January 1900. For development of this point, see my discussion of Elizabeth Vestris's Oberon in chapter 4.

137. *Vanity Fair*, 18 January 1900.

138. J. T. Grein, *Premieres of the Year* (London, 1900), 140.

139. Percy Fitzgerald, *Shakespearean Representation* (London, 1908), 74.

140. *Times*, 11 January 1900; *Punch*, 24 January 1900. This is confirmed by the photo of Tree in the souvenir program, Bristol University Theatre Collection.

141. Tree promptbook, Bristol University Theatre Collection, Shattuck *MND*, No. 30.

142. Margaret Webster remembered this as long-standing business in her *Shakespeare Today* (London: J. M. Dent, 1957).

143. The examples of business are taken from the two Tree promptbooks, Shattuck *MND*, Nos. 30 and 31.

144. *Times, Athenaeum,* and *Pall Mall Gazette*, 11 January 1900; *Saturday Review*, 20 January 1900.

145. See chapter 1.

146. Arthur Hutchinson, "The Shakespeare Memorial Theatre at Stratford-upon-Avon, a Decade of Its Work," in *The Shakespeare Revival*, ed. Reginald R. Buckley (London, 1911), 13–14; T. C. Kemp and J. C. Trewin, *The Stratford Festival: A History of the Shakespeare Memorial Theatre* (Birmingham, 1953), 26–27; J. C. Trewin, *Benson and the Bensonians* (London, 1960), provides a detailed account of Benson's career.

147. *Athenaeum*, 28 December 1889; Constance Benson, *Mainly Players* (London, 1926), 87; Frank Benson, *My Memoirs* (London, 1930), 298; Trewin, 104.

148. Benson promptbook, prepared by F. R. Ayrton, Shakespeare Centre Library, Stratford-upon-Avon, Shattuck *MND*, No. 27; Harcourt Williams, *Old Vic Saga* (London: Winchester, 1949), 157; and Constance Benson, 80.

149. London newspaper review, 1 March 1900, fugitive clipping, *MND* file, Harvard

Theatre Collection; Ben Iden Payne, *A Life in a Wooden O* (New Haven, Conn.: Yale University Press, 1977), 27 (Payne was at one time an attendant in Benson's production).

150. *Times*, 20 December 1889; Charlotte C. Stopes, "A Spring Pilgrimage to Shakespeare's Town," *Poet Lore* 4 (1892), 373–375; Sprague, vii.

151. *The Theatre*, 1 February 1890; Dan H. Laurence, ed., *Bernard Shaw, Collected Letters 1847–97* (New York, 1965), 240.

152. Constance Benson, 282.

153. Winifrid Isaac, *Ben Greet and the Old Vic* ([London, 1964]); this privately printed book must be regarded at best as a collection of valuable working notes.

154. Crosse, 9, 109, 111; Program, Oxford University, 18 June 1992, Crawford Theatre Collection, Yale University; Charles H. Shattuck, "Setting Shakespeare Free?," *Journal of Aesthetic Education* 17 (1983), 115; *A Midsummer Night's Dream*, arranged by Mr. Ben Greet (n.p., n.d.), Folger Shakespeare Library.

155. Greet playbills: 4 February 1895, 1914–15 (Old Vic), and other assorted bills, Greet file, Billy Rose Theatre Collection, NYPL; Greet playbill, June 1902, *MND* file, Harvard Theatre Collection; fugitive review, New York newspaper, 9 May 1932, Greet file, Billy Rose Theatre Collection, NYPL.

156. Odell, "*MND*," 156; Winter, *Shakespeare*, 277; program and fugitive clippings, *MND* file, Harvard Theatre Collection.

157. Fitzgerald, 58; Odell, "*MND*," 156; Charles Whibly, *Outlook*, 9 December 1905.

158. Odell, "*MND*," 158; *New York Times*, 22 October 1906; Winter, *Shakespeare*, 278–281; Henry C. Shelley, fugitive clipping, *Boston Globe*?, *MND* file, Harvard Theatre Collection.

159. Newton, 149; *Punch*, 26 April 1911; *Times*, 18 April 1911; *Illustrated London News*, 22 April 1911; *Sketch*, 3 May 1911; *Saturday Review*, 29 April 1911; *Outlook*, 6 May 1911; *Spectator*, 3 January 1925. No mention of the rabbits occurs in reviews that I have seen of the 1900 production, where most memories of Tree's production place them; in 1911, many critics testify to their presence, and in one Tree promptbook, on a separate list of "new" properties, there is the entry "3 rabbits" (Bristol University Theatre Collection, Shattuck *MND*, No. 30).

160. James M. Barrie, *Peter Pan*, in *The Plays of James M. Barrie* (New York: Charles Scribner's Sons, 1929), 74. Barrie drew somewhat on *A Midsummer Night's Dream* in his 1917 *Dear Brutus* (contained in this same collection), a sentimental drawing-room comedy in which older couples visit a guest house on midsummer eve and are given a second chance in love in their night in "Lob's wood," Lob being their Puck-like host, an immortal, supernatural figure.

161. Martin Gardner, *Science, Good, Bad and Bogus* (Buffalo, N.Y.: Prometheus Press, 1984), 118–119, 121, note 4. Doyle published a second, enlarged edition of the book (London: Psychic Press, 1922), to which he added more photographs. The photographs came to Doyle by way of a theosophist and occult journalist. Gardner follows the story up through a 1971 interview with the two childhood playmates, then elderly women.

7. The *Dream* of Modernism: The "New Hieroglyphic Language of Scenery" and the Theology of the Text

1. Barker's productions and his well-known prefaces to the plays figured prominently in J. L. Styan's influential *The Shakespeare Revolution, Criticism and Performance in the Twenti-*

eth Century (Cambridge: Cambridge University Press, 1977). Styan argued that twentieth-century Shakespearean production, having shed Victorian pictorialism and having evolved, from Barker to Peter Brook, toward less illusionistic stages, had moved ever closer to capturing the aesthetics of "the Shakespeare experience." While this was an important recognition of twentieth-century achievements, the analysis focused on staging choices as matters of style rather than locating them culturally and so allowed the implication that Shakespearean production had become more pure and less culturally mediated than it ever had been. In Dennis Kennedy's *Granville Barker and the Dream of Theatre* (Cambridge: Cambridge University Press, 1985), Barker was celebrated as a pioneer in modernist theatre practice who recovered the essence of Shakespeare for the twentieth century, as was the case in Christine Dymkowski's *Harley Granville Barker: A Preface to Modern Shakespeare* (Washington, D.C.: Folger Books, 1985). Dennis Kennedy's *Looking at Shakespeare* (Cambridge: Cambridge University Press, 1993) offered a brief reassessment of Barker's production (76–77).

2. Letter to *Daily Mail*, 26 September 1912, reproduced in Eric Salmon, *Granville Barker and His Correspondents* (Detroit: Wayne State University Press, 1986), 528.

3. Letter to *Play Pictorial*, November 1912, reproduced in Salmon, 556.

4. Ibid., reproduced in Salmon, 530.

5. Preface to Barker's single-volume edition of the play (London: William Heinemann, 1914), iii. Heinemann published paperback editions of the three Shakespeare plays Barker staged at the Savoy, each containing a short preface by Barker and photos of some of the costume designs.

6. W. B. Worthen, "Deeper Meanings and Theatrical Technique: The Rhetoric of Performance Criticism," *Shakespeare Quarterly* 40 (1989), 443. Performance criticism, as currently practiced, may be said to begin with Barker's prefaces to Shakespeare and, true to its source, seems little interested in the cultural transactions involved in specific historical productions.

7. C. B. Purdom, *Harley Granville Barker, Man of the Theatre, Dramatist and Scholar* (London: Rockliff, 1955), plate 29, opposite p. 138.

8. T. S. Eliot, *Selected Essays* (New York, 1964), 96. He added a slightly qualifying footnote, granting that an Old Vic production of Shakespeare "may add much to our understanding."

9. Harley Granville Barker, *Prefaces to Shakespeare* (Princeton, N.J.: Princeton University Press, 1946–1947), 1:22–23.

10. Harley Granville Barker, *Preface to A Midsommer Nights Dreame [The Players' Shakespeare]* (London: Ernest Benn, 1924), xii–xiii; also in Harley Granville Barker, *More Prefaces to Shakespeare*, ed. Edward M. Moore (Princeton, N.J.: Princeton University Press, 1974), 97–98.

11. Kennedy provides accounts of Barker's debt to the new scenic design in England and Germany in *Granville Barker*, 151–153, and in *Looking at Shakespeare*, chapter 3.

12. Interview with Wilkinson by Amelia Dorothy Defires, *New York Press*, 21 February 1915.

13. Harvard promptbook, Shattuck *MND*, Shattuck, No. 35a, in "Supplement." See also Trevor Griffths, "Tradition and Innovation in Harley Granville-Barker's *A Midsummer Night's Dream*." *Theatre Notebook* 30 (1976), 78–86.

14. See the discussions of textual cuts in chapters 5 and 6.

15. *Punch*, 18 February 1914. My description derives in part from Gary Jay Williams, "*A Midsummer Night's Dream*: The English and American Popular Traditions and Harley Granville Barker's 'World Arbitrarily Made,'" *Theatre Studies* 23 (1976/77), 40–52. In addition to the reviews cited hereafter, I have drawn on the Harvard promptbook, Shattuck *MND*, No. 35a, in Shattuck, "Supplement"; University of Michigan promptbook, Shattuck *MND*,

No. 35, which includes photographs; photographs in *Illustrated London News*, 14 and 28 February 1914, and *Sketch*, 25 February 1914; and color photographs in *Illustrated London News*, 11 April 1914.

16. Walter P. Eaton, *Plays and Players* (Cincinnati, 1916), 237.

17. *Times*, 7 February 1914.

18. *New Statesman*, 21 February 1914.

19. University of Michigan promptbook, Shattuck *MND*, No. 35.

20. Louis V. Defoe, fugitive clipping, hand-dated 21 February 1915, Scrapbook No. 24, Folger Shakespeare Library.

21. See, for example, the photographs of the costumes of Nijinski in *Sheherazade* and Boulgakov in *The Firebird* in Martin Hurlimann, ed., *Das Atlantisbuch des Theaters* (Zurich: Atlantis Verlag, 1966), 299, 316.

22. Eaton, 237.

23. Harvard promptbook, Shattuck *MND*, No. 35a, in Shattuck, "Supplement."

24. The University of Michigan promptbook, Shattuck *MND*, No. 35, contains Sharp's score; Sharp's published score was reviewed in the *Times*, 11 February 1914; see also Sharp's own essay on his music for the Savoy Shakespeare series in *Athenaeum* 7 February 1914, 210–211. The score is discussed in Maud Karpeles, *Cecil Sharp, His Life and Work* (Chicago: University of Chicago Press, 1967), 121.

25. *Times*, 7 February 1914.

26. See the discussion of futurism in the theatre in Michael Kirby, *Futurist Performance*, with manifestos and playscripts translated by Victoria Nes Kirby (New York: Dutton, 1971), especially chapters 8 and 9.

27. Karl Schmidt, "How Barker Puts Plays On," *Harper's Weekly* 60 (30 January 1915), 115–116.

28. *Athenaeum*, 14 February 1914. According to the critic for the *New York Press* (17 February 1915), the production ran three hours and ten minutes, even with the swift scene changes, so the impression of rapid speaking may need to be understood relative to the previous very slow, measured intoning of Shakespeare.

29. *Athenaeum*, 14 February 1914.

30. Harvard promptbook, Shattuck *MND*, No. 35a, in Shattuck, "Supplement."

31. In the New York production, Horace Braham played Oberon.

32. Although women usually had played the role, Calthrop was not the first male to play the role on the English-speaking stage. The Pucks of Phelps and Burton were boys, as was the Puck in Tree's 1911 revival (Burford Hampden), and an adult, George Vivian, played Puck for Ben Greet in 1911.

33. Griffiths, 83.

34. *Times*, 7 February 1914.

35. *New Statesman*, 21 February 1914.

36. John Gielgud, with John Miller and John Powell, *An Actor and His Time* (London, 1979), 121, 44.

37. John Palmer, *Saturday Review*, 14 February 1914.

38. Crosse, 48.

39. *Nation*, 14 February 1914.

40. William Archer, letter to Barker [11 February 1914], in Salmon, 60.

41. *New York Press*, 17 February 1915.

42. G. Wilson Knight, *Shakespearian Production* (London: Faber, 1964), 227.

43. Kennedy, *Granville Barker*, 180.

44. Odell, *Shakespeare*, 2:468; Winter, *Shakespeare*, 290, 281–296.

45. Purdom, epilogue.

46. Kennedy, *Granville Barker*, 153.

47. Barker, *Preface to A Midsommer Nights Dreame*, xii.

48. Ibid., xii–xiii.

49. Henry Hewes, "How to Use Shakespeare," *Saturday Review of Literature* 40 (13 July 1957), 11.

50. Basil Dean, *An Autobiography, 1888–1927* (London, 1970), 226. Dean devotes a chapter to the production of *A Midsummer Night's Dream*.

51. *Sunday Times*, 28 December 1924.

52. Farjeon, 39.

53. *Observer*, 25 December 1949.

54. A photograph of the old Memorial Theatre interior and this drop is in Micheline Steinberg, *Flashback, a Pictorial History 1879–1979* (Stratford-upon-Avon: RSC Publications, 1985), 24.

55. Barker refers to Williams in 1911 as one of the "lieutenants" he is grooming (letter to Gilbert Murray, 5 September 1911, in Salmon, 276), and Williams recounts a fifteen-hour conversation with Barker on staging Shakespeare just before Williams began his first season at the Old Vic (Harcourt Williams, *Four Years at the Old Vic*, [London, 1935], 55); Margaret Webster, *The Same Only Different* (New York, 1959), 342.

56. Williams, *Four Years*, 52.

57. See chapter 1. E. K. Chambers had advanced the Stanley-Vere wedding or the Carey-Berkeley wedding as possible occasions of the play in 1916 and 1923, and John Dover Wilson and Arthur Quiller-Couch had suggested the Southampton-Vernon wedding in their 1924 Cambridge edition of the play.

58. Williams, *Old Vic Saga* 33; Webster, *The Same Only Different*, 339.

59. Ivor Brown, *Observer*, 15 December 1929; Williams, *Four Years*, 52–53.

60. James Agate, *Brief Chronicles* (London, 1943), 43; Williams, *Four Years*, 55; Ivor Brown, *Observer*, 15 December 1929; *Times*, 10 December 1929. The Elizabethan motif grew on reviewers, judging from reviews of the 1931 revival. A *Sunday Times* critic went twice to the 1931 revival to accustom himself to the Elizabethan manner (8 November 1931).

61. Williams, *Four Years*, 17–20, 36; Webster, *The Same Only Different*, 342. Webster was Williams's Hermia in this production.

62. Ronald Hayman, *John Gielgud* (New York, 1971), 58, 147.

63. Sally Beauman, *The Royal Shakespeare Company, a History of Ten Decades* (Oxford: Oxford University Press, 1982), 72–73, 93–105.

64. The name, in fact, of the factious group that ultimately backed a resident company at Stratford was the Shakespeare Memorial National Theatre Committee. Archer was active in it, and Barker was on an advisory committee for the building of the new theatre, though he remained at arm's length from it and ultimately was critical of the enterprise. See Beauman, 69–71, 102–104.

65. W. Bridges-Adams, *The Irresistable Theatre* (London: Secker and Warbridge, 1957), 205; *Athenaeum*, 8 and 15 August 1919, citing an interview with Bridges-Adams on the 1919 season of six plays; M. C. Day and J. C. Trewin, *The Shakespeare Memorial Theatre* (London, 1932), 162.

66. Bridges-Adams promptbook, Shattuck *MND*, No. 39. A note inside the cover identifies it as having been used for the 1928, 1928/29, Canadian tour, 1930, and 1932 productions. The interlinear cuts range from one to eight lines and total approximately sixty-five to seventy lines.

67. *Spectator*, 21 May 1921.

68. Beauman, 82–85.

69. Based on reviews of this and the later revivals in the *MND* clippings scrapbook, vol. 26, p. 36, Shakespeare Centre Library, Stratford-upon-Avon, including *Birmingham Post*, 29 April 1932; fugitive clipping, 1932, signed M.F. K.F.; *Stratford-upon-Avon Herald*, 8 June 1934; *Harrogate Herald*, *Midland Daily Telegraph*, *Birmingham Gazette*, *Birmingham Evening Dispatch*, and *Yorkshire Post*, 6 June 1934; *Times*, *Daily Telegraph*, *Morning Post*, *Daily Mail*, *Daily Herald*, and *Birmingham Post*, 30 March 1937. But by 1938, even local reviewers were calling for a change (e. g., *Stratford-upon-Avon Herald*, 29 April 1938).

70. Fugitive clipping, 1932, signed M.F. K.F., *MND* clippings scrapbook, vol. 26, p. 36, Shakespeare Centre Library, Stratford-upon-Avon.

71. *Stratford-upon-Avon Herald*, 8 June 1934.

72. Steinberg, 42.

73. Williams, *Four Years*, 36.

74. Other reviews consulted include the *Spectator*, *Saturday Review*, and *Illustrated London News*, 3 January 1925; *Nation* and *Athenaeum*, 10 January 1925; *Literary Digest*, 14 February 1925.

75. Guy Boas, *Shakespeare and the Young Actors* (London: Rockliff, [1955]), 47–48; the description is printed in full in O'Casey's *The Flying Wasp* (London: Macmillan, 1937), 163–167. Other O'Casey letters of this time establish the date of 1936; see David Krause, ed., *The Letters of Sean O'Casey* (New York: Macmillan, 1975), 1:620, 747.

8. The *Dream* of Modernism: The Sacred and the Secular

1. My sources on the number of Reinhardt's Shakespearean productions are Siegfried Jacobsohn, *Max Reinhardt* (Berlin: E Reiss, 1921), Appendix, 141–150; Ernst Stern and Heinz Herald, *Reinhardt und seine Bühne* (Berlin: Ensler, 1920); Franz Horch, "Die Spielpläne Max Reinhardts," in *Max Reinhardt, 25 Jahres Deutsches Theater*, ed. Hans Rothe (Munich: Piper, 1930), 72–74; Huntly Carter, *The Theatre of Max Reinhardt* (New York, 1914; reprint, 1964), appendix 5, 316–326; Heinz Kindermann, *Theatergeschichte Europas* (Salzburg: Otto Müller, 1968), 8:413–447; and J. L. Styan, *Max Reinhardt* (Cambridge: Cambridge University Press, 1982), chapter 5, and production list, 128–156. The number of Berlin performances of the play between 1905 and 1919 includes Carter's figure for the first Neues Theater production (150) and Horch's for the rest. Some thirteen Reinhardt productions of the play might be said to have been distinct by virtue of being staged in different theatres (or playing spaces) with new designers and/or new casts. Several are closely related scenically, such as the productions at the Neues Theater in 1905 and the Deutsches Theater in 1906, those at the Salzburg Festival and in New York in 1927, and the outdoor spectacles at the Boboli Gardens in Florence, Headington Hill in Oxford, and the Hollywood Bowl in California.

2. Oscar G. Brockett and Robert Findlay, *Century of Innovation, a History of European and American Theatre and Drama Since the Late Nineteenth Century*, 2d ed. (Boston: Allyn and Bacon, 1991), 124.

3. George R. Marek, "The Lord of Leopoldskron I," in *Max Reinhardt 1873–1973*, ed. George E. Wellwarth and Alfred G. Brooks (Binghamton, N.Y.: Max Reinhardt Archive, 1973), 92.

4. Gottfried Reinhardt, *The Genius* (New York: Alfred A. Knopf, 1979), 17, 217–219.

5. Gusti Adler, *. . . aber vergessen Sie nicht die chinesischen Nachtigallen* (Munich and Vienna, 1980), 45 f., cited in *Max Reinhardt, the Magician's Dreams*, ed. Edda Fuhrich and Gisela Prossnitz, trans. Sophie Kidd and Peter Waugh (Salzburg: Residenz Verlag, 1993), 28. This

collection of documents was published in connection with exhibitions in Europe and America celebrating the fiftieth anniversary of Reinhardt's death.

6. Interview with Arthur Kahane, Berlin, 1901, in Fuhrich and Prossnitz, 31.

7. Ibid., 33.

8. Letter from Reinhardt to Berthold Held, 21 July 1904, in Ibid., 45.

9. Transcribed notes from the 1905 *Regiebuch*, in Hugo Fetting, ed., *Max Reinhardt, Leben für das Theater* (Berlin: Argon Verlag, 1989), 377.

10. Stern and Herald, 38.

11. *Regiebuch*, in Fetting, 375.

12. Stern and Herald, 43.

13. *Regiebuch*, in Fetting, 378. See, for example, the account in Jacobsohn, 1–3; and George Brandes's comments in Oliver M. Sayler, ed., *Max Reinhardt and His Theatre* (New York: Brentano's, 1924), Appendix 2, 330.

14. Simon Williams, 1:210.

15. The *Regiebuch* reads: "Zuerst erscheint Oberon au einem Fabeltier reitend (weisser Hirsh mit grossem Geweih)" (Fetting, 377). Styan (58) takes the passage to mean that Oberon literally entered on a white stag.

16. Hofmannsthal, cited in Jacobsohn, 3; also in F. Hadamovsky, ed., *Max Reinhardt, Ausgewählte Briefe, Reden, Schriften und Szenen aus Regiebüchern* (Vienna, 1963), 3.

17. Jacobsohn, 2.

18. The best photographs may be seen in Rothe, plates 43 and 48; see also Kennedy, *Looking at Shakespeare*, 59.

19. Interview with Reinhardt in the *Nieuwe Rotterdamsche Courant*, 1 May 1916, cited in Fuhrich and Prossnitz, 80–82.

20. Donald Freedman, review of Reinhardt's 1925 production in Vienna, *New York Times*, 8 March 1925.

21. Maximilian Harden, "The Genius of Max Reinhardt," in Sayler, 218, 219, 217.

22. Frank E. Washburn-Freund, "The Evolution of Reinhardt," in Sayler, 52.

23. Michael Patterson, "Reinhardt and Theatrical Expressionism," in *Max Reinhardt: The Oxford Symposium*, ed. Margaret Jacobs and John Warren (Oxford: Oxford University Press, 1986).

24. Stern and Herald, 37; *Regiebuch*, in Fetting, 377; Letter to Berthold Held, 21 July 1904, in Fuhrich and Prossnitz, 44.

25. Jacobsohn, 1.

26. *Reigiebuch*, in Fetting, 376, 384.

27. Harden, 217–218.

28. Rudolf Kommer, "The Magician of Leopoldskron," in Sayler, 7.

29. Walser's watercolor design is reproduced in color in Fuhrich and Prossnitz, 102; and in Henning Rischbieter, ed. *Art and the Stage in the Twentieth Century* (Greenwich, Conn., 1970), 29.

30. Jacobsohn, 1; see also Washburn-Freund, 52.

31. For coverage of the designs for these productions, see Kennedy, *Looking at Shakespeare*, 60–65.

32. A photograph and ground plans are reproduced in Brockett and Findlay, 236–237.

33. See Reinhardt's comments of about 1911, after his *Oedipus Rex*, on his hopes for Schumann productions, in Fetting, 446 ff.

34. Kindermann, 8:417–418.

35. Herman J. Mankiewicz, review and report on Berlin reviews of Reinhardt productions, *New York Times*, 15 May 1921.

36. Fuhrich and Prossnitz, 54–55, 105.

37. Donald Freedman, *New York Times*, 8 March 1925.

38. Kindermann, 8:419–420; Saloma Pekka, "Max Reinhardt's Productions of *A Midsummer Night's Dream*," *Players Magazine* 11 (May 1964), 257–258.

39. Kindermann, 8:421–422 and photographs; Lincoln Eyre, *New York Times*, 8 August 1927.

40. Kurt Pinthus, "Max Reinhardt and the U.S.A.," *Theatre Research/Recherches Theatrales* 5 (1963), 154.

41. *Wall Street Journal*, 19 November 1927; *Commonweal*, 30 November 1927.

42. *Commonweal*, 30 November 1927; similar sentiments, not so well expressed, are to be found in *Time*, 28 November 1927; and *Outlook*, 7 December 1927.

43. *New York Times*, 4 December 1927.

44. Brooks Atkinson, *New York Times*, 18 November 1927.

45. Joseph Wood Krutch, *Nation*, 7 December 1927, 666.

46. Reinhardt had directed the play with students of his theatre school, setting scenes outside and within the palaces at Kressheim and Leopoldskron (Kindermann, 88:423).

47. Reinhardt, 234.

48. For background on how Reinhardt dealt with the rise of the Nazi regime, see Ibid., 237–243.

49. Felix Felton, "Max Reinhardt in England," *Theatre Research/Recherches Theatrales* 5 (1963), 140; letter from Oxford University to Max Reinhardt, 2 May 1933.

50. Cited in Humphrey Carpenter, *OUDS, a Centenary History of the Oxford University Drama Society, 1885–1985* (Oxford: Oxford University Press, 1985), 133.

51. Felton, 141.

52. Edwin Schallert, *Los Angeles Times*, 18 September 1934; Carolyn Anspacher, *San Francisco Chronicle*, 2 October, 1934. I am indebted here to Helen Deese's paper, "Max Reinhardt's California *Dream*," for the 1985 Shakespeare Association of America seminar on performance.

53. Felton, 142; Rupert Hart-Davis, *Spectator*, 23 June 1933. There is some confusion about who carried off whom. Felton named Michael Martin Harvey as the one who carried off the First Fairy; Styan mistakenly says it was Puck, but Puck was played by Peter Glenville; Hart-Davis thought it was Titania who was abducted.

54. I am partially indebted for this suggestion to Helen Deese's paper.

55. Wayne Kvam, "The Nazification of Max Reinhardt's Deutsches Theater Berlin," *Theatre Journal* 40 (1988), 357–359.

56. The letter is cited in Hugo Fetting, ed., *Max Reinhardt Schriften* (Berlin: Henschel Verlag, 1974), 223–225. In the letter, Reinhardt writes somewhat plaintively that only one possibility remains to him, "and that is to invite GERMANY to take over my life's work."

57. Letter from Reinhardt to Einar Nilson, 18 October 1934, in Fuhrich and Prossnitz, 172.

58. *Los Angeles Times*, 9, 10, and 16 September 1934.

59. Reinhardt, 297; Cantor was mentioned by *Newsweek*, 28 September 1934, 27.

60. *New York Times*, 19 September 1934.

61. *Los Angeles Times*, 18 September 1934.

62. Ibid.; *San Francisco Chronicle*, 6 October 1934.

63. *Los Angeles Times*, 18 September 1934.

64. *New York Times*, 17 September 1934.

65. Reinhardt, 298–299.

66. Jack J. Jorgens, *Shakespeare on Film* (Bloomington: Indiana University Press, 1977),

38–50. Seven short silent-film versions of the play preceded the Reinhardt film, which have been described by Robert Hamilton Ball in *Shakespeare on Silent Film: A Strange Eventful History* (London: Allen and Unwin, 1968).

67. *A Midsummer Night's Dream*, with a foreword by Max Reinhardt (New York: Grosset and Dunlap, [1935]), v. This text does not represent the heavily cut and rearranged shooting script. Like eighteenth- and nineteenth-century editions, this edition would have functioned in part as a legitimization of the film.

68. For a full tracing of this, see Alexander Vardac, *Stage to Screen: Theatrical Method from Garrick to Griffith* (Cambridge: Harvard University Press, 1949).

69. A line-by-line comparison with Shakespeare's text remains to be done, but I estimate that the interlinear cutting amounts to somewhat over half of the text.

70. Robertson Davies, "*A Midsummer Night's Dream,*" in *The Stratford Scene, 1958–1968,* ed. Peter Raby (Toronto: Clarke, Irwin, 1968), 181.

71. Katherine Best, "Puck in Luck," *Stage* (May 1935), 24–26.

72. Jorgens, *Shakespeare on Film*, 45.

73. Of the five publicity stills reproduced here to represent the film, only this one does not seem to come from a frame in the prints of the film I have seen.

74. Souvenir program, Reinhardt film, Robert Hamilton Ball papers, Folger Shakespeare Library.

75. Jorgens, *Shakespeare on Film*, 47.

76. Interview with Reinhardt in the *Neues Wiener Journal*, 25 July 1935, cited in Fuhrich and Prossnitz, 175.

77. Sidney W. Carroll, *Times*, 10 October 1935, and *Sunday Times*, 13 October 1935.

78. Roger Manvell, *Shakespeare and the Film* (New York: Praeger, 1971), 26.

79. Fred K. Prieberg, *Musik in NS-Staat* (Frankfurt: Fischer, 1982), 144; Werner, 38. Prieberg devotes a full chapter, entitled "Ein Sommernachtstraum — arish," to the Mendelssohn story.

80. Prieberg, 157–158.

81. Ibid., 163, 159.

82. Letter of 10 June 1938, from Orff to Fritz Krebs, a major figure in the National Socialist Worker's Party in Frankfurt, reproduced in Ibid., 159.

83. Carl Orff, "Musik zum Sommernachtstraum," *Shakespeare-Jahrbuch* 100 (1964), 117–134.

84. Ibid., 133; Stanley Sadie, ed., *The New Grove Dictionary of Music and Musicians* (London: Macmillan, 1980), 13, 709. On the Bochum production, directed by Sellner and derivative of his 1952 staging, with new scenery by Franz Merz, see Wolfgang Stroedel, "9th Anniversary Celebration of the Deutsche Shakespeare-Gesellschaft," *Shakespeare Quarterly* 5 (1954), 317–322. For information on the Orff scores, see Gootch and Thatcher, 2: 1033–1034.

85. Andreas Liess, *Carl Orff*, trans. Adelheid and Herbert Parkin (New York: St. Martin's Press, 1966), 107–110. Liess provides a characterization of the later work. He reports that three Orff scores have been published, but I have not been able to examine these. To my knowledge, no performance of his score for the play has ever been recorded.

86. Ibid., 109.

87. *Variety*, 6 December 1939, 50; *New York Amsterdam News*, 25 November 1939.

88. *New York Herald Tribune*, 26 November 1939.

89. *Variety*, 6 December, 1939; the Freeman sketch is in the *New York Herald Tribune*, 26 November 1939; *New York Daily News*, 30 November 1939; *New York Times*, 24 November 1939.

90. Brooks Atkinson, *New York Times*, Richard Watts Jr., *New York Herald Tribune*, and John Mason Brown, *New York Post*, 30 November 1939.

91. Donald Bogli, *Toms, Coons, Mulattoes, Mammies, and Bucks, an Interpretive History of Blacks in American Film* (New York: Continuum [Ungar], 1989), 38–44.

92. Ibid., 75.

93. Brooks Atkinson, *New York Times*, and John Chapman, *New York Daily News*, 30 November 1939.

94. *New York Times*, 10 December 1939.

95. Guthrie's program note, cited in Audrey Williamson, *Old Vic Drama* (London: Rockliff, 1948), 77.

96. Farjeon, 46–47; Williamson, 78–79; Williams, *Old Vic Saga*, 157, 165 — photo of the young lovers.

97. Reginald P. Mander, "Stage History of 'The Dream,'" note in the souvenir program of the 1954 Old Vic production, private collection.

98. Williams, *Old Vic Saga*, 157.

99. Williamson, 80; Williams, *Old Vic Saga*, 157.

100. Harold Hobson, *Theatre 2* (London, 1950), journal entry for 23 April 1949.

101. My description is based partially on the production photographs in the Shakespeare Centre Library; ten were published in Angus McBean's *The Shakespeare Memorial Theatre* (London: Reinhardt and Evans, 1951).

102. Kemp and Trewin, 234–235. Other reviews of the 1949 production that I have consulted include *Birmingham Post Dispatch*, *Manchester Guardian*, and *Daily Telegraph*, 25 April 1949; *Sunday Times* and *Times*, 24 April 1949; *Punch*, 4 May 1949; and *Royal Leamington Spa Courier*, 29 April 1949.

103. Souvenir program, Old Vic 1954, Crawford Theatre Collection, Yale University. This was one of two such ads in the program; the other showed a ballerina on stage in a bra-slip.

104. Una Ellis Fermor, *Frontiers* (London: Methuen, 1945), 40–45.

105. James Agate, *Sunday Times*, 21 January 1945. Other reviews consulted include W. A. Darlington, *New York Times*, 25 March 1945; *Times*, 26 January 1945; and Ivor Brown, *Observer*, 28 January 1945. The *Sketch* carried ten photographs of the production on 21 March.

106. Ronald Hayman, *John Gielgud* (New York, 1971), 147.

107. Ibid.

108. Ivor Brown, *Observer*, 28 January 1945.

109. James Agate, *Sunday Times*, 4 February 1945.

110. *Sketch*, 16 January 1952; Ivor Brown, *Observer*, 30 December 1951.

111. Photo feature on the "air-lifting" of the scenery to New York, *New York Times*, 1 September 1954.

112. *New York Times*, 19 October 1954. The production played twenty-nine performances at the Metropolitan Opera, with a gross of $380,000, which the *Times* reported as record-breaking.

113. Walter Kerr, *New York Herald Tribune*, 23 September 1954; Brooks Atkinson, *New York Times*, John McClain, *New York Journal American*, Richard Watts Jr., *New York Post*, John Chapman, *New York Daily News*, Robert Coleman, *New York Daily Mirror*, William Hawkins, *New York World Telegram and Sun*, 22 September 1954; Arthur Colby Sprague, "Shakespeare and the New York Stage, 1954–1955," *Shakespeare Quarterly* 6 (1955), 423–427; Alan Downer, "A Comparison of Two Stagings: Stratford-upon-Avon and London," *Shakespeare Quarterly* 6 (1955), 428–429.

114. Walter Kerr, *New York Herald Tribune*, 23 September 1954.

115. Ibid.

116. Souvenir program, Crawford Theatre Collection, Yale University. According to this text, Benthall, like Daly over half a century before, omitted the scene of the reunion of the mechanicals.

117. Richard David, "Plays Pleasant and Plays Unpleasant," *Shakespeare Survey* 8 (1955), 136–137.

118. *Sunday Observer*, 28 March 1954. Other reviews consulted include *Times, Birmingham Gazette*, and *Daily Worker*, 24 March 1954; *Daily Telegraph* and *Bolton Evening News*, 26 March 1954; *New Statesman* and *Evesham Journal*, 27 March 1954; and *Times*, 1 April 1954.

119. Roberta Kerensky Cooper, *The American Shakespeare Festival Theatre* (Washington, D.C.: Folger Books, 1986), 34, 14, 56.

120. See chapter 7.

121. John Houseman and Jack Landau, *The American Shakespeare Festival: The Birth of a Theatre* (New York: Simon and Schuster, 1959), 67–68, with four photographs; Cooper, 35–36.

122. Clair McGlinchee, "Stratford, Connecticut, Shakespeare Festival, 1958," *Shakespeare Quarterly* 9 (1958), 541.

123. Cooper, 70.

124. At Ashton's death in 1988, *Washington Post* dance critic Alan M. Kriegsman wrote that "Ashton was to British ballet what Shakespeare was to British drama and Handel was to British music" ("Steps of a Giant," *Washington Post*, 20 August 1988).

125. George Balanchine and Francis Mason, *Balanchine's Complete Stories of the Great Ballets*, rev. ed. (Garden City, N.Y.: Doubleday, 1977).

126. Ibid., 359–360. Balanchine notes that in his seventies, he was still able to recite passages from the play in Russian.

127. Ibid., 360. These are, in the first act, the overtures to *Athalie, The Fair Melusine*, and *The First Walpurgis Night* and, in the second act, *Symphony No. 9* and the overture to *Son and Stranger*.

128. A revival of the 1976–1977 season was recorded in a published collection of seventy photographs by Martha Swope in Nancy Lassalle, ed., *"A Midsummer Night's Dream," the Story of the New York City Ballet's Production* (New York: Dodd, Mead, 1977).

129. Anna Kisselgoff, "In That Woodsy Dream with a Mystical Donkey," *New York Times*, 22 June 1995.

130. Igor Stravinsky and Robert Craft, *Dialogues and a Diary* (London, 1968), 115n.

131. Space does not allow discussion here of a minor twentieth-century opera inspired by the play, Marcel Delannoy's 1950 *Puck, an opera féerique en trois actes.* . . . For further information, see Carroll and Williams, entries T1001A, T1107A, and T1128.

132. Peter Evans, *The Music of Benjamin Britten* (Minneapolis: University of Minnesota Press, 1979), 256.

133. Christina Burridge, "'Music Such as Charmeth Sleep': Benjamin Britten's *A Midsummer Night's Dream*," *University of Toronto Quarterly* 51 (1981–1982), 149; see also Peter Evans, "Britten's New Opera: A Preview," *Tempo* 53–56 (1960), 34–35 (Evans later modified his analysis, as noted later).

134. Philip Hope-Wallace, *Guardian*, 4 February 1961; *New York Times*, 13 June 1960; Eric Walter White compares Britten's accomplishment to Verdi's in chapter 11 of his *Benjamin Britten, His Life and Operas* (Los Angeles: University of California Press, 1970). See also the reviews in *Musical America*, September 1960; and *New Yorker*, 25 February 1961. The list of reviews offering such praise could be extended considerably.

135. Christopher Headington, *Peter Pears: A Biography* (London: Faber and Faber, 1992), 200.

136. Evans, *The Music of Benjamin Britten*, 236–237.

137. Pears preferred the implied pronunciation of the Quarto spelling (White, *Benjamin Britten*, 194).

138. For my discussion, I have drawn on the 1967 Decca recording of the opera, conducted by Britten; on Imogene Holst and Martin Penney, eds., *A Midsummer Night's Dream, Opera in Three Acts*, Op. 64 by Benjamin Britten (London: Hawkes and Son, 1960); and on Benjamin Britten, *A Midsummer Night's Dream: Vocal Score* (London: Boosey and Hawkes, 1960).

139. Philip Hope-Wallace, *Guardian*, 4 February 1961.

140. Burridge, 150.

141. *Daily Mail*, 3 February 1961. On Oberlin, see also *Guardian*, 4 February 1961; *Times*, 2 February 1961. On Deller, see *New York Times*, 13 June 1960; *Spectator* 204 (24 June 1960), 918; *Musical Times*, 101 (August 1960), 503; *Musical America* 30 (September 1960), 25.

142. Evans, *The Music of Benjamin Britten*, 239, 256.

143. Anthony Tommasini, *New York Times*, 24 November 1996.

144. Evans, *The Music of Bejamin Britten*, 237.

145. William Godsalve, *Britten's* A Midsummer Night's Dream: *Making an Opera from Shakespeare's Comedy* (Madison, [N.J.]: Fairleigh Dickinson University Press, [1995]), see chapters 2 through 5 for an extensive analysis of the reshaping of the libretto.

146. Anthony Tommasini, *New York Times*, 24 November 1996. As we have seen, the eighteenth century, too, used *Pyramus and Thisbe* to parody operatic form, although in skits detached from the play.

147. Burridge, 158–159.

148. See, for example, Gary Schmigall, *Literature as Opera* (New York: Oxford University Press, 1977), 5; and Evans, *The Music of Benjamin Britten*, 236. For a table of performances, 1960–1988, see Godsalve, appendix A, with supplementary notes on performances in the United States and the United Kingdom, 1988–1992.

9. Postmodernism: "The Fierce Vexation of a Dream"

1. Cited in Arthur Holmberg, "Erotic Dreams," *American Theatre* (April 1989), 15–16.

2. For a list of the cities, see Glenn Loney, ed., *Peter Brook's Production of William Shakespeare's* A Midsummer Night's Dream *for the Royal Shakespeare Company* (Chicago: Dramatic Publishing Company, 1974), 104.

3. John Russell Brown (*Free Shakespeare* [London: Heinemann, 1973]), for example, offered a critique of some of the more egregious examples of the contempory treatments of the plays and seemed to advocate returning to what he saw as the idyllic, directorless Elizabethan acting ensemble. See especially chapters 6 and 8.

4. Robert Weimann, "Shakespeare on the Modern Stage: Past Significance and Present Meaning," *Shakespeare Survey* 20 (1967), 115; Weimann's full argument came in his 1967 *Shakespeare und die Tradition des Volkstheaters*, published in East Berlin. This was translated and updated as *Shakespeare and the Popular Tradition in the Theatre: Studies in the Social Dimension of Dramatic Form and Function*, trans. and ed. Robert Schwartz (Baltimore: Johns Hopkins University Press, 1978).

5. Tyrone Guthrie, *A Life in the Theatre* (New York: McGraw-Hill, 1959), 210.

6. The development wants analysis, as Dennis Kennedy has noted in his overview of it (*Looking at Shakespeare*, 157–164).

7. Herbert Whittaker, *Toronto Globe and Mail*, 29 June 1960.

8. Michael Langham, "Introduction/Twelve Years at Stratford," in Raby, 12.

9. Peter Hall, "Shakespeare and the Modern Director," in *The Royal Shakespeare Company 1960–1963* (London, 1964), 41–46. For overviews of Hall's RSC work, see David Addenbrook, *The Royal Shakespeare Company: The Peter Hall Years* (London, 1974); and Beauman, chapters 10 and 11.

10. Review by W. A. Darlington, *Daily Telegraph*, 3 June 1959.

11. Lewis Funke, "Stage Is a World to Avon Director," *New York Times*, 31 August 1959.

12. John Russell Brown, "Three Adaptations," *Shakespeare Survey* 13 (1960), 143.

13. Muriel St. Clare Byrne, "Shakespeare at Stratford-upon-Avon, 1959," *Shakespeare Quarterly* 10 (Autumn 1959), 554–556.

14. Based on production photographs, Shakespeare Centre Library, Stratford-upon-Avon.

15. *Observer* and *Sunday Times*, 7 June 1959.

16. Photographs, RSC souvenir program of the 1962 revival, Crawford Theatre Collection, Yale University.

17. Kenneth Tynan, *Curtains* (New York, 1961), 239. For a photograph by Angus McBean of Laughton as the translated Bottom, see Ivor Brown, *The Shakespeare Memorial Theatre, a Photographic Record* (London: Max Reinhardt, 1959).

18. St. Clare Byrne, 554–556.

19. Tynan, 238.

20. Reviews of the 1962 and 1963 productions consulted include *Shakespeare Quarterly* 12 (1962), 514–515; *Times*, and *New York Times*, 18 April 1962; *Observer*, 22 April 1962; *Times*, *Guardian*, *Evening News*, *Daily Mail*, and *Daily Express*, 14 June 1963; *Sunday Times*, 16 June 1963; and *Shakespeare Survey* 16 (1963), 143–151. For fuller lists of reviews of this and other productions discussed in this chapter (through 1983), see the appropriate entries in Carroll and Williams.

21. For a full description and analysis of Hall's 1969 film, see Jorgens's *Shakespeare on Film*, chapter 3 and 255–258. See also Manvell, chapter 10; and Peter Hall, "Why the Fairies Have Dirty Faces," *Sunday Times*, 26 January 1969. For a discussion analyzing the text in relation to directorial choices in both the 1959 production and the 1969 film, see Roger Warren, A Midsummer Night's Dream: *Text and Performance* (London: Macmillan, 1983), 47–54.

22. *Times*, 18 April 1962.

23. Beauman, 238.

24. *Times*, 18 April 1962 and 14 June 1963; Tynan, *Observer*, 22 April 1962.

25. *Times*, 14 June 1963.

26. Brooks Atkinson, *New York Times*, 30 June 1960; Arnold Edinborough, *Shakespeare Quarterly* 11 (1960), 455–459.

27. John Gardiner, *Windsor Star*, 29 June 1960.

28. Based on photographs of the production in the Stratford Festival Archives.

29. Kenneth Tynan, *Observer*, 25 December 1960.

30. *Times*, 25 January 1962; *Observer*, 28 January 1962; other reviews consulted include *Spectator* and *New Statesman*, 2 February 1962; and *Illustrated London News*, 10 February 1962.

31. Tony Richardson, "Spare, Simple and Naive," *Plays and Players* 9 (February 1962), 5.

32. Irving Wardle, *Observer*, 10 June 1962. Other reviews consulted include *Times*, 5 June 1962; and *New York Times*, 2 July 1962. The production was revived in 1963 with similar reviews, for example, *Times*, 18 July 1963; *Observer*, 21 July 1963; and *Plays and Players* 10 (September 1963), 47.

33. *New York Times*, 30 June 1964; *New York Times*, 12 July 1964; *New York Herald Tribune*, 16 October 1964.

34. A study of the mobile theatre by sociologists, sponsored by Papp to see if the production was reaching the masses, suggested that the effort was rather patronizing ("To bring an integrated cast to a Negro neighborhood is to say 'you, too, belong'") and noted that *Blues for Mr. Charlie*, recently seen by most of the blacks in the audience, had had more of an impact than *A Midsummer Night's Dream* (Richard Faust and Charles Kadushin, *Shakespeare in the Neighborhood: Audience Reaction to* A Midsummer Night's Dream *as Produced by Joseph Papp for the Delacorte Mobile Theatre* [New York: Twentieth Century Fund, 1965], 33, 37).

35. I am grateful to Barbara Mowatt, editor of *Shakespeare Quarterly*, for her memory of this show. It aired in England in May and June and was shown in the United States in November. A photograph of the performance is in Mark Lewisohn, *The Complete Beatles Chronicle* (New York: Harmony Books, 1992), 159.

36. *Babes in the Woods*, a musical adaptation with music and lyrics by Rick Besoyan, opened on 28 December 1964 at the Orpheum Theatre, New York City, directed by Besoyan. The libretto was published by Broad Play Publishing in 1984.

37. Antonin Artaud, *The Theatre and Its Double*, trans. Mary Caroline Richards (New York: Grove Press, 1958). Key chapters are "The Theatre and the Plague," "On the Balinese Theatre," and "No More Masterpieces." A good, brief summary is in Marvin Carlson, *Theories of the Theatre*, expanded ed. (Ithaca, N.Y.: Cornell University Press, 1993), 392–393.

38. Kott.

39. Brecht actually uses the adjective to describe opera in his notes to the *Aufsteig und Fall der stadt Mahagonny*, in *Brecht on Theatre*, ed. John Willett (New York: Hill and Wang, 1964), 33.

40. Studies are needed on the influence of Artaud, Kott, and Brecht on Shakespearean production in general.

41. Artaud, 7.

42. Ibid., 13, 74–83, 76.

43. For Artaud's influence on Mnounchkine, see Adrian Kiernander, *Ariane Mnouchkine and the Théâtre du Soleil* (Cambridge: Cambridge University Press, 1993), 5, 36, 60. For Artaud's influence on Brook, see Peter Brook, *The Empty Space* (New York: Avon Books, 1968), where he writes (in chapter 2) of creating a group within the RSC to experiment with Artaud's ideas, an experiment assisted by Charles Marowitz and which resulted in, among other things, the 1963 production of Peter Weiss's *The Persecution and Assassination of Marat as Performed by the Inmates of the Asylum of Charenton under the Direction of the Marquis de Sade*. See also Beauman, 272–277.

44. Samuel Leiter, ed., *Shakespeare around the Globe* (New York: Greenwood Press, 1986), 484–485; Dennis Kennedy, ed. *Foreign Shakespeare* (Cambridge: Cambridge University Press, 1993), 10.

45. Kott, 220.

46. Ibid., 219.

47. Kennedy, *Foreign Shakespeare*, 9.

48. The Actor's Workshop production opened at the Marines Theatre on 11 March 1966, at the Pittsburgh Playhouse on 25 November 1966, and at the Theatre De Lys on 29 June 1967 (with major cast changes each time). Theodore Mann and Paul Libin offered it in New York as a Circle in the Square production. John Willis, ed., *Theatre World* (New York, 1967), 212; playbills for the Pittsburgh Playhouse and the Theatre De Lys, Billy Rose Theatre Collection, NYPL.

49. Production photographs and Virgina Allen's "Introduction," in *jim dine designs for* A

Midsummer Night's Dream, ed. William S. Lieberman (New York: Museum of Modern Art, 1968), 30, 5–8; Gordon Gow, "A Feeling in the Throat," *Films and Filming* 25 (1979), 13 (interview with Hancock on the occasion of the release of his film *California Dreaming*). In 1970, Jorgens ("Studies in the Criticism and Stage History of *A Midsummer Night's Dream*") provided the first lengthy characterization and discussion of this production.

50. Michael Smith, *Village Voice*, 6 July 1967.

51. The production, at the Jan Hus Auditorium, was directed by Norman Peck. Robert Rietz played Theseus and Oberon and Mel Dowd played Hippolyta and Titania. Philip Lawrence also doubled as Philostrate and Puck. Brooks Atkinson, *New York Times*, 14 January 1956.

52. Gow, 13; *New York Times*, 30 June 1967; Alan N. Bunce, *Christian Science Monitor*, 3 July 1967.

53. *Sen Noci Svatojanske [A Midsummer Night's Dream]* was an eighty-minute, 35-mm animated film in Cinemascope, with puppets. The 1961 re-release with an English sound track was narrated by Burton and featured Jack Gwylim as Oberon, Barabara Jefford as Titania, and Alec McCowen as Bottom.

54. Donna Lange, *Valley Independent* [Pittsburgh], 29 November 1966; Allen, 5.

55. Dine design for Titania, Museum of Modern Art, New York; *New York Times*, 30 June 1967; Mildred C. Kuner, *Shakespeare Quarterly* 18 (1967), 412.

56. *Pittsburgh Post-Gazette*, 28 November 1966; *Village Voice*, 6 July 1967.

57. Gow, 13.

58. *Village Voice*, 6 July 1967.

59. Designs for Snout, Quince, Snug, and Bottom and a production photograph of them, in Lieberman, 24–29.

60. George Oppenheimer, *Newsday*, and Dan Sullivan, *New York Times*, 30 June 1967; *Variety*, 5 July 1967; *Shakespeare Quarterly* 18 (1967), 411–415; see also Richard Cooke, *Wall Street Journal*, 1 July 1967; Jerry Tallmer, *New York Post*, 5 July 1967; Whitney Bolton, *Morning Telegraph*, 1 July 1967; and Allen, 8.

61. Dan Sullivan, *New York Times*, 30 June 1967.

62. See Robert Hughes, *The Shock of the New* (New York: Alfred A. Knopf, 1982), 365–366 and chapter 8, passim; and Hilton Kramer, *The Age of the Avant-Garde* (New York: Farrar, Straus, 1973).

63. This point has been made by many, including Margaret Croyden, who traces the developments in her *Lunatics, Lovers & Poets, the Contemporary Experimental Theatre* (New York: McGraw Hill, 1974).

64. For a discussion of the production and its reception, see Iris Smith, "Mabou Mines's *Lear*: A Narrative of Collective Authorship," *Theatre Journal* 45 (1993), 279–302, especially 290–296; see also Gary Jay Williams, "Queen Lear: Reason Not the Need," *Theater* 22 (1990–1991), 75–78.

65. The essay was later republished in Susan Sontag, *Against Interpretation* (New York: Dell, 1967), 275–292.

66. See chapter 1.

67. Although I use some poststructural terms in describing the production, I do not mean to suggest that Hancock was influenced by Jacques Derrida and poststructural theory. This production does intersect in time, however, with Derrida's groundbreaking lecture at Johns Hopkins University in 1967, "Structure, Sign and Play in the Discourse of the Human Sciences." "After the rupture," writes Derrida, "it was necessary to begin thinking that there was no center, that the center could not be thought in the form of a present-being, that the center had no natural site, that it was not a fixed locus but a function, a sort of nonlocus in

which an infinite number of sign-substitutions came into play." "Structure, Sign, and Play," in *Critical Theory Since 1965*, ed. Hazard Adams and Leroy Searle (Tallahassee: Florida State University Press, 1986), 83–94. Derrida's *De la grammatologie* was also published in 1967 (translated into English by Gayatri C. Spivak in 1976).

68. Michael Smith, *Village Voice*, 6 July 1967.

69. Andreas Huyssen, "Mapping the Postmodern," *New German Critique* 33 (1984), 16.

70. Allan Lewis, "*A Midsummer Night's Dream* — Fairy Fantasy or Erotic Nightmare?" *Educational Theatre Journal* 21 (1969), 257.

71. Ibid., 256–257; Walter Kerr, *New York Times*, 18 June 1967; Julius Novick, *Nation*, 25 September 1967; Bernard Beckerman, "The Season at Stratford, Connecticut, 1967," *Shakespeare Quarterly* 18 (1967), 406–407.

72. Kiernander discusses the influences of Vilar, Copeau, Artaud, and Kott on Mnouchkine at various points in his account; see especially his overview, 3–6. See also the characterization of Mnouchkine and the company's work in Claude Roy, "Ariane Soleil," *Double Page* 21 (1982), [3–11], with photographs by Martine Franck of *Richard II* and *La nuit des roi*; and in Ruby Cohn, "Ariane Mnouchkine: Twenty-one Years of *Théâtre du Soleil*," *Theater* 27 (Winter 1985), 78–84.

73. Following her success with *The Kitchen*, she won a government subsidy of one hundred thousand francs that helped make her production of *A Midsummer Night's Dream* possible (Kiernander, 70).

74. Ibid., 51–57; David Bradby and David Williams, *Directors' Theatre* (London: Macmillan, 1988), 84–87.

75. Conversation with René Saurel, cited by Kiernander from Jean-Pierre Bégot, "Recherches sur une création collective au Théâtre du Soleil, *Les Clowns*" (Master's thesis, Institut d'Etudes Théâtrales, 1968–1969), 215.

76. Kiernander, 58.

77. Ibid., 59–62, photographs 10 and 11; Marie-Louise Bablet and Dennis Bablet, *Le Théâtre du Soleil ou la quête du bonheur* (Paris: CNRS, 1979), 29; Roy, [7].

78. Kiernander, 59; Pierre Lacreux, *Theater der Zeit* 23 (November 1968), 30; Bradby and Williams, 87.

79. B. Poiret-Delpech, *Le Monde*, 24 January 1968; Nicole Zand, *Le Monde*, 13 February 1968.

80. Henri Gouhier, "L'Année Claudel. *Le Songe d'une Nuit d'Eté*," *La Table Ronde* 244 (May–June 1968), 92–93; August Strindberg, "*A Midsummer Night's Dream*," in *Open Letters to the Intimate Theatre*, trans. Walter Johnson (Seattle: University of Washington Press, [1966]), 223. Strindberg also notices other dark threads in the "complex" play in his essay, written about 1908: Puck "muddles the intrigue" so that the action becomes "nightmarishly twisted"; Theseus has conquered Hippolyta by sword; Hermia is condemned to marry Demetrius under pain of death or the convent; and in general, the course of love never runs smoothly. Strindberg also praises parts of Carl August Hagsberg's translation as superior to the original.

81. Lacreux, 30.

82. Gouhier, 93.

83. Bradby and Williams, 87–88.

84. Caution is wanted, of course, in the attributions of "influence" throughout this discussion. The creative process is often one of unconscious assimilation and the irrational synthesis of many sources and not subject to any arithmetic. Mnouchkine herself has said that the influence of Artaud on her was "not conscious," that when she first read him, "I realized that I wanted to find by myself what he had discovered already. . . . And so I didn't keep on

reading him. I only read him quite recently, and some of what he says is exactly what I need, in a way." (Kiernander, 141).

85. Mnouchkine's oriental appropriations elsewhere have raised postcolonial issues. For an attempt at critical distinctions on the subject of intercultural productions in our era, see Patrice Pavis, *Theatre at the Crossroads of Culture* (London: Routledge, 1992), especially chapter 8.

86. Jacques Derrida, *Writing and Difference*, trans. Alan Bass (Chicago: University of Chicago Press, 1978), chapters 6 and 8.

87. Bablet and Bablet, 30.

88. Kiernander, 63.

89. J. W. Lambert, "Plays in Performance," *Drama* 87 (Winter 1967), 18–31; Irving Wardle, *Times*, 22 August 1967; *Observer*, 27 August 1967.

90. The program (Stratford Festival Archives) offered brief notes by Hirsch; his preproduction working notes were published in Raby, 176–178. His program notes barely hint at the Kottian vision that informs the first part of his preproduction notes. Dan Sullivan thought Hirsch was influenced by Kott (*New York Times*, 13 June 1968).

91. Arnold Edinborough, "Stratford, Ontario — 1968," *Shakespeare Quarterly* 19 (1968), 381–384.

92. Dan Sullivan, *New York Times*, 13 June 1968. So, too, do Hirsch's preproduction notes begin in Kott-like vision but move toward conventional romantic concerns and conclusions, for example, "The lovers emerge from their forest dream with greater self-knowledge; the eyes and the mind, the senses and imagination have been reconciled" (Raby, 178).

93. Other reviews consulted for this production include Herbert Whittaker, *Toronto Globe and Mail*, 13 June 1968; *Toronto Star* and *Toronto Telegram*, 13 June 1968; Walter Kerr, *New York Times*, 23 June 1968; and Richard Coe, *Washington Post*, 13 June 1968.

94. The production opened on 27 August 1970 at the Royal Shakespeare Theatre, Stratford-upon-Avon; on 20 January 1971 at the Billy Rose Theatre, New York; and in June 1971 in London. The world tour was in 1972–1973.

95. Lionel Trilling, *Sincerity and Authenticity* (Cambridge: Harvard University Press, 1971), 169 and chapter 6, passim.

96. Brook, 88.

97. Ibid., 103.

98. Peter Ansorge, "Director in Interview: Peter Brook," *Plays and Players* 18 (October 1970), 18.

99. John Kane, "Plotting with Peter," *Flourish* [RSC newspaper] 2, (Summer 1971), [5, 6]. The essay is also reprinted in Loney. A full account of the rehearsals, accompanied by the texts of the scenes they explored, is in David Selbourne, *The Making of Peter Brook's* "A Midsummer Night's Dream" (London: Methuen, 1982); it includes twenty-four photographs of the final production.

100. Kane, [5].

101. Ansorge, 19.

102. Nunn has said: "Our sense of discovery made us use our theatre in a new way — new to us — a big white void, a free-ranging use of the space defined only by the actors' use of it, a celebration of what was consciously allegoric in the play and not an uncomfortable naturalistically localized series of symbolic nudges" (in Judith Cook, *Director's Theatre* [London: Harrap, 1974], 117).

103. John Mahoney, "Even Dreams Need Technicians to Make the Magic Happen," in Loney, 87.

104. Jacobs's original design did not include the vertical slots in the middle of the right

and left walls, which were necessary in the final setting to accommodate the dropping of a fire curtain, so far downstage was the whole structure placed. When installed, they were made just wide enough for entrances. See Sally Jacobs's essay on the design process in Loney, 49.

105. My account is drawn from my own viewings of the production at the Eisenhower Theatre, Kennedy Center, Washington, D.C., in April 1973; from the photographs and the business and blocking production book in the Shakespeare Centre Library, Stratford-upon-Avon (71.21/1970 MND/S.1435); and from Loney. (The latter is a conflation of notes from the original and the touring productions. I have indicated some of the differences in the notes.) I have also consulted fifty reviews of the production in England and the United States, a number of which are cited later. Others will be found in Carroll and Williams, entry T1314.

106. Walter Kerr, *New York Times*, 31 January 1971.

107. This was not the case on the world tour, perhaps because of the danger the stilts posed in varying conditions.

108. Irving Wardle, *Times*, 12 June 1971 (at the Aldwich). Among the other critics who praised the delivery explicitly were Herbert Kretzmer, *Daily Express*, 28 August 1970; Peter Roberts, *Plays and Players* 18 (October 1970), 43; Peter Thomson, "A Necessary Theatre: The Royal Shakespeare Season 1970 Reviewed," *Shakespeare Survey* 24 (1971), 125; Jack Kroll, *Newsweek*, 1 February 1971; Martin Gottfried, *Women's Wear Daily*, 22 January 1971; and John J. O'Connor, *Wall Street Journal*, 22 January 1971.

109. Walter Kerr, *New York Times*, 31 January 1971.

110. Thomson, 125.

111. Oberon's incantation, "What thou seest when thou dost wake" (2.2.33), was inserted after the first chorus of the fairies' song (Loney, 30b).

112. Ansorge, 19.

113. Croyden, 253.

114. John Russell Brown, "Free Shakespeare," *Shakespeare Survey* 24 (1971), 133.

115. Croyden, 254. Croyden offers a lengthy characterization of the whole production (251–258).

116. I take the era of the 1960s in America to be the years bracketed by the assassination of John F. Kennedy in 1963 and the resignation, amid the Watergate scandal, of Richard M. Nixon in 1974.

117. The differences between the Quarto and Folio touching this issue are explained in chapter 1, with consideration of Barbara Hodgdon's theory.

118. Loney, 67b; the scene was played this way in the Washington, D.C., performances that I saw.

119. Ansorge, 18–19.

120. "MSND at the Drama Desk: Peter Brook and Major Players Discuss the Production in New York," in Loney, 31.

121. This was the business in the two Kennedy Center performances I witnessed in April 1973.

122. The actors who played the mechanicals were: Quince, Philip Locke; Flute, Glynne Lewis; Snout, Norman Rodway (Patrick Stewart in the New York production); Starveling, Terrence Hardiman; and Snug, Barry Stanton.

123. Thomson, 125; Roberts, 42.

124. Harold Hobson, *Sunday Times*, 30 August 1970; Jack Kroll, *Newsweek*, 1 February 1971; Clive Barnes, *New York Times*, 28 August 1970; Barnes also reviewed the New York opening on 22 January 1971.

125. Stanley Kauffmann, *New Republic*, 20 February 1971, in Stanley Kauffmann, *Persons of the Drama, Theatre Criticism and Comment* (New York: Harper and Row, 1976), 57–58.

126. Walter Kerr, *New York Times*, 31 January 1971.

127. Benedict Nightingale, *New Statesman*, 4 September 1970.

128. Douglas Watt, *Daily News*, 31 January 1971.

129. Promptbook, Shakespeare Centre Library, Stratford-upon-Avon. This was true of the tour performances that I witnessed at the Kennedy Center in Washington, D.C. I followed the text closely during one performance and found no lines cut; some were slightly rearranged in sequence, and a few lines were set to music; both kinds of alterations are noted earlier in my account.

130. John Simon, *New York Magazine*, 21 February 1971.

131. Brown, "Free Shakespeare," 133; John Simon, *Uneasy Stages* (New York: Random House, 1976), 318–319. For other negative critiques of the production, see T. A. Kalem, *Time*, 1 February 1971; and Richard Proudfoot, "Peter Brook and Shakespeare," in *Drama and Mimesis*, ed. James Redmond (Cambridge: Cambridge University Press, 1980), 157–189.

132. Jonathan Miller, introduction to the broadcast of the BBC Television Shakespeare series production of *A Midsummer Night's Dream*, directed by Elija Moshinsky, 1981.

133. William Henry III, "Moonbeams and Menaces," *Time*, 26 August 1985, 65 (review of Liviu Ciulei's production at the Guthrie Theatre).

134. Joseph Morgenstern, *New York Herald Tribune*, 3 August 1961.

135. Jean Peterson, *Shakespeare Bulletin* (Winter 1993), 13–14; Mel Gussow, *New York Times*, 2 August 1991.

136. Lawrence Guntner, "Brecht and Beyond: Shakespeare on the East German Stage," in Kennedy, *Foreign Shakespeare*, 122–123.

137. Maik Hamburger, "New Concepts of Staging *A Midsummer Night's Dream*," *Shakespeare Survey* 40 (1988), 53; Guntner, 128–129. Hamburger's essay is accompanied by five photographs of German productions of the 1970s and 1980s.

138. Guntner, 123.

139. For some of these details, I am grateful to the notes of Gary Taylor, who saw the Lang production in 1986.

140. Martin Linzer, "*A Midsummer Night's Dream* in East Germany," *Drama Review* 25 (1984), 45–54.

141. Guntner, 125, 123–126, photographs 4 and 5.

142. Ibid., 127.

143. Hamburger, 59; Linzer, 52.

144. Linzer, 49–52.

145. Guntner, 127.

146. For allusions to or brief descriptions of other continental productions in the 1970s and 1980s, see Leiter, 466–470, 484–485, 488–491, 493–494.

147. Mike Steele, "For His Guthrie Finale, Ciulei Picks a 'Dream,'" *Minneapolis Star and Tribune*, 26 July 1985.

148. Robert Brustein, *New Republic*, 23 September 1985, 33; Henry, 65.

149. Henry, 65; Thomas Clayton, "Shakespeare at the Guthrie," *Shakespeare Quarterly* 37 (1986), 230–231.

150. Clayton, 231.

151. Cited in Holmberg, 16.

152. Brustein, 33.

153. Clayton, 233.

154. Henry, 65.

155. Brustein, 33.

156. Steven LaVigne, KFAI, 8 August 1985, cited in Clayton, 236.

157. Hap Erstein, "Romanian Director's 'Dream' Is Dark Vision," *Washington Times*, 28 September 1989.

158. Hap Erstein, *Washington Times*, and David Richards, *Washington Post*, 9 September 1989; also, Louise Sweeney, *Christian Science Monitor*, 24 October 1989 (Arena Stage production); Mel Gussow, *New York Times*, 15 July 1986; and Moira Hodgson, *Nation*, 30 August 1986 (Pepsico production).

159. Frank Rich, *New York Times*, 4 October 1989.

160. Holmberg, 17.

161. Mel Gussow, *New York Times*, 15 May 1975.

162. Holmberg, 17.

163. Other reviews from which my characterization has been drawn are, for the Yale production: Walter Kerr, *New York Times*, 25 May 1975; Michael Feingold, *New York Times*, 8 June 1975 (rejoinder to Kerr's review); Harold Clurman, *Nation*, 31 May 1975; and Jack Kroll, *Newsweek*, 20 October 1975; for the ART production: Mel Gussow, *New York Times*, 24 March 1980; Jack Kroll, *Newsweek*, 24 April 1980; and Elizabeth Hageman, *Shakespeare Quarterly* 32 (1981), 190–193.

164. Holmberg, 15–16.

165. Ibid., 14.

166. Ibid.

167. Souvenir progam of the Stratford Festival, 1977, Stratford Festival Archives, presumably by the literary manager, Urjo Kareda. The 1976 program notes on the production emphasized the associations of the play with a court wedding but did not yet develop the idea of the play as Elizabeth's dream.

168. Warren, 62.

169. Ralph Berry, "Stratford Festival, Canada," *Shakespeare Quarterly* 29 (1978), 222–226.

170. Warren, 62.

171. Berry, 222–226.

172. The first and last phrases are from Audrey M. Ashley, *Ottawa Citizen*, 7 June 1977; the middle phrase is from Ronald Bryden, "A Former Light Restored," *Macleans*, 11 July 1977, 58.

173. Richard Eder, *New York Times*, 8 June 1977.

174. Kevin Kelly, *Boston Globe*, 8 June 1977.

175. Bryden, 58. Others critical of the concept were Audrey Ashley, *Ottawa Citizen*, 7 June 1977; John Fraser, *Toronto Globe and Mail*, 8 June 1977; Maureen Peterson, *Ottawa Journal*, 7 June 1977; and Berners A. W. Jackson, *Shakespeare Quarterly* 28 (1977), 197–206.

176. Eyewitness account of Jack Hrkach, seminar paper, Catholic University of America, 1979.

177. Letter to the author, 2 March 1982.

178. Michael Billington, *Guardian*, 17 July 1981.

179. Robert Cushman, *Observer*, 19 July 1981.

180. Michael Coveney, *Financial Times*, 17 July 1981. Other reviews consulted include Benedict Nightingale, *New Statesman*, 24 July 1981; Sheridan Morely, *International Herald Tribune*, 30 July 1981; Nicholas Shrimpton, *Times Literary Supplement*, 31 July 1981; Gareth Lloyd Evans, *Shakespeare Quarterly* 33 (1982), 184–188; and Roger Warren, "Interpretations of Shakespearian Comedy," *Shakespeare Survey* 35 (1982), 141–152.

181. "A Dance for Our Disbeliefs: The Current *A Midsummer Night's Dream* of the RSC," *Theater* 13 (1982), 60–64. Letter to the author, 2 March 1982.

182. Letter to the author, 2 March 1982.

183. Warren, "Interpretations," 144–147.

184. Discussion of the play for the International Shakespeare Congress, Shakespeare Institute, Stratford-upon-Avon, August 1981.

185. In a production in August 1981 at the Edinburgh Festival by the Leicester Youth Theatre, Theseus and Hippolyta were played as Charles and Diana by the teenage cast members (Gerald Berkowitz, "Edinburgh: Festival and Fringe," *Shakespeare Quarterly* 33 (1982), 161–170).

186. Michael Coveney, *Financial Times*, 26 November 1982.

187. Irving Wardle, *Times*, 26 November 1982.

188. Michael Billington, *Guardian*, 27 November 1982.

189. Robert Cushman, *Observer*, 28 November 1982.

190. Other reviews consulted include James Fenton, *Sunday Times*, 5 December 1982; and Roger Warren, "Shakespeare in England, 1982–83," *Shakespeare Quarterly* 34 (1983), 334–335.

191. John Beaufort, *Christian Science Monitor*, 18 August 1982.

192. Quoted in Jennifer Dunning, "The 'Dream' Comes to Central Park," *New York Times*, 8 August 1982.

193. The video is available from Films for the Humanities, Princeton, N.J. Other reviews consulted include Howard Kissel, *Women's Wear Daily*, and Jerry Tallmer, *New York Post*, 16 August 1982; and Richard Schickel, *Time*, 30 August 1982.

194. H. R. Coursen, "Shakespeare in Maine," *Shakespeare Quarterly* 34 (1983), 96–98.

195. Produced by Orion and released by Warner Brothers, the film opened 16 July 1982 with Woody Allen as Andrew, Mia Farrow as Ariel, José Ferrer as Leopold, Julie Hagerty as Duley, Tony Roberts as Maxwell, and Mary Steenburgen as Adrian.

196. See chapter 6.

197. Roger Warren, "Moonshine," *Times Literary Supplement*, 13 April 1984. The production toured schools and colleges in 1983–1984 and came back to play Stratford-upon-Avon's Other Place.

198. For an analysis of this film, see Warren, A Midsummer Night's Dream: *Text and Performance*, 72 ff.

199. Nicholas Shrimpton, *Times Literary Supplement*, 25 December 1981.

200. Susan Willis, *The BBC Shakespeare Plays* (Chapel Hill: University of North Carolina Press, 1991), 107–108.

201. Ibid., 10–13. For other discussions of the BBC series and Shakespeare for television in general, see J. C. Bulman and H. R. Coursen, *Shakespeare on Television* (Hanover, N.H.: University Press of New England, 1988).

202. For a general overview of the development, see Taylor, *Reinventing Shakespeare*, chapter 6, especially 311–321 and 356–362.

203. By director, they were: Ron Daniels, 1981; Sheila Hancock, 1983; Bill Alexander, 1986; and John Caird, 1989.

204. Roger Warren, "Shakespeare at Stratford-upon-Avon, 1986," *Shakespeare Quarterly* 38 (1987), 86–89.

205. John Higgins, "Dreaming for Everyone," *Times*, 30 June 1986.

206. Reviews consulted include H. R. Woudhuysen, *Times Literary Supplement*, 18 July 1986; Irving Wardle, *Times*, 10 July 1986; Robert Hewison, *Sunday Times*, Francis King, *Sunday Telegraph*, and Michael Ratcliffe, *Observer*, 13 July 1986.

207. Ralph Berry, *On Directing Shakespeare*, 2d ed. (London, 1989), 183.

208. Paul Taylor, *Independent*, 13 April 1989.

209. See, for example, Michael Coveney, *Financial Times*, 13 April 1989.

210. Paul Taylor, *Independent*, and Nicholas de Jongh, *Guardian*, 13 April 1989. Other reviews consulted include Jeremy Kingston, *Times*, and Michael Schmidt, *Daily Telegraph*, 13 April 1989; Paul Lapworth, *Stratford-upon-Avon Herald*, 14 April 1989; D.A.N. Jones, *Sunday Telegraph*, 16 April 1989; and Peter Kemp, *Independent*, 12 June 1989 (Barbican performance).

211. Donal O'Connor, "Festival a Beacon in the Face of Cultural Gloom," [*Stratford, Ontario*] *Beacon Herald*, 1993.

212. Ben Brantley, *New York Times*, 10 September 1993.

213. Production photographs and costume designs in the playbill and the festival souvenir program.

214. Stratford Festival playbill, 11 .

215. Ben Brantley, *New York Times*, 10 September 1993.

216. George L. Geckle, *Shakespeare Bulletin* (Spring 1983), 27–28.

217. Jay Halio describes the production in detail in *A Midsummer Night's Dream in Performance* (Manchester: Manchester University Press, 1995), 117–125.

218. Interview of Lepage by Charles Spencer, *Daily Telegraph*, 6 July 1992.

219. Marvin Carlson, "Karin Beier's *A Midsummer Night's Dream* and *The Chairs*," *Western European Stages* 7 (Winter 1995/1996), 71.

220. My characterization is drawn largely from a viewing of a video of the stage production, taped with a live audience for broadcast in Germany. For some details, especially the cast and their origins, I am indebted to Carlson, 71–73, and to Daniel Mufson, "Berlin Theatertreffen," *Theatre Journal* 48 (1996), 504–505.

221. Carlson, 73.

222. Mufson, 505.

223. Matt Wolf, "Dreaming of Shakespeare," *Stagebill*, program for the Kennedy Center, Washington, D.C., 11–12. Noble told Wolf, "I was very inspired by the Surrealists, and obviously Magritte is sort of glaring."

224. On the relationship of Magritte and Foucault, see James Harness's introduction to Michel Foucault, *This Is Not a Pipe*, trans. James Harness (Berekely: University of California Press, 1983), 2–12.

225. Photographs of this production are to be found in many theatre texts, including Oscar Brockett and Robert Findlay, *A Century of Innovation*, 2d ed. (Boston: Allyn and Bacon, 1991), 183.

226. Wolf, 11.

Epilogue

1. Catherine Belsey, *The Subject of Tragedy: Identity and Difference in Renaissance Drama* (New York: Methuen, 1985), 9–10.

2. Montrose, 32. See chapter 1.

3. 1 Corinthians 2:9–10.

INDEX

Mellor, Cherith, 250

Mendelssohn, Felix, xii, 4, 92, 93, 99, 103–
 109, 112, 117, 121, 133, 140, 141, 144,
 146, 150, 156, 157, 158, 160, 164, 168,
 171, 173, 174, 176, 178, 185–186, 187,
 188, 192, 193, 195, 198–199, 201, 208,
 212, 216, 223, 227, 241, 249, 252

Merchant, W. Moelwyn, 42, 280n, 290–
 291n, 293n, 295n, 297n, 298n

Mercouri, Melina, 85

Meres, Francis, 36

Merivale, Herman Charles, 122

Messel, Oliver, 188

Metamorphoses, 1, 28

Metropolitan Opera House, 193, 203

Meyerhold, Vsevolod, 157, 219, 226, 256

Michell, Keith, 192

Middleton, Thomas, 11

Midsummer Night's Dream, A (Balanchine's
 ballet), 109

Midsummer Night's Dream, A (Britten's
 opera), 62, 164, 199–203, 245, 287n,
 291n

Midsummer Night's Dream, A (Garrick-
 Colman adaptation, 1763), 66, 70–73,
 fig. 4, 77, 78, 291n

Midsummer Night's Dream, A. See
 Shakespeare, William

Midsummer Night's Sex Comedy, A, 249, 321n

Milhous, Judith, 59, 282n, 283n

Mille, Agnes de, 186

Miller, Jonathan, 233, 250

Milton, John, 67, 68, 71, 115

Mirren, Helen, 250

Mitchell, Arthur, 198

Mnouchkine, Ariane, 214, 215, 219, 223,
 233, 260, 316–317n

modernism and modernist theatre practice,
 114, 143–146, 156, 157, 164, 165, 174,
 199, 200, 202, 205–207, 218

Moiseiwitsch, Tanya, 193, 206

Moissi, Alexander, 165, 168, 173, 176

Mollison, William, 137

Montgomery, George, 127

Montresor, Beni, 238

Montrose, Louis, 1, 3, 11, 17, 18, 21–22,
 96, 218, 260, 274n

Moore, John, 101, 117, 300n

Moore, Robert, 42, 43, 48, 53

Morley, Henry, 113, 121

Moscoso, Roberto, 220

Moshinsky, Elija, 249, 250

Moth, 33, 102. *See also* fairies

mothers, in the play, 21

Mowatt, Barbara, 314n

Mufson, Daniel, 255

Muir, Jean, 180

Murphy, Arthur, 69

Murphy, Gerard, 251

music: Elizabethan, 5, 15, 26–27; concept
 of semi-opera, 38, 42, 45–46, 47, 66;
 eighteenth-century musical adaptations,
 see chapter 3, passim; Reynolds-Bishop
 opera, see chapter 4, passim; in Vestris's
 production (1840), 98–99; use of Horn's
 melody and others' for "I know a
 bank . . . ," 99, 117, 135, 141, 292n;
 Tieck-Mendelssohn (1843), 103–109; in
 Phelps (1853), 111, 112, 296n; Simpson
 (1841), 114; Barry (1854), 117; Burton
 (1854), 117, 296n; Daly, 129–130; Tree
 (1900), 133, 135; Benson (1889–1912),
 141; Goodwin (1903), 141; Barker (1914),
 144, 146, 150; Reinhardt (1905–1935),
 168, 171, 173, 174, 175; the Nazis and
 Mendelssohn's score, 185–186; Carl
 Orff's scores for the play, 186; *Swingin'*
 the Dream, 186–187; in Coghill's production (1945), 192–193; Benthall–Old
 Vic (1954), 193, 195; Landau–Stratford,
 Conn. (1958), 197; Balanchine's and
 Ashton's ballets (1962, 1964), 198–199;
 Britten's opera (1960), 199–203; Hall
 (1959), 208; Hancock (1962), 216;
 Mnouchkine (1968), 221; Cleo Laine as
 Titania, 222; Brook-RSC (1970), 225,
 226–227, 229; Ciulei-Guthrie (1985),
 238; Yale Repertory Theatre (1975), 240;
 Daniels-RSC (1981), 243; Caird-RSC
 (1989), 252; Dowling–Stratford, Ontario
 (1993), 253; list of nineteenth- and
 twentieth-century operas derived from
 the play, 287n; Restoration, see *The Fairy*
 Queen. See also under composers' names

Mustardseed, 6, 32, 33, 102. *See also* fairies

Myerscough-Jones, David, 250

STUDIES IN THEATRE HISTORY AND CULTURE